Global Sceptical Publics

Global Sceptical Publics

*From non-religious print media
to 'digital atheism'*

Edited by Jacob Copeman and Mascha Schulz

First published in 2022 by
UCL Press
University College London
Gower Street
London WC1E 6BT

Available to download free: www.uclpress.co.uk

ISBN: 978-1-80008-346-2 (Hbk.)
ISBN: 978-1-80008-345-5 (Pbk.)
ISBN: 978-1-80008-344-8 (PDF)
ISBN: 978-1-80008-347-9 (epub)
DOI: https://doi.org/10.14324/111.9781800083448

Contents

List of figures

Notes on contributors

Stefan Binder is a Postdoctoral Researcher and Lecturer in the Department of Social Anthropology and Cultural Studies (ISEK), University of Zurich. He has published on secular activism and lived atheism in South India and on the aesthetic production of multiple temporalities in the context of Shi'i mourning rituals and media practices in Hyderabad. He is currently developing a research project on ethics and generational change in queer and trans communities in South Asia and Europe.

Joseph Blankholm is Associate Professor of Religious Studies at the University of California, Santa Barbara, and author of *The Secular Paradox: On the religiosity of the not religious* (New York University Press, 2022). His research focuses on secularism, atheism and religious change.

Frank Bosman is Senior Researcher at the Tilburg School of Catholic Theology, Tilburg University. He is currently involved in multiple research projects concerning cultural theology and video games. He has published various articles on theology and gaming in journals such as *Games and Culture*, *Gamevironments* and *Online: Heidelberg Journal of Religions on the Internet*, and the series Studies in Theology and Religion. Further key publications include *Gaming and the Divine: A new systematic theology of video games* (Routledge, 2019) and, as editor, *The Sacred & the Digital: Critical depictions of religions in video games* (Multidisciplinary Digital Publishing Institute, 2019).

James Bradbury completed his PhD in Social Anthropology at the University of Manchester in 2019. His doctoral dissertation, entitled 'Hinduism and the Left: Searching for the secular in post-communist Kolkata', was based on fieldwork in parts of the city that were settled by Hindu refugees from what is now Bangladesh, and which became bastions of the regional communist movement. Through these neighbourhoods, the thesis explored the city's distinct formulations of secularism, as well as how they have begun to transform in the post-communist period. He is now the editor for Synaps, a research and training organisation based in Beirut, Lebanon. (ORCID: 0000-0002-7501-244X.)

Eric Chalfant is Adjunct Assistant Professor in the Department of Film & Media at Queen's University in Kingston, Ontario. He received his PhD in Religion and Modernity from Duke University in 2016. He also has an MA in Religious Studies from Wake Forest University, NC (2011) and a BA in Religious Studies from Whitman College, WA (2008). He has previously taught at Portland Community College, OR and Elon University, NC. His current research unearths the affective elements underlying the history of atheist uses of media in the United States from the nineteenth to the twenty-first centuries.

Jacob Copeman is Research Professor, University of Santiago de Compostela, and Distinguished Researcher (Oportunius). His most recent monograph, co-authored with Dwaipayan Banerjee, is *Hematologies: The political life of blood in India* (Cornell University Press, 2019). His most recent edited collection, co-edited with Giovanni da Col, is *Fake: Anthropological keywords* (HAU Books, 2018). He is principal investigator of the ERC-funded project 'Religion and its others in South Asia and the world: Communities, debates, freedoms'.

Neelabh Gupta is a PhD candidate in anthropology at the Centre for South Asian Studies, University of Edinburgh. His work focuses on digital media and atheism in North India, exploring various ways in which the lives of non-religious individuals are joined together by digital media. His primary research interests are media, non-religion and visual cultures.

John Hagström is a PhD student in Social Anthropology at the University of Edinburgh. His research is on apostate refugees – atheist, humanist, rationalist and other non-religious asylum seekers in England and Scotland – with a concomitant focus on the various organisations and networks that support them. More broadly, his research interests include secularisation, ethics and morality, wonder, and non-religious movements worldwide. He is co-author of 'The absence of the divine' (*HAU: Journal of Ethnographic Theory*, 2018). (ORCID: 0000-0002-6902-8197.)

Pierre Hecker is Senior Researcher and Lecturer at the Centre for Near and Middle Eastern Studies at the Philipps University of Marburg. He holds a PhD from Leipzig University and is the author of the book *Turkish Metal: Music, meaning, and morality in a Muslim society* (Ashgate, 2012). Recent publications include 'Islam: The meaning of style' (*Sociology of*

Islam, 2018) and 'The "Arab Spring" and the end of Turkish democracy', in E. Mohamed and D. Fahmy (eds) *Arab Spring: Critical political theory and radical practice* (Palgrave Macmillan, 2019). He heads the research group 'Atheism and the politics of culture in contemporary Turkey' funded by Stiftung Mercator, and co-edited the volume *The Politics of Culture in Contemporary Turkey* (Edinburgh University Press, 2021).

Natalie Khazaal (PhD, UCLA) is Associate Professor at the Georgia Institute of Technology and an American Council of Learned Societies (ACLS) fellow for her work on Arab atheists. She has contributed to the topic of atheism with publications on the use of pseudonyms by Arab atheists and the embedded atheism in Mohamed Choukri's literary oeuvre. Her latest books, *Pretty Liar: Television, language, and gender in wartime Lebanon* (Syracuse University Press, 2018), which studies how audiences affect media legitimacy during violent crises, and her co-edited volume on borders and the displacement of human refugees and non-human animals, *'Like an Animal': Critical animal studies approaches to borders, displacement, and othering* (Brill, 2020), explore different forms of disenfranchisement.

Evelina Lundmark holds a postdoctoral position at Agder University in Norway, where she studies the intersection of Christian nominalism, Scandinavian secularism and national identity in relation to public broadcasting and children's television. She holds a PhD from the Faculty of Theology at Uppsala University, where she looked at how atheist women and gender-queer people speak about their unbelief in a US context on YouTube. Her research interests lie in the areas of non-religion and secular studies, digital religion, gender studies and critical theory. She has previously researched how religion is negotiated in discussions on reddit.com/r/atheism, worked within the Understanding Unbelief programme based at the University of Kent, and collaborated on projects that explored the modern graveyard in Sweden and examined how the Swedish Christian magazine *Vår Lösen* impacted on the daily press during Anne-Marie Thunberg's tenure as editor-in-chief.

David Nash is Professor of History at Oxford Brookes University. He has published monographs in the areas of blasphemy, secularism and secularisation and on British criminal history, and is an internationally renowned specialist in the history of blasphemy in Europe and the English-speaking world. He has also published *Cultures of Shame: Exploring crime and morality in Britain 1600–1900* (with Anne-Marie Kilday) (Palgrave Macmillan, 2010).

Johannes Quack is Professor of Social Anthropology at the University of Zurich. He is the author of *Disenchanting India: Organized rationalism and criticism of religion in India* (Oxford University Pres, 2012). He co-authored the book *The Diversity of Nonreligion: Normativities and contested relations* (Routledge, 2020), and co-edited the volumes *The Problem of Ritual Efficacy* (OUP, 2010), *Religion und Kritik in der Moderne* (LIT, 2012), *Asymmetrical Conversations: Contestations, circumventions and the blurring of therapeutic boundaries* (Berghahn, 2014) and *Religious indifference* (Springer, 2017), and he co-edits the book series Religion and Its Others: Studies in religion, nonreligion, and secularity (De Gruyter).

Lena Richter is a PhD researcher at Radboud University, Nijmegen. She has a background in anthropology and migration studies, with a regional specialisation in the Maghreb. As part of the Mediating Islam in the Digital Age (MIDA) project, she conducts qualitative research about the experiences of non-believers in Morocco and the Moroccan diaspora. Her research explores how the less religious urban youth normalise this taboo topic, by using humour, embracing a 'liberal' lifestyle and narrating their experiences online.

Mascha Schulz is a postdoctoral research fellow on the ERC project 'Religion and its others in South Asia and the world (ROSA)' and is based in the Department of Anthropology of Politics and Governance, at the Max Planck Institute for Social Anthropology, Halle. She is a political anthropologist currently working at the intersection of politics, economics and non-religion. Drawing on long-term ethnographic research in urban Sylhet (Bangladesh), she is working on a book titled *Cultivating Secularity: Politics, embodiment and criticism of religion in Bangladesh*. She has also published on the state, political parties and student politics in South Asia. (ORCID: 0000-0002-9053-5134.)

Acknowledgements

This volume was made possible through the support of the European Research Council (ERC) under the European Union's Horizon 2020 research and innovation programme (grant agreement no. 817959) and the Leverhulme Trust (RPG-2018-145). It grows out of a workshop funded by the same grants held (virtually) at the University of Santiago de Compostela in May 2021. We would like to thank the participants in that workshop for their feedback. Particular thanks are due to Stefan Binder, Amelie Blom, Koonal Duggal, Meera Gopakumar and Arkotong Longkumer. We would also like to thank Joseph Blankholm and Johannes Quack for generously taking up our invitations to reflect on the chapters, Lindsay Graham for her help in preparing the final manuscript and Chris Penfold at UCL Press for his support for this project.

Foreword: the frustrating and wonderful ambiguity of sceptical publics

Joseph Blankholm

This volume explores important questions. As a scholar of American secularism and secular people, I give lectures about non-believers to public audiences several times a year, both in person and broadcast via media. I receive certain questions often. Does more access to information make people less religious? Has the internet led more people to become atheists? Has a medium like the internet helped non-believers find others like them and feel less alone? These questions are surprisingly loaded, which makes them tougher to answer than they appear. Who counts as a non-believer? Why do they want to talk about what they don't believe? Why do they form communities – publics – online and in person? The persistence of these questions belies their simplicity, which is why I don't always have great answers, and why I'm grateful for this volume's perspicacity and breadth.

As an ethnographer of very secular people, including secular activists, I also hear questions non-believers ask in conversations, in person, but also in print and online. I ask these questions in my voice, but they capture the gist. Are atheists simply people who don't believe in God? Or people who don't believe in the supernatural? Is atheism anything more? (Maybe now we're talking about humanism!) Did ancient philosophers know the truth about the gods? Was that truth lost in the dark ages and rediscovered in the Renaissance? Was it the Enlightenment that revealed it fully? Is it enough to make this truth known? Or should a good atheist try to convince people there is no God? Would the world be a better place without religion? Questions like these are pressing for people trying to understand atheism, secularism and secularisation. They are even more important for the secular people trying to create a more secular world. Their answers provide the basic assumptions that constitute secularism and animate secular life.

Scepticism, media and publics are great starting points for finding answers. This volume begins a subfield; it does not summarise one. Its essays enter into an emerging terrain for which there is, as yet, no map. The paths they blaze are several and fantastically ambiguous; they lead one way, turn suddenly, then turn again; they dead-end. These paths' progress is circuitous, even as it remains important to follow where they lead. As the authors in this volume attempt to map the secular terrain, they are mired in a special set of challenges that it would be helpful for readers to recognise. Why are sceptical publics, of all things, so difficult to understand?

Publics, sceptics, non-religious and *media* are all ambiguous, even paradoxical, concepts. They warrant a little examination before we embark with them as our guide.

Public and *publics* depend on privacy for their meaning, just as secrets depend on disclosure. As scholar Michael Warner has made clear, public is distinguished from private more easily in theory than in practice. Secrets can be told in public just as private life can be aired publicly. Particular publics can be open to outsiders and still insular. As the authors in this volume repeatedly observe, publics are not necessarily public, in the sense of available to everyone. This is all the more true in the case of counterpublics, which are defined by their relationship to more dominant publics because they are spaces where people who feel marginalised interact with one another. A public can be open, but closed, and in any public, discourse usually has its limits.

Sceptics are no less ambiguous, and likewise in more than one sense. If sceptics are doubters then on what grounds? Anyone can doubt, as many faithful Christians will attest. Ancient sceptics like Pyrrho and Sextus Empiricus doubted as much as they could and urged a state of indecision, *ataraxia*, which questions even the conditions of their doubting. Modern sceptics are different because they are decidedly empirical. They doubt the veracity of claims that are not falsifiable by science, but they do not question that science provides the best way of knowing and that claims about reality should be subjected to its methods first and foremost. In other words, modern sceptics are sceptical of some epistemological sources and not others. Divine revelation, inspired scripture and mystical experiences cannot be trusted because they cannot be verified by microscopes, telescopes or the Large Hadron Collider. Sceptical faith lies in the empirical testing of reality even as social reality tends to confound science at nearly every turn. Here I should admit that I share sceptics' secular faith in the empirical even as I find ancient sceptical critiques both compelling and maddening. My ambiguity remains unresolved.

Non-religious is at its core paradoxical, as are 'non-belief', 'atheism', 'secularism', and any other term we use to describe religion's absence. Yes, any negative identity bears within it that which it is not, but where does that observation really get us? The 'non-religious' are so strange because they might share something more than what they lack. Negative epithets are often mere slander; they are more uncanny when they become self-appellations. After all, early Christians called the Romans atheists, and the Romans did the same to the early Christians. That they called each other heretics doesn't tell us much about who they actually were. But what happens when people begin to call themselves heretics, to call themselves atheists?

In the negative, those who do not believe are only unified by what they oppose, and defining their opposition broadly can too easily swell their ranks. The rise of the religiously unaffiliated, or so-called 'nones', has been described by some secularists as a growth in secularism, though a lack of religious affiliation can only tell us about how people don't belong. What about their beliefs and behaviours? And what about atheists who consider themselves religious, like many members of the Satanic Temple? More complicated still is atheism's presence as a worldview of its own. Is atheism merely the rejection of the 'God hypothesis', or does it name the consequences of a worldview, such as materialism or physicalism, which is atheistic only incidentally? Atheism is of course both a name for heresy and a name for a way of seeing the world and being in it. We must have it both ways if we're to see it rightly.

Media is a filter and a conduit. Or are media filters and conduits? I labour the point, which is of course media's overwhelming ambiguity as it simultaneously enables and constrains communication. Twitter's 280 characters, broadcast television's inability to receive and ancient texts' lacunae are at once methods of delivery and message-shaping constraints. Interpretations reflect these limits, too. In the media of sceptical publics, there are implications between the lines and allusions perceived only by those in the know. For historians of atheism, the constraints of persecution loom large. Did he really believe in God, or did he hold back the truth of his atheism? Philosopher Leo Strauss is right to argue there's an art to writing when certain sentences are punishable by death, though paranoia might be getting the better of us if we believe that any contradictions in a systematic thinker's oeuvre hold the keys to their hidden truth. Even in the absence of media's mediation, wondering whether a speaker is sincere can make a labyrinth of understanding. As this volume shows, the risks of non-belief are not the same everywhere, and those risks condition how, where and to whom atheists speak their minds. Media enables their speech even as the publics it reaches, sometimes via surveillance, impose their own restrictions.

The ambiguity of these four concepts is confusing, but it should motivate us to look at them more closely, as this volume does, rather than turn away. Ambiguities are the best starting points because they show the seams of social reality and reveal how it's stitched together. They dare us with loose threads we might pull, which fill us with the thrilling but false hope of taking everything apart to understand it more clearly. Alas, we're stitched in, too, and this is why our words so often betray us.

The challenge of ambiguity is basic and unavoidable for those who study people, and all the more for scholars using secular, empirical methods to study the secular people who are most empirical. In actual life, we have to contend with what the authors in this book face head-on. A certain type of philosopher might indulge in the luxury of settling these disputes by stipulating a definition and placing sceptics or non-believers in one category or another: yes, they are religious because they have faith in an epistemology; no, they are not because they claim they are not religious. Those of us who want to make sense of living people must do our best to understand them as we find them, in all their contradictions, even as our own ideas and language betray us by failing to capture what we find. To make matters worse, those we study are always entangling our terms with theirs in an ouroboros of emic and etic.

That social life so often resists description in language tells us as much about the latter as it does the former. The language and concepts we bring to bear on an object we seek to understand have a material history just as rich as that of the people and things we study. Vibrations like those that emanate from the mouth of someone reading these words aloud are aural shapes that resonate in our ears as comprehension. They have been learned through repetition, and what they mean or signify has not only changed over time but is also the product of accretion. Meanings linger, mixing old and new into remarkably dense signs.

Publics, sceptics, non-religious and media are overladen concepts, which makes them as useful as it makes them confusing. They help us understand the world better even if they also refuse us the satisfaction of fixity. The authors of this volume do the important work of stitching these concepts to a social world that exceeds containment but nonetheless demands explanation, at least for anyone reading these words. Its essays are timely, which of course means they will one day be less relevant than they are now. All the more reason to read them soon.

Introduction: non-religion, atheism and sceptical publicity

Jacob Copeman and Mascha Schulz

On 15 January 2013, Asif Mohiuddin, a secular activist, was stabbed in Dhaka, Bangladesh, allegedly because of his blogging activism, particularly his critical writings on religion, and for being an atheist. Having, luckily, survived, he now lives in exile in Germany. The incident, however, marked the beginning of a wave of attacks between 2013 and 2015 on activists who engaged critically with the Islamist party Jamaat-e-Islami and Islamic fundamentalism, promoted secularism or lobbied for LGBTQ rights, which subsequently became known as the killings of the 'atheist bloggers'. Several of the nearly 20 victims were self-declared atheists, who wrote on blogs such as *Mukto-Mona* ('freethinking'), while others were not necessarily known as atheists but rather as progressive activists in a broader sense. In the national media coverage, these people were sometimes referred to simply as 'the bloggers'; blogging thus became increasingly associated with being an apostate or an atheist. As a report in the Bangladeshi newspaper *The Daily Star* stated, 'Islamist groups have branded them [bloggers] "atheists" …. They have launched a propaganda campaign against the bloggers, utilising the lack of understanding of the concepts – blog, blogging and blogger'. The report contextualised the intensification of sentiments around 'blogging' and 'atheism' as part of wider power struggles concerning the war crimes tribunals that were taking place at the time, which put on trial prominent leaders of the Jamaat-e-Islami.[1] The trials were accompanied by popular mobilisations around issues of secularism, non-religion and Islam staged by the Shahbag movement and the Hefajat-e-Islam (see for example Chowdhury 2019). But of particular interest for us here is that the article points out how a certain medium, namely blogging, became in this context associated, and even partially synonymous, with 'atheism'. This is further specified in the article (Haque 2013):

> If you introduce yourself as a blogger, social media illiterate people take you to be an atheist! Because of this, all bloggers are now facing such kind of trouble though they (Muslims bloggers) have full faith in the Almighty Allah and Islam. Blogging is not a sin. ... Before [the] introduction of blog[s], there were some self-proclaimed atheists but they did not have any open sources for writing. But now they have such open sources. So, blogging is not a practice of atheism and every blogger is not an atheist. It depends on what type of content is posted at a blog and whether it is hurting Islam or other religions.

Bangladesh is not the only country in which digital media has provided new spaces for religion-sceptical publicity, which has subsequently led to controversies. The social media activism that accompanied the Arab Spring in 2011, for instance, seems to have resulted in a marked increase in online exchanges about religion and secularism (see for example Al Hariri, Magdy and Wolters 2019; Schielke 2015), which resulted in intensified visibility and, similar to what happened in Bangladesh, increasing contestation regarding atheism in countries like Tunisia, Egypt and Morocco. Moreover, Ayala Fader has vividly documented how, since the mid-2000s, the Jewish blogosphere has created new opportunities for sceptical ultra-Orthodox Jews to cultivate and communicate doubt, and crucially to find like-minded community. This led the rabbinic authorities to campaign against the internet as such, fearing that what they perceived as an 'anonymous heretical public' could bring about a general crisis of faith (Fader 2020). Striking a balance between increasing visibility and providing the possibility of remaining anonymous, blogs and social media like Facebook, Twitter, YouTube, Quora forums and Reddit have formed crucial spaces for communication and activism among agnostics, freethinkers, sceptics and atheists in a wide range of places, including those where such media have not provoked the same degree of controversy, such as Indonesia (Schäfer 2016; Duile 2020), Egypt (van Nieuwkerk 2018), Morocco (Richter 2021), Kyrgyzstan (Louw 2019), the US (e.g., Cimino and Smith 2014; Laughlin 2016; Lundmark and LeDrew 2019), the

Middle East (Al Zidjaly 2019; Khazaal 2017) and the Philippines (Blechschmidt 2018).

It is thus not surprising that there has been a surge in research on 'digital atheism' in recent years (e.g., Bosman 2019; Fader 2017, 2020; Richter 2021; Rashid and Mohamad 2019). So far, however, there has been little attempt to engage at a more systematic level with questions of the relation between different forms of media and non-religiosity, and how they may produce what we call sceptical publics. While there has been extensive scholarly engagement with and theorisation of how certain media affordances affect religious community formation and shape religious subjectivities (e.g., Engelke 2011; Houtman and Meyer 2012; Meyer and Moors 2006), we know little about the significance of different media for the (re)production of non-religious publics and publicity.

The above-quoted newspaper article helps us see what is novel about dynamics provoked by the increase in formats and use of digital and social media. Though they did not promote the emergence of atheism as such, they did equip atheists, agnostics, rationalists and religious sceptics with potentially novel forms of publicity, in particular with regard to scale, interactivity and accessibility. As a result of the often semi-anonymous affordances of these media, different forms of non-religious activism and community became more visible and, hence, more easily accessible for religious sceptics – as well as researchers – especially in contexts in which non-religious positions tend to be marginalised and silenced. Yet, in contrast with the view put forward in the newspaper article quoted above, digital media is only the latest means of expressing non-religiosity. Sceptical publicity has, of course, a very long history and utilised a wide range of different media, such as discussion circles, print media such as books, pamphlets and other textual forms (see Nash 1995; Minois 2012; Whitmarsh 2016), atheist archives and cartoon strips (Luehrmann 2011, 2015; Schmidt 2016), advertisements on buses (Tomlins and Bullivant 2016), billboards (Blankholm 2018), and films and TV shows, to name just a few. Even in Bangladesh the violent campaign targeting 'atheist bloggers' can be understood as being in continuity with similar, earlier campaigns against writers such as Taslima Nasrin, Shamsur Rahman and Humayun Azad (a point we will return to below), and the blogging we have discussed is contemporary with other forms of non-religious expression less prone to provoking controversies or violent attacks by Islamists (see for example Bradbury and Schulz in this volume).

This book seeks to further understanding of the remarkably diverse ways in which a variety of religious sceptics, doubters and atheists engage with different forms of media as means both of communication and of forming non-religious publics. Some varieties, such as books in English ranging from early scepticism (for example, those of Bertrand Russell) to the New Atheism[2] literature, had a far-reaching influence, informing debates and subjectivities in diverse places. Other forms, such as the use of Bengali theatre for secularist projects, have remained highly idiosyncratic to specific contexts. The volume brings together scholars from different disciplines in order to initiate debates on media, materiality and non-religion. It thus contributes to the recently growing social science literature on humanism, atheism and other varieties of non-religion, but expands its thematic reach and theoretical concerns by extending prevailing insights from studies of non-religion to media contexts. How do changes in media forms affect modes of anti-atheist activism and vigilantism? How does non-religious publicity differ according to medium and locale? What can geographically dispersed non-religious literature and visual art, from theatre to video production, tell us about non-religious subjectivities, communities and activisms, past and present?

Any attempt to engage with these questions must take account of the diversity and heterogeneity of the various forms of mediated scepticism and non-religious publicity that make a single, uniform reply to these questions unrealistic. In doing so, the book makes three key conceptual interventions.

First, if most previous studies typically treated media (mostly texts) 'as transparent vehicles for ideas' (Chalfant 2020, 4), simply transporting rationalist and religion-sceptical ideologies into new or existing domains, several programmatic works have emphasised the need to attend to the role of materiality and media in the study of non-religion (e.g., Lee 2012; Copeman and Quack 2015; Nash 2019; Binder 2020; Chalfant 2020). Building on these works, and extending them, we explore how various media produce different ways of circulating and mediating discourses for specific audiences, and also how these mediated discourses are closely interlinked with the properties and materiality of different media, and also to embodiment and emotional encounters. This book shows that the mediated formation of sceptical, atheist or secularist subjectivities cannot be analysed merely at a cognitive level; rather, affective and material (technological) dimensions must also be taken into account. Which forms and materials are used to sustain and promote sceptical publicity? How have different media forms facilitated the travel and exchange of non-religious ideas across contexts, and how does this facilitation relate to the specific properties of certain media? When are issues of non-religion addressed directly and when are more indirect forms such as humour used?

Examining diverse media, but with a focus on digital technologies, the book aims, secondly, to make a conceptual contribution to contentious debates on religion, secularism and 'the public sphere' by highlighting how media – including those considered 'public' and 'liberal', such as print media and the internet – tend to facilitate engagement with criticism of religion and communications among highly specific and limited 'publics', rather than by contributing to intellectual debates in a more generalised public sphere. By paying close attention to the material and technological properties of different forms of media, not only their role in circulating ideas and ideologies but also their affective potentials, the book seeks to rethink the relation between the 'secular' and 'public(s)' in diverse contexts. Acknowledging the centrality of the role of script and print media in the formation of non-religious thought and community, but also moving beyond these media forms, it asks the following questions. What other means do non-religious people employ to publicise their scepticism? What kinds of publics are created thereby? Are such publics directed primarily at educating 'the public' or do they serve as a means of seeking like-minded individuals for community creation? How do the dynamics of mediated non-religious publics and publicity vary, depending on the location and time? How does consideration of these dynamics allow us to rethink the relationship between 'the secular' and 'the public sphere'?

Thirdly, given that digital and social media is receiving a growing amount of attention – both popular and scholarly – because of how it apparently assists the formation of sceptical publics, this book makes a particular effort to bring different studies of 'digital atheism' into conversation. It does so by attending to questions such as the following. Might the internet, in markedly religious countries, have a community-building function in allowing formerly isolated individual atheists to locate and interact with like-minded persons, without necessarily meeting them face to face, becoming, thereby, a key atheist technology for the imagining and construction of non-religious communities in sometimes hostile locales? How do such digital dynamics differ from other forms of 'underground press' that have published periodicals critiquing religious orthodoxy and fundamentalism? How and when do digital or offline media become means of socio-political mobilisation, building up advocacy networks within and across national borders? Taken together, the contributions show that despite this transnational and supposedly non-local, 'liberal', open and democratic form of communication, the role that the internet plays for atheist and religious sceptics varies considerably depending not only on specific communities, which display a surprisingly strong sense of geographical belonging and often engage with specific forms of religious tradition, but also on the kinds of digital space used (closed Facebook groups, openly accessible activist statements and so on).

In this introduction we first explain our use of the term 'sceptical publics' in reference to still prevalent understandings of the secular public sphere, arguing that configurations of sceptical publicity always appear as *a* public rather than *the* public. We suggest that although a number of the sceptical publics we discuss are not outward-facing (the ambivalent relation of sceptical publics to visibility is a marked theme across the book), pursue only indirect forms of publicity, and do not resemble formal communities, this does not mean that they are a- or anti-political. We then address discourses of newness (New Atheism, new media, new opportunities for sceptical publicity), questioning the novelty that is frequently imputed to both medium and message in such contexts. Media innovations tend to renew or rework rather than transform extant modes of sceptical publicity. A historically informed approach allows us to see that spreadable media and virtual networking are far from being confined to the digital world.

We then turn our focus to materiality. Rather than taking non-religion as negation or absence of religion or as a neutral ground, we argue for a focus on *non-religious fabrications* as a means of allowing us to ask pertinent questions about how non-religiosity is produced and made tangible and socially significant in different contexts.

Our final section, on digital atheism, shows that though the digital can be vital for apparently offering socially and politically isolated atheists a safe place for finding like-minded fellowship, digital privacy breaches can make such communities vulnerable to discovery. Further, engaging with Daniel Miller et al.'s (2016) theory of attainment, we present evidence showing that digital affordances can go beyond enabling the fruition of latent non-religious attitudes or desires to actively produce varieties of non-religion.

Public(s) and publicity

It can seem that whenever the word 'public' appears in scholarly writing, it evokes an association with, and impulse to position oneself towards, Habermas's influential work on the public sphere, as well as debates on public(s) that emerged in its wake (e.g. Fraser 1992; Warner 2002; Cody 2011). According to Habermas, the emergence of the public sphere in eighteenth-century Europe was strongly connected with bourgeois coffee house culture and the rapid development of mass media. The argument that it provided a space for 'rational' debate on society and politics has of course been widely criticised, not only for its Eurocentrism and for ignoring existing power inequalities and exclusions, but also because its normative presumptions of a 'secular' and 'rational' space discount the significance of affect and local discursive traditions and positionality, including religious belonging (see Calhoun 1992; Meyer and Moors 2006; Salvatore and Eickelman 2004). As already indicated, the concept of 'sceptical publics' seeks to move beyond this debate to take inspiration from recent critical works on publics, publicity and media in order to 'examine how [sceptical] publics are brought about into being through historically specific media practices' (Hirschkind, de Abreu and Caduff 2017, S3).

This book's focus on non-religion, media and 'sceptical publics' forces us to question notions of the public sphere that associate it closely with 'the secular' and which posit the emergence of publics as an integral part of modernisation and secularisation. While Habermasian notions assume, and normatively posit, that the public sphere is in principle 'secular', several studies have shown how public(s) might be created through religiously informed media. One of the most renowned works here is Charles Hirschkind's *The Ethical Soundscape* (2006), in which he explored how cassette sermons reinforce Islamic traditions of both ethical discipline and deliberation, resulting in what he conceptualised as an 'Islamic counterpublic' in Egypt, thereby questioning not only the association with 'the secular' but also 'the hierarchy of senses underpinning post-Kantian visions of the public sphere' (Cody 2011, 42). Similarly, Arvind Rajagopal (2001) argues that media, most notably the telecast serial version of the Hindu epic *Ramayana*, was crucial for fashioning a Hindu public that enabled the rise of Hindu nationalism in India in the 1990s (see also Rao 2011; Lewis 2016). Moreover, numerous recent studies explore how certain religious groups or authorities publicly reposition themselves through the use of media technology, such as televangelism in the Americas (Birman 2006), audiovisual media in Ghana (Meyer 2006) and Islamic televangelism in India (Eisenlohr 2017). These studies often seek, like Tania Lewis in her research on religious and spiritual television, explicitly to enhance a 'non-secular or more correctly a post-secular conception of contemporary publics' (2016, 284) and to 'challenge such narrow associations between the public and the liberal-secular' (Lewis 2016, 295). Thus, much scholarly effort has gone into empirically disproving any direct association between publics and secularity by highlighting intersections between emergent forms of religion, media and publics.

We aim to extend this debate, albeit through approaching it from a slightly different angle, suggesting that problematic assumptions about close links between 'the secular' and the public sphere can fruitfully be rethought through a focus on non-religious or sceptical publics, as witnessed by the contributions to this book. In view of the different modalities of 'sceptical publics' explored here, one necessarily has to leave behind the idea of the public sphere as 'secular' *qua* default. Instead, the focus on non-religious media, materiality, publics and publicity allows us to explore how secularist, atheist or religion-sceptical stances are substantive, and in fact contested, ethical-political positions which themselves are mediated – and actively produced or fabricated – in diverse forms by actors who seek recognition, legitimacy or visibility to different degrees. Moreover, the different 'sceptical publics' assembled in this book more often than not reflect specific religious contexts that are marked by Christianate, Islamicate or Hindu influence. The degree of legitimacy these stances are able to claim varies considerably depending on the context – temporal, spatial and social – as does, interrelatedly, the extent to which actors seek or avoid publicity.

The term 'sceptical publics', therefore, is not a descriptive term that attempts to capture a clearly delimited phenomenon or necessarily similar forms of community. Instead, it is used here as a heuristic for exploring the diverse ways in which publicity and creating publics matter for non-religious and secularist actors and configurations – or not. The question, assuredly, is not just how certain media are used to further criticism of religion and advance atheists stances in society, but under what circumstances people choose to use them for this purpose.

Mediated publics, community formation and identity politics

In contrast to notions of a secular public sphere, all non-religious publics or configurations of sceptical publicity in this book appear as *a* public rather than *the* public. This does not mean, however, that people do not seek to position themselves in diverse ways towards an imagined dominant opinion, or what they perceive as *the* public. But if we accept the now relatively established notion of publics as multiple, unstable, fragmentary, interconnected and diverse in their formation, what are the main characteristics that mark a 'public'? There are of course many answers to this in the vast literature on the subject. In his essay on 'the various, seemingly contradictory, uses of the public as a concept' (Gilmartin 2015, 371) in historical and contemporary South Asia, David Gilmartin has argued that, despite such a plurality, 'the paradoxical tension of the public – as an arena for open debate and displays of difference and for the production of an image of imagined community unity – is central to its modern meanings' (Gilmartin 2015, 386). Similarly, David Marshall emphasises in his discussion of 'the plurality of publics' that 'most (if not all) iterations of "public" have contained this overriding communicative relationship of the individual to unity' (2016, 2). Imagined communities and communication figure also in the chapters in this book. Yet the precise relationship between them differs substantially in each case.

Certain chapters (for example Gupta's) explicitly address how particular media, more often than not digital media, provide a space in which to talk about non-religious convictions, and to share affective communications like memes or jokes, and thereby create a form of (imagined) community for religion-sceptics, rationalists and atheists despite the lack of face-to-face contact. These digital spaces thereby provide such atheists with a sense of community despite their anonymity and internal heterogeneity. Participants are provided with online space for debate and recognition of their scepticism, precisely because they are closed and limited and their privacy settings carefully guarded by most members in order, ironically, 'to limit its public reach'.

Tellingly, a sense on the part of atheists of marginality and exclusion from what is commonly understood as 'the public' is present in many of the chapters. In the light of this, several of the chapters (see also Dick 2015) characterise mediated atheist communities as forms of counterpublic, drawing on the influential work of Nancy Fraser (1992) and Michael Warner (2002).[3] This is done most explicitly in Eric Chalfant's chapter, which focuses on several subreddit atheist communities, the combination of which can be considered a mode of counterpublic not only because it 'marks itself off unmistakably from the dominant public' while voicing a sense of being subordinated, but also because the relation it embodies between stranger communication and identification results in the provision of 'an alternative space for the performance of (non)religious identity as neither fully public nor fully private'.

In interesting tension with Chalfant's analysis is Evelina Lundmark's chapter, which also focuses on US atheist Reddit users as well as animated discussions beneath the line of YouTube videos. Focusing on one discussion following a video in which the public commentator Ana Kasparian rejected identification as an atheist, Lundmark shows how such a closed digital public allows users to distinguish themselves from, and imagine themselves as rational through opposition to, supposedly irrational Others (both atheist and religious), while not necessarily imagining themselves as forming part of a community in the sense of evoking a sense of shared identity. Indeed, the point for such users is precisely to resist shared identity, even as they congregate virtually to do so.

Lundmark's chapter also prompts reflection about the supposedly 'political' nature of publics. It has been argued that in 'conjunction with communities, publics emerged as political entities related to visible cultural movements' (Marshall 2016, 6). Yet in the cases outlined so far we have seen how non-religious actors' principal aim is communication within the group rather than 'going public' beyond such spaces: 'coming in' rather than 'coming out', as Chalfant puts it. At the same time, the lack of 'publicness' of these publics should not be equated with an absence of the political. As Warner (2002, 63) has argued, even if it is possible only for limited or 'damaged forms of publicness' to develop since '[c]ounterpublics are, by definition, formed in conflict with the norms and contexts of their cultural environment', they can nevertheless transform non-religious subjectivities since they offer a space where 'private life can be made publicly relevant' (Warner 2002, 62). For Warner, it is precisely such processes of 'world making' that allow us to determine whether collections or assemblies of people are 'just "communities"' or 'mediated publics' (ibid., 61). Indeed, for Rosalind C. Morris such a form of speaking, which 'is no longer to be understood in the terms of communicative action' (2013, 95) – that is, it does not address strangers with a (political) message – is a property of the contemporary moment beyond counterpublics. Its emergence is connected with the opportunities presented by new mass media, which require us to rethink 'publicness beyond the public sphere, in the nonspaces of a networked world' (Morris 2013, 100).

Richter's chapter complicates further the question about power relations and communication between a sceptical public and *the* public by paying attention to diverse, partially contradictory forms of communication, and, crucially, different audiences. While Richter points out that the internet provides a space for many of her Moroccan interlocutors to connect with like-minded religious sceptics and to gain visibility, she also explores their ambivalence towards such visibility. She shows that non-religious people might have good reason for remaining silent or for not going public beyond the boundaries of the sceptical public. While some of her interlocutors avoid such publicity, having in mind the sensibilities of family members or threats from third parties, such a decision might also be based on political considerations, such as the wish of diasporic Moroccan ex-Muslims to avoid inflaming anti-Islamic sentiment in Belgium. Thus, an increased sense of community emerging in online and offline spaces does not necessarily result in an activist stance that attempts to challenge its marginal position. Rather, these spaces are marked by diverse forms of communicative register, among them 'talking among' more or less like-minded persons and 'talking with' other marginalised groups, for instance when non-religious groups speak up for gender or LGBTQ rights.[4]

The question of community formation via such publics is of course vital for many non-religious interlocutors because of a lack of established formal organisations. While religious communities, and especially religious reform movements, create community and thus limited publics through their religious activities (for example in churches or mosques, or through listening to sermons transmitted through loudspeakers; Stille 2020), this is not true to the same degree of non-believers, agnostics, atheists or religious sceptics. Recent years have seen the publication of numerous studies on organised non-religion across the globe (e.g., Quack 2012; Engelke 2012, 2015; Kind 2020; Blechschmidt 2020). At the same time it is widely acknowledged that the majority of non-religious people globally have engaged in more diffuse ways of cultivating doubt and non-religious community. However, in seeking to conduct research on less visible or less formally organised non-religious subjectivity formation, scholars face challenges, as we have discussed elsewhere (Schulz and Binder 2023; Copeman and Quack 2019). Digital spaces, such as closed forums like the Atheist Republic and those on Reddit, might be one way of engaging productively with these more diffuse non-religious publics (see also Lundmark and LeDrew 2019), especially since most digital spaces are entangled with offline sociality, as the chapters in this volume by Gupta and Richter demonstrate (see also Duile 2020; Blechschmidt 2020).[5] In Gupta's chapter on WhatsApp discussion groups and Instagram meme sharing among young Indian atheists, it is striking how little engagement exists between them and the modes of organised atheism discussed in the chapters by Binder and by Copeman and Hagström. Though the organised variants have attempted to form online presences (Quack 2012, 97, 165; Binder 2020, 239), the situation appears to reflect Daniel Loxton's general assessment that while 'digital outreach may bring new grassroots support to traditional skeptical organizations, … realizing that potential requires facing up to a more fundamental shift: traditional skeptical organizations are no longer the default leaders of the popular movement. Indeed, new skeptics may not even realize the traditional skeptical groups exist' (2009, 24; see also Smith and Cimino 2012, 27).

We should not, then, limit our approach to forms of sceptical publics that resemble more or less formal communities. Instead, a wide range of different genres is involved in the production of sceptical publics. Rather than dialogue-centric interaction, often associated with public spheres, it has been suggested that 'genre-specific communication might be producing specific forms of consensus and truth that aim to persuade not everyone, but those involved in this particular communication' (Stille 2020, 15). David Nash in this volume surveys how media and genre innovations and the historical prominence of different media have shaped 'sceptical publics' in the UK and the US over time. He reminds us that besides the most obvious form of publicity, that is, 'reading publics' fostered via publication of pamphlets and other print media, imagined communities have also been created through oral formats, though it can be challenging to find historical sources for this. Nash shows that court records of blasphemy or similar cases can be a particularly productive genre for reconstructing difficult-to-trace sceptical histories.

Several other chapter authors highlight the significance of particular genres for sceptical publicity. Frank Bosman's chapter offers an in-depth discussion of the serial *Rick and Morty* as an example of American popular entertainment that prominently engages in criticism of religion. James Bradbury and Mascha Schulz explore why their secularist interlocutors in Bangladesh and West Bengal, India, often choose theatre and Bengali cultural activism rather than communist politics, in which they are also engaged, in order to promote a secular society. Direct criticism of religion can result in threats or unpopularity; hence such statements and actions are discouraged in formal politics. Theatre allows activists to address these issues more indirectly. A 'secular public' is not only created through performances in front of different audiences, but also, in another sense, by providing a space for cultural activists to cultivate secular sentiments and to come together as 'seculars'. Further, argue Bradbury and Schulz, the degree of publicity associated with performances is strongly regulated depending on its content and the expected audience. The supposedly 'public' medium of street theatre is therefore marked by what Martin Zillinger (2017) has called a 'graduated publicness'.

The chapter by Copeman and Hagström focuses on how Indian rationalists see an opportunity in TV and film formats, including talk shows and video slow motion, to renew attempts to expose religion as 'fake' and superstitious. While the rationalists have scored some notable successes, the chapter also highlights significant audience-related ambivalences concerning these highly visual modes of sceptical publicity; the spectacle of broadcast exposure of spiritual gurus on popular TV does not always lead to the intended result: audiences might ask questions about the particular guru under scrutiny, but not about guru-ship in general; or, even worse, they may assume that rationalists themselves hold some kind of special power. Recalling the case of a mid-nineteenth-century US sceptic withdrawing from a project of publicly exposing spiritualism after realising his efforts were helping to create new spiritualists (Walker 2013, 31), such unintended side effects of increased publicity can result in ambivalence towards mass mediation among rationalists, despite their inherent activist desire for publicity.

Hecker's chapter discusses another case of unwarranted publicity, or publicity of the wrong sort. The Turkish cartoons and satirical comic books on which his chapter focuses form part of a long tradition of providing critical engagement with and humorous reflections on religion dating back to the late Ottoman era. Indeed, they have played a central role in the formation in the country of sceptical publics, which, as Hecker argues, in contemporary Turkey constitute a mode of counterpublic because of the increasing hegemony of political Islam and pious conservatism. Reflecting this hegemony, popular Turkish cartoonists are increasingly under threat of legal action for denigrating religious values 'in public'. Hecker's historical discussion illuminates not only considerable ambivalences concerning publicity but also important shifts over time in what it is deemed acceptable to say about religion, or Islam, 'in public'.

The focus on sceptical publicity in these chapters, rather than sceptical publics in respect of mediated community formation, raises questions of reception, diversity of audience and 'regimes of circulation' (Cody 2009). Though it might be true that publicity is integral to secularisation (Lebner 2018), this does not mean that sceptical publics seek publicity necessarily or in an unqualified way. As several chapters in this volume show, there can be good reasons for avoiding 'going public'. In particular, dangers can arise if digital communications move beyond their intended audiences: consequences range from their appropriation in support of right-wing anti-Islamic agendas (Richter), to the unintended provocation of outrage. Therefore publicity is often sought indirectly, for instance through humour or entertainment media (Bosman), via media that specialise in implicit messaging (Bradbury and Schulz), or by targeting publicity at certain segments of society. Indeed, focusing on non-religiously inflected indirection, silences and 'public secrets' (Taussig 1999) is likely to be productive in the further study of global sceptical publics.

At the same time, many non-religious people do of course actively and explicitly seek publicity in order to advance an activist stance, despite running the risk of provoking harsh reactions; we see this in Gupta's chapter in relation to meme sharing, and also in cases where the agenda of sceptical communities is explicitly to make rationalism, secularism or atheism more acceptable to what they understand to be *the* public, which despite being fictitious exerts powerful effects on these dynamics. The chapter by Natalie Khazaal is concerned with such individuals, who engage in media strategies to promote acceptance of apostasy and atheism in Lebanon. Her chapter provides insight into the implicit rules of how one can speak in public in order to make legitimate claims to be an atheist and nevertheless a moral person, reminding us that the strategies employed, be they calculated or habituated practices in the form of gendered dispositions, matter for how an atheist testimony might be evaluated.

Sceptical publicity designed to emphasise the 'nevertheless moral' character of atheists in the face of the tenacious argument that 'atheists are unable to be moral because they lack belief in the religious faiths that define morality for many in society' (Linneman and Clendenen 2010, 101) has long been a key public-facing concern for atheists, sceptics and humanists. The notable nineteenth-century British sceptic George Holyoake rejected the term 'atheism' precisely because it might lend credence to the widely held assumption that abandonment of religion is synonymous with abandonment of morality (Zuckerman and Shook 2017, 4). Media employed for 'good without god' publicity have included print (e.g. Epstein 2009), billboards (Blessing 2013), the body (Copeman and Quack 2015), charities (as in the establishment of organisations like Aid Without Religion), and miracle demonstration (to show that atheists conduct such exercises to foster scientific literacy whereas others do so to exploit (Binder 2020)). Yet, in dramatic contrast to projects that seek to promote acceptance of atheism among *the* public via 'good without god' publicity, Bosman's chapter demonstrates how the *Rick and Morty* TV show has no interest in such a project at all, instead foregrounding its atheist protagonists' ethical nihilism: precisely the perception atheists are usually so keen publicly to counter. With Rick 'generally portrayed as an amoral atheistic genius' (Hummel 2019), the programme comes to look like a kind of sceptical anti-publicity, actively lending credence to stereotypes of the morally unmoored atheist without meaning and purpose.

Yet non-religious modes of 'going public' need not be primarily directed towards 'the public'. John Hagström's chapter highlights the significant emergence and prominence in UK humanist circles of a discourse, stimulated by a recent increase in non-religious asylum seekers in the country, centring on the global plight of apostates. While such an 'apostate politics of visibility' is directed towards a secularising public in which the suffering of individuals leaving religion has become far less visible, such apostates have sought publicity particularly among their more privileged non-religious peers, which reminds us of the importance of taking into account the internal heterogeneity of any given 'sceptical public'.

New atheism, new publics?

Scholarly interest in relations between publicity, media and non-religiosity has grown in parallel with increased research on non-religion in more diverse geographic locations. It is no coincidence, we suggest, that this research has emerged alongside, or subsequent to, two significant interrelated popular developments at the beginning of the twenty-first century: first, the appearance of a public debate concerning 'New Atheism' after the publication of high-profile works by Sam Harris, Daniel Dennett, Richard Dawkins and Christopher Hitchens (2004–7) that provoked substantial controversies, especially in the US and the UK, but which have nevertheless, or possibly for that reason, been highly influential around the globe (for example in the Philippines (Blechschmidt 2018)); secondly, the emergence of what is called 'new media' and interrelated debates on how this has shaped our possibilities of forming communities, and our relation to space and the dynamics of political participation (Hirschkind, de Abreau and Caduff 2017; Kelty 2017; Morris 2013).

The word 'new' figures in both these popular developments and also prominently in academic discourses that discuss different (digital) media and their role in allowing atheists and other non-religious people to raise their voices or seek community. This is also true of contributions in this book: Richter, for instance, concludes that 'the internet has set in place the basic conditions for a *new* counterpublic of non-believers'. Copeman and Hagström discuss how film and TV 'offer rationalists *new* techniques of vision' and Chalfant discusses how a specific form of digital media (Reddit) has enabled 'users to develop *new* forms and formations of intimacy'. Most prominently, digital media has been associated with 'newness' and with cutting-edge technology that brings about change. For now, we bracket the question of whether (or not) and to what extent digital atheism creates new forms of sceptical public and publicity, as we attend to it in detail below. Instead, we would like to draw attention to the discourse of 'newness' that accompanies such writings.

Of course, the word 'new' immediately invites caution. As the authors of the introduction to a journal special issue on 'New media, new publics?' say of ongoing innovation in digital technology and interactive formats, 'scholars increasingly wonder what is "new" in new media' (Hirschkind, de Abreu and Caduff 2017, S4). The 'novelty' of New Atheism has also been subject to debate (Flynn 2010; see also Pigliucci 2014). Most prominently, Tom Flynn questioned the novelty of the arguments made by so-called New Atheists, arguing that there are substantial continuities between present-day atheist arguments and those made within a long tradition of freethinking, which includes figures such as Robert Ingersoll and Bertrand Russell. He contended that 'there's nothing new about the new atheism' besides its key texts being massively accessible because of their publication by mainstream presses and their prominence as bestsellers (Flynn 2010). One could argue whether even this is innovative or novel given its continuity with the earlier media strategy of rationalist 'cheap editions' in operation since the late nineteenth century (see Nash, this volume). Our aim here is not to take up a position in this debate. Instead, we dwell on it in order to highlight the significance within it of media circulation, and its consequences for non-religious visibility and publicity. While Flynn downplays the role of media as insignificant compared to the main arguments of New Atheism, it strikes us as a central characteristic of the phenomenon and one of the main reasons for its controversial influence. A key aim of this book is to attend to the different affordances and characteristics of media without overemphasising the cutting-edge technology of digital formats, which have figured prominently in research on atheism in the last decade. Instead, we attempt to bring into conversation different media genres as well as contemporary and historical research.

In fact, New Atheists have employed a number of media beyond renowned book publications such as *The God Delusion* (2006) to facilitate publicity and promote radical atheist politics, ranging from Twitter to YouTube videos and Richard Dawkins's large personal investment in bus advertisements (see Tomlins and Bullivant 2016). It was the combination of this large-scale publicity, supported by the considerable financial means of a few of its members, the appearance in a post-9/11 era of increased concern about the public role of religion, and surging anti-Muslim sentiment in the US and the UK (see also Kettell 2013) that made it such a visible and controversial movement. While the 'new' publicity of 'New Atheism' has resulted in increased academic interest (Bullivant 2020), studies of non-religion have largely covered countries in Europe and North America, and the variants of non-religion explored have often been comparatively hard-line, organised, or both. This book has a larger geographical purview, with chapters including but not limited to contemporary Euro-American contexts, and also considers more diverse modes of non-religiosity, though we acknowledge that the contributions remain, despite their 'global reach', limited to certain regions, reflecting the asymmetries of existing scholarship.

In locations hitherto barely considered by scholarship on non-religion, such as Bangladesh or Morocco, the visibility of non-religious publics and publicity has often been considered a novel development or, at least, as reaching 'a new stage of atheist and irreligious publicity', as Khazaal argues for the Arabic-speaking world, and this is frequently put down to the prevalence of new media formats. Yet we would not wish to reiterate this popular diagnosis without reservation. It is an obvious but still important point that media forms in practice often nest within one another rather being isolable, with no obvious boundary between 'traditional' and more recent forms such as social media, and, certainly, different media forms do not emerge successively in any simple sense as substitutions for one another (Hirschkind, de Abreu and Caduff 2017). A particularly prominent mode of this is the reposting on YouTube of TV clips which thereby become subject to different dynamics of circulation and publicity (see Khazaal in this volume). Recognising this, Daniel Miller et al. (2016, x) propose the term 'polymedia' as a means of emphasising 'our inability to understand any one platform or media in isolation'.

Thus, while we need to acknowledge the 'new' dynamics that attend what Francis Cody calls the 'networked publicity of satellite television and "spreadable media"' (2020, 394), these dynamics neither fully replace extant media forms nor necessarily fundamentally transform sceptical publicity. Instead, sceptical publics tend to have diverse histories and multiple geographic origins liable to be renewed, reworked or reconfigured in the light of media innovations. We thus agree with Kajri Jain that we need 'to disentangle the idea of newness in "new media" from the much-critiqued modernist narratives of linear progress and evolutionary succession in whose terms it is still too often unwittingly framed – or rather to provincialize this as just one of the temporalities at work when thinking about what enables newness to emerge' (2017, S13).

We illustrate this by returning to the Bangladeshi case of the so-called atheist bloggers. Despite the novelty of blogging as a form of Bengali sceptical publicity, this development was not exclusively new but 'layered itself over existing infrastructures', to employ Cody's phrase (2020, 394). The newspaper article we cited earlier suggested, in accordance with popular sentiment at the time, that the figure of the blogging atheist was a new phenomenon, since the blog form, for the first time, provided an 'open source of writing' for religious sceptics. Yet such a 'new' development has a long intellectual history in Bengal, as has writing more broadly. One of the main targets of Islamist condemnation was the *Mukto-Mona* ('freethinking') blog, which, according to its self-description, 'is an Internet congregation of freethinkers, rationalists, skeptics, atheists & humanists of mainly Bengali and South Asian descent[6] who are scattered across the globe'.[7] As a moderated blog, it gave religious sceptics and secularists an opportunity to exchange views and share thoughts mostly through longer-form writing, with a strong intellectualist leaning. While the weblog genre certainly offered 'new' affordances, such as the relatively short period between writing and publication, it should be seen in continuity with older traditions of freethinking and writing in Bengali such as the freethinker 'Young Bengal' movement in Calcutta, and the radical humanist movement Buddhir Mukti Andolon ('Freedom of Intellect Movement') in Dhaka in the 1920s, which began under Kazi Abdul Wadud's leadership (see Khan 2001; Murshid 1997), and other forms of publication such as the journal *Sikha* ('education'). Moreover, such blogs were not particularly 'new' when they became a nationally controversial issue in 2013 in the context of the polarisation following the Shahbag movement: *Mukto-Mona*, for instance, had been founded in 2001.[8] The outrage focused on 'the bloggers' in 2013 thus needs to be understood in the light of the socio-political context of the time (see also Hasan and Ruud 2021; Chowdhury 2019). While the 'new' technology of blogging certainly had its own effects in Bangladesh, it did so in continuity with older patterns to create a media of 'layered temporalities' (Jain 2017, 2021).

Following this, the book includes chapters that bring historical trajectories to the fore. Nash's chapter on the changing nature of non-religious media engagements in the US and the UK illustrates how many patterns and challenges continue, albeit with modifications, despite innovations in technology. Other chapters explore how certain genres have historically been linked with 'sceptical publics'. Copeman and Hagström, for instance, demonstrate how the advent of TV was mobilised by Indian rationalists, while Bradbury and Schulz examine how understandings of Bengali street theatre as a form of 'secular media' result from its significant historical legacy and the role it played in anti-communal and resistance movements. Hecker's chapter, too, is sensitive to the long history of critical engagement with religion in Turkey and how the social evaluation and acceptability of this engagement have changed over time.

While the chapters by Hecker and Nash are focused on printed texts and their circulation, the existence of reading (and writing) publics is also a precondition for the forms of mediated non-religion explored in digital contexts by Chalfant, Gupta, Richter and Lundmark. Jack Goody (Goody and Watt 1963; Goody 1996) famously made the case for literacy and writing as pivotal for the development of sceptical thinking. For instance, he connected a rise in reflexivity and criticism of religion in sixth-century India with the introduction of an alphabetic script (1996, 674).

Objectifying and codifying myths and other religious narratives via writing enhances one's ability to critically scrutinise and discern incongruities in them. The approach has been criticised for its division of oral and literate cultures according to relative levels of credulity (Barber 2007, 68–9), with orality and literacy in any case frequently hybrid practices (Binder 2020, 129). In his later work, Goody clarified that literacy merely 'seizes' upon kernels of doubt that already existed in oral cultures (1996, 678). Literacy does not invent scepticism, but it can extend it.

Focusing (as did Goody and Watt) on ancient Greece and Rome, Tim Whitmarsh (2016) similarly connects growth in criticism of the epics with the emergence of a sophisticated literate culture that sought out 'naturalistic plausibility'. Moreover, literacy allowed a form of 'virtual network' to form, comprising the 'scattered dots' of individual Hellenic and Roman atheists across time and space. These ancient atheists initiated no large-scale movement, community or public face, but writing and literacy did allow a form of 'detached fellowship' or linking together of scattered dots at particular times, especially in the pre-Christian Roman Empire. That is to say, literate culture allowed atheists of this era to sustain 'a fantasy of connection' to the great classical atheists (Diagoras, Protagoras, Socrates, Critias). Returning in the light of this to our earlier discussion of media novelty and layering, the chapters by Nash and Hecker, which explore licit and illicit circulations of printed documents (including pictorial representations) among literate publics, remind us that spreadable media and virtual networking are far from being confined to the digital world. Moreover, if ancient 'disbelievers were not concerned to leave physical traces of their absence of belief, [with] no shrines, statues, inscriptions, coins, or graffiti indicating their presence' (Whitmarsh 2016, 142), these circulations perhaps indicate that the material culture of atheism should be considered more in terms of 'books, pamphlets, books and more books' (Nash 2019, 7). The physical circulation of books and pamphlets among clandestine and other networks of literate publics is certainly a central part of the material culture of many non-religious communities across time and space (see for example Minois 2012). However, if there still lingers an association between the phenomenon of written language and 'peculiarly abstract and autonomous qualities of cognition' (Mertz 2007, 23), analytically coupling written language too tightly with non-religion runs the risk of reducing non-religion to the status of an abstract intellectual position. In contrast, the next section seeks to highlight just how multifaceted non-religious material engagements can be.

Non-religious fabrication: media, aesthetics and the material

Contributions to this book highlight the diversity of non-religious aesthetic and affective encounters, ranging from the aesthetics of propagation via speech, film and street theatre (Binder; Copeman and Hagström, Bradbury and Schulz) to the strategies employed by Lebanese atheists on social media and their affective implications (Khazaal), and the role of humour and ridicule in the criticism of religion in a US TV series (Bosman) and 'ungodly visuals' in the form of memes (Gupta). Thus, *Global Sceptical Publics* reflects and extends emerging approaches to non-religion that no longer treat it as a domain divorced from aesthetics and the sensory.[9] This is important for any analysis of 'sceptical publics' because, although it is widely agreed that debate and dialogue are critical features of publics, equally important is how publics constitute themselves through aesthetic styles and material signs (Prince 2019, 136). Here we address these styles and signs with reference to chapters in the book and recent key works in aesthetic theory, in particular those by anthropologist Birgit Meyer.

A widely noted problem confronted by scholars of non-religion working in the area of non-religious sensoria and aesthetics has been the conventional assessment of secular humanism as a hyper-intellectual exercise (Lee 2012; Engelke 2012) that is antithetical to aesthetics (Binder 2020) and so unconcerned with, indeed divorced from, matter, affect and the senses. This is ironic given the normative commitment of secular humanists to materialism (Copeman and Quack 2015). On the one hand, such understandings of secular disembodiment and dispassion were only possible because so many scholars already assumed they knew how secular humanists think and operate, with no further investigation required (Luehrmann 2015, 101). It is no accident that the aforementioned stereotypes began to be challenged almost as soon as ethnographic studies of non-religion began in earnest in the 2010s. On the other hand, there does indeed exist 'a kind of "Enlightenment story", in which bodies, affects and emotions are supposed to play minor roles' (Engelke 2019, 200). This is a story that should be taken seriously as informing some atheists' self-understandings and that indeed is reflected in certain self-ascribed labels such as 'freethought', 'scepticism' and 'rationalism' (Lee 2012, 142), but it is a story that should not be treated uncritically or taken for granted, and its bias in terms of European intellectual history should be recognised.

A number of studies question positions that assume the very idea of secular aesthetics is a contradiction (Binder 2020, 10) and that non-religion is 'all in the mind'. Lois Lee (2012) argued early on that studies of non-religion should not fail to address the rich material culture of non-religion. Taking inspiration from the concept of 'banal nationalism' and approaches to religion that emphasise its lived dimensions, she persuasively challenged the assumption that 'nonreligious forms are primarily intellectual rather than social, practical, symbolic, aesthetic and/or material' (2012, 136). This was an important shift. To focus on lived non-religion rather than abstract formal doctrine – on *atheists* rather than on *atheism* (Chalfant 2020, 6; see also Copeman and Hagström, this volume) – is to be more likely to avoid the unilluminating stereotypes we pointed out above. Leigh Eric Schmidt's (2016) emphasis, in his work on nineteenth-century atheists and freethinkers in the US, on the earthiness or 'mundane materiality' (p. 18) that marked these atheists' alienation from religion, is exemplary here. Other key works – such as those by Engelke (2015), Copeman and Quack (2015), Chalfant (2020), Binder (2020) and Schulz (2021) – that have sought to take forward Lee's agenda or propose adjacent ones often cite in passing the work of Birgit Meyer, who is well known for her substantial body of work on religious media, aesthetics and materiality. We think, however, that it is worth explicating more fully the conceptual possibilities for studies of non-religion generated by her work.

With an ethnographic focus on Christianity in West Africa, Meyer has been key to the scholarly endeavour to foreground the mediated, material and affective basis of religion as a counter to dematerialised belief-centred approaches that define it in terms of internalised mental representations and propositional assents (Engelke 2005; Morgan 2009; Chidester 2018). Valuable though it is, such work on 'material religion' runs the risk of perpetuating unhelpful perceptions of the immateriality of non-religion (Binder 2020, 10). We suggest that the most productive response to this risk is to creatively apply concepts developed by material religion scholars to the field of non-religion. The first step is to recognise the shared concern of scholars of religion and non-religion to counter overemphasis on mentalistic representations of their objects of study; to acknowledge that 'atheists, like religionists, are more than what they do or do not believe' (Chalfant 2020, 3). There is thus, at the outset, a quite evident symmetry or overlap between Meyer's agenda and that of scholars seeking to engage material *non*-religion.

Proceeding from this, we suggest that Meyer's (2014, 209) emphasis on the significance of 'form' – 'not as a vehicle but as a generator of meaning and experience' – is as apt for non-religion as it is for religion. Related to this is Meyer's interest in processes of fabrication (via texts, sounds, pictures, objects, etc.) as means of generating a sense of the sublime or transcendent. If this might appear unhelpful for describing those 'who neither affirm nor long for the transcendent' (Blankholm 2017), we suggest that a sense of the immanent, of the non-religious, should not be considered the neutral ground from which such religious fabrications begin, but that it is a sense that itself must be fabricated. This, too, can often take the form of a beyond in respect of a (from the perspective of the active non-believer) problematically de-secularised, or incompletely secular, here and now. To paraphrase Meyer (2014, 213), foregrounding fabrication prompts very concrete empirical questions about the specific practices, materials and forms employed in generating a sense of the non-religious. Which materials are used and how are they authorised as suitable? What steps are involved in procedures of de-sacralisation? How does a *non-religious fabrication* inspire or help sustain non-belief? Posing such questions allows us to study attempts both to dispose of extraordinary (religious) presences and to create immanent ones. In such processes we are often able to register a kind of non-religious 'moving beyond': what, to repurpose a concept proposed by Stef Aupers, Dick Houtman and Peter Pels (2008, 702), we call the engineering of *immanent, 'this-worldly other worlds'*.

Consider how secular humanists across time and space have sought to fabricate selves, spaces and events free from – beyond – religious iconography. In present-day England, for instance, 'the first thing that a [humanist] celebrant does, when he or she arrives at the chapel [to conduct a funeral], is take away or have covered any religious symbols that may be present' (Engelke 2015, 39). An Indian example of non-religious fabrication consists of atheist activists attempting 'to overcome [caste and religious] communalism by mobilising a social imaginary or an "aesthetic formation" (Meyer 2009) of atheist humanism' (Binder 2016, 205) that centres on sharing food among communities for which restrictions on food sharing are a key means of maintaining community distinctions. Activists thereby attempt to materially engineer an immanent, this-worldly other world that both represents and hopes to eventuate a condition of achieving freedom from – going beyond – normative religious identities.

The chapters by Gupta, Binder and Khazaal each depict non-religion as an embodied practice of the human senses which, to paraphrase Binder (this volume), aesthetically produces varied affects: group-binding humour, offence and silencing in the case of memes (Gupta), ridicule and arrogance in the case of speeches propagating non-religion by Indian activists (Binder), and affective responses to religious discrimination as a spur to emotive non-religious messaging in the case of Lebanon (Khazaal).

Bradbury and Schulz, in their chapter, coin the term 'secular media' to stress the point where secular humanism and media merge through 'performative embodiments of secularity' in Bengali street theatre. A genre and material practice that criticises religion, opposes divisive communalism and, critically, simultaneously advocates and arouses an atmosphere of autonomy from religion, it is fabricated out of Bengali aesthetic genres old and new – demonstrating again how non-religious fabrication can seek to bring forth a richer, more palpable immanence or 'phenomenal secularity' (Lee 2019, 44), however temporarily or imperfectly, to form immanent, this-worldly other worlds.

Meyer (2014, 216) approvingly cites Robert Orsi's (2012, 147) definition of religion as 'the practice of making the invisible visible, of concretizing the order of the universe, the nature of human life and its destiny, … in order to render them visible and tangible, present to the senses in the circumstances of everyday life'. Yet tackling invisibility and making it available to the senses can be just as much a concern for disbelievers as for the faithful. For example, some atheists are keen to have their dead bodies publicly donated to medical science – thereby circumventing death rituals and contributing to science – because it can make atheist commitments tangible. With scurrilous rumours often circulating about deathbed recantations, successfully enacted body donations palpably objectify the reality of the deceased atheist's unwavering irreligiosity, making it available for inspection (Copeman and Quack 2015). Precisely because non-religion is so often interpreted in terms of mental attitudes and interiority, it is often essential for claims of non-religion to be given material form.

Following this, it is important to explore the different media through which these claims are made tangible, whether oral, material, documentary or affective, and how these change over time and space, an endeavour this book contributes to. For instance, in Binder's chapter on atheist verbal propagation in India the principal aesthetic forms at stake are sonality, oratorical mastery (involving, for example, memorisation and fluency) and a 'hyperliteral' attitude towards religious texts in order to expose absurdities therein. The resultant speeches are intended not only to persuade via logical exposition but to be means of fabricating – making perceptible – secular difference, that is, secularity as a figuration of perceptible difference. We find literal visualisations of non-religion in the chapter by Hecker, which describes the materialisation in popular comic books of a comic aesthetics of resistance to the increasing de-secularisation of the Turkish state. These centre on vulgar bodily images and transgressive retellings of Muslim and religious myths. Consider too the illustrations of the American secularist

Watson Heston, whose provocative drawings featured in the American freethinker publication *Truth Seeker* in the late nineteenth century: 'His lifework had been the visualization of a secular republic, the bountiful provision of emblems – of enlightened rationality, anti-Catholicism, women's emancipation, anti-evangelicalism, scientific progress, intellectual freedom, and strict church-state separation – designed to render freethinking liberalism tangible' (Schmidt 2016, 84). The evidence of the senses and the requirement to make the invisible visible also lie at the heart of Copeman and Hagström's chapter, which describes how Indian rationalists employ video slow motion and replay to make visible their otherwise immaterial (and therefore unconvincing) claims of religious malfeasance. In addition to seeing, audience involvement in miracle-debunking performances entails use of the so-called lower senses of taste, smell and touch as important ingredients in rationalist projects of exposé. If the 'process of acquiring conviction through the senses' is frequently discussed in terms of religion (Stolow 2008, 684; van de Port 2011; Meyer 2014, 212), it is also patently a central component of non-religious sensoria.

While the resignification and redeployment of religious aesthetic forms (myths, imagery) for secular purposes described by Hecker are not novel secular techniques, they warrant our consideration as a key mode of material fabrication of senses and spaces of the non-religious (here through drawing, printing, pictures and viewing). Indeed, secular redescription, or non-religious aesthetic appraisal, can be a significant component of non-religious aesthetics, with secular actors seeking to clarify which aspects of culture – though they may 'present' as religious – possess an essentially human and therefore valuable basis independent of religious premises.[10] Such cultural forms are made 'visible and tangible, present to the senses' (Orsi) in a manner that authorises their de-sacralisation. But this is not a hard and fast rule: Bradbury and Schulz's chapter shows how clarification between 'the secular' and 'the religious' need not be significant for secular protagonists: reference to, and appreciation of, certain aesthetic traditions on their own might be considered sufficient to demarcate oneself as secular and to further one's secularity.

Digital atheism

From anthropology (Oosterbaan 2011), to sociology (Slater 2007), religious studies (Caputo 2001) and media theory (Mitchell 2015), much recent scholarship has emphasised the potential of digital technologies for evangelical outreach and visions of a globally connected religiosity.

Yet digital technologies are just as capable of fostering atheist visions of globality and future successful outreach as they are religious ones. As one influential US atheist blogger put it: '[The Internet's] a religion destroyer as much as anything else we've ever seen – open access to information, the ability to prove your pastors wrong, the overwhelming number of atheists who make their case online' (cited in Laughlin 2016, 320). A further exemplary expression of this kind of liberatory digital atheism is Iranian-born activist and commentator Maryam Namazie's statement that 'Social media and the internet are doing to Islam what the printing press did to Christianity' (Jacobsen 2017). Such claims form part of a narrative that some atheists tell about the internet and its ability to prove the validity of their claims and promote their message, forming part of a larger long-standing propensity to view the internet as a kind of 'transparency machine' (Mazzarella 2006, 489), and digital and social media as promising a 'universal political enfranchisement in the form of "access"' (Hirschkind, de Abreu and Caduff 2017, S4). At the same time, existing studies in the field of digital atheism, both those in this volume and others, demonstrate ambivalence and heterogeneity with regard to the modes of engagement of religious sceptics with the internet concerning questions of visibility, identity formation and community building. But noting such diversity is not to say there are no patterns within these engagements, as we shall see. Discussing such patterns, but also variations that depend on particular platforms or geographic regions, this book aims to advance comparative discussions of non-religious engagements with and experiences of digital media.

As we have already noted, digital technologies have played an important community-building function in allowing formerly socially isolated individual atheists in markedly religious countries to locate and interact with like-minded persons without necessarily meeting them face to face, thereby further decoupling geographical and moral proximity. This dynamic, considered by Simmel more than a century ago in his reflections on modern urban societies (1908; O'Hara et al. 2014, 2), has since accelerated because of many factors, including, especially, the rise of digital communication technologies. In places where public expressions of atheism may be treated as blasphemous and so pose physical and social dangers, digital technologies have seemed to offer a safe place for atheists to anonymously 'gather' and engage in dialogue, or to find moral closeness apart from their immediate geographic locales, or indeed simply to assuage loneliness, as reported for Kyrgyzstan (Louw 2019). Digital technologies can thus be a key tool for the imagining and construction of non-religious communities in sometimes uncongenial or even hostile locales.

The anonymity characteristic of many digital interactions can be central to non-religious digital experiences, with many users engaging anonymously because of the social costs of publicly being known to be an atheist, though certainly not all of them do this. Where online anonymity *is* preserved a critical doubleness may result, the atheist's online presence reflecting their non-religious attitudes while their visible bodies and public practices remain religious. Chalfant's chapter in this book provides a striking example of this doubleness, with US-based Reddit contributors deliberating over whether or not to 'come out' to their devout families as atheists, while Gupta's chapter, too, explores the sometimes parallel lives of young Indian atheists who, though active participants in digital atheist spaces, may refrain from expressing themselves on these matters elsewhere (for example in domestic contexts).

In such instances, use of online pseudonyms can be crucial for enabling a degree of security, for example when used among Arab ex-Muslims as a technology of destigmatisation (Khazaal 2017) or by US Reddit users as a necessary condition for the creation of 'atheist intimacies' (Chalfant, this volume). Euro-American governments are currently engaged in policy debates that raise the prospect of removing rights of anonymity on social media as a means of reducing trolling and ensuring accountability.[11] If such measures are adopted, it is not hard to imagine the deleterious effects they will have on numerous kinds of non-religious social media user.

The differentiated nature of covert engagements has been teased out by Al Zidjaly (2019, 10) for the case of Arab Twitter. If the main action takes the form of tweeted interactions between well-known ex-Muslims and current Muslims, lurkers who silently observe such debates also read along. Fear of prosecution in a region in which criticism of religion is punishable by law leads to 'followers withholding response'; this extends even to refraining from 'light practices' (Blommaert 2018) such as liking or sharing. This refraining further complicates the distribution of silence we have contemplated in previous sections, with silenced doubt associated principally with face-to-face lives (e.g., Fader), as opposed to the ability to find voice (and community, moral propinquity, etc.) in digital environments. Here we see how offline silences are not necessarily countered but replicated online (see also Richter's chapter). Voice, community and moral proximity are disaggregated: we find a kind of 'silenced community' marked by moral propinquity but not by the ability to have a voice or engage in dialogue.

Regarding the central question of digitally enabled doubleness and covert identities, it is precisely because digital technologies have assisted atheists by affording moral proximity and visions of community that some religious groups have identified these technologies as a generalised threatening 'blasphemous space'. Consider a 2017 newspaper report on atheism-related moral panics concerning social media in Pakistan: 'An Islamabad High Court (IHC) judge has called for a ban on social media sites in Pakistan, due to the spread of "blasphemous" images online. ... [The Justice] appealed for the support of Pakistan's Interior Minister ..., asking him to "take some steps in his own supervision to eliminate the evil, even at the cost of blocking the entirety [of] social media"' (Sulleyman 2017). In this way, the internet paradoxically can make atheists more visible to non-atheists even as it seems to afford them anonymity and a safe place for discussion. Thus, as we have already seen, in Bangladesh atheist bloggers have become the target of violence, in Pakistan atheist bloggers have been arrested and associated Facebook groups taken down, and in Pakistan and India internet users have publicly sought to uncover the identities of participants in atheist online forums. Another important case is that of Saudi Arabian blogger Raif Badawi, who in 2022 was released from prison after completing a ten-year sentence that included 1,000 lashes (though he received 'only' 50 after global condemnation).[12] Nevertheless, access to digital communication technologies has been particularly important for those whose voices traditionally have been constrained, as van Nieuwkerk (2018) has also argued in the case of atheist digital engagements in Egypt. Indeed, the way atheists have found refuge in private groups online but also come to be newly vulnerable to discovery through participation in them strongly reflects the significant wider argument that has been made about digital media, that it both affords greater capacities of privacy to users and has the strong potential to threaten such privacy (Miller et al. 2016, 212).

Yet, if digital technologies have undoubtedly enabled dialogues between differently located non-religious people, that is not to say they always find common ground. The ability of digital technologies to grant atheist users instant access to 'other' atheists can force acknowledgement of separateness and aversion just as much as it facilitates productive exchange. For instance, Richter (this volume) finds that many Moroccan atheists come to be 'critical of French secularism and cannot identify with the most vocal non-believers, who are overwhelmingly middle-aged Western men', while the Kyrgyz atheists discussed by Louw (2019) are as likely to be disillusioned by the divisive atheist rhetoric in global online spaces as inspired by thinkers such as Richard Dawkins. This shows once again that, despite the supposedly 'global' reach and de-territorialising potential of digital media, social and geographic location continues to matter substantially for digital atheism.

Further, while Chalfant shows how digital atheist community can seem to coalesce around discursive exaltation of the atheist individual and that individual's agency, notably in celebrating the individual atheist's heroic resolve in overcoming conformity to come out as an atheist, he also points out that users are not unaware of the role of Reddit's algorithms in manipulating their online preferences and behaviour, undermining their agentive free will even as they continue to exalt it as the pivot of their hard-won atheist subjectivities. Committed to free will versus determinism, they employ quasi-automated socio-technical structures to express and form that commitment. The point is not simply to contrast algorithms and individual human judgement (Gillespie 2016) but to recognise how embedding the latter within systems highly structured by the former can provoke novel challenges to non-religious values. With a different 'higher power' in play than the one atheists are usually concerned with, the danger faced by users is that 'the notion of the individual atheist making a rational choice to disbelieve based on available information is replaced with that of the atheist hivemind conditioned by algorithmic feedback loops and echo chambers' (Chalfant 2016, 22).

Despite perceptions of digital media as a space for disembodied forms of communication, various scholars have noted the gendered dimensions of non-religious digital engagements. Al Zidjaly (2019, 21) has examined the gendered dimension of the harbouring of covert digital identities, with Arab male atheists struggling under the burden of having to publicly perform daily acts of prayer they no longer believe in. On the other hand, social media is reportedly facilitating a challenge to traditional male dominance within atheist communities, disrupting its 'boys' club' culture 'in part because it is now easier for like-minded women to realise they are not alone in their inclinations' (McAnulla, Kettell and Schulzke 2019, 97).[13] This is reminiscent of Fader's analysis of gendered language in the Jewish blogosphere, even though it leads in that case, by contrast, to a sceptical counterpublic which 'remained almost exclusively for men, reproducing women's exclusion from the ultra-Orthodox religious public sphere' (2017, 729). Khazaal also focuses on gender differences in her chapter on expressions of atheism on Arabic YouTube, Twitter, TV shows and literature, finding that male and female atheists quite consistently account for their rejection of religion in different ways. Men tend to present their journey as one of a gradual increase in logical thinking and curiosity, with critical appraisal of religious contradictions leading to intellectual growth. This approach often fails to provoke public sympathy. By contrast, female tellings that dwell on religion-related restrictions to freedom and the consequent suffering they have endured gain far more resonance and traction, so modelling a successful form of atheist public engagement in the region.

Contrasting with the previously outlined discourse of newness, Miller et al. (2016, 205) approach digital technologies via a 'theory of attainment', which highlights how digital technology expands users' capacities without necessarily changing their pre-existing wants and desires: 'Typically new media are first used conservatively, to attain something already desired but more easily achieved with the help of this new media.' With regard to digital atheism this raises the question: do these media provide new ways of representing atheism and accentuating already existing atheist identities, as the theory would suggest, or do they assist in actively producing these phenomena? It is a question atheists themselves have posed: 'Would you be an atheist without the internet?', asked one noted atheist blogger. Laughlin (2016, 320) summarises Smith and Cimino's analysis of the responses received (2012, 27), namely, that 'the Internet is not so much responsible for making atheists as it is for the intensification of this identification', a finding that supports the theory of attainment.

Yet we also want to suggest – without denying its value in many cases – that a theory of attainment cannot always account for the generativity of non-religious digital engagements. To return to Fader's (2017, 745) work on the heretical Jewish blogosphere: she argues persuasively that doubt is not simply an unpersuasive discourse or state internal to the individual, but is 'rather produced intersubjectively in interaction' in these digital spaces, that is, through digital mediation. Further, in her work on Arabic Twitter, Al Zidjaly (2019, 10) compellingly argues that expressions of atheism are not just extensions of already existing offline attitudes, but emerge from new identities and attitudes formed from within those very spaces. Responses to the hashtag #WhyILeftIslam explicitly reference particular memes and other discrediting actions native to Twitter as key catalysts of their apostasy. Al Zidjaly suggests that 'online forbidden actions taking place on Twitter are, in a clandestine and slow, yet steady manner, taking roots and shifting the very fabric of Islamic societies in yet unforeseen ways'. Cases such as these show how digital affordances can go beyond enabling the fruition of latent attitudes or desires to actively produce varieties of non-religion.

So far we have shown how the digital can be good to think with for atheists (not just for practitioners of religion; cf. Slater 2007), deliver a means of communication to atheists whose voices have hitherto been constrained, foster global visions of non-religious connection, offer a variety of meaningful modes of non-religious association, and in certain circumstances go further than actualising already existing atheist latency to generate atheist attitudes, understandings and affects 'from within'. Yet we have also sought to highlight problems and limitations concerning silencing, threats to privacy, and algorithmic disruption of non-religious values and global frictions, and we finish by proposing a further qualification concerning the potentially constraining nature of discussion forums and their prescription of identity.

Scholars have, with good reason, emphasised a connection between global intensification of engagements with digital media and a burgeoning of non-religious identity politics (e.g. Smith and Cimino 2012; Addington 2017; Bullivant 2020). Yet we want to caution against the presumption of such a relation and to note how, even where such a relation unquestionably exists, it may be shot through with ambiguity and ambivalence, as we saw earlier in our discussion of Lundmark's chapter in this volume. Consider also the UK-based closeted ex-Muslims studied by Simon Cottee, for whom anonymous online discussion forums are important for ameliorating loneliness, offering support and providing an appropriate language for defining their journey away from Islam. At the same time, online discussion can trigger difficult emotions in users, and even lead to depression, while for others the usefulness of such forums is strictly time-bound, in part because it is too definitional in terms of identity: not wanting to be defined by their atheism only, apostates may leave the forums to re-engage with 'real life'. As Cottee was told by one of his interlocutors: 'There's more to me than being someone who used to be a Muslim' (2015, 207). This does not gainsay the pivotal role of these forums in apostates' journeys, but rather suggests they can play a role akin to the proverbial ladder that can be kicked away after the ascent, and that non-religious identity can be something to be resisted via digital engagements as well as fostered by them.

Acknowledgements

We would like to thank John Hagström, Michael Vine and Jakub Zahora for valuable feedback on earlier versions of this chapter.

Notes

1　The War Crimes Tribunal of Bangladesh was set up in 2009 to prosecute crimes committed during the Independence War in Bangladesh. It was criticised by the opposition as being politically motivated and resulted in a considerable polarisation around issues of secularism, atheism and Islam.
2　'New Atheism' denotes the impact of ostensibly novel arguments against religion that saw widespread popular diffusion in the first decade of the twenty-first century as a result of the publishing successes of predominantly US- and UK-based atheist and humanist thinkers such as Richard Dawkins, Daniel Dennett, Christopher Hitchens and Sam Harris, who are often collectively referred to as the 'New Atheists'.
3　See Chalfant (2016) and Laughlin (2016) for earlier applications of the concept. Laughlin's is distinctive for arguing that US digital atheism 'is far less a counterpublic, in Warner's sense, than it imagines itself to be' (p. 334).
4　Richter is drawing on bell hooks's concepts here.
5　Founded by Iranian Canadian ex-Muslim Armin Navabi in 2012, Atheist Republic has developed into a prominent and influential multiplatform digital community with many national branches. Growing out of the Orkut-hosted 'Iranian Atheists' group, its name was coined to contrast with that of the Islamic Republic of Iran.
6　Notably, Bangladeshis with residence in the US took a leading role in initiating and promoting this digital platform. The significance of expatriate citizens for digital platforms such as Mukto-Mona has parallels in many other regions, such as Morocco (Richter) and India (Gupta).
7　https://mm-gold.azureedge.net/new_site/mukto-mona/muk-aboutus.html, accessed 19 May 2022.
8　It was a Yahoo group for a short time before being transformed into a website.
9　Aesthetics is understood here as 'a methodological framework for integrating the analysis of sensory, embodied, mediated, and cognitive aspects of religious practices within specific historical and political contexts' (Binder 2019, 285 fn.3).
10　See Engelke (2014) for a related argument. The corollary of discerning which modes of religiosity are to be considered legitimate cultural or human artefacts is the marking for disposal of those aspects of culture which cannot thus be determined (that is, superstitious and potentially harmful mystical practices and understandings); see Hagström and Copeman (2023).
11　Other states have trialled or adopted such laws, e.g. Egypt and South Korea. The Geek Feminism Wiki has compiled a list of groups likely to be harmed by the introduction of 'Real Names' mandates. It includes 'those whose religious beliefs, lack thereof, or experiences place them at risk' and 'people who are questioning their religious beliefs': https://geekfeminism.fandom.com/wiki/Who_is_harmed_by_a_%22Real_Names%22_policy%3F (accessed 20 August 2022).
12　'Saudi blogger Raif Badawi released from prison', Al Jazeera, 11 March 2022. https://www.aljazeera.com/news/2022/3/11/saudi-blogger-raif-badawi-released-from-prison (accessed 20 May 2022).
13　The relationship between non-religion and progressive politics is of course multifaceted and contested. Studies by Laughlin (2016), Quack (2012) and Bradley and Tate (2010) provide starkly different perspectives on this question.

References

Addington, Aislinn. 2017. 'Building bridges in the shadows of steeples: Atheist community and identity online', in *Organized Secularism in the United States: New directions in research*, Ryan T. Cragun, Christel Manning and Lori L. Fazzino, eds, 135–49. Berlin and Boston, MA: De Gruyter. https://doi.org/10.1515/9783110458657-008.
Al Hariri, Youssef, Walid Magdy and Maria Wolters. 2019. 'Arabs and atheism: Religious discussions in the Arab Twittersphere', in *Social Informatics: 11th International Conference, SocInfo 2019, Doha, Qatar, November 18–21, 2019, Proceedings*, Ingmar Weber, Kareem M. Darwish, Claudia Wagner, Emilio Zagheni, Laura Nelson, Samin Aref and Fabian Flöck, eds, 18–34. Cham: Springer.

Al Zidjaly, Najma. 2019. 'Digital activism as nexus analysis: A sociolinguistic example from Arabic Twitter.' *Tilburg Papers in Culture Studies.* Paper 221: 1–28.

Aupers, Stef, Dick Houtman and Peter Pels. 2008. 'Cybergnosis: Technology, religion, and the secular', in *Religion: Beyond a concept*, Hent de Vries, ed., 687–703. New York: Fordham University Press.

Barber, Karin. 2007. *The Anthropology of Texts, Persons and Publics.* Cambridge: Cambridge University Press.

Binder, Stefan. 2016. '"Let us become human through beef and pork": Atheist humanism and the aesthetics of caste.' *Südasien-Chronik/South Asia Chronicle* 6: 205–27.

Binder, Stefan. 2019. 'Magic is science: Atheist conjuring and the exposure of superstition in South India.' *HAU: Journal of Ethnographic Theory* 9 (2): 284–98.

Binder, Stefan. 2020. *Total Atheism: Secular activism and the politics of difference in South Asia.* New York and Oxford: Berghahn.

Birman, Patricia. 2006. 'Future in the mirror: Media, evangelicals, and politics in Rio de Janeiro', in *Religion, Media, and the Public Sphere*, Birgit Meyer and Annelies Moors, eds, 52–72. Bloomington: Indiana University Press.

Blankholm, Joseph. 2017. 'The ghost of immanentism.' *The Immanent Frame*, 14 November 2017, https://tif.ssrc.org/2017/11/14/the-ghost-of-immanentism/ (accessed 21 May 2022).

Blankholm, Joseph. 2018. 'Secularism and secular people.' *Public Culture* 30 (2): 245–68. https://doi.org/10.1215/08992363-4310874.

Blechschmidt, Alexander. 2018. 'The secular movement in the Philippines: Atheism and activism in a Catholic country.' PhD thesis, University of Zurich.

Blechschmidt, Alexander. 2020. 'Collective nonreligiosities in the Philippines', in *The Diversity of Nonreligion: Normativities and contested relations*, Johannes Quack, Cora Schuh and Susanne Kind, eds, 77–104. Abingdon and New York: Routledge.

Blessing, Kimberley, 2013. 'Atheism and the meaningfulness of life', in *The Oxford Handbook of Atheism*, Stephen Bullivant and Michael Ruse, eds, 104–18. Oxford: Oxford University Press.

Blommaert, Jan. 2018. *Durkheim and the Internet: On sociolinguistics and the sociological imagination.* London: Bloomsbury Academic.

Bosman, Frank. 2019. *Gaming and the Divine: A new systematic theology of video games.* Abingdon: Routledge.

Bradley, Arthur and Andrew Tate. 2010. *The New Atheist Novel: Philosophy, fiction and polemic after 9/11.* London: Continuum.

Bullivant, Stephen. 2020. 'Explaining the rise of "nonreligion studies": Subfield formation and institutionalization within the sociology of religion.' *Social Compass* 67 (1): 86–102. https://doi.org/10.1177/0037768619894815.

Calhoun, Craig, ed. 1992. *Habermas and the Public Sphere.* Cambridge, MA: MIT Press.

Caputo, John. 2001. *On Religion.* Abingdon: Routledge.

Chalfant, Eric. 2016. 'Practicing disbelief: Atheist media in America from the nineteenth century to today.' PhD dissertation, Duke University.

Chalfant, Eric. 2020. 'Material irreligion: The role of media in atheist studies.' *Religion Compass* 14 (3): 1–11. https://doi.org/10.1111/rec3.12349.

Chidester, David. 2018. *Religion: Material dynamics.* Oakland: University of California Press.

Chowdhury, Nusrat Sabina. 2019. *Paradoxes of the Popular: Crowd politics in Bangladesh.* Stanford, CA: Stanford University Press.

Cimino, Richard and Christopher Smith. 2014. *Atheist Awakening: Secular activism and community in America.* New York: Oxford University Press.

Cody, Francis. 2009. 'Daily wires and daily blossoms: Cultivating regimes of circulation in Tamil India's newspaper revolution.' *Journal of Linguistic Anthropology* 19 (2): 286–309. https://doi.org/10.1111/j.1548-1395.2009.01035.x.

Cody, Francis. 2011. 'Publics and politics.' *Annual Review of Anthropology* 40: 37–52. https://doi.org/10.1146/annurev-anthro-081309-145626.

Cody, Francis. 2020. 'Millennial turbulence: The networking of Tamil media politics.' *Television & New Media* 21 (4): 392–406. https://doi.org/10.1177/1527476419869128.

Copeman, Jacob and Johannes Quack. 2015. 'Godless people and dead bodies: Materiality and the morality of atheist materialism.' *Social Analysis* 59 (2): 40–61. https://doi.org/10.3167/sa.2015.590203.

Copeman, Jacob and Johannes Quack. 2019. 'Contemporary religiosities', in *Critical Themes in Indian Sociology*, Sanjay Srivastava, Yasmeen Arif and Janaki Abraham, eds, 44–61. New Delhi: SAGE Publications India.

Cottee, Simon. 2015. *The Apostates: When Muslims leave Islam*. London: Hurst & Co.

Dawkins, Richard. 2006. *The God Delusion*. Boston, MA: Houghton Mifflin.

Dick, Hannah. 2015. 'Atheism in religious clothing? Accounting for atheist interventions in the public sphere.' *Culture and Religion* 16 (4): 372–91. https://doi.org/10.1080/14755610.2015.1090466.

Duile, Timo. 2020. 'Being atheist in the religious harmony state of Indonesia.' *Asia Pacific Journal of Anthropology* 21 (5): 450–65. https://doi.org/10.1080/14442213.2020.1829022.

Eisenlohr, Patrick. 2017. 'Reconsidering mediatization of religion: Islamic televangelism in India.' *Media, Culture & Society* 39 (6): 869–84. https://doi.org/10.1177/0163443716679032.

Engelke, Matthew. 2005. 'Sticky subjects and sticky objects: The substance of African Christian healing', in *Materiality*, Daniel Miller, ed., 118–39. Durham, NC: Duke University Press.

Engelke, Matthew. 2011. 'Material religion', in *The Cambridge Companion to Religious Studies*, Robert A. Orsi, ed., 209–29. Cambridge: Cambridge University Press.

Engelke, Matthew. 2012. 'Angels in Swindon: Public religion and ambient faith in England.' *American Ethnologist* 39 (1): 155–70. https://doi.org/10.1111/j.1548-1425.2011.01355.x.

Engelke, Matthew. 2014. 'Christianity and the anthropology of secular humanism.' *Current Anthropology* 55 (S10): S292–S301.

Engelke, Matthew. 2015. 'The coffin question: Death and materiality in humanist funerals.' *Material Religion* 11 (1): 26–48. https://doi.org/10.2752/205393215X14259900061553.

Engelke, Matthew. 2019. 'Afterword: Getting hold of the secular', in *Secular Bodies, Affects, and Emotions: European configurations*, Monique Scheer, Nadia Fadil and Birgitte Schepelern Johansen, eds, 199–207. London: Bloomsbury Academic.

Epstein, Greg. 2009. *Good without God: What a billion nonreligious people do believe*. New York: William Morrow.

Fader, Ayala. 2017. 'The counterpublic of the J(ewish) Blogosphere: Gendered language and the mediation of religious doubt among ultra-Orthodox Jews in New York.' *Journal of the Royal Anthropological Institute* 23 (4): 727–47. https://doi.org/10.1111/1467-9655.12697.

Fader, Ayala. 2020. *Hidden Heretics: Jewish doubt in the digital age*. Princeton, NJ: Princeton University Press.

Flynn, Tom. 2010. 'Why I don't believe in the New Atheism.' *Free Inquiry* 30 (3): 7–43.

Fraser, Nancy. 1992. 'Rethinking the public sphere: A contribution to the critique of actually existing democracy', in *Habermas and the Public Sphere*, Craig Calhoun, ed., 109–42. Cambridge, MA: MIT Press.

Gillespie, Tarleton. 2016. 'Algorithm', in *Digital Keywords: A vocabulary of information society and culture*, Benjamin Peters, ed., 18–30. Princeton, NJ: Princeton University Press.

Gilmartin, David. 2015. 'Rethinking the public through the lens of sovereignty.' *South Asia: Journal of South Asian Studies* 38 (3): 371–86. https://doi.org/10.1080/00856401.2015.1055422.

Goody, Jack. 1996. 'A kernel of doubt.' *Journal of the Royal Anthropological Institute* 2 (4): 667–81. https://doi.org/10.2307/3034302.

Goody, Jack and Ian Watt. 1963. 'The consequences of literacy.' *Comparative Studies in Society and History* 5 (3): 304–45. https://doi.org/10.1017/S0010417500001730.

Hagström, John and Jacob Copeman. 2023. 'Clarification and disposal as key concepts in the anthropology of non-religion.' *Religion and Society* 14.

Haque, Mahamudul. 2013. '"Black propaganda": Is blogging a sin?' *The Daily Star*, 12 April. https://www.thedailystar.net/news/black-propaganda-is-blogging-a-sin (accessed 30 June 2022).

Hasan, Mubashar and Arild Engelsen Ruud. 2021. 'The state and the construction of the "blasphemer" in Bangladesh', in *Blasphemies Compared: Transgressive speech in a globalised world*, Anne Stensvold, ed., 175–91. Abingdon: Routledge.

Hirschkind, Charles. 2006. *The Ethical Soundscape: Cassette sermons and Islamic counterpublics*. New York: Columbia University Press.

Hirschkind, Charles, Maria José A. de Abreu and Carlo Caduff. 2017. 'New media, new publics? An introduction to supplement 15.' *Current Anthropology* 58 (S15): S3–S12.

Houtman, Dick and Birgit Meyer, eds. 2012. *Things: Religion and the question of materiality*. New York: Fordham University Press.

Hummel, Tyler. 2019. 'Flawed faith: Rick and Morty, existential angst, and millennials.' *Geeks under Grace*, 9 November. https://geeksundergrace.com/christian-living/flawed-faith-rick-and-morty-existential-angst-and-millennials/ (accessed 21 May 2022).

Jacobsen, Scott Douglas. 2017. 'Extended interview with Maryam Namazie', *Humanist Voices*, 23 September. https://medium.com/humanist-voices/extended-interview-with-maryam-namazie-a60070ee804d (accessed 30 June 2022).

Jain, Kajri. 2017. 'Gods in the time of automobility.' *Current Anthropology* 58 (S15): S13–S26.

Jain, Kajri. 2021. *Gods in the Time of Democracy*. Durham, NC: Duke University Press.

Kelty, Christopher M. 2017. 'Too much democracy in all the wrong places: Toward a grammar of participation.' *Current Anthropology* 58 (S15): S77–S90.

Kettell, Steven. 2013. 'Faithless: The politics of new atheism.' *Secularism and Nonreligion* 2: 61–72. http://doi.org/10.5334/snr.al.

Khan, Shahadat H. 2001. 'Radicalism in Bengali Muslim thought: Kazi Andul Wadud and the "religion of creativity"', in *Understanding the Bengal Muslims: Interpretative essays*, Rafiuddin Ahmed, ed., 153–78. New Delhi: Oxford University Press.

Khazaal, Natalie. 2017. 'The cultural politics of religious defiance in Islam: How pseudonyms and media can destigmatize.' *Communication and Critical/Cultural Studies* 14 (3): 271–87. https://doi.org/10.1080/14791420.2017.1296170.

Kind, Susanne. 2020. 'Contested humanist identities in Sweden', in *The Diversity of Nonreligion: Normativities and contested relations*, Johannes Quack, Cora Schuh and Susanne Kind, eds, 35–76. Abingdon and New York: Routledge.

Laughlin, Jack C. 2016. 'Varieties of an atheist public in a digital age: The politics of recognition and the recognition of politics.' *Journal of Religion, Media and Digital Culture* 5 (2): 315–38. https://doi.org/10.1163/21659214-90000084.

Lebner, Ashley. 2018. 'On secularity: Marxism, reality, and the Messiah in Brazil.' *Journal of the Royal Anthropological Institute* 25 (1): 123–47. https://doi.org/10.1111/1467-9655.13000.

Lee, Lois. 2012. 'Locating nonreligion, in mind, body and space: New research methods for a new field', in *Annual Review of the Sociology of Religion. Volume 3: New Methods in the Sociology of Religion*, Luigi Berzano and Ole Preben Riis, eds, 135–57. Leiden: Brill.

Lee, Lois. 2019. 'Observing the atheist at worship: Ways of seeing the secular body', in *Secular Bodies, Affects and Emotions: European configurations*, Monique Scheer, Nadia Fadil and Birgitte Schepelern Johansen, eds, 43–60. London: Bloomsbury Academic.

Lewis, Tania. 2016. 'Spirited publics? Post-secularism, enchantment and enterprise on Indian television', in *Contemporary Publics: Shifting boundaries in new media, technology and culture*, P. David Marshall, Glenn D'Cruz, Sharyn McDonald and Katja Lee, eds, 283–99. London: Palgrave Macmillan.

Linneman, Thomas and Margaret Clendenen. 2010. 'Sexuality and the secular', in *Atheism and Secularity. Volume 1: Issues, Concepts, and Definitions*, Phil Zuckerman, ed., 89–112. Santa Barbara, CA: Praeger.

Louw, Maria. 2019. 'Atheism 2.0: Searching for spaces for atheism in contemporary Kyrgyzstan.' *Central Asian Affairs* 6 (2–3): 206–23. https://doi.org/10.1163/22142290-00602007.

Loxton, Daniel. 2009. 'The paradoxical future of skepticism.' *Skeptical Inquirer* 33 (6) November/December: 24–7.

Luehrmann, Sonja. 2011. *Secularism Soviet Style: Teaching atheism and religion in a Volga republic*. Bloomington: Indiana University Press.

Luehrmann, Sonja. 2015. 'Antagonistic insights: Evolving Soviet atheist critiques of religion and why they matter for anthropology.' *Social Analysis* 59 (2): 97–113. https://doi.org/10.3167/sa.2015.590206.

Lundmark, Evelina and Stephen LeDrew. 2019. 'Unorganized atheism and the secular movement: Reddit as a site for studying "lived atheism".' *Social Compass* 66 (1): 112–29. https://doi.org/10.1177/0037768618816096.

Marshall, P. David. 2016. 'Introduction: The plurality of publics', in *Contemporary Publics: Shifting boundaries in new media, technology and culture*, P. David Marshall, Glenn D'Cruz, Sharyn McDonald and Katja Lee, eds, 1–13. London: Palgrave Macmillan.

Mazzarella, William. 2006. 'Internet X-Ray: E-governance, transparency, and the politics of immediation in India.' *Public Culture* 18 (3): 473–505. https://doi.org/10.1215/08992363-2006-016.

McAnulla, Stuart, Steven Kettell and Marcus Schulzke. 2019. *The Politics of New Atheism*. Abingdon: Routledge.

Mertz, Elizabeth. 2007. *The Language of Law School: Learning to 'think like a lawyer'*. New York: Oxford University Press.

Meyer, Birgit. 2006. 'Religious revelation, secrecy, and the limits of visual representation.' *Anthropological Theory* 6 (4): 431–53. https://doi.org/10.1177/1463499606071596.

Meyer, Birgit, ed. 2009. *Aesthetic Formations: Media, religion, and the senses*. New York: Palgrave Macmillan.

Meyer, Birgit. 2014. 'Mediation and the genesis of presence: Toward a material approach to religion.' *Religion and Society* 5: 205–54. https://doi.org/10.3167/arrs.2014.050114.

Meyer, Birgit and Annelies Moors, eds. 2006. *Religion, Media, and the Public Sphere*. Bloomington: Indiana University Press.

Miller, Daniel, Elisabetta Costa, Nell Haynes, Tom McDonald, Razvan Nicolescu, Jolynna Sinanan, Juliano Spyer, Shriram Venkatraman and Xinyuan Wang. 2016. *How the World Changed Social Media*. London: UCL Press.

Minois, Georges. 2012. *The Atheist's Bible: The most dangerous book that never existed* (trans. Lys Ann Weiss). Chicago: University of Chicago Press.

Mitchell, W. J. T. 2015. *Image Science: Iconology, visual culture, and media aesthetics*. Chicago: University of Chicago Press.

Morgan, David. 2009. 'Introduction: The matter of belief', in *Religion and Material Culture: The matter of belief*, David Morgan, ed., 1–17. Abingdon: Routledge.

Morris, Rosalind C. 2013. 'Theses on the new Öffentlichkeit.' *Grey Room* 51: 94–111. https://doi.org/10.1162/GREY_a_00108.

Murshid, Tazeen M. 1997. 'State, nation, identity: The quest for legitimacy in Bangladesh.' *South Asia: Journal of South Asian Studies* 20 (2): 1–34. https://doi.org/10.1080/00856409708723294.

Nash, David. 1995. '"Look in her face and lose thy dread of dying": The ideological importance of death to the secularist community in nineteenth-century Britain.' *Journal of Religious History* 19 (2): 158–80. https://doi.org/10.1111/j.1467-9809.1995.tb00254.x.

Nash, David. 2019. 'Secularist history: Past perspectives and future prospects.' *Secularism and Nonreligion* 8 (1): 1–9. http://doi.org/10.5334/snr.113.

O'Hara, Kenton P., Michael Massimi, Richard Harper, Simon Rubens and Jessica Morris. 2014. 'Everyday dwelling with WhatsApp', in *CSCW '14: Proceedings of the 17th ACM conference on computer supported cooperative work & social computing*, 1131–43. https://doi.org/10.1145/2531602.2531679.

Oosterbaan, Martijn. 2011. 'Virtually global: Online evangelical cartography.' *Social Anthropology* 19 (1): 56–73. https://doi.org/10.1111/j.1469-8676.2010.00138.x.

Orsi, Robert. 2012. 'Material children: Making God's presence real through Catholic boys and girls', in *Religion, Media and Culture: A reader*, Gordon Lynch and Jolyon Mitchell, eds, 147–58. Abingdon: Routledge.

Pigliucci, Massimo. 2014. 'A muddled defense of New Atheism: On Stenger's response.' *Science, Religion and Culture* 1 (1): 10–14.

Prince, Ruth. 2019. 'Pandemic publics: How epidemics transform social and political collectives of public health', in *The Anthropology of Epidemics*, Ann H. Kelly, Frédéric Keck and Christos Lynteris, eds, 135–53. Abingdon: Routledge.

Quack, Johannes. 2012. *Disenchanting India: Organized rationalism and criticism of religion in India*. New York: Oxford University Press.

Rajagopal, Arvind. 2001. *Politics after Television: Religious nationalism and the reshaping of the Indian public*. Cambridge: Cambridge University Press.

Rao, Ursula. 2011. '"Inter-publics": Hindu mobilization beyond the bourgeois public sphere.' *Religion and Society* 2: 90–105.

Rashid, Radzuwan Ab and Azweed Mohamad. 2019. *New Media Narratives and Cultural Influence in Malaysia: The strategic construction of blog rhetoric by an apostate*. Singapore: Springer.

Richter, Lena. 2021. 'Laughing about religious authority – but not too loud.' *Religions* 12 (2), art. no. 73: 1–18. https://doi.org/10.3390/rel12020073.

Salvatore, Armando and Dale Eickelman. 2004. *Public Islam and the Common Good*. Leiden: Brill.

Schäfer, Saskia. 2016. 'Forming "forbidden" identities online: Atheism in Indonesia.' *Austrian Journal of South-East Asian Studies* 9 (2): 253–68. https://doi.org/10.14764/10.ASEAS-2016.2-5.

Schielke, Samuli. 2015. *Egypt in the Future Tense: Hope, frustration, and ambivalence before and after 2011*. Bloomington: Indiana University Press.

Schmidt, Leigh Eric. 2016. *Village Atheists: How America's unbelievers made their way in a godly nation*. Princeton, NJ: Princeton University Press.

Schulz, Mascha. 2021. 'Convoluted convictions, partial positionings: Non-religion, secularism, and party politics in Sylhet, Bangladesh.' PhD thesis, University of Zurich.

Schulz, Mascha and Stefan Binder. 2023. 'Introduction: An anthropology of nonreligion?' *Religion and Society* 14.

Simmel, Georg. 1908. *Soziologie. Untersuchungen über die Formen der Vergesellschaftung* ['Sociology: investigations on the forms of sociation']. Leipzig: Duncker and Humblot.

Slater, Don. 2007. 'Glimpsing God in the Internet', in *Cultural Politics in a Global Age: Uncertainty, solidarity and innovation*, David Held and Henrietta Moore, eds, 88–97. Oxford: Oneworld.

Smith, Christopher and Richard Cimino. 2012. 'Atheisms unbound: The role of the new media in the formation of a secularist identity.' *Secularism and Nonreligion* 1: 17–31. http://doi.org/10.5334/snr.ab.

Stille, Max. 2020. *Islamic Sermons and Public Piety in Bangladesh: The poetics of popular preaching*. New York: I.B. Tauris.

Stolow, Jeremy. 2008. 'Salvation by electricity', in *Religion: Beyond a concept*, Hent de Vries, ed., 668–86. New York: Fordham University Press.

Sulleyman, Aatif, 'Pakistan considers social media ban due to blasphemous content online', *The Independent*, 8 March 2017. https://www.independent.co.uk/tech/pakistan-social-media-ban-fears-blasphemous-content-online-islam-muslim-faith-a7619076.html (accessed 30 June 2022).

Taussig, Michael. 1999. *Defacement: Public secrecy and the labor of the negative*. Stanford, CA: Stanford University Press.

Tomlins, Steven and Spencer Culham Bullivant. 2016. 'Introduction', in *The Atheist Bus Campaign: Global manifestations and responses*, Steven Tomlins and Spencer Culham Bullivant, eds, 1–23. Leiden: Brill.

van de Port, Mattijs. 2011. '(Not) Made by the human hand: Media consciousness and immediacy in the cultural production of the real.' *Social Anthropology* 19 (1): 74–89. https://doi.org/10.1111/j.1469-8676.2010.00139.x.

van Nieuwkerk, Karin. 2018. 'Religious skepticism and nonbelieving in Egypt', in *Moving In and Out of Islam*, Karin van Nieuwkerk, ed., 306–32. Austin: University of Texas Press.

Walker, David. 2013. 'The humbug in American religion: Ritual theories of nineteenth-century spiritualism.' *Religion and American Culture* 23 (1): 30–74. https://doi.org/10.1525/rac.2013.23.1.30.

Warner, Michael. 2002. *Publics and Counterpublics*. New York: Zone Books.

Whitmarsh, Tim. 2016. *Battling the Gods: Atheism in the ancient world*. New York: Alfred A. Knopf.

Zillinger, Martin. 2017. 'Graduated publics: Mediating trance in the age of technical reproduction.' *Current Anthropology* 58 (S15): S41–S55.

Zuckerman, Phil and John R. Shook. 2017. 'Introduction: The study of secularism', in *The Oxford Handbook of Secularism*, Phil Zuckerman and John R. Shook, eds, 1–17. New York: Oxford University Press.

Aesthetics and visual culture
of non-religion

1
Rationalist camera: non-religious techniques of vision in India

Jacob Copeman and John Hagström

There now exist many scholarly accounts that demonstrate how adept religious practitioners have been at employing the latest forms of media for their own purposes (e.g., de Vries and Weber 2001; Pinney 2004; Dwyer 2006; Meyer 2009; Eisenlohr 2011). In the case of India, writes Kajri Jain, 'most new media and technologies made their initial appearances with religious or mythological themes – indeed, one might argue that in India, religion has been the most responsive arena for new technologies of all kinds' (2012, 188). In this chapter, we provide examples of Indian rationalist visual media interventions that contrast Jain's diagnosis. They range from locally specific uses of video slow motion, replay and hidden cameras to successful mass-mediatised campaigns of exposé that demonstrate both the growth and the ambivalent nature of the rationalist movement's influence on Indian public culture. These examples of how rationalist activists have used technological media (film) to unmask superstitious phenomena rub up against well-established trends in occult anthropology and largely Western-centric histories of communication. In these two areas of enquiry, ethnographic and historical data have been used to argue that technology – especially photography, film and telegraphy/telephony – has inexorably spectral dimensions (e.g. Leathem 2019). Meanwhile, considerable scholarly effort has been expended on demonstrating how the emergence and expansion of various technological forms has inhibited the proliferation of secular sensibilities and impaired secularisation (in Ashley Lebner's (2018) sense, as projects and processes that create domains and practices that are distinct from religious, mystical and superstitious premises). To be sure, anthropology has accumulated a rich bank of insights that rightly undermine secular-modern triumphalism and, in particular, have radically unsettled the idea that a specifically *technological* modernity allows for critical secular affordances. In this chapter, we raise a provocation against these disciplinary habits of mind and suggest that they risk saddling analysts with a blinkered approach to contexts in which it is necessary to critically examine yet also recognise the secular achievements and effects that technological forms can engender.

While secularism and detachment from religious forces and premises are long-standing concerns in the sociology and anthropology of South Asia, existing scholarship on this region, as on others, frequently invokes secularism as an abstract intellectual doctrine or in terms of its legal-constitutional status. If anthropology is philosophy with the people left in (Ingold 1992), secularism has mostly been analysed with the people left out. This tendency has, however, begun to change, with an increasing number of studies seeking to move beyond intellectualised debates to access the lived, practical dimensions of secularism. These studies form part of a growing discussion of non-religion globally that seeks to take its manifestations seriously in ethnographic terms (see for example Blanes and Oustinova-Stjepanovic 2015; Schulz and Binder 2023). Research on the topic in India has focused on the organised criticism of religion, delineating the particularities of Indian rationalism and non-religion as ways of life.[1] This work has entailed a kind of balancing act: acknowledging the pervasiveness of religion and the prevailing importance of caste without corroborating the frequently unchallenged assumption that all Indians are 'notoriously religious' and only to be understood as *homines hierarchici*. Studies of Indian rationalism have not omitted discussion of media, matter, aesthetics and publicity: for example, its often mediatised anti-superstition and miracle exposure campaigns (Quack 2012; Binder 2019), its promotion of body donation as a means of enacting materialism and social reform (Copeman and Quack 2015), and the aesthetics of naming (Copeman 2015) and speech (Binder, this volume), have all been explored. However, the modalities of publicity it pursues have not formed the primary subject matter of these studies.

While studies of non-religion have much to learn from recent generative works on affinities and dependencies between religion and various forms of media (see Copeman and Schulz, this volume), it is also the case that richly entangled histories of non-religion, media and matter have constituted a blind spot in this proliferation of works (Copeman and Quack 2015, 55). Moreover, we question the emphasis of this research on the deeply (even essentially) woven-together nature of media and religion (e.g. Mitchell 2015, 116), an emphasis that militates against any suggestion that media can be deployed to produce secular(ising) effects. Helpful here is Ashley Lebner's (2018) argument concerning the inextricability of publicity and *secularity*. Lebner defines secularity as 'the condition of living *with* secularization', with secularisation understood not in conventional (yet now long discredited) terms of a putative growth in atheistic attitudes but instead as the enlargement of spaces of action and reflection distinguishable from religion (p. 127). These secular domains and sensibilities are marked by a 'will to publicity' because of their attitudes to 'reality'. The demarcations of secularisation, albeit roughly drawn and subject to dispute, make reality subject to public argument and contestation (pp. 129–30). Secularisation, by necessity, involves 'encounters with other views of reality and politics – and with other publics – and thus makes reality and politics themselves publicly contestable' (p. 142). Hence 'the will to publicity, the desire to go public, arise under conditions of secularity' (p. 129).

The Indian rationalist, humanist, and atheist activists we are concerned with here seek to contest and remedy the non-naturalistic understanding of reality they see as predominating in the country.[2] Secularising publics do not necessarily see themselves as such (Lebner 2018, 129); however, in this case the mode of secular publicity at stake is explicitly and reflectively so. The will to publicity is instantiated in the ways activists have sought simultaneously to define their own reality and to mould others' conceptions of it. Such a reality, roughly speaking, is one that is 'exhausted by nature [and] contain[s] nothing "supernatural"'. Its proponents argue that 'the scientific method should be used to investigate all areas of reality, including the "human spirit"' (Papineau 2007, para. 1). Oratory and writing have traditionally been central to invoking this reality (Quack 2012; Binder, this volume). The movement's use of written media, earlier in the form of printed periodicals and pamphlets and more recently as blogs and articles on dedicated websites, has been prolific and wide-ranging.[3] To contest realities fraught with supernatural premises, a key approach has been to launch public challenges; in this chapter, we refer to these as 'tournaments of reality'. Celebrated anti-superstition campaigner Abraham Kovoor (1898–1978) was pivotal in developing this mode of publicity, with 'purveyors of superstition' such as astrologers and palmists challenged to prove their dubious claims under scientific conditions (Yongjia 2008, 9; Quack 2012). Such challenges would be advertised in newspapers and the results subsequently reported.[4] Another prominent means of overtly contesting supernatural claims on reality, as noted, has been the public performance of miracle demonstrations, the aim being to set up a kind of 'theatre of proof' (Ecks 2010) in which to expose the trickery of holy men who gain followers and funds through the performance of miracles. Activists demonstrate the 'science behind miracles' before audiences – most often schoolchildren – who are shown how to perform them and encouraged to replicate the work of exposé themselves.

Eric Chalfant (this volume) notes that atheist publics in the modern West, since their inception as self-identified communities roughly 300 years ago, have been preoccupied with a politics of visibility centring on how to make themselves, and atheism more broadly, visible to a wider religious public. Meanwhile, James Bradbury and Mascha Schulz (this volume) propose the notion of secular media as that which simultaneously expresses, and has the potential transformatively to embody (instantiate), secular convictions. These insights, taken together with Lebner's on the inextricability of secularity and publicity, set the stage for the central focus of this chapter: the possibilities and perils afforded to activist reality contestation by new developments in visual media. What happens when the staple techniques of exposure we have outlined are filmed and subjected to mass mediatisation?

Chalfant's chapter explores questions of the visibility of atheist identity through discussion of the public appearances of Madalyn Murray O'Hair in the US in the twentieth century – her priority being to challenge prevalent negative understandings of atheism, to re-present it in destigmatised form, and to claim certain rights for atheists – and also of Reddit's atheist community, in which questions of visibility are discussed more equivocally, because 'coming out' as an atheist can entail profound family tensions. This kind of atheist visibility is something to be thought through carefully and even discouraged. Building on Chalfant's analysis, this chapter identifies further dimensions of an atheist politics of visibility in India. Similar to members of the atheist Reddit community's ambivalence concerning visibility[5] (see also Gupta, this volume), there are drawbacks for Indian rationalists in becoming visible via mass media. It can place a target on their backs; they become exposed even as, or precisely because, they seek to expose superstitions. Further, the fact that private TV is driven in part by a commercial profit motive can jeopardise and actively undermine the messages that rationalists seek to convey. Yet film and TV offer rationalists new 'techniques of vision' (Hirsch 2004), techniques that are less about causing atheism to be seen than about prompting mass audiences to see better the nature of reality. Adapting Hirsch (pp. 19–20), we highlight how film and TV – in the form of video slow motion, the hidden camera, replay and massification of exposé – offer rationalists new techniques of vision conducive to the public disclosure of naturalistic reality. By using the term 'techniques of vision', we draw attention to the capacity of film and TV to 'bring forth' vision: the word 'technique' derives from 'techne' – 'a form of poiesis, something that brings forth' (Weiner 2001, 87).[6] Rationalists view such techniques as forms of secular media in the sense discussed by Bradbury and Schulz (this volume): inherently disposed to both mediating and producing secular sentiments. We refer here to the possibilities and hoped-for effects of these media – their potential as secular media to provide new ways of rendering revelations of reality.

Rationalist camera

In discussing what he calls registers of incontestability – modes and means of authentication, of communicating the unarguability of a given claim – Mattijs van de Port (2004) emphasises the power of the *how* over the *what* of communication; indeed, the latter's relationship to the former is depicted as being one of complete dependency. For the rationalists, the *how* of filmic techniques of vision has the potential to bring forth the 'unarguable truthfulness' (p. 20) of their claims concerning reality – a kind of felicity condition underscoring the veracity of the naturalist message transmitted. While many rationalists today harbour a sense of having been left behind as religious figures such as spiritual gurus have proceeded with notable entrepreneurial prowess to seize the expansive possibilities of television and film, rationalists of the 1980s and 1990s were in some ways ahead of the game in exploring the possibilities of film to realise their agendas, in particular, film's apparent ability to uncover the truth because of the indexical relationship (direct connection, fidelity) it affords between image and object.

Use of hidden cameras to forcefully demonstrate religious wrongdoing has been common practice among rationalist groups since at least the 1990s. Activists carried out early variants of the 'sting' journalism that the Indian media would embrace in the 2000s (with incriminating footage uploaded onto online news sites) as a means of collecting visual evidence of crime (Mazzarella 2006). They, too, contributed to the 'optical turn' (Roy 2015, 5) taken by contemporary Indian democracy, and more generally a strong case could be made for treating their work together with, or at least adjacent to, studies of the anti-corruption movement (Khandekar and Reddy 2015) and transparency activism such as the influential *Jan Sanwais*, village-based public hearings, centring on 'informational transparency', that resulted in the Right to Information Act (Sen 2016). Indeed, India's rationalists can be viewed as an idiosyncratic segment of the consumer protection movement: both seek to counter mis-selling and to promote transparency and disclosure (Schwarcz 2014; Gold 2016). Rationalists specialise, of course, in the mis-selling of religion. It is no accident that probably the leading figure in present-day Indian rationalism, Narendra Nayak, was prominent in the consumer movement in the 1980s that resulted in the landmark Consumer Protection Act, 1986 ('Consumer protection is also about scientific thinking', Nayak told us). Following from this, a proposed anti-superstition law in Andhra Pradesh and Telangana employs the framework of consumer protection in seeking to criminalise disprovable claims made by religious practitioners as false advertising and fraud (Binder 2020, 135). Activists seek to bring wrongdoing to *light*. 'Consumer champion' activists seek to employ the techniques of vision offered by contemporary media to provide visual evidence of religious crimes.

In addition to handing to the police any footage they obtain of criminal wrongdoing committed by religious figures so that they can take action, rationalists frequently rely on TV to expose their findings to a broad audience: their footage is nested within another form of media – a televisual ecosystem – whose priorities sometimes accord with the rationalists' and sometimes do not, which causes activists to have a conflicted view of TV. An account from 2007 provides an example of what was, from the rationalists' point of view, a successful collaboration with TV producers. Rationalists from the Maharashtra Andhashraddha Nirmoolan Samiti (Blind Faith Eradication Committee; ANS) used a hidden camera to expose the falsity of claims by a guru, Shivanand, that he was enacting a penance of standing on nails for 82 days while refraining from speaking or taking food and water. With the assistance of TV executives 'who took [an] interest in [ANS] activities', the footage was ultimately aired on a popular TV channel. The account, published in the ANS in-house journal *Thought and Action*, concludes: 'ANS activists thanked Sahara TV for their cooperation in exposing Shivanand. If media joins hands with ANS activists a lot can be done!' (Mandape 2007, 3). This optimism about the possibilities of TV is reflected in some rationalists' enthusiasm for what we earlier called the massification of exposé afforded by TV: 'TV is more convenient and more effective, I have found', one rationalist told us. He was probably referring to how activist mass communication via TV – and its perpetual storage and replayability in a kind of 'archive of reason' on YouTube – can seem to promise liberation from 'the constraints of material form' (Hirschkind, de Abreu and Caduff 2017, 10), that is, the everyday labour of secular publicity involving repetition of miracle demonstration and science education before teachers and schoolchildren across the land. Rationalist media activism certainly does possess the contemporary indicator of value that is 'citability' – 'the capacity to circulate' – which we see in the hundreds and sometimes thousands of comments below the line of clips of rationalist media appearances.

Some activists, however, have been left demoralised by their encounters with TV. A female activist from Patna describes TV appearances by rationalists as producers' 'alibi': 'Every day you have something: a tree secreting holy water, or some other bullshit. They report all this. But the broadcast code says you can't propagate superstition, so they invite us. They describe some bullshit for the whole programme, and then give us 30 seconds at the end. What's the point?' Another said: 'TV uses us as puppets.' They fear they are being used by TV channels precisely as a means of screening more superstitious programming. They could decline to participate, but then the 'bullshit' would go completely unchallenged. They are damned if they do and damned if they don't.

A technique of vision that held out particular promise, for rationalists, of publicly contesting the version of reality claimed by miracle-enacting holy men was that of video slow motion: indeed, it was integral to their investment of hope in film as a potentially secular medium. Michael Wesch (2009, 25) cites Marshall McLuhan (Fallon 2008) on the replay of sound and video recordings as offering a means of re-cog – recognition – of an event. He compares this to Catholic ritual, the repetition, or replay, of which is intended to elicit 'a deepening for the devotee'. Rationalists envision a different kind of deepening for devotees, to be brought about through enrolling replay into a project of reality contestation. Devotees must be made to re-cognise their guru's miracles as fraudulent by way of second-order observations of them via slow-motion replay.

At the turn of the twentieth century, slow motion was used in scientific cinematography for Pathe (Sobchack 2006, 350); similarly, work on early film culture and dance has explored its educational potential (Guido 2006, 144). The 'detailed reproduction of specific phases of technical gestures' afforded by slow motion can 'give an exact idea of the different phases in movement, phases that escape even the most trained eye', and so 'allow "progress to those in training"' (p. 143). It was also used as a kind of military technology by the British during the First World War for observing the flight of artillery shells in minute detail. Early film-makers, likewise, employed the technology 'as a major mode of detailing and inspecting violence (a major civil concern at the time)' (Sobchack 2006, 350 n. 20). The use of slow motion by rationalists to enact 'truth-events' (Banks and Harris 2004, 10) echoes these earlier uses, with motion slowed to allow scientific observation of the technical skill required for enacting sleight-of-hand miracles and inspection of a kind of double-pronged violence: the violence of exploiting people who make offerings to those who demonstrate such (false) powers, and the violence done to naturalist reality. However, if slow motion apparently holds the capacity to make the reality of this violence incontestable, the problem remains of the nesting of this secular medium within another (TV) that is more ambiguous, mercurial, and less amenable to control by rationalists.

Video slow motion featured prominently in the attempts of rationalist Basava Premanand (1930–2009) to discredit the eminent South Indian guru Sathya Sai Baba (d. 2011).[7] One of the most celebrated Indian rationalists of the latter half of the twentieth century, Premanand founded the Federation of Indian Rationalist Associations (FIRA) in 1997, and the monthly magazine *The Indian Sceptic*, and was a key figure in institutionalising rationalist activism in India in the tradition of Abraham Kovoor. Sathya Sai Baba famously designated his ability miraculously to materialise sacred ash (*vibhuti*) as his 'calling card', while a CNN journalist described it as the guru's 'signature illusion' (Marshall 2004). Given the guru's popularity and the extraordinary fetishisation of this substance among his devotees (Srinivas 2015), *vibhuti* has taken on the status, for activists, as the number one superstitious substance and therefore figures prominently in their programmes. If *vibhuti* is a fetish in the classic sense – the objectivised form of devotees' desire – for activists it forms a kind of reverse or 'rationalist fetish' as the objectification of devotees' superstition and so a primary object of desire for rationalists in terms of its debunking. Such a reverse fetish is layered, with slow motion itself a kind of fetishistic technology: 'the desire to be able to view the same images again and again points to the fetishist dimension in the act of watching in a continuous loop' (Guido 2006, 144), which is exactly what Premanand does in order to access the secrets of the *vibhuti* fetish, a procedure that, in turn, is encompassed within a rationalist process of 'fetishistic inversion' (Žižek 1991, 30) as the concept applies to interpersonal relationships: if rationalists assume they focus on this powerful guru because he is already in himself a powerful guru, in reality this person is a powerful guru at least in part because they treat him as one in their continual preoccupation with debunking him.

In interviews with us, Premanand explained how he obtained as much film footage of the guru as he could find, particularly footage in which he is shown performing miracles. Meticulously and repeatedly playing the footage and slowing it down to observe and learn how the guru performed his craft, Premanand confirmed what, as a rationalist, he already knew, namely that the guru's miracles were merely magic tricks: 'I took all of his films and proved it [*vibhuti*] is taken from his fingers from his left hand – with slow motion it was very easy.' But it also, crucially, allowed him to learn the skills himself and to teach them to others, who, it was supposed, would no longer be taken in by the guru; furthermore, they would be capable of demonstrating the sleight of hand to others. In the documentary film *Mystery Hunters*, Premanand explains how what he learned from slow motion gave a new impetus to efforts to expose Sathya Sai Baba 'in real time': 'I wrote an article, "You too can be a godman", and I trained lots of girls and boys. I said to them, "You go to [the guru's residence in] Puttarparthi, and say, 'Oh! Oh! Oh!' and fall at his feet and he will think you are *bhaktas* [devotees], and when he gives you *vibhuti* you knock his hand." One girl from Hyderabad University did it.'

This ethnographic material is notable in part because it contrasts with prevailing scholarship that links the proliferation of technological forms with the continuity, modification and entrenchment of religious and superstitious premises. The myriad global entanglements of the occult and the modern have been standard anthropological fare for quite some time (e.g., Geschiere 1997); these entanglements are exemplified by the rate at which 'such long-standing practices as reading oracular designs' are given an 'electronic update' by embracing the television, for example, as a technology of mystical mediation (Comaroff and Comaroff 1999, 287). In Gabon, Bonhomme has shown how the communicative ambiguities of mobile phones have suffused such devices with occult risk and he describes them as 'witchcraft technology by design' (2012, 223). Bubandt's inquiry into the 'witchcraft nature of technology' is also telling (2014, 241). In Buli, the *gua* is a cannibal witch capable of assuming 'the shape of an animal or a plant, and it can become any object, mechanical or inanimate. The *gua* in that sense can become technology: a motorbike or a boat, for instance' (pp. 222–3). In these contexts, researchers have sought to unsettle the ostensibly secularising telos of technological modernity. Rather than advancing disenchantment, technology – even when, as we have seen, it is recruited into the service of scientific demonstration – is not the 'causal engine dragging the gods [and the gurus] into retirement' (Stark 1999, 251). It is the spectral and occult potentialities of early and recent communications technology that have tended to occupy the forefront of analysis. As John Durham Peters put it in his study of the history of communication – a work filled to the brim with contemplation of the ghosts invariably conjured by phonographic and filmic media – 'Every new medium is a machine for the production of ghosts' (1999, 139).

The combined weight of ethnographic findings, critical studies in the history of thought, and common contemporary critiques of anything that resembles outmoded modernisation theory, has instilled – as Lebner suggests – an unproductive 'trepidation, sometimes even confusion, around "secularization" as a theme for anthropological investigation' (2018, 129). From a different historical location, however, the critical interrogative and unmasking work pursued by rationalist activists looks distinctly anthropological. Richard Baxstrom's depiction of the 'mastery of nonsense' undertaken by early anthropologists in the late nineteenth and early twentieth centuries is relevant here: a 'privileged space was claimed by early anthropology … through the discipline's purported ability to understand the seeming "nonsense" of "the native". The *empirical mastery* of domains consigned to the illogical [and superstitious?] realm of human social life' was at the 'foundation of an empirical method … that would allow field-workers to "see" [and expose?] unknown or irrational forces' (2014, 4, our emphasis). Central to Baxstrom's argument is that early anthropologists, like present-day rationalist activists, seized on the irrational, superstitious and fake as legitimising spaces for rationalist activity.

In their miracle demonstrations before schoolchildren, activists often screen a film called *Sai Baba Seduced Me*. The children are told the film is 'very serious'. Sai Baba is shown before a crowd that includes the Prime Minister of Thailand. His signature miracle – the materialisation of sacred ash – is shown in slow motion so that one can see him perform, quite clearly, the sleight of hand. Close-ups are shown of an ash pill in the guru's hands (compressed cow dung, according to activists) and a graphic encircles it on the screen. There can be no doubt of the guru's trickery. 'Is it a miracle?' asks the sceptical narrator. We are then shown another trick in which Sai Baba materialises a gold chain before offering it as a gift to an awestruck dignitary. The activist keeps stopping and replaying the footage to make sure the audience has had every opportunity to see, in slow motion, how the guru has taken the chain out from under a 'memento' (a large cup standing on a square wooden base) – something that is easy to see in slow motion, and next to impossible without it.

In fact this footage was shot not by rationalists but by the state broadcaster Doordarshan. As was the case with ANS and Sahara TV, Premanand availed himself of contacts at the channel who were rationalist sympathisers. Having advance warning of the event at which Sai Baba would produce the chain, Premanand contacted the producers, who were careful to secure footage of the sleight of hand which, slowed down on film, is clearly visible. The guru was 'caught' by a secular medium. Yet the next part – the planned exposé on national television by Doordarshan of the guru – did not go to plan. Doordarshan was inaugurated in 1976 but only became a widely accessible mass medium in the mid-1980s (Ganti 2009, 119). Despite its state ownership and formal pedagogical mission, it was not completely non-commercial and did not regard 'the popular' as off limits. It screened content that was often 'lustily corporeal' (Mazzarella and Kaur 2009, 17), and though the channel was under central control, much of its programming was produced in the private sector. Despite its imperfections, however, the Doordarshan of these years is remembered by activists as being characterised by an ethos of restraint and anti-commercialism of which, generally, they approved.

What transpired in this case, however, is recalled by rationalists as a promising moment for the movement thwarted. According to Premanand, 'because VVIPs were involved, the [Doordarshan] Director said he had to go higher [for permission to screen the materialisation in slow motion and so discredit the guru]. They called the Prime Minister [Narasimha Rao] and the concept was removed.' The former Prime Minister P. V. Narasimha Rao is regarded by rationalists as a politician notorious for his indulgence of holy men, astrology and other superstitions (Yongjia 2008), but he is far from alone: at least one other Prime Minister and a President of India have been Sathya Sai Baba devotees, and Prime Minister Indira Gandhi famously consulted holy men (Jaffrelot 2012). The case foregrounds, then, both the hopes that were invested in film and TV and how the nesting of the former within the latter leaves ample space for sabotage. This dynamic of filmic hope coupled with recognition of an all-too-real potential for televisual spoliation is captured in the words of an activist from Uttar Pradesh who was speaking about the episode before a cohort of trainee science teachers in the state: 'On Doordarshan [Sai Baba] materialised a gold chain on air, but TV cameras have no faith and [in slow motion] the footage showed him handling the chain and taking it out. But Doordarshan edited the trick out [of the telecast footage]. They are all in cahoots.'

If cameras 'have no faith' – the secular medium perfectly rendering the incontestability of the guru's deceit – the reality they so compellingly convey is sabotaged (in the eyes of rationalists) by the imperatives of a second-order medium (TV). In consequence, the imperfect secularism of the secular state is once again foregrounded. Thomas Hansen understands 'perceptions of the state as always/already split into a "profane" and a "sublime" dimension, one imperfect and corrupt, the other a more durable ideal form relatively impervious to real-life imperfections of *sarkari* practice' (Hansen 2019, 10). The state's handling of the footage was, from rationalists' point of view, the state at its most profane. Conversely, the Constitution of India, which mandates that citizens foster 'scientific temper', is the state at its most sublime, and it is by no means the case that the state is consistent in obstructing rationalists' activities.[8] Rationalists must work with and through both of its dimensions as outlined by Hansen.

Yet all was not lost. A sympathetic cameraman sent the slow-motion footage to Premanand, who, afraid that state authorities might confiscate it, had 12 copies made and sent to different locations outside the country. 'One copy went to the BBC. The BBC immediately came and made the *Guru Busters* documentary which made me famous',[9] and the rationalists, as we have seen, make suitable use of the footage in their education programmes outside of any necessity to nest it within the televisual domain. Notably, the footage features in Video CDs (VCDs) distributed by Mumbai-based activists as part of a strategy of 'deception to expose deception'. The aim is to distribute, to devotees who might not otherwise be willing to accept them, revelatory VCDs featuring slow-motion unveilings of their spiritual masters' sleights of hand. But to highlight gurus' sleights of hand activists engage in some of their own. As one activist told us, 'I will talk piously about that baba [guru] to [devotees] on the train, and ask them, "Have you seen the baba's new VCD?" And they say "No! You have it?" And I say, "Please take it!" I hand it over very religiously.' The footage lives on, then, in other ways, including now on YouTube, where Sathya Sai Baba's miracles can in theory be infinitely re-cognised, and the reality of which they are symptoms contested.

In his account of the denigration of listening within modernist narratives, Charles Hirschkind (2006) discusses the historical affinity between rationality and vision. The other senses, such as hearing, were considered too immersive and risked engulfing the individual in a manner that might compromise their independence and detachment. As a fidelity requirement for the visual discernment of the real, a distance was required between 'the eye and its objects of perception', thereby grounding 'the masculine spectatorial consciousness' (13). The flesh-and-blood rationalists we are discussing – as opposed to narratives concerning the purported claims of reason – both reflect and depart from such a characterisation. On the one hand, this chapter endorses the centrality of vision to the rationalist project as it manifests in India. Watching is integral to the process of debunking; new media provide new rationalist techniques of vision. On the other hand, audience involvement in miracle demonstrations entails use of the so-called lower senses of taste, smell and touch as important ingredients in rationalist projects of exposé (Copeman and Quack 2015, 42). More significantly, the very means of achieving objectively seeable, knowable reality requires the immersion – even engulfment – that in Hirschkind's account is anathema to that reality. Recall Premanand's repeated rewatching of the guru's sleight of hand in slow motion and the replay of similar film before schoolchildren. Scholars of South Asia – where seeing can be intimately tactile, a kind of touching or even drinking of the seen object (Vidal 2006) – are perhaps more aware than most that seeing need not always maintain a distance between the eye and its objects of perception. In other words, Hirschkind recalls the requirement of distance or detachment as a guarantor of vision's fidelity, but it is the untrained eye's insensitivity to registers of velocity – requiring *slow* motion – that matters more.

The remainder of this chapter presents more recent case studies of rationalist engagements with TV, and considers how the rationalist politics of visibility has adapted to a context in which deregulation led to the introduction of at least 300 satellite TV networks between 1995 and 2007 (Udupa and McDowell 2017, 2). It is important to note that market imperatives have stimulated both 'profitable provocation' – composed not just of heightened representations of sex but also 'irrational' religious appeals – *and* forces opposed to it (Mazzarella and Kaur 2009, 4). The Cable Television Network Rules, issued in 1994, which forbid the broadcast of content that encourages superstition, theoretically continue to apply. Indian rationalists, however, are convinced that the state is no longer interested in promoting the scientific temper that such codes nevertheless ritually invoke. How, then, have they responded?[10]

The great tantra challenge

On 3 March 2008, on the set of a live show on India TV, one of the country's major Hindi-language news channels, celebrity rationalist Sanal Edamaruku and a tantric priest named Pandit Surinder Sharma, who claims to advise leading politicians and is well known from his TV shows, faced off in a show named *The Great Tantra Challenge* (the GTC henceforth).

Headlined 'India TV exposé of guru's stunt' on India TV's YouTube channel, the description reads: 'Holy man Pandit Surender Sharma had claimed he could murder a man using simply his mind. So, after hearing his boasts of the lethal talent, sceptic Sanal Edamaruku challenged him to kill him there and then. Mr Edamaruku – head of the Indian Rationalist Association – said calmly: "Go on then – kill me." The mystic was at first unwilling but finally relented and agreed to prove his powers'.[11]

The India TV presenter begins by announcing the contest between the two: 'Aur aaj TV pe ho raha hai tantra aur tark ke beech bohot bada ghamasan' ('Today is the biggest battle between magic and reason on TV'). The set background represents the different sides through a display of competing symbols: 'scientific' images connoting atomic energy and the sun on one side, and images of a human figure in a classic yogic posture and of a human skull crosscut with bones (resembling signage warning of danger) connoting black magic and psychedelic effects on the other. The headline, in massive text, calls attention to the event as the final day of reckoning between the two sides – 'Aaj faisla ho kar rahega' ('Today the final decision will be made') – and to its sensational unfolding live in front of a TV audience. Drama and suspense are prompted by headlines – 'Jyotish bada ya vigyan?' ('What's greater – astrology or science?'); 'TV par tark aur tantra amnay-samnay' ('TV faceoff between tantra and reason'); 'Studio mein tantra aur tark ki ladai' ('In the studio – battle between reason and tantra'); 'Tantra jeetega ya tark?' ('Will tantra or reason win?') – flashing and replacing one another in a cycle, as if they conveyed breaking news, with a background score akin to that of a horror film or thriller. Indeed, the programme was originally to have ended with discussion of a controversy centring on the politician and Hindu ascetic Uma Bharti, 'but the "breaking news" of the ongoing great tantra challenge was overrunning all program schedules.'[12]

Inside the studio, the battle lines were drawn. With Uma Bharti's face in the background, Edamaruku and Sharma are shown standing on two opposing sides, with the news presenter, between them, acting as a kind of referee; indeed, the presenter struggled to protect the boundary between them from foul play, with Sharma constantly attempting to violate it. The comportments of the contestants are starkly contrastive. While Edamaruku, pillar-like, stands firm and still, Sharma appears restless and desperate as he vigorously chants the mantra Om Aim Hreem Kleem Chamundaye Viche while ritualistically sprinkling water on his opponent for all of 15 minutes in the first bout. If Edamaruku repeatedly smiles and mocks the tantric's actions, explaining how their ineffectiveness demonstrates or reconfirms the truth of reason – 'Yeh sab andhvishwas *hai, is tantra-mantra mein koi shakti nahi hai'* ('There is no power in the magic, all this is superstition') – Sharma, in his defence, declares *'Jo aapke marg par chalega woh depression ka shikar hoga'* ('Whoever would follow your path will get into depression').

Television rating points (TRPs) measure audience numbers in real time, and maximising them is crucial for a channel's advertising revenue. With India TV's TRP ratings soaring, the channel allowed the GTC to overrun and roll on and on in 'breaking news' mode. With the construction of suspense and unfolding drama drawing in millions of viewers all over India, the channel was moved to announce another round of 'our epic battle' for the night show. The contest eventually shifted location from the inside of the studio to an open-air setting in which the tantric had prepared a *havan kund* (sacred fire). The struggle between the rationalist and the tantric continued for several more hours, with Edamaruku emerging each time as the fearless victor and Sharma the fearful loser anxiously trying to manipulate the situation in his favour. More and more desperate to save face, the tantric shifts from seeking to kill Edamaruku to causing him merely to faint or become ill. Finally, with the attempt at harming Edamaruku through the invisible power of *mantra* clearly failing, the tantric tries to apply physical force to injure him in a less 'supernatural' way. Still very much alive at the end of the evening, Edamaruku was proclaimed the victor, and the guru a fake.

'We love rational investigations!'

Thus was the activist challenge pioneered by Kovoor in the 1970s adjusted to fit a tabloid TV format, and because it was enacted in real time as a kind of duel, it had a certain gripping quality that was reflected in the viewing figures. With the two sides resembling dogs fighting over the same bone, namely truth (Quack 2012, 307), the rationalist tournament of reality came of age as a mass-mediated spectacle.

The GTC case begs the question, is it simply that the rationalist theatre of proof is now larger, or does the shift in scale cause a qualitative reshaping of its politics of visibility? We have already mentioned that the GTC retained the form of the public challenge. This was not premeditated and setting it up required some quick thinking on the part of Edamaruku. Referring to a TV show on which the subject of 'Tantric power versus science' was debated, he said:

Both of us were invited to comment on the claims of Uma Bharti, former chief minister of Indian state Madhya Pradesh, that her political opponents were using tantrik powers to damage her. It was a staged controversy. After screening a video clip about the troubles of the superstitious politician, my counterpart elaborated with the standard routine of a tantrik specialist; he demonstrated various techniques for causing harm to any person, such as burning their photo or torturing a little doll made from wheat flour that is named after the intended victim. Suddenly half of the 30-minute show was over without me having an opportunity to say a single word to counter these absurdities. While I was watching Sharma 'strangling' his sticky clot of dough with a thin red thread, I suddenly knew what I had to do. My casually expressed doubts provoked him to boast about his personal tantrik powers: he could, he claimed proudly, kill anyone with mantras in just three minutes. That was where I caught him. I challenged him to demonstrate his powers there and then, on me. At first, he tried to ignore my proposal, but I insisted, and after repeating 'I challenge you!' five times it could not be ignored. Still, the anchor and I took the whole of the commercial break to pin Sharma down. Finally, the trap clicked.

(Edamaruku 2008)

As with the use of hidden cameras and video slow motion that we have discussed, film remains here the medium for rendering incontestable the illegitimacy of supernatural reality, Edamaruku's filmed aliveness at the end of the evening apparently proving black magic's inefficacy. But there are key differences. Ever since Kovoor, it has been a requirement for all but the most intellectualised variants of Indian rationalism to generate audiences by making their programmes entertaining. Here, however, the televisual setting of 'rationalist entertainment' is much less within the control of rationalists and might draw proceedings in a direction dangerous to the cause, while the massification of televised exposé on a tabloid channel draws rationalism into the attractive but dangerous orbit of popular culture, with attendant fandom and heightened vulnerability to attack and vilification. The trustworthiness of tabloid channels is generally understood to be questionable. If they are the setting for rationalist techniques of disclosure, does this corrupt the ability of those techniques to bring forth the proper understanding of reality rationalists seek?

The Indian Journalism Review described the event as 'an unprecedented experiment in rationalism – and television', claiming that it offered a win–win combination of enlightenment and entertainment:

'Over a couple of hours, a dangerous and widespread Indian superstition had been slayed in the studios, while the channel laughed all the way to the top of the ratings' chart.'[13] If, after liberalisation and deregulation, the citizen-subject must be seduced into consuming enlightening information (Mazzarella 2003; Rao 2010), Edamaruku seemed to have hit upon a winning formula for rationalist communication.[14] Though almost certainly tongue in cheek, YouTube comments such as 'We love rational investigations!' and 'Temple of Doom live on television! Awesome' point to the enjoyable nature of the episode.[15] Meanwhile, commenters both Indian and non-Indian post triumphalist comments on Edamaruku's GTC feat: 'This video wants to say FUCK OFF to all the religious fanatics and idiots. ... Great Job Sanal', 'A victory for rationalists everywhere', '*Kya bakwaas hai. Photo jalaa kar, mantar bol kar, aur loongi pehan kar aadmi nehi marta. Bandook ki goli se baat kar, pandit :P*' ('What a load of nonsense. After burning a photo, after chanting mantras, and after wearing a lungi a man doesn't die. Talk with bullets from a gun, pandit'), 'Take a time machine back to the 14th century where you belong, you [tantric] LUNATIC', 'Only good thing India TV's ever done ... normally they show "*naag naagin ka pyaar*" [lit. love of shape-shifting serpents, a phrase used here to refer to trashy superstitious TV].' The comedic impact of the programme is also registered in comments such as: 'He should have faked a heart attack, that would have been hilarious', and the reply: 'And then rise as a super zombie sceptic. lol'.

Edamaruku's calls from media companies increased and India TV began a regular series on debunking holy-man tricks that ran for over a year. It might have seemed that the 'experiment in rationalism – and television' had succeeded and that a new template for mass-mediated rationalism had been established. However, we turn now from the triumphalism that marked the immediate aftermath of the GTC to our earlier discussion of the ambivalence at the heart of the rationalist politics of visibility. A number of different registers of scepticism emerged in response that were markedly distinct from the kind of scepticism Edamaraku's 'victory' was meant to encourage: the 'wrong' kind of sceptical public(s) were formed, so to speak.

When we spoke about the programme with the residents of a predominantly Sikh and Hindu mixed-income neighbourhood of West Delhi a few months later, it still seemed fresh in their minds. They had found it amusing and entertaining; some even watched the whole thing, which lasted for several hours, gripped. However, to return to the *Indian Journalism Review* write-up, they were not at all convinced that 'a dangerous and widespread Indian superstition had been slayed'. Some residents, distrustful of India TV, regarded it as 'a put-up show' that proved nothing (we return below to the allegation that the tantric was an actor). However, for those who took the programme at face value, a different problem (from rationalists' point of view) emerged, which is simply that Edamaruku's demonstration of invulnerability revealed no broader truth beyond itself, but proved only his own adeptness at withstanding tantric assaults. Edamaruku, as one of them put it, simply 'had the stronger magic'. Perhaps they took seriously the defeated tantric's claim that his inability to kill the rationalist was due to the latter's own tantric defensive abilities.

Such responses reflect a problem of efficacy faced by all forms of rationalist challenge and miracle demonstration, mass-mediated or not: a problem of (lack of) exemplarity. Everyone knows there are fake gurus, many of whom make false claims to possess supernatural powers. Rationalists who debunk a given holy man's claims require spectators to treat the debunking as exemplary, a synecdoche standing for any and all such claims. But the hope or assumption is frequently misplaced. Audiences already know particular holy men are charlatans, but why extrapolate beyond such cases? The very work of exposé that successfully designates someone a fake guru can seem to rest on the assumption (and reconfirm as fact) that real or true gurus do exist; debunkers' very success may be their failure. What audiences learned from the GTC, then, was not that tantra is false but that this particular tantric is, or at least that he is not a very good one.

If such a problem of efficacy linked to refusal to extrapolate is not unique to the GTC or TV,[16] it might have been made worse by the mass-mediated setting. Here we encounter a critique from Edamaruku's fellow rationalists, who explain that debunking works best in person through audience participation. Rationalists from Bihar and Karnataka we spoke with were dismissive of miracle demonstration on TV because 'Talking isn't enough – it only works when you do and show', and 'Demonstration only on ourselves has no value – the audience has to come and demonstrate it'. This is important for circumventing a key problem faced by rationalists (as we have seen in response to the GTC), namely the possibility that rationalists will themselves be taken to be supernaturally powerful on account of their ability to perform miracles in the very act of exposing them. As one activist emphatically stated to us: 'When I burn myself they think I'm magical, but when they do it – that is the proof.' Indeed, where Kovoor gave lectures about the science behind miracles, and was able to demonstrate several of them, the novelty and reported effectiveness of Premanand's approach were to combine this approach with getting the audience to demonstrate them, too. This is now a key activist principle, borne out at least in part by viewer responses that consider Edamaruku to have emerged victorious because of his better magic. If the audience is taken away or is in front of a TV screen, the key participatory element is foiled and the reality contestation less effective.

Tom Boland (2019) notes that in public debates about New Atheism, science and climate change, promotion of critical attitudes by New Atheists ironically provides tools for climate change deniers to critique the claims of mainstream science regarding the reality of climate change. Those whom the New Atheists or scientists would term climate change deniers or conspiracy theorists see themselves as the sceptics as they adopt and deploy the supposedly universal elements of logic and science to produce doubt about mainstream scientific claims (p. 97): sceptical publicity is directed at the sceptics. Similarly, Indian rationalists, in a time and country in which everything seems ripe for debunking, are not exempt. 'Was it genuine?' asked many of those we spoke with about the GTC; indeed, there are grounds for at least broaching the subject. Tantric acts in general are strongly associated with secrecy (White 2000; Urban 2003). A tantric openly operating in front of TV cameras – and with everything to lose – raises questions. To take just one comment beneath the YouTube video: 'A true black magician will never cast spells openly on others. Black magic is the most secretive. Even entire villages become sick and die when a true black magician passes by.'

Further, a website associated with Sathya Sai Baba – a prominent rationalist target, as we have seen – claimed that nobody had ever heard of this supposedly very famous tantric guru and that the Sanskrit mantras he chanted were in fact life-giving rather than life-taking.[17] Rationalists, moreover, are well known for dressing up and acting out the parts of those they seek to expose.[18] For these reasons, the website asserts, the GTC proved nothing about the efficacy of tantra: 'Surprising how so many people and so many websites blindly jumped on this bandwagon. … It is ironic how those who ask the general public to embrace rationalism, logic, skepticism, the scientific process and free thinking do not subject stories that advance their beliefs to the same standards they apply to stories that advance spiritual people's beliefs.' In seeking to debunk the televisual debunking the website enacted a kind of negative reciprocity, thereby adding a further dimension to a tournament of reality in which sceptical subject positions are by no means restricted to avowed sceptics.[19] This partly reflects Boland's (2019, 2) observations concerning critique of critique, or the unmasking of unmasking, as a self-undermining exercise. But that is not quite right. The authors on the Sathya Sai Baba website are not critiquing critique per se but rather bad critique; it is Edamaruku's critique, as they see it, that is self-undermining in its being at least as fraudulent as the tantric he seeks to expose.

Even if the GTC was not a hoax, rationalists, too, worried that India TV's wish to make the most of its popularity might result in fraudulence. For the ratings success of the GTC meant it was now not only rationalists but also media companies and others who had an interest in the spectacular debunking of holy men, and in ways that might have the potential to reflect badly on the movement whose methods of exposé it borrowed from. As we noted earlier, India TV sought to capitalise on the success of the GTC by screening almost nightly exposés of fraudulent holy men, often via the use of hidden cameras. If at first glance the strategy seemed to mimic (albeit crassly), while provoking a strange kind of nostalgia for, an age of broadcasting in which it was imperative to impart information that could further national growth and development (Sen 2016, 133), the debunking of course had very little to do with the cultivation of 'scientific temper' and everything to do with entertainment. Well aware of this, far from gaining the approval of the movement, many rationalists suspect that the holy men subjected to televisual exposé were actors; that is, India TV was debunking *fake* fake holy men. Here is where the critiques of Edamaruku's fellow rationalists and those found on saisathyasai.com find common ground. While rationalists were not directly involved in the serial exposés screened by India TV in the aftermath of the GTC, they nonetheless feel compromised by the (alleged) duplicity of the TV producers. The attempt to unmask fraudulent spiritual practices as entertainment on commercial TV comes to seem less of a win–win. Rationalists' entrance into a domain in which it is apparently expected that no one plays by the rules potentially compromises their reputation and brings the movement into disrepute.

Reality TV and the meta-politics of atheist visibility

To borrow from the *Indian Journalism Review* article quoted above, 2018 witnessed a still more radical experiment in rationalism and television, with the famous Hyderabad-based rationalist Babu Gogineni appearing as a contestant on the Telugu version of *Bigg Boss*, the Indian adaptation of a globalised format known in the UK as *Celebrity Big Brother*, in which well-known contestants are confined to a house fully equipped with surveillance cameras to become 24/7 objects of the voyeuristic viewing public.[20] Viewers interact with the show by voting to eliminate a contestant each week; the last person remaining wins. 'Staging a TV show as if it was not a TV show', in the form of a 'dream of immediacy' (van de Port 2011, 76), reality TV defines a form of subjectivity 'which equates submission to comprehensive surveillance with self-expression and self-knowledge' (Andrejevic 2002, 253). Meanwhile differences between individual participants are key to selection criteria and exaggerated by producers to generate controversy and resultant 'eyeballs' (Sen 2016, 147). *Bigg Boss* is renowned for the extraordinary level of social media coverage it generates, with contestants often viciously trolled by fans organised into campaign 'armies' (*senas*) who owe allegiance to their rivals.

Gogineni was an apt choice by the show's producers. Comparatively youthful, outspoken, active on social media, a campaigner within the broader movement to up its media game, and with experience of presenting his own TV show, he was probably better equipped than any other public-facing rationalist to engage a youthful audience. He was also more likely than other rationalists to view the invitation as an opportunity rather than as something that would further 'subordinat[e] the priorities of a movement for mental revolution to the agendas of profit-oriented, privately owned media networks' (Binder 2020, 240); reality TV has, after all, been described as the single biggest phenomenon of Indian TV of the past two decades (Sen 2016, 134).[21] We have discussed Indian rationalism's predilection for contests and challenges as central planks of its sceptical publicity. It intersects here with the 'series of contests and confrontations' (Sen 2016, 147) that is the standard fare of reality shows. What would come of this novel intersection? Could supernatural reality be contested on reality TV?

If Gogineni was already a well-known figure, since his appearance on *Bigg Boss* he has been subject to elements of the fan *bhakti* (devotion) for which South India is famous (Prasad 2009; S. V. Srinivas 2009). YouTube comments beneath his videos proclaim: '*Babu Gogineni Zindabad*' ('Long live Babu Gogineni'), 'I am a big fan of babu gogineni', 'I love you babu Thank you sir', 'Babu rocks', 'Babu garu … first things first, mee new look bagundi [very nice]. Now, we all rationalists owe you big time sir. Your courage, unrelenting fight against these cheaters is a parallel [unparalleled?] in Telugu world Sir. Thank you and we all owe you.'[22] Gogineni and his fans have certainly made rationalism more visible in Telugu public spaces and, to refer back to Chalfant's argument about an atheist politics of visibility, that is at least part of the point. If *Bigg Boss* itself is dominated by the notion of popularity, the result of his participation is ambiguous. On the one hand reportage drew attention to his popularity among youthful viewers: 'It's now increasingly becoming clear that many had underestimated Babu Gogineni's popularity before *"Bigg Boss-2"* ... In India, large sections of youngsters are atheists ... In Babu Gogineni, atheists in the Telugu States see one of their own. Since the media usually don't give rationalists much of a voice, only a few very sophisticated rationalist speakers have made a name in the country. Gogineni is one of them.'[23] On the other hand, while he did last for 63 days in the house, he did not come close to winning.

In press interviews after his elimination, Gogineni spoke of how 'it gave me a huge platform to air my views'. Recalling the initial invitation, he said: 'I chose to go only because they said I could be myself. In fact, I told them, "I can't sing, dance or perform. ... I can't even comb my hair. So what will you do with me 24 hours a day?" That's when they said they are inviting because I am a humanist and a rationalist. I liked that.' He considered his stay in the house a success, noting that he

> broke many stereotypes, questioned many conventions and superstitions in the *Bigg Boss* house. I stepped my left leg into the show first,[24] opposed the pumpkin-breaking custom[25] in the movie-making task, gave equal wages to the hero and heroine and offered a share to the labours from the producer's profit too.[26] I believe these are victories for a humanist in the house. This is indeed a message to the film industry as well.[27]

Recalling his interactions on the show with the legendary film actor Kamal Haasan, who had entered the house to promote his latest film, Gogineni records the thrill of having Haasan discuss 'humanism in front of tens of millions of viewers with me'. Flattered that Hassan knew his name 'even though we have had no prior contact', he recalls how Haasan singled him out as a kindred spirit: 'We are both connected by our rationalist mind.' Star-struck, but also sensing an opportunity to make more visible a true icon's sympathy for rationalism, Gogineni presented Haasan with his T-shirt, which even before the interaction with Haasan had formed a small part of Gogineni's atheist visibility strategy. For the text on the T-shirt read 'REASONOTRELIGION'. Accepting the gift, Haasan 'said that he would cherish it'.[28]

As we have noted, however, the show demands controversy and seeks to establish the conditions for achieving it. The principal controversy featuring Gogineni concerned an earlier criticism he had made of acclaimed Telugu film director and avowed atheist S. S. Rajamouli. The year before, in 2017, Rajamouli had visited a temple in Mantralayam where he prayed with his family before the village deity Manchalamma and Raghavendra Swamy to give thanks for the success of his films. On a talk show at the time, Gogineni had 'criticised Rajamouli for maintaining dual standards. He added that [he] has no objection if Rajamouli visits [a] temple but on one side he is claiming [to be] an atheist but on the other side he is visiting temples[,] which is questionable.' It was on account of this criticism that he was nominated for eviction by another of the contestants who claimed – apparently without irony – that for him Rajamouli 'is like god'.[29] Gogineni had committed, then, what counts as a kind of blasphemy in the Telugu world of fan *bhakti*. If the matter was raised quite cynically by his fellow contestant as a means of eliminating a rival, the fact that Gogineni was voted off by viewers nevertheless seemed to demonstrate their dislike of Gogineni's criticisms. The host, Nani, also weighed in, revealing that his own grandmother was 'a converted Christian and [that] he used to go to Church every Sunday with her even though he himself is not a Christian because he respects her belief and he loves her. Then Nani used this analogy to defend Rajamouli's visit to temples[, because], even though Rajamouli is an atheist, he might have visited temple on the request of his family members as he loves them and he respects their beliefs.'[30] While any kind of criticism of a Telugu hero such as Rajamouli was unlikely to be well received, viewers apparently also found unappealing the glimpse it afforded of 'internal' rationalist policing (see Hagström and Copeman 2023) with its militant demand for self-consistency in a domain they intuit and may know from their own experience – especially in sensitive domestic contexts that may require delicate manoeuvring between one's own private disbelief and the religiosity of one's family members – to be marked by the kinds of compromise, accommodation and ambivalence that are rarely reducible to the religion versus atheism binary that Gogineni apparently seeks to police and maintain.[31]

What resulted, then, was a kind of meta-politics of atheist visibility, with Gogineni's prior criticism of atheist (in)visibility in the case of Rajamouli's temple visit the principal form that atheist visibility took in the *Bigg Boss* house. As Gogineni himself put it, 'You can't claim you don't believe and yet be *seen* praying at temples' (our emphasis).[32] If Gogineni is concerned that atheists should not be seen to be hypocritical, this very concern with (and attempted enforcement of) how things should appear is strategically made visible by another contestant in such a way that the designated spokesperson for rationalism on the programme – and rationalism itself? – is made to appear unappealing. While we must recall that an atheist politics of visibility is not concerned solely with popularity or even acceptance, Gogineni's experience highlights an obvious peril of this kind of rationalist visibility, namely that viewers might be put off by what they see. Indian rationalists have long been accused by their critics of arrogance and condescension (see Binder, this volume, on atheist arrogance as an aesthetically produced affect), and Gogineni was criticised, too, along precisely these lines. One article drew attention to Gogineni's haughtiness in telling another contestant that 'Living in the same house and talking Telugu doesn't make us equal. I am an international figure',[33] and rival contestants' social media armies made similar complaints via Twitter:

> I used to have some respect on #BabuGogineni before #BiggBossTelugu2 show but i completely lost it because he doesn't looks a humanist and looks like egoist for me with his behaviour in the house and in the news channels
>
> Hi big boss team … babu Gogineni is the wrong contestant in the house … From first day he is not at all participating any tasks … unnecessarily he is analysing the things … making every one mentally disturbed.
>
> Babu gogineni shd be evicted from Big boss and sent to Ramana Maharshi Ashram where he will learn the very purpose of our life.
>
> Any sane and rational person know Babu Gogineni got the Big Boss 2 opportunity on his stance 'reason not religion' and eliminated because of his arrogant and irrational behavior.[34]

If such comments enact quite typical critical moves in respect of atheism, such as denying the reality of the avowed humanists' humanism, claiming the irrationality of their rationalism, and underscoring their arrogance and egoism, it is difficult to gauge how representative they are of Gogineni's overall reception: he was never going to receive a sympathetic hearing from members of rival contestants' social media armies. However, such comments are worth noting here to give a sense of how the perceived arrogance of the 'aloof' atheist is apt to be reproduced even as (and perhaps because) rationalists seek to make themselves more accessible and approachable in pop culture contexts, a perceptual reproduction that adds a further stratum of ambivalence to the politics of atheist visibility.

Mass-media visibility strategies can also make public-facing rationalists more vulnerable to legal action and even violence. A key element of the *Bigg Boss* formula is the creation of a kind of hothouse bubble, with contestants cut off from the publicity the show generates. Therefore, Gogineni was not aware until his elimination that during his confinement he had been charged with a range of offences by the Madhapur police that included sedition, outraging religious feelings, cheating, and intent to provoke a breach of the peace.[35] Though the charges did not directly relate to comments he made during the programme, it appears that its raising of his public profile led the private petitioner to search online for his speeches, on the basis of which the petition was filed. Though the charges – condemned by local and international humanist groups as spurious and malicious – were quickly dismissed by the Hyderabad High Court, for International Humanist and Ethical Union President Andrew Copson they were nevertheless 'dangerous' for potentially 'painting a target' on his back for religious extremists.[36] Edamaruku, too, is in exile in Finland because of both the legal cases he faces and death threats; once again, it seems that rather than the content of the GTC (it is a Christian group that has charged him with blasphemy) it is the way it enhanced his visibility that made him vulnerable.[37] More broadly, while Indian rationalists have for several decades been reviled by Hindu nationalist groups for being 'anti-Hindu' (that is, for their alleged concentration on Hindu practices rather than those of other religions), the recent advance of South Asian outrage politics – in which the 'emotional subject' (Blom 2008, 21) enacts politics on the basis of an 'experience of indignation' (Blom and Jaoul 2008, 2), and 'hurt religious sentiments' are strategised and distributed as a means of cultural regulation (Zecchini 2020, 243) – can cause atheist visibility projects to become particularly fraught with danger. Maharashtrian rationalist leader Dr Dabholkar was killed in 2013. Edamaruku, as noted, has had threats made on his life (not just by the tantric). Rationalists in Karnataka were killed in 2015 and 2017. Others employ bodyguards. If the era of private TV has offered new opportunities to rationalists to make rationalism visible, the recent exceptional level of violence directed towards them is perhaps a perverse measure of their success. It is not far-fetched to suggest that there is a relation between this violence and the increased media visibility of rationalists; that is, the violence is an extra-legal form of 'vigilante censorship' (Pohjonen and Udupa 2017, 1178).

Conclusion

For some time, there has existed a considerable scholarly impetus to 'radically revise the purported status of media as secularizing machines' (Udupa and McDowell 2017, 9), when media has in fact been completely normalised as the reverse.[38] Whatever the unwelcome outcomes and compromises of televised and mediatised rationalist exposés, their sometimes widely publicised successes should invite recognition of the power and – dare we say, at least from the point of view of rationalist activists and their supporting publics in India and elsewhere – the *emancipatory* secular potential of technological media, an ethnographic as well as analytical thematic that has generally been pushed aside in favour of counter-examples that drive home media's imbrication with the radically non-secular.

Building on works by Lebner, Chalfant, and Bradbury and Schulz, we have shown how the rationalist will to publicity has employed various visual media both to contest supernatural reality and to make rationalism visible to a wider public. Adapting Kovoor's model of the public challenge to new media formats, spectacles of reason are enacted as massified 'ideological events' (Nash 1995) with explicit instructional value. Film and TV have offered rationalists new techniques of vision for bringing forth naturalistic reality, with the indexicality of film, in particular, marking it out as having 'no faith' and therefore being potentially a secular medium: video slow motion, replay and hidden cameras have all been key filmic techniques of vision to enact truth-events, inspiring viewers to re-cognise reality. We have also seen, however, that the requirement to nest faithless footage within potentially 'less' secular media can subvert its hoped-for communicative efficacy. In spite of their ambivalent interactions with TV before liberalisation, rationalists have sought to adapt their politics of visibility to the imperatives of private TV, with high-profile coups such as the GTC and *Bigg Boss*, on channels, too, that rationalists recognise have little or no interest in promoting 'scientific temper'.

In the case of the GTC, rationalism seemed to triumph not just against tantra but against its own and others' expectations of its ability to retain relevance and visibility in the age of commercial TV: the rationalist tournament of reality as a mass-mediated spectacle was a huge ratings success. However, once more the matter of media within media, or mediatic nesting, raised questions of efficacy. If India TV is entertaining but not trustworthy, the GTC in the opinion of many viewers could not be distanced from the agreed-upon characteristics of the channel on which it was broadcast; a kind of unmasking of unmasking ensued. The *Bigg Boss* experiment also embedded rationalism in a pop culture format in which its penchant for controversy and contest could find new expression. Certainly successful in making rationalism highly visible in Telugu public space, Gogineni's appearance also occasioned the revival of hoary accusations of atheist arrogance, saw controversy turned against public perceptions of rationalism, and underscored how a new mass-mediated visibility for rationalism is likely to be accompanied by new vulnerabilities in an era of 'religious outrage as spectacle' and 'blurred distinctions between the emotional and the orchestrated' (Ruud 2019, 107).

Acknowledgements

We would like to thank Stefan Binder, Johannes Quack, Mascha Schulz and the audience at the Centro de Investigación Interuniversitario en Paisaxes Atlánticas Culturais (CISPAC), Santiago de Compostela, for their helpful feedback. We are particularly indebted to Koonal Duggal for his insights and help with this chapter.

Notes

1 See in particular works by Quack (2012), Binder (2020) and Copeman (2015). Renny Thomas (2017) has conducted related work on atheism and unbelief among Indian scientists.

2 While we use the term atheist activists here to describe these figures, the reticence with which most rationalists use the term 'atheism', or its closest Hindi equivalent *nastika*, in public must be noted. The public use of these terms is discouraged since they have the potential to prevent activists from getting a sympathetic public hearing. As in rationalist organisations globally, there is an unequal representation of the sexes in the Indian movement. Roughly, active women constitute less than a quarter of the group's membership. The caste make-up of activists is quite diverse, but leaders tend to hail from upper-caste and -class backgrounds.

3 The London-based Rationalist Press Association (RPA), founded in 1899, made available cheap copies of classic Western humanist texts in the mid-twentieth century, and 'One of the most influential successes of Indian atheist publishers was to translate much of the Thinker's Library, and many other classics of humanism, into local languages like Malayalam' (Melville 2007). Periyar, himself an extremely influential and prolific anti-Brahminical and atheist pamphleteer, had translated into Tamil important critical works on religion (Manoharan 2020: 4). The tradition continues apace.

4 Kovoor was originally from Kerala, but much of his work was in Sri Lanka. See Wijeyewardene's (1979) account of Kovoor and Sri Lankan rationalist challenges to supernatural understandings of fire walking. Such challenges are a point of connection between the Indian movement and rationalists elsewhere (Quack 2012).

5 This ambivalence is strongly reminiscent of the dynamic of disclosure ('coming out') and concealment ('staying in'), which is found in many studies of apostasy (e.g., Brooks 2018).

6 Paraphrasing Hirsch (2004, 20).

7 See T. Srinivas (2015) for a full account of the Indian rationalist encounter with Sathya Sai Baba.

8 Most notably, Prime Minister Indira Gandhi's Emergency suspension of democracy in the 1970s is remembered by many rationalists as a time of productive cooperation with the state.

9 IMDb summary of *Guru Busters* (dir. Robert Eagle, 1995): 'On the road with India's anti-superstition campaigners confronting fraudulent gurus and quacks. The film reveals the trickery behind pseudo-magical phenomena such as levitation, materialization and walking on fire and questions the credibility of leading "god men" such as Satya Sai Baba.' https://www.imdb.com/title/tt0472100/plotsummary?ref_=tt_ov_pl (accessed 23 May 2022).

10 We can compare this with comparable fears elsewhere among rationalists concerning a perceived takeover of the media by adept religious entrepreneurs; for example, 'as one prominent British freethinker has confided, the proliferation of Christian computer and Internet resources has been seen within secularist circles as a perceived "threat that must be countered"' (Nash 2002, 280).

11 https://www.youtube.com/watch?v=AfJPYzxHM4g (accessed 23 May 2022). Our thanks to Koonal Duggal for this and other references on and insight into the GTC.

12 'The great tantra challenge', *Rationalist International*, 18 March 2008. https://web.archive.org/web/20080318045751/http://www.rationalistinternational.net/article/2008/20080310/en_1.html (accessed 23 May 2022).

13 *Indian Journalism Review*, 18 March 2008. https://indianjournalismreview.com/2008/03/18/how-indian-tv-slayed-a-dangerous-superstition/ (accessed 23 May 2022).

14 Here we paraphrase Ursula Rao's (2010, 189) discussion of political information and infotainment.
15 A reference to one of the Indiana Jones Hollywood blockbusters.
16 There are many comparable instances from the ethnographic record. See, for example, Shipley (2009, 524) and Evans-Pritchard (1976, 107).
17 Sathya Sai Baba, '"Great tantra challenge" hoax? Rationalist International, India TV & Sanal Edamaruku', 2 August 2008. https://sathyasaibaba.wordpress.com/2008/08/02/great-tantra-challenge-hoax-rationalist-international-india-tv-sanal-edamaruku/ (accessed 21 August 2022).
18 See Copeman and Ikegame (2012, 295–7).
19 See Copeman (2018) on debunking and cycles of negative reciprocity.
20 The 'hugely popular format … originated in the Netherlands and has since been implemented in over 50 countries' (Sen 2016, 156). It is to be distinguished from the 'civilian' version of *Big Brother*.
21 See Binder (2020) on Gogineni's show *The Big Question with Babu Gogineni*, which 'has been airing successfully from 2014 to 2015 on 10TV, a private news channel with close ties to the Communist movement' (p. 241).
22 https://www.youtube.com/watch?v=B4_mH_sbPX8 (accessed 1 July 2022).
23 https://www.ntvtelugu.com/en/post/thats-what-strikes-for-babu-gogineni (accessed August 2021).
24 Stepping into a house left foot first is a well-known bad omen in India.
25 Ritual performed at house-warming ceremonies.
26 See Quack's (2012) important reflection on the centrality of social justice efforts within Indian manifestations of rationalism.
27 *Times of India*, 31 August 2018.
28 *Times of India*, 31 August 2018.
29 Telugu360, 29 July 2018, '*Bigg Boss* tidbits: Rajamouli's atheism was central topic in show this week'. https://www.telugu360.com/bigg-boss-tidbits-rajamoulis-atheism-was-central-topic-in-show-this-week/ (accessed 24 May 2022).
30 Telugu360, 29 July 2018, 'Bigg Boss tidbits: Rajamouli's atheism was central topic in show this week'. https://www.telugu360.com/bigg-boss-tidbits-rajamoulis-atheism-was-central-topic-in-show-this-week/ (accessed 24 May 2022).
31 On such familial compromises and ambivalences, see Quack 2017.
32 'Rajamouli, who is also an atheist like me, went to a temple and prayed after his movie became a success. So, I said that either you say you belong to a religion or admit that you're an atheist and stick to it. You can't claim you don't believe and yet be seen praying at temples' (Gogineni cited in Suhas Yellapantula, 'Inside *Bigg Boss*' house, it felt like I was in North Korea on a starvation diet: Babu Gogineni', *Times of India*, 31 August 2018. https://timesofindia.indiatimes.com/tv/news/telugu/inside-bigg-boss-house-it-felt-like-i-was-in-north-korea-on-a-starvation-diet-babu-gogineni/articleshow/65621383.cms (accessed 24 May 2022).)
33 ManuaTeluguMovies, 24 July 2018, 'Babu Gogineni's true colors exposed'. http://manatelugumovies.cc/babu-goginenis-true-colors-exposed/ (accessed 24 May 2022).
34 Sakshi Post, 'Kaushal army slams Babu Gogineni over paid fans comment', 3 September 2018. https://english.sakshi.com/entertainment/2018/09/03/kaushal-army-slams-babu-gogineni-over-paid-fans-comment (accessed 24 May 2022).
35 *The News Minute*, 14 August 2018, '"Kamal Haasan said we share a rational mind": *Bigg Boss* contestant Babu Gogineni': https://www.thenewsminute.com/article/kamal-haasan-said-we-share-rational-mind-bigg-boss-contestant-babu-gogineni-86559 (accessed 24 May 2022).
36 Hemant Mehta, 'Two notable South Asian atheists face blasphemy charges in their countries', *Friendly Atheist*, 22 July 2018. https://friendlyatheist.patheos.com/2018/07/22/two-notable-south-asian-atheists-face-blasphemy-charges-in-their-countries/ (accessed 24 May 2022).
37 See P. Thomas (2020) for further details of Edamaruku's plight.
38 Not only in anthropology. See, for instance, art historian W. J. T. Mitchell's (2015, 116) suggestion that contemporary media 'is simply the latest version of that image of the divinity in which "we live and move". Perhaps that is why the rhetoric of religion is so deeply woven into the discourse on media, why concepts like media and mediation so easily turn into god-terms even in secular, technical contexts, why the concrete materiality of a medium is so easily abstracted and spiritualized by the terminology of media and mediation.'

References

Andrejevic, Mark. 2002. 'The kinder, gentler gaze of Big Brother: Reality TV in the era of digital capitalism.' *New Media & Society* 4 (2): 251–70. https://doi.org/10.1177/14614440222226361.

Banks, Kathryn and Joseph Harris. 2004. 'Introduction', in *Exposure: Revealing bodies, unveiling representations*, Kathryn Banks and Joseph Harris, eds, 9–20. Oxford: Peter Lang.

Baxstrom, Richard. 2014. 'Knowing primitives, witches, and the spirits: Anthropology and the mastery of nonsense.' *Republics of Letters* 3 (2): 1–22.

Binder, Stefan. 2019. 'Magic is science: Atheist conjuring and the exposure of superstition in South India.' *HAU: Journal of Ethnographic Theory* 9 (2): 284–98.

Binder, Stefan. 2020. *Total Atheism: Secular activism and the politics of difference in South Asia*. New York and Oxford: Berghahn.

Blanes, Ruy L. and Galina Oustinova-Stjepanovic, eds. 2015. 'Being Godless: Ethnographies of atheism and non-religion.' *Social Analysis* 59 (2) (special issue).

Blom, Amélie. 2008. 'The 2006 anti-"Danish cartoons" riot in Lahore: Outrage and the emotional landscape of Pakistani politics.' *South Asia Multidisciplinary Academic Journal* 2. https://doi.org/10.4000/samaj.1652.

Blom, Amélie and Nicolas Jaoul. 2008. 'Introduction: The moral and affectual dimension of collective action in South Asia.' *South Asia Multidisciplinary Academic Journal* 2. https://doi.org/10.4000/samaj.1912.

Boland, Tom. 2019. *The Spectacle of Critique: From philosophy to cacophony*. Abingdon: Routledge.

Bonhomme, Julien. 2012. 'The dangers of anonymity: Witchcraft, rumor, and modernity in Africa.' *HAU: Journal of Ethnographic Theory* 2 (2): 205–33.

Brooks, E. Marshall. 2018. *Disenchanted Lives: Apostasy and ex-Mormonism among the Latter-day Saints*. New Brunswick, NJ: Rutgers University Press.

Bubandt, Nils. 2014. *The Empty Seashell: Witchcraft and doubt on an Indonesian island*. Ithaca, NY: Cornell University Press.

Comaroff, Jean and John L. Comaroff. 1999. 'Occult economies and the violence of abstraction: Notes from the South African postcolony.' *American Ethnologist* 26 (2): 279–303.

Copeman, Jacob. 2015. 'Secularism's names: Commitment to confusion and the pedagogy of the name.' *South Asia Multidisciplinary Academic Journal* 12: 1–26. https://doi.org/10.4000/samaj.4012.

Copeman, Jacob. 2018. 'Exposing fakes', in *Fake: Anthropological keywords*, Jacob Copeman and Giovanni da Col, eds, 63–90. Chicago: HAU Books.

Copeman, Jacob and Aya Ikegame. 2012. 'Guru logics.' *HAU: Journal of Ethnographic Theory* 2 (1): 289–336. https://www.journals.uchicago.edu/doi/10.14318/hau2.1.014.

Copeman, Jacob and Johannes Quack. 2015. 'Godless people and dead bodies: Materiality and the morality of atheist materialism.' *Social Analysis* 59 (2): 40–61. https://doi.org/10.3167/sa.2015.590203.

de Vries, Hent and Samuel Weber. 2001. *Religion and Media*. Stanford, CA: Stanford University Press.

Durham Peters, John. 1999. *Speaking into the Air: A history of the idea of communication*. Chicago: University of Chicago Press.

Dwyer, Rachel. 2006. *Filming the Gods: Religion and Indian cinema*. London: Routledge.

Ecks, Stefan. 2010. 'Spectacles of reason: An ethnography of Indian gastroenterologists', in *Technologized Images, Technologized Bodies*, Jeanette Edwards, Penny Harvey and Peter Wade, eds, 117–35. Oxford: Berghahn.

Edamaruku, Sanal. 2008. 'Death on air.' *New Humanist*, 6 May. https://newhumanist.org.uk/1773 (accessed 25 May 2022).

Eisenlohr, Patrick. 2011. 'Introduction: What is a medium? Theologies, technologies and aspirations.' *Social Anthropology* 19 (1): 1–5. https://doi.org/10.1111/j.1469-8676.2010.00134.x.

Evans-Pritchard, E. E. (1937) 1976. *Witchcraft, Oracles, and Magic among the Azande*, abridged with an introduction by Eva Gillies. Oxford: Clarendon Press.

Fallon, Peter K. 2008. 'Fr. Patrick Peyton interviews Marshall McLuhan (part 1).' 24 January. http://youtube.com/watch?v=1uZYR3jmMng (accessed 25 May 2022).

Ganti, Tejaswini. 2009. 'The limits of decency and the decency of limits: Censorship and the Bombay film industry', in *Censorship in South Asia: Cultural regulation from sedition to *seduction*, Raminder Kaur and William Mazzarella, eds, 87–122. Bloomington: Indiana University Press.

Geschiere, Peter. 1997. *The Modernity of Witchcraft: Politics and the occult in postcolonial Africa.* London: University Press of Virginia.

Gold, Howard R. 2016. 'Consumer protection takes more than transparency.' *Chicago Booth Review* 31 August. https://review.chicagobooth.edu/behavioral-science/2016/article/consumer-protection-takes-more-transparency (accessed 25 May 2022).

Guido, Laurent. 2006. 'Rhythmic bodies/movies: Dance as attraction in early film culture', in *The Cinema of Attractions Reloaded*, Wanda Strauven, ed., 139–56. Amsterdam: Amsterdam University Press.

Hagström, John and Jacob Copeman. 2023. 'Clarification and disposal as key concepts in the anthropology of nonreligion.' *Religion and Society* 14.

Hansen, Thomas Blom. 2019. 'The state as an ethnographic object', in *Critical Themes in Indian Sociology*, Sanjay Srivastava, Yasmeen Arif and Janaki Abraham, eds, 1–18. New Delhi: SAGE Publications India.

Hirsch, Eric. 2004. 'Techniques of vision: Photography, disco and renderings of present perceptions in highland Papua.' *Journal of the Royal Anthropological Institute* 10 (1): 19–39.

Hirschkind, Charles, 2006. *The Ethical Soundscape: Cassette sermons and Islamic counterpublics.* New York: Columbia University Press.

Hirschkind, Charles, Maria José A. de Abreu and Carlo Caduff. 2017. 'New media, new publics? An introduction to supplement 15.' *Current Anthropology* 58 (S15): S3–S12.

Indian Journalism Review. 2008. 'How Indian TV slayed a dangerous superstition.' 18 March. https://indianjournalismreview.com/2008/03/18/how-indian-tv-slayed-a-dangerous-superstition/ (accessed 25 May 2022).

Ingold, Tim. 1992. 'Editorial.' *Man* (N.S.) 27 (4): 693–6.

Jaffrelot, Christophe. 2012. 'The political guru: The guru as éminence grise,' in *The Guru in South Asia: New interdisciplinary perspectives*, Jacob Copeman and Aya Ikegame, eds, 80–96. Abingdon: Routledge.

Jain, Kajri. 2012. 'Mass reproduction and the art of the bazaar', in *The Cambridge Companion to Modern Indian Culture*, Vasudha Dalmia and Rashmi Sadana, eds, 184–205. Cambridge: Cambridge University Press.

Khandekar, Aalok and Deepa S. Reddy. 2015. 'An Indian summer: Corruption, class, and the Lokpal protests.' *Journal of Consumer Culture* 15 (2): 221–47. https://doi.org/10.1177/1469540513498614.

Leathem, Hilary M. V. 2019. 'Ghostly excesses: Ethnography and experimental cinema.' Visual and New Media Review, *Fieldsights*, 30 December. https://culanth.org/fieldsights/everything-is-full-of-ghosts-experimental-cinema-and-ethnography?fbclid=IwAR29KA8-1d1eaPOu43u952_Nv8-JDYYwN2X-_Yg9d6HfQJsOC-Ih4okh6-4 (accessed 25 May 2022).

Lebner, Ashley. 2018. 'On secularity: Marxism, reality, and the Messiah in Brazil.' *Journal of the Royal Anthropological Institute* 25 (1): 123–47. https://doi.org/10.1111/1467-9655.13000.

Mandape, Kumar. 2007. 'Sting operation of Shivanand Maharaj.' *Thought and Action* 2 (7): 1–3.

Manoharan, Karthick Ram. 2020. 'Freedom from God: Periyar and religion.' *Religions* 11 (10): 1–12. https://doi.org/10.3390/rel11010010.

Marshall, Andrew. 2004. 'Hoax-busters.' *CNN Traveller.* http://www.exbaba.com/articles/hoaxbusters.html.

Mazzarella, William. 2003. *Shovelling Smoke: Advertising and globalization in contemporary India.* Durham, NC: Duke University Press.

Mazzarella, William. 2006. 'Internet X-ray: E-governance, transparency, and the politics of immediation in India.' *Public Culture* 18 (3): 473–505. https://doi.org/10.1215/08992363-2006-016.

Mazzarella, William and Raminder Kaur. 2009. 'Between sedition and seduction: Thinking censorship in South Asia', in *Censorship in South Asia: Cultural regulation from sedition to seduction*, Raminder Kaur and William Mazzarella, eds, 1–28. Bloomington: Indiana University Press.

Melville, Caspar. 2007. 'The debunkers.' *New Humanist*, 31 May (first published in 2005).

Meyer, Birgit, ed. 2009. *Aesthetic Formations: Media, religion, and the senses.* New York: Palgrave Macmillan.

Mitchell, W. J. T. 2015. *Image Science: Iconology, visual culture, and media aesthetics.* Chicago: University of Chicago Press.

Nash, David S. 1995. '"Look in her face and lose thy dread of dying": The ideological importance of death to the secularist community in nineteenth-century Britain.' *Journal of Religious History* 19 (2): 158–80. https://doi.org/10.1111/j.1467-9809.1995.tb00254.x.

Nash, David S. 2002. 'Religious sensibilities in the age of the Internet: Freethought culture and the historical context of communication media', in *Practicing Religion in the Age of the Media: Explorations in media, religion, and culture*, Stewart M. Hoover and Lynn Schofield Clark, eds, 276–90. New York: Columbia University Press.

Papineau, David. 2007. 'Naturalism', *The Stanford Encyclopedia of Philosophy (Spring 2007 edition)*, Edward N. Zalta, ed. https://plato.stanford.edu/ archives/spr2007/entries/ naturalism (accessed 25 May 2022).

Peters, John Durham. 1999. *Speaking into the Air: A history of the idea of communication*. Chicago: University of Chicago Press.

Pinney, Christopher. 2004. *'Photos of the Gods': The printed image and political struggle in India*. London: Reaktion Books.

Pohjonen, Matti and Sahana Udupa. 2017. 'Extreme speech online: An anthropological critique of hate speech debates.' *International Journal of Communication* 11: 1173–91.

Poonjar, Hariharan. 1980. 'Dr. Kovoor: A profile.' In A. T. Kovoor, *Gods, Demons and Spirits*, edited by V. A. Menon, vii–xii. Mumbai: Jaico Publishing House.

Prasad, M. Madhava. 2009. 'Fan bhakti and subaltern sovereignty: Enthusiasm as a political factor.' *Economic and Political Weekly* 44 (29): 68–76.

Quack, Johannes. 2012. *Disenchanting India: Organized rationalism and criticism of religion in India*. New York: Oxford University Press.

Quack, Johannes. 2017. 'Bio- and ethnographic approaches to indifference, detachment, and disengagement in the study of religion', in *Religious Indifference: New perspectives from studies on secularization and nonreligion*, Johannes Quack and Cora Schuh, eds, 193–218. Cham: Springer.

Quack, Johannes and Cora Schuh, eds. 2017. *Religious Indifference: New perspectives from studies on secularization and nonreligion*. Cham: Springer.

Rao, Ursula. 2010. *News as Culture: Journalistic practices and the remaking of Indian leadership traditions*. Oxford: Berghahn

Roy, Srirupa. 2015. 'Angry citizens: Civic anger and the politics of curative democracy in India.' *Identities* 23 (3): 362–77. http://dx.doi.org/10.1080/1070289X.2015.1034131.

Ruud, Arild Engelsen. 2019. 'Religious outrage as spectacle: The successful protests against a "blasphemous" minister', in *Outrage: The rise of religious offence in contemporary South Asia*, Paul Rollier, Kathinka Frøystad and Arild Engelsen Ruud, eds, 103–22. London: UCL Press.

Schulz, Mascha and Stefan Binder. 2023. 'Introduction: An anthropology of nonreligion?' *Religion and Society* 14.

Schwarcz, Daniel. 2014. 'Transparently opaque: Understanding the lack of transparency in insurance consumer protection.' *UCLA Law Review* 61 (2): 394–462.

Sen, Biswarup. 2016. *Digital Politics and Culture in Contemporary India: The making of an info-nation*. Abingdon: Routledge.

Shipley, Jesse Weaver. 2009. 'Comedians, pastors, and the miraculous agency of charisma in Ghana.' *Cultural Anthropology* 24 (3): 523–52. https://doi.org/10.1111/j.1548-1360.2009.01039.x.

Sobchack, Vivian. 2006. '"Cutting to the quick": *Techne, physis*, and *poiesis* and the attractions of slow motion', in *The Cinema of Attractions Reloaded*, Wanda Strauven, ed., 337–54. Amsterdam: Amsterdam University Press.

Srinivas, S. V. 2009. *Megastar: Chiranjeevi and Telugu cinema after N. T. Rama Rao*. New Delhi: Oxford University Press.

Srinivas, Tulasi. 2015. 'Doubtful illusions: Magic, wonder and the politics of virtue in the Sathya Sai movement.' *Journal of Asian and African Studies* 52 (4): 381–411. https://doi.org/10.1177/0021909615595987.

Stark, Rodney. 1999. 'Secularization, R.I.P.' *Sociology of Religion* 60 (3): 249–73. https://doi.org/10.2307/3711936.

Thomas, Pradip. 2020. 'Journalism and the rise of Hindu extremism: Reporting religion in a post-truth era', in *The Routledge Handbook of Religion and Journalism*, Kerstin Radde-Antweiler and Xenia Zeiler, eds, 232–44. Abingdon: Routledge.

Thomas, Renny. 2017. 'Atheism and unbelief among Indian scientists: Towards an anthropology of atheism(s).' *Society and Culture in South Asia* 3 (1): 45–67. https://doi.org/10.1177/2393861716674292.

Udupa, Sahana and Stephen D. McDowell. 2017. 'Introduction: Beyond the "public sphere"', in *Media as Politics in South Asia*, Sahana Udupa and Stephen D. McDowell, eds, 1–18. Abingdon: Routledge.

Urban, Hugh B. 2003. *Tantra: Sex, secrecy, politics, and power in the study of religion.* Berkeley: University of California Press.

van de Port, Mattijs. 2004. 'Registers of incontestability: The quest for authenticity in academia and beyond.' *Etnofoor* 17 (1/2): 7–22.

van de Port, Mattijs. 2011. '(Not) Made by the human hand: Media consciousness and immediacy in the cultural production of the real.' *Social Anthropology* 19 (1): 74–89. https://doi.org/10.1111/j.1469-8676.2010.00139.x.

Vidal, Denis. 2006. '*Darshan*.' http://www.soas.ac.uk/south-asia-institute/keywords/file24803.pdf (accesssed 22 August 2022).

Weiner, James. 2001. *Tree Leaf Talk: A Heideggerian anthropology.* Oxford: Berg.

Wesch, Michael. 2009. 'YouTube and you: Experiences of self-awareness in the context collapse of the recording webcam.' *Explorations in Media Ecology* 8 (2): 19–34.

White, David Gordon. 2000. 'Introduction', in *Tantra in Practice*, David Gordon White, ed., 3–38. Princeton, NJ: Princeton University Press.

Wijeyewardene, Gehan. 1979. 'Firewalking and the scepticism of varro.' *Canberra Anthropology* 2 (1): 114–33. https://doi.org/10.1080/03149097909508639.

Yongjia, Liang. 2008. 'Between science and religion: An astrological interpretation of the Asian tsunami in India.' *Asian Journal of Social Science* 36 (2): 234–49. https://doi.org/10.1163/156853108X298716.

Zecchini, Laetitia. 2020. 'Hurt and censorship in India today: On communities of sentiments, competing vulnerabilities and cultural wars', in *Emotions, Mobilisations and South Asian Politics*, Amélie Blom and Stéphanie Tawa Lama-Rewal, eds, 243–63. Abingdon: Routledge.

Žižek, Slavoj. 1991. *Looking Awry: An introduction to Jacques Lacan through popular culture.* Cambridge, MA: MIT Press.

2
Performing the secular: street theatre and songs as 'secular media' in Bangladesh and West Bengal
James Bradbury and Mascha Schulz

Shomapti Debi:[1] My father was passionate about left politics. Because he was a socialist and engaged with Marxism and Leninism. For this reason, he told us from our childhood onwards that before getting directly involved with politics, you have to go via culture [cultural activism] ... You get closer to the people [through culture] than would be possible via engagement with formal politics. You can reach them [via party politics] but not at first. It is for this reason that he encouraged us to practise music and songs [*gān-bājnā*].

Shomapti Debi, a Hindu woman in her late thirties, is staunchly political and works towards a more equal and 'secular' society in Bangladesh. She ascribes a central, even predominant role to cultural activism in the promotion of her political viewpoints among the broadest possible public, alongside party politics. For Shomapti, as for many of our interlocutors in Bangladesh and West Bengal, leftist or communist 'formal politics' and cultural activism seem inherently interlinked. Following her parents' example she is engaged in communist party politics, cultural organisations and other forms of activism, such as women's rights advocacy. Shomapti stood as her party's candidate in recent local elections, is an elected member of the coordination committee of the United Theatre Council (sammilita nāṭya pariṣad) in Sylhet, Bangladesh, and has engaged in various other cultural activities for many years. However, Shomapti attributes different potential and moral qualities to each activity. Following her father's advice, she emphasises 'culture' or cultural activism as a medium for effectively protesting against inequalities and promoting a progressive and secular society, free from communal divisions and conflict. Cultural activism allows her to advocate these political values and secular vision in relative freedom from the compromises and corrupting tendencies that seem to come with party politics. As Shomapti explained, 'Change will occur through culture, through political awareness. This does not mean that everybody will be an active member of a political party, and this is not necessary.'

The notion that culture could be used to advance secularism or 'dharmanirapekṣatā' (lit., neutrality towards religion(s)),[2] and to promote progressiveness and political awareness, is widespread in both Bangladesh and West Bengal, which share vibrant secular political cultures despite many differences between the two regions. West Bengal, an Indian state with a Hindu majority and a sizeable Muslim population (roughly 30 per cent), has harboured diverse institutional and ideological commitments to secularism, reinforced through the dominance of the Left Front coalition that governed from 1977 to 2011 (Bradbury 2019). The coalition's leading partner, the Communist Party of India (Marxist) (CPI(M)), brands itself as the 'secular alternative' in contemporary India's political landscape.[3] More broadly, various socialist parties, associated cultural groups and rationalist associations have fostered non-religious cultural activities. Despite this historical commitment to secularism, the increasing significance of Hindu nationalism cannot be ignored, and younger generations of activists in West Bengal now strive to counter the Hindu right's promotion of religiously divisive narratives.

In Bangladesh, by contrast, secularism is most strongly associated with the struggle to gain independence from Pakistan in 1971, which entailed a rejection of a shared Islamic identity as the basis for statehood (in part because of Bangladesh's substantial Hindu minority population) in favour of Bengali nationalism.[4] Communist parties and ideologies played a major role in the mobilisation for the country's independence, and during the first years after it, but are now comparatively marginal and embraced mostly by a tiny cultural-intellectual elite. Instead, the ruling Awami League party draws on the significant role that it played during the Independence War to portray itself as a liberal, left-leaning and secularist party, and is commonly perceived as such, despite common complaints about its policy decisions among some self-identified secularists (see also Schulz 2020). Being thus intertwined with party politics, secularism and criticism of (certain forms of) religion have long been significant yet contentious issues in Bangladesh, as revealed through several constitutional changes that have installed, eliminated and reinstated secularism as a constitutional principle.[5] At the same time, secularism continues to constitute a strong point of identification and social imagination that is supported and shared by different segments of society, especially by an educated and culture-oriented middle class.

Despite the divergent trajectories on either side of the Bengal border, so-called left-leaning and progressive interlocutors in both Bangladesh and West Bengal advocate secularism most strongly through culture, which they see as a potent medium for fighting communalism and religious extremism. Although the umbrella term 'culture' or its Bengali equivalent *sanskṛti* is often used in this context, it mostly refers to specific performative art genres such as *gaṇasaṅgīt* (folk songs), *rabīndrasaṅgīt* (songs in the tradition of Rabindranath Tagore), Baul songs[6] and theatre, especially street theatre (*pather nāṭak*). These specific genres, rather than, for instance, Bengali rock music or Islamic song forms (e.g., *gajal, murśidī gān, kāoẏāli*), are associated with a sense of being secular, with a secular Bengali cultural identity (or 'Bengaliness'), and with an inherent potential to transform self and society. Like Shomapti, many secular-minded interlocutors have engaged in these kinds of performative arts in order to advance their fight for a secular society. For them, culture is not only a form of political engagement complementary to party politics, but also often more effective, 'purer' or more honest, and thus morally superior.

In this chapter, we explore how cultural forms – specifically theatre performances, but also related performative genres – function as articulations of the secular for our interlocutors. We analyse the specific kinds of secular imaginations that are produced through cultural work, as well as the ways in which such activism contributes to the fostering of secular and non-religious publics in the region. In our analysis, cultural activism is not only, nor necessarily, a vehicle for explicit secularist messages, nor is it a monolithic project that aims to produce a singular secularised public sphere. Instead, culture provides a medium through which secular conversations, self-cultivation and identification among a certain group of secularly oriented interlocutors can take place. Ultimately, we argue that cultural secularism should be understood in terms of the subjectivities, communities, genres and publics that become constituted, and recognised as secular per se, through such performances.

Secular culturalism: the preferred means of promoting a secular society

The notion that culture is closely interlinked with politics in Bengal is not coincidental. The region has a long history of using performative arts as a tool for political movements and protests. Among its diverse and long-standing performative traditions (*kabi gān*; *paṭuẏā*; *bāul*; *pālā gāmbhīrā*, etc.) is *jatra* theatre (*yātrā*), which before the nineteenth century mostly portrayed different episodes of the life of the Hindu god Krishna, but later also engaged with more 'secular' socio-political themes. Playhouses emerged in the colonial period; the first one was built in Kolkata in 1753 (Kunz 2006, 284), with colonial officers making up most of the theatre-going audience. During the nineteenth century, the *bhadralok* elite increasingly appropriated this theatre culture, while simultaneously incorporating many elements of *jatra*, especially its emphasis on musical elements (Kunz 2014), which resulted in the distinctive aesthetics of a 'Bengali theatre'.

The first dedicated Bengali-language theatre venue opened in Kolkata under the name 'National Theatre' in 1872, amid rising anti-colonialism. Starting as a temporary stage in a courtyard, it aimed to be accessible to urban middle- and lower-middle-class audiences. Its first performance, *Nīl Darpaṇ* ('The indigo mirror', written in 1858–9 by Dinabandhu Mitra and published in Dhaka), drew attention to the oppression of indigo cultivators and their revolt against colonial rule, and thus inaugurated a powerful new medium for changing political consciousness. This new public role of the theatre was, according to Partha Chatterjee (2012, 232), one of the most important tools for cultivating political consciousness at a time when 'formal politics' was off limits to most:

> Denied equal participation in a racially divided civil society, the nationalist elite proceeded to carve out a separate public cultural sphere for itself. But in doing so, it also hoped to reach out to a wider urban public, educate it in its new and sophisticated tastes, and persuade it to listen to the new doctrines of social reform and nationalism. Of all the means employed by the Indian nationalist elite to create a base of mass support in the cities, the theater was one of the most effective.

The British government brought in the Dramatic Performances Act of 1876, granting authorities the power to censor performances that challenged, criticised or mocked colonial rule. However, less institutional theatre continued to foster nationalism and create new kinds of public cultures. *Jatra*, street theatre and other performative art genres played a crucial part in the popular mobilisation of the Swadeshi movement (1906–11), a forerunner of the independence movement that mobilised against the partition of Bengal in 1905 along religious lines (that is, into a Hindu-majority West Bengal and a Muslim-majority East Bengal) (Kunz 2014). Bengali nationalism and non-communalism were promoted at that time through political protest songs (*gaṇasaṅgīt*, lit. people's songs) by writers such as Rabindranath Tagore, Kazi Nazrul Islam, Rajanikanta Sen and Atulprasad Sen, many of which are still used by secularist cultural activists today.

Throughout the twentieth century, stage theatre (*mañca nāṭak*) and street theatre (*pather nāṭak*) continued to inform each other, both forms being committed to exploring contemporary socio-political issues, albeit in different ways. The former is associated with 'progressiveness' and has incorporated diverse influences, including those of Bengali writers, Rabindranath Tagore being one of the most renowned, but also European traditions such as Shakespeare, French political theatre (especially Sartre, Molière) and German theatre, most explicitly the Brechtian *Lehrstücke*. Although undoubtedly political in its content and the intentions of its performers, stage theatre remained a largely urban and middle-class culture, as it took place mostly in playhouses, community halls and auditoria attached to educational institutions. The street theatre tradition, by contrast, explicitly seeks to address diverse audiences by performing short plays in open spaces, often (though not exclusively) without a stage or props. These plays are more experimental, draw on aesthetic traditions from different Bengali music, dance and theatre genres, and are explicitly didactic and politicised in nature. Some contemporary forms have also adopted elements of the Theatre of the Oppressed of Augusto Boal (see also Mohan 2004).

The street theatre approach was central to anti-colonial nationalist mobilisations in the mid-twentieth century. This is particularly true of the Indian People's Theatre Association (IPTA), which emerged in the late 1940s out of the independence struggle and as part of a growing Marxist cultural movement that sought to promote 'cultural awakening' in rural areas of the subcontinent (Kunz 2014; Bharucha 1983). Being directly linked to the Communist Party of India, it laid the groundwork for the strong association between theatre and progressive, left-wing politics that is today observable throughout South Asia (e.g., Arora 2019; Bharucha 1983; Eldhose 2014; on Nepal, see Mottin 2017; on Pakistan, see Rashid 2015). Even as the IPTA became beset with internal tensions around the party's interference in cultural productions, it gave rise to many independent left-leaning theatre groups, including the renowned Jana Natya Manch in Delhi, associated with Safdar Hashmi. Street theatre likewise played a role in fostering the Bengali language movement in East Bengal, and, later, the struggle for Bangladesh's independence. The diverse array of cultural groups that used theatre in such ways consolidated the association of certain cultural genres with Bengali nationalism, secularism and non-communalism.

In contemporary Bengal, this history of political theatre, which continues to be widely perceived as liberal and left-leaning, inspires a diverse range of theatre groups that share in broadly left-wing, secular political aspirations. These can be large organisations with branch structures, such as Bangladesh's Udichi Shilpigosthi, which is now international in scope, but also small groups in which young middle-class people gather in their neighbourhoods to rehearse and stage amateur plays. Given their relative autonomy from party politics, neighbourhood theatre groups sustain a left-leaning culture of performance while largely circumventing partisan dynamics, such as the violence surrounding elections. Theatre has also been taken up by NGOs in order to promote human rights and campaign against practices such as dowry, child marriage and religious fundamentalism. These 'forum theatre' groups, along with independent, politically inclined street theatre performers, have moved through Bengal in recent decades, bringing plays that focus on diverse social and political issues to villages and to less affluent and educated urban populations.

There is therefore a long tradition of political theatre in Bengal, and yet the contemporary entanglements between 'culture', (left) politics in a broad sense, political parties and secularism require further attention. Shomapti, like many other activists, sees cultural activism and party-political engagement as two different but complementary means of bringing about a change in society and fighting for a non-communal society. Yet many of our interlocutors saw a tension between these two approaches, often considering cultural activism less 'dirty' (see Ruud 2001), corrupt and compromising than party politics. At the same time, they distanced themselves from supposedly apolitical forms of art.

Souvik Bose, a member of the CPI(M) in his mid-thirties in Howrah, West Bengal, emphasised that he was not a cultural person per se. He was not like some in his neighbourhood who wrote, acted in and produced plays for some of Kolkata's premier venues. However, cultural work became a way of expressing his politics at a time when he was not fully accepted by the party, as someone deemed too radical. For several years, he ran a small, informal theatre group for young people in his neighbourhood, for which he wrote the plays himself. He thus saw himself as a facilitator who organised performances, but also provided mentorship to the group members in ways that served his political cause. He was also an active member of his local branch of IPTA, the party's cultural wing. Even after gaining party membership, he continued to invest energy in his theatre activities, because he felt that he could express his political convictions more effectively through this medium. His plays explicitly critiqued religion, often to a degree that is unusual even for secularist cultural activists. Souvik's idea of performance was not concerned with professional standards and settings, but was a more self-consciously amateur, agitprop medium that would impart messages to his audience.

Although Souvik would have preferred to disregard religion entirely, his domestic life was indelibly marked by Hindu symbols and practices. He lived in a small house with his mother, a pious woman who did her rituals (*pūjā*) every morning, and the walls were covered with framed prints of Hindu gods, goddesses and guru figures. Souvik recalled that, in his youth, political figures came to consult his grandfather, who was a well-known astrologer (*jyotiṣ*). However, his life was also shaped by the influence of communism: his father, family members and many neighbours were supporters of the CPI(M). Many of these people saw no contradiction between support for the secularist party and their religious commitments. But, for Souvik, religious practices went against his materialist convictions. He refused to conduct the Hindu last rites when his father died, even though the local party comrades had urged him to do so for the sake of his mother. He felt that the party delayed his membership because of such 'radicalism', which could harm their image among the electorate. Later, in 2018, he married a non-practising Muslim woman from rural northern West Bengal whom he had met at a state-level party rally. Souvik was frustrated that many comrades saw her first and foremost through her religious identity, especially given that she was also a party member. For him, and indeed many in the CPI(M), party belonging should override any sense of religious affiliation. However, in practice, some CPI(M) members talked and behaved in ways that reflected the wider polarisation of society along religious lines, and interreligious (and inter-caste) marriages within the party's ranks were always rare.

Many in Souvik's neighbourhood were frustrated by the constraints of party politics, and preferred to express their politics through culture. Besides the local branch of the IPTA, which is directly linked to the CPI(M) and participates in their campaigns through songs and street theatre (see Ghosh 2005), Souvik's friends and neighbours also frequented a local social club which had vibrant cultural events, and counted several prominent communist theatre personalities among its members. Some of these activists had had relationships with the IPTA in the past, but resented the party's control over creative work, and left to work 'without any party flag'. These tensions, in which left-wing culture coexisted in complicated and even antagonistic relationships with the local party institutions, are very familiar to Kolkata's cultural activists. Nevertheless, the latter's historical links to left-wing political parties have reinforced in West Bengal a strong association between secularism and cultural activism. The political and the cultural are thus seen as co-constitutive and distinct at the same time.

Likewise, theatre activists in Sylhet frequently sought distance from Bangladesh's party politics and guarded against any interference from the two largest parties, the Awami League and the BNP. They distinguished themselves from cultural organisations that are formally or informally considered the cultural wing of a political party, such as JASAS (Jatiyatabadi Samajik Sangskritik Sangstha), the cultural wing of the BNP, whose committees are directly approved by the party's leaders and who tend to be active only when their party is in power. For the most part, secular theatre groups in Sylhet do not maintain direct affiliations with mainstream political parties but have generally taken an oppositional stance towards the Islamist party, Jamaat-e-Islami. Although cultural activism is widely associated with left-wing politics, few groups are explicitly committed to communism or any particular left-wing party. The United Theatre Council, in which Shomapti is a committee member, is an umbrella organisation for 21 lay theatre groups in Sylhet, and takes tremendous pride in not being affiliated to any single party, maintaining links to politicians of various parties in an effort to avoid partisanship. According to its constitution, the Council aims to advance the theatre culture in Sylhet and to 'improve the cultural consciousness of general people for the sake of progressive development of society', to 'always keep up the value of our independence', and to 'be active against all kind of backwardness like bigotry, communalism, regionalism through practising theatre and enforcing the dynamic development of society'. Shomapti's other main engagement, Udichi Shilpigosthi, is one of the largest and most active cultural organisations in Bangladesh. Founded in 1968 by the renowned writers and Marxist-influenced activists Satyen Sen and Ranch Das Gupta, the organisation is committed to a left-leaning or 'communist' stance but is not directly affiliated to any party.

Shomapti regards her engagement with a communist party and cultural activism as two complementary means of political commitment. Both forms of engagement matter to her but fulfil different roles in her vision of advancing a more equal, secular and just society. However, she remains concerned about party interference in cultural activism, contending that 'if anyone in the leadership of cultural activities has a political [i.e., partisan] bias, then it will not be pure (*śuddha*) culture'. She shares the common view that this 'contamination' of culture through party politics occurs because of the pragmatics of political manoeuvring: 'The main aim of the Awami League is to remain in power, voter politics. They always need to calculate. … And this is why, in my view, the Awami League can never take a clear stance towards secularism.' According to her, anyone affiliated directly to a party needs to consider how their actions as a cultural activist will reflect on the party, and consequently affect their public reputation. Any open criticism of religion, she contends, is thus very unlikely to occur. In her view, partisan 'bias' dissuades cultural activists from clearly and openly articulating their political perspective, including their secularism, something that she believes is at the core of actual or pure (*śuddha*) culture. She thus keeps both activities explicitly and intentionally separate, even though her party comrades and fellow performers broadly share the same cause and convictions.[7]

Culture is therefore deeply enmeshed with political activities in the Bengal region. The historic associations of specific performative genres with national independence and left-wing movements, both of which have strong secularist components, carry into the present. Moreover, they have provided relatively free spaces in which to express secular values, which would otherwise pose a problem for party activists who have much to lose when it comes to votes, in societies where religion remains politically salient. However, how and why are theatre and certain other genres of Bengali culture actually considered 'secular'? What does it entail to publicly promote secularism through cultural performance rather than party politics? These are questions we explore more explicitly in the next section.

Performative arts as a secular medium

Some 'secular' cultural performances in Bengal address religion directly and critically, with an educational and political purpose. Such performances tackle issues of interreligious conflict, corrupt godmen or dangerous superstitions head-on, in fictional but very accessible formats. This is part of a long tradition of scepticism and critical engagement with religion in mainstream Bengali culture. Examples include: plays, such as Rabindranath Tagore's *Bisarjan* (1890), in which animal sacrifice to a Hindu goddess brings down a kingdom; novels like Syed Waliullah's *Lālsālu* (1948, film 2001), which critically engages with superstition and the authority of Islamic leadership through the story of a man who takes advantage of people with his fabricated religious teachings; and Satyajit Ray's film *Devī* (1960), in which a father worships his daughter as an incarnation of the goddess Kali. In recent years many novels, poems, plays and films continue to tackle superstition, religious authority, fundamentalism, communalism and terrorism, with some, like the films of Tareque Masud, becoming internationally renowned.

As noted above, Souvik engaged in cultural performances as a way of disseminating his secularist, Marxist values among broader publics. When the Bengal Platform of Mass Organisations, an umbrella body of outfits that supported the Left Front, organised a major rallying march through rural West Bengal in 2016, Souvik's group decided to perform a play on roadsides along their itinerary through Howrah district. Souvik was not only the play's author but also played one of the central characters, a corrupt godman associated with the Rashtriya Swayamsevak Sangha (RSS), the paramilitary arm of India's Hindu nationalist party, the BJP. The plot, according to Souvik, saw this religious figure (*sādhu-bābā*) go to 'a specific area where the majority were backward classes, devoted to *ślōkas*, *sūtrās*, things like that [i.e., passages from Hindu religious texts]'. The godman made a deal with the local political leader, and they told the residents of the village to go around collecting something that he called 'the elixir of life'. The villagers misunderstood, and went around collecting waste from the roadsides. When they realised that they had been sent on a fool's errand, they threw the collected sewage over the godman.

> It was a comic play, but the message was: those *sādhus*, the whole Indian structure of religion, will put people in that state. The people don't understand anything, they are just following [their religious

leaders]. And if you do that for one or two thousand years, you'll just gather shit.

Through the medium of satire, Souvik was able to express what otherwise would certainly be seen as offensive, and even dangerous. For an Indian audience, he taps into everyday grumbles about the exploitative activities of some renunciants, who go round asking for food and monetary donations (sevā, lit. 'service'). He associates such behaviour with the BJP, the Hindu nationalist party, which counts several prominent renunciants among its leaders, as well as its support base. The very language that he uses suggests his dismissal of religion: sādhu-bābā is a colloquial turn of phrase for a religious figure, devoid of any reverence; the phrase 'ślokas, sūtrās, things like that' undermines any sense of the sacred in these Hindu texts. Most explicitly, the supposedly god-given elixir is revealed to be a deeply polluting substance; even calling it 'shit' is an affront to the cultural tastes of many respectable Hindus. The image of people from 'backward classes' pouring sewage over a corrupt godman is a sort of communist wish fulfilment which could be gleefully performed, with none of the repercussions that could be expected if it happened in real life.

There is perhaps no more visceral demonstration of a secular positionality than embodying a religious figure who is punished for his own moral failings. Souvik was proud of a photo that showed him dressed up in the white *dhuti* (lower-body garment) and sacred thread, the attire of a religiously conservative, upper-caste Hindu man, during the performance described above. Being born into a family with strong religious convictions but also an atheist himself, Souvik's choice to not only write such a play but also act in the role of a religious villain was a rebellious act for him personally. When asked how his performance was received in Muslim areas of Howrah, he seemed to feel vindicated: 'Over there, the people really stood and clapped. There was loud laughter, they were really happy that Hindu people like me were playing the role of a *sādhu* and criticising.' However, Souvik's desire to frontally criticise religion was not always given free rein. He recalled that the local CPI(M) secretary had reluctantly approved his play for the rally, asking Souvik to tone down the slang and obscenities. This reflected the uneasiness among much of the party rank and file with upfront criticism concerning such sensitive issues, which could have negative reputational consequences for the party and ultimately cost them popular support.

While there are certainly more examples of plays that explicitly confront hegemonic forms of religion, they are comparatively rare and often criticised, as we can see by the secretary's reaction, for being too provocative. Notably, these plays tend not to oppose religion as such, but certain forms of religiosity or what is considered a 'misuse' of religion. Furthermore, the plays tend to target forms of religiosity that are dominant in their part of the Bengal region, or that are considered by critics to be potentially dangerous. Therefore, while the problem of superstition and Hindu guru figures is commonly addressed in West Bengal, plays in Bangladesh tend to focus on Islamic fundamentalism or the role of Bengali Islamic leaders in opposing the independence movement in 1971 and encouraging violence against Hindus. The kinds of religiosity that are targeted through theatre thus reflect contemporary debates and the political climate.

More often than not, performances articulate a secularist critique in a much more indirect way. Furthermore, many plays reflect notions of secularism that are quite different from the one articulated by Souvik. For instance, the notion of secularism as non-communalism is arguably more widespread – and, socially, far more acceptable, even respectable – than overt criticism of religion. Such a notion is linked to the Bengali term *dharmanirapekṣatā*, which may be glossed as neutrality or impartiality towards religion or different religious groups as well as ethnic minorities. It implies a commitment to the equal treatment of all religions in the public sphere, and opposition to religious division and exclusivism. Despite the different meanings and connotations that secularism acquires in colloquial usage, this idea of equal treatment of religions is very prominent and feeds into the English-language term. In this form, 'secularism comes to be defined as a form of pluralism with metaphysical foundations and not, in any sense, as the replacement of religious values by irreligious ones' (Cannell 2010, 93).

A typical example of promoting this distinct form of secularism through theatre is the play *Blood Test*, which was performed by a theatre group in Sylhet. The main storyline of the play sees a person arrive in a particular place to take blood tests from the whole population. The person claims that through blood tests they will be able to determine the religion (*dharma*) of an individual and thus check whether the person 'belongs to this country'. They will subsequently divide people according to religion, thereby preventing any supposedly undesirable mixing. Moreover, the blood tester, it is revealed, aspires through this endeavour to attain high political office in the country. Ultimately, he fails to determine whether a person is Muslim, Hindu, Christian or Buddhist, and in his rage accuses some of the test subjects of being atheists (*nāstik*), a term with negative connotations in Bengal. The simple moral of the play is voiced by those characters who contest the blood tester's authority, namely that religion cannot be determined by blood because 'all humans are one [kind]', 'we are all equal', and that the harmony between different religious groups will be destroyed by persons like him. While the play promotes, in a nutshell, universal humanity and a form of humanism that invokes familiar secularist slogans in Bangladesh, it also touches on a couple of more tangible political issues. For instance, the play indirectly accuses politicians of dividing the country along communal lines, and addresses how citizenship has become entangled with religious belonging throughout South Asia.[8] Though only a side note, the sudden, and apparently arbitrary, accusation that a test subject is 'atheist' seems to comment on how a person who criticises powerful leaders or hegemonic ideas can easily be defamed as such. The audience would immediately associate this kind of accusation with a number of killings of so-called atheist bloggers in the years preceding the play's writing.

However, a substantial proportion of plays staged by cultural activists do not touch upon the issue of religion at all. If 'secular' performances in Bengal are indeed often about staking out a different identity, they do not necessarily or always refer to the supposedly constitutive Other, namely religion. Indeed, cultural activists tend to address a wide range of issues related to contemporary political discourse, from environmental pollution, corruption and gender politics to specific policy debates, such as expressing opposition to the building of a nuclear power plant in Rampal. Theatre and other forms of 'culture' favoured by activists are nevertheless seen as inherently 'secular' by activists themselves, as well as by other people in Bengal. This understanding is linked to how certain genres index 'Bengali culture' and the (secular) history that has become associated with particular aesthetic practices, traditions and references.

On World Drama Day 2017, one of the theatre groups in Sylhet staged a martial dance known as a *bratacārī nṛtya* (Bratachari dance), in which the performers (male in this case, but not always) wore white and red *dhutis*. This performance stood out in a programme that was otherwise made up of street theatre plays with a clear didactic approach. It was distinct in its aesthetics and its impressive rhythmic choreography inspired by martial arts, but also for the absence of any narrative or explicit message. It is not unusual for theatre performances to be accompanied by more artistic-leaning dance or music performances, especially at cultural events that take place on national days. However, in this case the dance was performed by a theatre group that is well known for its radical progressive agenda, for its political street theatre and for drawing on different aesthetic registers.

When asked by the researcher, one of the leaders of the group explained that they had chosen this performance because it was a Bengali rural 'folk dance', and that it was important for them to cultivate a cultural tradition that might otherwise be forgotten. For him, this performance was both highly political and part of a secular cultural repertoire. Through engagement with this physically demanding choreography one could become a whole human, he suggested, irrespective of class and caste. The link that he makes between engaging with an aesthetic and cultural genre, supposedly indexing 'Bengaliness', and the cultivation of a certain universalist humanism is related to the fact that the dance emerged in the Bratachari movement, which was initiated by Gurusaday Dutt (1882–1941) in the 1930s in undivided Bengal. The Bratacharis sought a spiritual and social renewal of the Bengali 'nation' irrespective of sex, religion or caste through engagement with folk traditions and physical exercise. Dutt, like many cultural activists, saw folk culture as contributing 'significantly to the development of a national culture by providing indigenous models of secularism' (R. Chatterji 2016, 101).

Following Talal Asad (2003), many studies of the secular have explored how 'religion' and 'the secular' emerge in relation to each other and how such taxonomies and imaginaries of a secularising modernity have shaped power dynamics in different social contexts. Despite widespread criticism of such a dichotomy (e.g., Bangstad 2009; Dressler and Mandair 2011; Schielke 2010), scholarly approaches nevertheless struggle to account for a mode of being secular that might not fit into this binary or relate to religion in any direct way. One promising solution to this problem has emerged in recent scholarship that attends to the aesthetic, embodied and performative dimensions of the secular (see Binder, this volume; Chalfant 2020; Gholami 2015; Schulz 2021). Stefan Binder (2020) has identified scholarly attention to material religion as one factor that reinforces an immaterial, ideological understanding of secularism that ignores its material, embodied and performative dimensions. He also suggests that the seeming defeat of the secularisation thesis has further weakened our ability to identify an autonomous secularist position. According to Binder (2020, 10),

> The critical impetus to deconstruct the intellectualist and disembodied bias of secular ideology has been immensely productive for 'rescuing' the aesthetics of lived religion but, in so doing, it has been unable to address the materiality and embodied nature of lived secularity as anything other than a *contradiction* or

shadow of secularity's own normative insistence on its autonomy from the realms of the material, the corporeal, the social, the traditional, and so on. (Italics in original.)

Binder attends to the material dimensions of atheist lives, accounting for how difference from religion is expressed in ways which deal with the negativity of the secular. He describes 'secular difference as an *aesthetic quality* and the outcome of a *performative positionality*, both being more complex than a conceptual dependence or relationality vis-à-vis the category of religion' (p. 13, italics in original). Such an approach, which allows us to account for secularism ethnographically through cultural expression without relegating it to an epiphenomenon of religion, and without having to see secularist culture in reference to religion, also enables us to conceive of performative cultural forms here as secular media, regardless of whether religious critique forms the content of the performance per se. This is true of the above-mentioned Bratachari dance, but similar cases could be made for a wide range of other genres (Baul music, *gaṇasaṅgīt*, etc.) used by cultural activists, along with aesthetic styles that are commonly associated with street theatre, such as specific kinds of clothing (e.g., *dhutis*) and musical instruments (the *ektārā* and the harmonium).

This aesthetic repertoire is often seen as secular insofar as it manifests as a tradition that is perceived as distinct from, though sometimes in competition with, and at other times complementary to, the religious. The kind of secularism that is articulated through 'culture' – or rather the specific forms evoked by cultural activists – is entwined with the aesthetic affordances of these genres or media, as well as the specific histories, traditions and understandings of cultural secularism in the region that are linked to the historical legacy described above. Attention to aesthetics suggests that the 'how' may be as important as, or more important than, the 'what' for a performative secular positionality. As Charles Hirschkind explains in relation to Islamic cassette sermons, these performances 'create the sensory conditions of an emergent ethical and political lifeworld, with its specific patterns of behavior, sensibility, and practical reasoning' (2006, 8). We therefore suggest that specific cultural repertoires allow activists to 'perform the secular' not only through overt messages but also as instantiated by the media themselves and the secularity that they enact. In both Bengals, 'culture' has thus become the preferred medium for expressing and advocating for secularist politics.

Furthermore, the aesthetic and affective dimensions of these performances accrue secular meaning from their ongoing associations with recent 'secularist' and non-communal causes. In the case of West Bengal, for instance, communist parties effectively 'secularised' the significant five-day-long annual Hindu festival Durga Puja, by focusing on its aesthetic and artistic dimensions (Guha-Thakurta 2015). The poetry recitations, art exhibitions and theatre performances that take place around Durga Puja allowed the CPI(M), and indeed the wider public, to think of the festival as a predominantly 'cultural' event, and therefore secular, in a mutually reinforcing loop. In Bangladesh, cultural performances are often used as a tool to counter Islamist leaders and movements. This has been observable in incidents ranging from protests against attacks on Hindus to the opposition to the demands of Islamic leaders that sculptures be removed from public places (see Schulz 2021), and most prominently in the significant role that cultural activists played in the 2013 Gonojagoron Moncho ('platform for people's awakening') or Shahbag movement,[9] which was widely celebrated as 'secular' and drew heavily on the particular cultural genres and aesthetics of these activists.[10]

As an aesthetic tradition, certain supposedly secular cultural genres coexist with other traditions, notably religious ones, each drawing upon established aesthetic norms and affective relations. Thus, while many performances may say little about religion per se, they are understood as secular because of the role that they fulfil in the public sphere, gathering around them audiences on the basis of non-religious affective experiences. While an openly secularist or even atheist position is often problematic because of the socio-political role of religious belonging and symbols, cultural activism creates a space in which to articulate, identify with and make perceptible secularist convictions and practices through distinct genres and aesthetics. This space becomes the basis of a 'secular public', to which we now turn.

Secular publics as mediated through culture

Cultural activism, by its very nature, seeks to impart a political message to a public. As noted above, Souvik and Shomapti took pride in the fact that their groups did not confine themselves to the theatre halls and *bhadralok* audiences; they both aspired to reach new audiences to promote a secularist standpoint that emphasised common interests over religious divisions and superstitions. This was precisely because they saw these audiences as being both in need of such messages and capable of effecting changes in people's opinions, as Souvik explains:

What is the point of performing this RSS *sādhu* in [a middle-class Hindu area]? It will serve nothing. I can get some applause, but that applause will come from the so-called rich people, the middle or upper-middle class. They will always find a comfortable corner in their life. If I claim myself as left or progressive, I should take my theatre to those people who are the agents of revolution.

Such comments were very common among our interlocutors and most cultural activists aimed at distinguishing themselves from 'fine arts' that target mostly an educated middle class. Theatre workers in both Bengals often emphasised the need to reach the *sādhāraṇ mānuṣ* (ordinary people) or *janagaṇ* (crowds, people, public) to bring about change. Such statements might be read as a reminder of the apparently obvious and intended publicness of theatre and an indicator that politically engaged plays seek to address a general public to inspire critical debates, reminiscent of what Habermas conceptualised as a 'public sphere'. Such a reading would resonate with the Indian literature scholar Adakkaravayalil Yoyakky Eldhose's conception of street theatre in Kerala as a 'space for democratic discourse in order to create an active public sphere' and as an 'agent of political conscientisation' (2014, 340).[11] The fact that many activists emphasised the importance of being neutral, with regard to both political and religious affiliations, evokes such an idealised notion of a public sphere.

Yet this Habermasian understanding of the relation between theatre or cultural activism and 'the public' is misleading for various reasons, not least given the various criticisms of his concept as Eurocentric and for its normative presumption of self-reflective critical subjects engaging in rational debates, apparently on equal terms, irrespective of existing inequalities and power structures (e.g., Cody 2011; Fraser 1992; Warner 2002). Despite their rhetorical references to the masses, our interlocutors were certainly aware of different audiences, as we can see in Souvik's statement. He was enthusiastic about addressing Muslim audiences, rather than 'the public' as such. This is in part because Muslims as a socio-economic group are underprivileged in contemporary India and the target of Hindu-nationalist rhetoric and violence, which he criticises through his performance, making them a receptive audience for his message. However, it also points to the fact that religious traditions have diverging relationships to different Bengali art genres for historical reasons, such as the close association of *jatra* with Hindu traditions, or the banning of Tagore songs by what was then the East Pakistan government for being 'un-Islamic'. Indeed, different Islamic theological standpoints have diverging attitudes to music; while the kinds of music genres used by activists closely resemble the aesthetics and religious practices of certain Sufi sects, they are opposed by other Islamic religious authorities. As a result, Muslims are on average less likely to engage in such forms of culture. Consequently, theatre performances have been not only oriented towards the middle class but also considerably Hindu-dominated, even in Bangladesh, where Hindus constitute a minority. Venturing into working-class and Muslim-populated neighbourhoods was for Souvik thus a practical way of enacting secularism, not only through his play's message but also as a performative act of outreach in itself.

Furthermore, his statement partakes of a long-standing discourse in which he distinguishes himself from those performers who, in his view, only seek artistic validation. The frequency with which we encountered such normative and moralising statements among cultural activists suggests that their ideal of 'reaching the masses' was an ambition more than a reality, and one that they did not always expect to fulfil. Our interlocutors did make efforts to move beyond the typical audiences of the educated secular-leaning elite and often explicitly sought to perform in front of unprivileged strata of society. Examples of this include performances in Muslim neighbourhoods of Kolkata, cultural activists' collaborations with tea workers in Sylhet and the organisation of performances in rural areas and at urban spots visible to rickshaw drivers and passers-by. Nevertheless, more often than not 'street theatre' did not take place at street corners as much as at established venues for cultural and other 'secular' activities – such as the Shaheed Minar in Sylhet, or on the campuses of College Street and Jadavpur University in Kolkata – and in front of sympathetic, mostly left-leaning, audiences. In fact, the Kobi Nazrul auditorium in Sylhet, which was the main venue for stage theatre, dances, musical and other artistic performances targeting a *bhadralok* middle class, had an outdoor space that was frequently used for street theatre performances, which were mostly attended by other cultural activists and what may be called a 'theatre-going public' (Shimko and Freeman 2012, 6). This space was crucial, one of the Udichi activists explained, because even though it was outside, it offered a secure and protected environment for cultural performances, just like other established secular-cultural venues.

Indeed, despite the supposed publicness of street theatre, certain plays were deemed too radical and provocative to be performed in front of a 'general' audience of passers-by, and were reserved for events at more explicitly secular spaces. The cultural activists were aware that their powerful tool for political education and awareness raising was not universally approved and at times even violently opposed, as in infamous incidents such as the killing of Safdar Hashmi by a political party cadre during a Jana Natya Manch performance on the outskirts of New Delhi in 1989 or the Islamist bomb attack on the Udichi office in Jessore, Bangladesh, in 1999; many much smaller incidents did not make it into the headlines (van Erven 1989). Consequently, theatre activists tend to anticipate their audiences and take into account which plays and speech acts might be appropriate. They are, thus, very much aware that they are not addressing any singular, abstract 'public sphere' but rather several distinct, and in this case physically embodied, publics. For instance, several years ago one theatre group in Sylhet split into two after a controversy over whether or not to perform a script written by the rationalist Ananta Bijoy Das, a so-called atheist blogger who was later killed by an Islamist, in 2015. Das's play was a biography of Giordano Bruno, the sixteenth-century polymath who was persecuted as a heretic because of his promotion of scientific knowledge and freethinking. Hasan Islam, one of the leading members of the Sylhet group, who had strongly opposed the proposal, explained his perspective on the controversy:

> This character [Giordano Bruno], he does not practise [religion]. He is against religion. … That's fine. But what is the issue here? If this is written for intellectuals, that is fine. But if you think about the general audience [sādhāraṇ darśak], then there is a problem. If the play was only for specific people and intellectuals, it would work. But will ordinary people understand it in the same way that you understand it? … An uneducated or moderately educated audience will assume that I have insulted their religion. Even if he [Bruno] does not protest for the sake of politeness … he and his family [i.e., members of a general audience] might decide to never see any theatre again.

As we can see, Hasan Islam did not oppose the script in principle but rather considered it inappropriate for a 'general audience'. He reflects on the possible reception of the play by the audience and unintended consequences, being concerned especially that the message might be distorted in this process. Even though this highly controversial play was a particular case, considerations concerning audiences and the particular locations of performances were common among theatre activists. They often maintained what Martin Zillinger has called a 'graduated publicness' by being concerned about the 'constantly changing mediation practices that constitute, negotiate, and shape the Öffentlichkeit [publicity]' (2017, S43) of their performances and regulate the degree of publicness not only with regard to the specific play at hand but also the political moment and the socio-political climate.

In anthropology and related disciplines, debates about 'publicness' have long moved beyond criticisms of Habermas's idea of a public sphere and have instead focused on how different mediating practices and 'regimes of circulation' (Cody 2009) serve to constitute diverse, fluid, competing and often overlapping publics. Such publics are often structured along lines of class, gender, ethnicity, religion, educational background, language group and, as Robert Shimko and Sara Freeman suggest, 'by shared interests in cultural matters' (2012, 6). In our case, we would also emphasise aesthetic preferences, political visions and commitment to socio-political projects. Ethnographic exploration of such mediating and media practices have resulted in a reconceptualisation of the role of 'media' in such processes as well as a renewed interest in their material and technological preconditions (e.g., Abu-Lughod 2004; Eickelman and Anderson 1999; Meyer and Moors 2006; Rajagopal 2001). For instance, Charles Hirschkind's (2006) emphasis on the medium of dissemination (in his case, cassette sermons), their affective affordances and significance for emergent forms of political community in Egypt provides a profound 'challenge to the hierarchy of the senses underpinning post-Kantian versions of the public sphere' (Cody 2011, 42). This is particularly important when we analyse the relationship between media and non-religious publics, considering the 'cognitivist bias' and tendency to 'treat media as a transparent vehicle for ideas' that have thus far typified scholarly approaches (Chalfant 2020, 1, 4; see also Binder in this volume).

Our interlocutors certainly envision street theatre and other Bengali cultural genres as tools for transmitting a message to 'masses', as they clearly explain. Yet if we take the insights from the anthropology of religions and publics seriously, it becomes apparent that such aspirations to publicity and, arguably, the creation of a 'secular' public sphere are not the only way we can understand the role of performance. If publics emerge through mediating practices, as has been widely argued (see Meyer and Moors 2006), the very engagements with certain Bengali cultural genres produce a specific and limited public, constituted through the medium of theatre among its activists, in which the cultivation and articulation of radical secularist or other non-religious stances are possible and at the same time inextricably linked with their aesthetic preferences and what is understood by them as 'Bengali culture'. It is for this reason that street theatre and genres like *gaṇasaṅgīt* or *bratacārī nṛtya* are often considered to be tools to promote secularism, even though such performances do not address, at least in any direct way, issues related to religious traditions, rationalism or superstition.

Habermas's concept of the 'public sphere' is inherently linked to narratives of secularisation. It stipulates a normative expectation that the public is inevitably and necessarily a secular space from which individuals, who may or may not be religious in their 'private' lives, separate any religious convictions in order to participate in supposedly impartial and rational debates. The widespread criticism of this prescriptive model for its lack of empirical significance was taken up in Habermas's later proposal of the 'post-secular', which, however, fails to fully transcend the normative and liberal binaries inherent in his theory (see Casanova 2013; Cooke 2010). For South Asia, even more than elsewhere, it has been argued that many publics are structured both religiously and, more specifically, communally, for a number of historical and structural reasons, many of which are rooted in colonial policy (Embree 2002; Scott and Ingram 2015). They range from the partial intersection of language or print communities with religious affiliation[12] to legal pluralism and the significance of contested religious nationalisms that are partially a legacy of the divide-and-rule policy, including the two-state solution of the British colonial government. In contemporary India and Bangladesh, religious traditions play a significant role, with the majority religions, Hinduism and Islam respectively, often exerting substantial normative power over people's lives. Cultural activists like Shomapti and Souvik are critical of such influence and the importance attributed to publicly performed piety. They thus conceptualise their own activities as part of what might be called a 'counterpublic'. Ironically, the common utopian vision of cultural activists, namely the establishment of a society in which all members are equal irrespective of religious convictions and belonging, seems to resemble Habermas's notion of a 'secular' public sphere in notable ways. Yet the activists are very aware that this secular space is a utopian aspiration, while their activities suggest secular publics of a limited, but more immediately tangible, nature.

We should therefore conceptualise cultural activism not as an intervention in a singular public sphere, but rather as a secular medium that allows conversations, self-cultivation and identification among a certain group of secularly oriented interlocutors to take place. And it is arguably for this reason that cultural activism creates spaces in which people feel they can actually raise their voices, openly articulate 'secular attitudes', and translate such aspirations into action, without being constrained by partisan interests and considerations of propriety.

However, this is the case because performative arts, rather than being mere media through which secularist 'messages' are transmitted to an audience, are in themselves cultural forms that are capable of mediating secular sentiments. Such performances thereby create – through a combination of the activists' intentional actions and the affordance of the medium itself as well as the regional history inscribed into it – local, limited but identifiably 'secular' publics for our interlocutors in Bangladesh and West Bengal.

Conclusion

This chapter has argued that cultural performances – specifically, several genres that carry with them historical resonances of struggle – are privileged media for activists to cultivate secularism among themselves and in order to disseminate their values to a wider public. For activists, it is important to keep this cultural secularism separate from the efforts of secularist political parties, with which they share broad aims and values. This is because cultural activists (even if they are party members themselves) are sceptical of the level of commitment that can be fostered through groups and organisations that must seek public support and are therefore prone to compromises with dominant opinions and norms. Conversely, performative genres lend themselves more readily to expressions of secularism that are relatively free of compromises, while performance itself shapes the formulations of secularism that are possible.

The kind of secularism that emerges is thus tied to the specific medium that activists deploy, in this case Bengali theatre. We have identified three possible secular cultural modalities, of which (1) the overt critique of religion and (2) the humanist opposition to communalism are most readily perceptible. The third kind of secular performance is not transmitted as a message of iterated 'content' but is rather a product of the act of performing itself: (3) the community and performance of being apart from religion, understood in relation to the historical inheritances of political theatre, as well as performers' and audiences' contemporary contexts. This secularism as autonomy from the religious involves manifesting a kind of public that brings people together as 'seculars' through the social act of performance, drawing upon the historical associations of performative media with secularist ideas and positions.

The specific configuration of cultural politics in Bengal, in which certain genres have themselves historically taken on secularist resonances, draws attention to the fact that performances need not reference religion to constitute a 'secular performance'. This recognition expands our field of attention to consider the secularity of various kinds of embodiment, through acting, dialogue, costume and genre aesthetics, as well as the groups, audiences and publics that coalesce around performances. It also highlights the fact that the 'secular public' produced through cultural activism need not aspire to totality, but may constitute a space in which activists can perform, socially reinforce and disseminate their secular commitments in ways they deem safe. Thus performative embodiments of secularity – unlike more cognitive or ideological considerations of secularism, and especially when secular performance does not reference religion – reveal how tangible secular publics cohere with a much broader social milieu, in ways that exhibit rebellion and radicalism, but also threats of censorship and violence. The importance of accounting for secular publics in this manner, paying attention to the limits of their performances as much as their explicit demonstrations of secularism, cannot be overestimated in contexts in which exclusivist religious politics continue to assert themselves violently.

Notes

1 All interlocutors' names and identifiable information have been anonymised.
2 Like the English term, the Bengali concept takes on multiple meanings, which may include the ideal of equal treatment of all religions (by the state and in everyday interactions), the rejection of religion-based politics and political parties, and the opposition of certain forms of religiosity such as fundamentalist forms of Islam or Hinduism. Thus, being 'secular' often has the connotation of being less religious. These issues are highly contested in both Bengals, though differently in relation to their histories and the dominant religions, Hinduism and Islam. In this chapter, we focus on secularism as it is variously defined by secularist cultural activists through performances.
3 According to the CPI(M) programme, 'the Party should fight against all forms of intrusion of religion in the economic, political and administrative life of the nation and uphold secular and democratic values in culture, education and society.' It criticises other secularist parties that describe themselves as secular for a supposedly bourgeois pseudo-secularism, in which all religions can 'equally interfere' in political life (Communist Party of India (Marxist) 2001: 24–5).
4 The notion that Bengali nationalism (conceptualised as distinct from Bangladeshi nationalism) is 'secular', especially in the sense of being non-communal, has its roots in earlier anti-colonial movements, especially the Swadeshi movement against the division in 1905 along communal lines of Bengal by the British colonial administration (see Chatterjee 1999).
5 The 1972 constitution of Bangladesh mentioned secularism as one of the four core principles. However, the fifth amendment to the constitution in April 1979 during the BNP (Bangladesh Nationalist Party) rule removed secularism from the constitution, and the Arabic phrase *'bi-smi-llāhi r-raḥmāni r-raḥīm'* (in the name of God, the Most Gracious, the Most Merciful) was added. In 1988, under the Ershad regime, Islam became the state religion. In 2010, the Supreme Court declared that the fifth amendment was unconstitutional. Subsequently, the principle of secularism was reinstated in the constitution, but *'bi-smi-llāhi r-raḥmāni r-raḥīm'* and Islam as a state religion were retained.
6 Bauls (Bāul) are members of a devotional musical tradition in the Bengal region, drawing adherents from both Islam and Hinduism. They often intentionally and explicitly aim at transcending religious divisions and are associated with secularism in Bengal. See Openshaw 1997; Knight 2010; Schulz 2021.

7   This sense of shared political values prevails even though very few groups in the United Theatre Council have explicit communist leanings. For Shomapti, commitment to 'the spirit of the Independence War', non-communalism and secularism form the common ground between all the cultural activists in the council.

8   Such contested entanglement between citizenship and religious belonging should be seen in the context of the divide-and-rule policies of the British colonial government and the many partitions of Bengal, as well as the two-state theory in which the British Raj was divided into a Hindu-majority India and a Muslim-majority Pakistan (see Chatterjee 1999; J. Chatterji 1994). Contemporary ramifications can be found in religion-based and secular nationalisms, but also in contestations about who may hold legal citizenship, an issue that has been recurrently debated with regard to the Urdu-speaking minority Biharis in Bangladesh, and has regained urgency in recent years in India as changing citizenship legislation increasingly discriminates against Muslims, reinforcing a notion that they are disloyal to the nation, second-class citizens or 'infiltrators' from outside.

9   This movement was formed mostly by cultural activists, intellectuals and digital activists in February 2013 to demand harsher punishment of the war crimes committed in the 1971 Independence War and in opposition to the Islamist party Jamaat-e-Islami. While it was denounced as an 'atheist' platform by some of its opponents, it was widely perceived as progressive and secular by those who supported it.

10 Examples of such secular aesthetics include not only performance and songs but also visual arts such as ālpanā (colourful floor paintings), as well as protests in the form of candlelit vigils, which the Islamist groups explicitly opposed in reaction to the Shahbag movement. Such opposition illustrates the contentious and political nature of some aesthetic practices that may be considered 'Bengali', 'secular' or 'Hindu', depending on one's point of view.

11 Eldhose discusses the interrelation between street theatre and the rationalist movement in Kerala, another Indian state that has been governed intermittently by a CPI(M)-led coalition. For another example of rationalist and anti-superstition performances, see Quack 2012.

12 The division between Urdu and Hindi is one of the most obvious examples. For a fantastic introduction to the historically changing relationship between language, script traditions and religious identity in Bengal, see Uddin 2006.

References

Abu-Lughod, Lila. 2004. *Dramas of Nationhood: The politics of television in Egypt.* Chicago: University of Chicago Press.

Arora, Swati. 2019. 'Left to "*biyaasi* number": Cultural activism and political street theatre in Delhi.' *Contemporary Theatre Review* 29 (1): 71–90. https://doi.org/10.1080/10486801. 2018.1558219.

Asad, Talal. 2003. *Formations of the Secular: Christianity, Islam, modernity.* Stanford, CA: Stanford University Press.

Bangstad, Sindre. 2009. 'Contesting secularism/s: Secularism and Islam in the work of Talal Asad.' *Anthropological Theory* 9 (2): 188–208. https://doi.org/10.1177/1463499609105477.

Bharucha, Rustom. 1983. *Rehearsals of Revolution: The political theater of Bengal.* Honolulu: University of Hawaii Press.

Binder, Stefan. 2020. *Total Atheism: Secular activism and the politics of difference in South Asia.* New York: Berghahn.

Bradbury, James. 2019. 'Hinduism and the Left: Searching for the secular in post-communist Kolkata.' PhD thesis, University of Manchester.

Cannell, Fenella. 2010. 'The anthropology of secularism.' *Annual Review of Anthropology* 39: 85–100. https://doi.org/10.1146/annurev.anthro.012809.105039.

Casanova, José. 2013. 'Exploring the postsecular: Three meanings of "the secular" and their possible transcendence', in *Habermas and Religion*, Craig Calhoun, Eduardo Mendieta and Jonathan VanAntwerpen, eds, 27–48. Cambridge: Polity.

Chalfant, Eric. 2020. 'Material irreligion: The role of media in atheist studies.' *Religion Compass* 14 (3): 1–8. https://doi.org/10.1111/rec3.12349.

Chatterjee, Partha. 1999. 'On religious and linguistic nationalisms: The second partition of Bengal', in *Nation and Religion: Perspectives on Europe and Asia*, Peter van der Veer and Hartmut Lehmann, eds, 112–28. Princeton, NJ: Princeton University Press.

Chatterjee, Partha. 2012. *The Black Hole of Empire: History of a global practice of power*. Princeton, NJ: Princeton University Press.

Chatterji, Joya. 1994. *Bengal Divided: Hindu communalism and partition, 1932–1947.* Cambridge: Cambridge University Press.

Chatterji, Roma. 2016. 'Repetition, improvisation, tradition: Deleuzean themes in the folk art of Bengal.' *Cultural Analysis* 15 (1): 99–127.

Cody, Francis. 2009. 'Daily wires and daily blossoms: Cultivating regimes of circulation in Tamil India's newspaper revolution.' *Journal of Linguistic Anthropology* 19 (2): 286–309. https://doi.org/10.1111/j.1548-1395.2009.01035.x.

Cody, Francis. 2011. 'Publics and politics.' *Annual Review of Anthropology* 40: 37–52.

Communist Party of India (Marxist). 2001. *Programme*. New Delhi: Progressive Printers.

Cooke, Maeve. 2010. 'Salvaging and secularizing the semantic contents of religion: The limitations of Habermas's postmetaphysical proposal', in *Jürgen Habermas*, vol. 4, David M. Rasmussen and James Swindal, eds, 235–58. Los Angeles and London: SAGE.

Dressler, Markus and Arvind-Pal S. Mandair, eds, 2011. *Secularism and Religion-Making*. Oxford and New York: Oxford University Press.

Eickelman, Dale and Jon Anderson, eds, 1999. *New Media in the Muslim World: The emerging public sphere*. Bloomington: Indiana University Press.

Eldhose, Adakkaravayalil Yoyakky. 2014. 'Political conscientisation through street theatre: A study with reference to *Kalyanasaugadhikam*.' *Research in Drama Education: The Journal of Applied Theatre and Performance* 19 (4): 340–54. https://doi.org/10.1080/13569783.2014.954811.

Embree, Ainslie T. 2002. 'Religion in public space: Two centuries of a problem in governance in modern India.' *India Review* 1 (1): 52–76. https://doi.org/10.1080/14736480208404620.

Fraser, Nancy. 1992. 'Rethinking the public sphere: A contribution to the critique of actually existing democracy', in *Habermas and the Public Sphere*, Craig Calhoun, ed., 109–42. Cambridge, MA: MIT Press.

Gholami, Reza. 2015. *Secularism and Identity: Non-Islamiosity in the Iranian diaspora*. Farnham: Ashgate.

Ghosh, Arjun. 2005. 'Theatre for the ballot: Campaigning with street theatre in India.' *Drama Review* 49 (4): 171–82.

Guha-Thakurta, Tapati. 2015. *In the Name of the Goddess: The Durga Pujas of contemporary Kolkata*. New Delhi: Primus Books.

Hirschkind, Charles. 2006. *The Ethical Soundscape: Cassette sermons and Islamic counterpublics*. New York: Columbia University Press.

Knight, Lisa I. 2010. 'Bāuls in conversation: Cultivating oppositional ideology.' *International Journal of Hindu Studies* 14 (1): 71–120. https://doi.org/10.1007/s11407-010-9087-y.

Kunz, Hans-Martin. 2006. 'Schauspiele, Schaubühnen, Schauplätze: "Jatra" und Populäres Theater in Kalkutta', in *Mumbai, Delhi, Kolkata. Annäherungen an die Megastädte Indiens*, Ravi Ahuja and Christiane Brosius, eds, 283–97. Heidelberg: Draupadi.

Kunz, Hans-Martin. 2014. *Schaubühnen der Öffentlichkeit. Das Jatra-Wandertheater in Westbengalen (Indien)*. Heidelberg: Draupadi.

Meyer, Birgit and Annelies Moors, eds, 2006. *Religion, Media, and the Public Sphere*. Bloomington: Indiana University Press.

Mohan, Dia. 2004. '*Jana Sanskriti*'s theatre and political practice in rural Bengal: The making of popular culture.' *South Asia Popular Culture* 2 (1): 39–53. https://doi.org/10.1080/1474668042000210500.

Mottin, Monica. 2017. *Rehearsing for Life: Theatre for social change in Nepal*. Cambridge: Cambridge University Press.

Openshaw, Jeanne. 1997. 'The web of deceit: Challenges to Hindu and Muslim "orthodoxies" by "Bāuls" of Bengal.' *Religion* 27 (4): 297–309. https://doi.org/10.1006/reli.1997.0093.

Quack, Johannes. 2012. *Disenchanting India: Organized rationalism and criticism of religion in India*. New York: Oxford University Press.

Rajagopal, Arvind. 2001. *Politics after Television: Religious nationalism and the reshaping of the Indian public*. Cambridge: Cambridge University Press.

Rashid, Tahmina. 2015. 'Theatre for community development: Street theatre as an agent of change in Punjab (Pakistan).' *India Quarterly* 71 (4): 335–47. https://doi.org/10.1177/0974928415602604.

Ruud, Arild Engelsen. 2001. 'Talking dirty about politics: A view from a Bengali village', in *The Everyday State and Society in Modern India*, Chris J. Fuller and Véronique Bénéï, eds, 115–36. London: Hurst & Company.

Schielke, Samuli. 2010. 'Second thoughts about the anthropology of Islam, or how to make sense of grand schemes in everyday life.' *Zentrum Moderner Orient Working Paper* 2 (16 pp.).

Schulz, Mascha. 2020. '"That was a good move": Some remarks on the (ir)relevance of "narratives of secularism" in everyday politics in Bangladesh.' *Contributions to Indian Sociology* 54 (2): 236–58. https://doi.org/10.1177/0069966720914056.

Schulz, Mascha. 2021. 'Convoluted convictions, partial positionings: Non-religion, secularism, and party politics in Sylhet, Bangladesh.' PhD thesis, University of Zurich.

Scott, J. Barton and Brannon D. Ingram. 2015. 'What is a public? Notes from South Asia.' *South Asia: Journal of South Asia Studies* 38 (3): 357–70. https://doi.org/10.1080/00856401.2015.1052896.

Shimko, Robert B. and Sara Freeman. 2012. 'Introduction: Theatre, performance, and the public sphere', in *Public Theatres and Theatre Publics*, Robert B. Shimko and Sara Freeman, eds, 1–19. Newcastle upon Tyne: Cambridge Scholars Publishing.

Uddin, Sufia M. 2006. *Constructing Bangladesh: Religion, ethnicity, and language in an Islamic nation*. Chapel Hill: University of North Carolina Press.

van Erven, Eugène. 1989. 'Plays, applause, and bullets: Safdar Hashmi's street theatre.' *The Drama Review* 33 (4): 32–47. https://doi.org/10.2307/1145964.

Warner, Michael. 2002. *Publics and Counterpublics*. New York: Zone Books.

Zillinger, Martin. 2017. 'Graduated publics: Mediating trance in the age of technical reproduction.' *Current Anthropology* 58 (S15): S41–S55.

3

'There is no god, Summer': a critical evaluation of *Rick and Morty*'s approach to atheism and nihilism

Frank Bosman

As early as the third minute of the first episode of the first season, Rick Sanchez, *Rick and Morty*'s anti-hero, throws his calling card on the table for everyone to see: 'There is no god, Summer. You gotta rip that Band-Aid off now. You'll thank me later.' It is an adage that runs through the core of the adult animated sitcom *Rick and Morty*, already running for four seasons at the time of writing: God is dead and the universe is a cold and lonely place without any meaning or comfort.

The series combines pubescent dick jokes with philosophical themes primarily connected to the philosopher Friedrich Nietzsche (Abesamis and Wayne 2019). The show (2013–present), created by Justin Roiland (*Gravity Falls*, 2012–16) and Dan Harmon (*Community*, 2009–15), has been nominated for numerous awards, winning – among others – the IGN Awards of 2015 and 2016 for Best Animated Series, the Annie Awards of 2018 for Best General Audience Animated Television/Broadcast Production and Outstanding Achievement for Writing in an Animated Television/Broadcast Production, and the Primetime Emmy Awards of 2018 and 2020 for Outstanding Animated Program. The series has been praised by the public as well as by critics, applauding its dark overtones, mature themes and philosophical sharpness (Bisset 2020; Chandler 2019; Di Placido 2020; Philips 2015).

The show focuses on the adventures of the members of the Smith household, consisting of parents Jerry and Beth, children Summer and Morty, and Beth's father Rick Sanchez. Rick, indisputably the 'hero' of the series, is a super-brilliant, nihilistic, alcoholic scientist, who drags his reluctant and fearful sidekick and grandson Morty with him on countless, often highly dangerous adventures, taking place in one of the infinite realities of the multiverse (Carr 2007). Beth may be the more assertive force in the household, but is emotionally torn by her dissatisfying marriage to Jerry, a simple-minded and insecure person, and her urge to be validated by her absent father. Summer, in her turn, is crushed under the general uncertainties of high school and under the specific knowledge that her mother's (unwanted) pregnancy with her is the only reason for her parents' strained marriage.

The philosophy of *Rick and Morty* has been described as 'a never-ending fart joke wrapped around a studied look into nihilism' (Cobb 2017). An instructive example of this nihilism can be found in the first season of the series, identified by Dan Harmon as 'the meaning of life in *Rick and Morty*' (Marnell 2017). When Rick, quite unintentionally, has genetically altered the DNA of the whole of humankind, turning them into monsters, he and Morty 'bail out' from their original universe to take the place of their counterparts in another dimension, just seconds after the latter are killed by a failed scientific experiment (S1E6 'Rick Potion #9').

Rick and Morty bury their counterparts in the backyard, a fact which leaves Rick quite unaffected, but leads to considerable mental trauma for Morty. Two episodes later (S1E8 'Rixty Minutes'), Summer learns that her mother's pregnancy with her was not planned, that her parents considered an abortion, and that her parents would have been much better off without her. When she plans to run away from home, Morty confronts her in her room, referencing his earlier 'death':

> I kinda know how you feel, Summer. … That out there? That's my grave. … And every morning, Summer, I eat breakfast 20 yards away from my own rotting corpse. … Nobody exists on purpose. Nobody belongs anywhere. Everybody's going to die. Come watch TV.

This ethical and teleological nihilism also has a religious dimension, or, better formulated, has a specific influence on the show's depiction and discussion of (institutionalised) religion. *Rick and Morty* is a self-identified atheist show, as readily expressed by Rick to his granddaughter in the third minute of the first episode ever (quoted above). In the series as a whole, atheism – in this chapter defined as the explicit denial of and critique of any belief in any metaphysical entity or reality (Nielsen 2021) – is ubiquitous, usually expressed by and through Rick himself, as a kind of realisation of Nietzsche's idea of the self-realising Übermensch (Magnus 1983).

In this chapter, I want to explore and critically evaluate *Rick and Morty*'s atheism-based religion criticism. To do so, I will present and discuss the series' criticism under five different themes (and in the same number of sections): (1) the series' deconstructive intertextual relationship with the Christian Bible and its reductionist view of religion; (2) the series' depiction of religion as a kind of coping mechanism; (3) the absence of divinity in the face of the existence of evil; (4) Rick as the Nietzschean Übermensch and its evident impossibility; and (5) the series' specific criticism of religious people 'selling' their story particularly badly.

In the conclusion, I will formulate some final thoughts concerning *Rick and Morty*'s handling of religion and nihilism, which will prove to be rather unexpected, at least for some readers. To foreshadow these final thoughts, it is enough to indicate that while the series appears to propagate a nihilistic and atheist worldview, in the end – as I hope to show convincingly through the course of this chapter – *Rick and Morty* judges quite critically the possibility of attaining and maintaining a 'hard' Nietzschean (in terms of both atheism and nihilism) position in life on a personal and practical level.

Some preliminary remarks are in order here. Of course, *Rick and Morty* is not the only adult animated sitcom – as the genre has been labelled – that targets (institutionalised) religion in a critical manner. *The Simpsons* (Groening, 1989–present), for example, while not overtly religion critical, gave rise to what is called the 'Ned Flanders effect', named after the Simpsons' extremely religious neighbour, namely the idea that the more religious a person appears to be, the more likely a non-believer is to assume they are not open to new ideas and (thus) find them less attractive (Bingham 2015).

Futurama got its Robot Devil (Groening, 1999–2013) and *Solar Opposites* (Roiland and McMahan, 2020) its pseudo-religion from 'The Wall', a self-contained world where shrunken people are kept as house pets by alien children, but it is probably *South Park* (Parker and Stone, 1997–present) that is best known for its blatant and forceful attack upon everything related to religion (even though the targets of the series' criticism are certainly not limited to that). Episodes that include strong religion criticism are: 'Christian hard rock' (on the economics of praise music), 'A boy and a priest' (about child sexual abuse in the Roman Catholic Church) and 'The passion of the Jew' (on Christian anti-Semitism).

As a methodology, I opt for a communication-oriented analysis (COA) of the series' content (Wieringen 2020). COA makes a strong differentiation between text-external communication (between the so-called 'real author' and 'real reader'), and text-immanent communication (between the so-called 'text-immanent author' and 'text-immanent reader'). In my analysis of the series' content, I focus on text-immanent communication, thus methodologically excluding the position of the series' creators (real authors) and their intentions and interpretations of their work, as well as the position of the series' actual viewers (real readers) in the United States and elsewhere in the world, and their reaction towards and opinions concerning the series' content.

Last but not least, I discuss only the first four seasons of the series (2013–20), since the fifth season is still airing while I am writing this chapter.

'Our cup runneth over': biblical references and religious reductionism

Rick and Morty is a series that cannot be accused of biblical or religious illiteracy (Dinham and Francis 2015). More than once the series quotes – implicitly or explicitly – the Christian Bible. Over four seasons, a kind of (chronologically ordered) anthology can be compiled.

The first instance is found in the pilot (S1E1). When a drunken Rick drags Morty from his bed into his spaceship, he explains to his grandson that he will nuke the world, apparently to 'get a whole fresh start' for the earth. Morty objects, understandably, to which Rick answers he will pick up Jessica first, Morty's long-lasting (but one-sided) love interest. Rick says: 'I'm gonna make it like a new Adam and Eve and you're gonna be Adam. ... And Jessica's gonna be Eve.' It is a clear reference to a section of the creation story found in Genesis 2:5–25, where Adam and Eve are portrayed as living in the primordial paradise.

The invocation of the biblical first couple, however, refers not only to a paradise now presumably lost, as Milton called it, but also to the Christian concept of 'original sin' (Jacobs 2008, i–xv). There is a kind of hereditary 'sin' running through the Smith-Sanchez family. Beth, and to a lesser degree Summer and Morty, are constantly wrestling with the combination of an intrinsic brilliant intellect and a chronic lack of ultimate purpose in life, traits clearly inherited from Beth's father. This inheritance is jeopardising not only her own happiness, but also that of her husband and two children.

In 'Rick Potion #9' (S1E6), Morty and Summer's school principal announces the annual flu-season dance. To explain this somewhat odd concept, he adds: 'I don't know how many times I have to say this but if you have the flu, stay home. The flu-season dance is about awareness, not celebration. You don't bring dead babies to Passover.' The principal's announcement invokes, quite ironically, the Passover story from Exodus 12: the Israelites were instructed to smear the blood of a lamb on their doorpost in order to avoid being targeted by the angel of death, killing every firstborn in Egypt.

Another example of intertextuality between *Rick and Morty* and the Bible is found in 'The Wedding Squanchers' (S2E10). The Smith family has to flee an alien wedding and eventually Earth because of the Galactic Federation's hunt for Rick, whom they deem to be one of the most dangerous criminals in the galaxy. Rick directs the Smiths to an Earth-like planet to start again, an episode reminiscent of the Adam and Eve scene from the pilot episode mentioned above, including the difficult suggestion that Adam and Eve's children would have to have sex with their parents to produce the next generation (Stiebert 2016).

When Rick has found the perfect planet, he smiles and quotes Psalm 23:5 from the Authorised Version (King James translation) almost verbatim: 'See? Our *cup runneth over.* Now, who wants to go shopping for a brand-new motherfuckin' world?! All right!' Of course, in a true *Rick and Morty* way, all three planets that appear to be an ideal replacement have some sort of terrible fault. The biblical quote boomerangs: instead of a divine blessing, the family is 'welcomed' with trials and tribulations.

In one instance, the biblical quotation is directly tied to Rick seeing himself as a kind of godlike creature (see below). When Jerry fails to put the Christmas decorations on top of the Smiths' house (S4E5 'Rattlestar Ricklactica'), Rick makes his body float through the air and argues:

> I made your atomic matrix slightly lighter than air, and now your shoes are heavier than air, which makes you neutrally buoyant, which I find personally more impressive conceptually than walking on water, but what do I know? I wasn't born into the god business. I fucking earned it.

Rick refers to the famous story from the New Testament in which Jesus walks on the Sea of Galilee (Mark 6:45–54, Matthew 14:22–34, John 6:15–21), claiming he himself is more powerful than the son of God.

The most extensive intertextual discussion with the Bible (with the possible exception of S4E6 'Never Ricking Morty', see below), however, is found in 'Childrick of Mort' (S4E9). In this episode, Rick seems to have had sex with a whole planet, conveniently called Gaia, bringing forth a whole nation of clay-people, resembling him in appearance. Because of her own experience of abandonment, Beth forces her father to take up his responsibility towards his offspring. Together they massively speed up the natural evolution of the clay-people in order to bring their civilisation up to the level of spacefaring, apparently the collective galactic equivalent of a person coming of age.

The clay-people themselves refer to a combination between Genesis 2:7, in which God creates humankind out of 'the dust of the ground', and Genesis 1:26–7, where God declares that 'they' (the Bible uses a plural form here) will create humankind after their own image. It isn't hard to see the parallel here: the episode suggests that – as the God of the Old Testament created humankind – Rick is doing the same with the clay-people, created after his own image, making him – again – a godlike being. The clay-people may also be a reference to the concept of the golem from Jewish mystical lore: a human-made clay figure imprinted with a secret incantation and coming to life in order to protect the people (Idel 1990; Sherwin 1985).

However, some of the clay-people are not 'well' and are deemed 'unproductive' by Rick: 'DJs, foodies and influencers'. They are tossed outside the quickly developing city, where they accept the categorically unemployed Jerry, by implication the most unproductive creature of all, as their leader. Jerry leads them in what is turning out to be a fight between Rick and his city-dwellers versus Jerry and his outsiders, supported by a giant Zeus-like figure who claims to be the real father of Gaia's children. Eventually, Rick defeats this Zeus, whose fallen body destroys almost all the clay-people.

The whole episode is one very difficult intertextual reference to the books of Genesis and Exodus. The clay-people are a reference to the creation story in which God creates the first human out of clay (Genesis 2:7), portraying God as a divine potter (as for example in Jeremiah 18:1–6). Jerry is clearly portrayed as a kind of modern Moses: he is taken away by a river (Exodus 2:3; see figure 3.1), assembles his 'chosen people', as both Rick and Jerry express it (Deuteronomy 14:2), splits the river separating 'the wild' from Rick's city (Exodus 14:15–31), unleashes 'plagues' on Rick's people (Exodus 10:4–20), in this case locusts, and self-identifies as Moses, who is 'ready to burn some bush' (Exodus 3:2).

The interpretation is, as said before, very complex. *Rick and Morty* seems to identify Rick with the Egyptian pharaoh, the traditional antagonist of the Exodus narrative, and Jerry with the hero Moses.

3.1 Jerry plays the role of Moses, splitting the sea and allowing his clay people to get across, not to escape Egypt, but to conquer it by force. From 'Childrick of Mort' (S4E9). *Rick and Morty* (2020). The Cartoon Network, Inc.

However, the deity fighting on Jerry/Moses's side is not that of biblical Israel, but that of Greek mythology, identified by Rick as 'the off-brand Yahweh'. This Zeus gives Jerry's clay-people superhuman, magical powers to fight Rick's city folk, a clash between magic and religion on the one hand, and science and rationality on the other. Rick's killing of Jerry's Zeus/God is the image of science triumphing over religion and superstition, the first leading to a spacefaring civilisation, the second to a primitive life in the untamed wilderness.

This last 'biblical' episode indicates very clearly the standpoint of the show with regard to the relationship between religion and science, opting quite frankly for the second over the first. In Ian Barbour's famous typology of religion–science interrelationships (1990, 4–10), *Rick and Morty* clearly falls into the category of conflict, the first category Barbour describes. Religion and science are principally and irreversibly incompatible with one another, to the point at which only one can be adhered to, leaving the other void and meaningless.

Another episode focusing on this conflict is 'Something Ricked This Way Comes' (S1E9), notably in both sub-narratives of the story. First, Rick quarrels with Lucius Needful, the self-identifying as devilish ('I am the devil') owner of an antique shop, freely handing out odd objects that imbue their new owners with magical boons, but curse them at the same time (a not so veiled reference to Stephen King's famous 1991 horror novel *Needful Things*). Rick invents a machine that identifies and removes the curse without sacrificing its benefits. Rick is triumphant over magic and superstition because of his scientific mastermind. We will discuss this episode later on in more detail.

In the same episode, Jerry and Morty have their own father–son adventure, revolving around the discussion concerning the classification of Pluto as a planet, a reference to the real-life 2006 discussion by the International Astronomical Union of whether to classify it as a dwarf planet (Weintraub 2008). Jerry is convinced Pluto is still a planet and goes to great lengths to maintain that claim, up to the point where he is invited by the leading class of Plutonians to visit their 'planet'. They mine the interior of their own world for raw materials, constantly diminishing its size.

The Plutonians have cross-shaped irises, probably as a reference to their religious-fundamentalist zeal, with which they cling to their belief despite scientific evidence pointing elsewhere. The ruling class of Plutonians is well aware of the situation, but keeps it a secret from the ordinary citizens out of corporate greed, a probable reference by the series to the famous, but usually not well-interpreted, quotation from Karl Marx about religion being the opium of the people. Jerry, in his turn, has some very particular views on the nature of science. On the status of Pluto as a planet, he comments: 'Yeah, I heard about that, Morty. And I disagree. … It is possible to disagree in science. Pluto was a planet, some committee of fancy assholes disagree, I disagree back.'

When the Plutonian king compliments Jerry, whom he constantly identifies as an '(earth) scientist', he comments: 'You know, sometimes science is about conviction.' Both expressions seem to reposition the outcome of scientific inquiry from the realm of empirical knowledge to that of subjective opinion, a tendency we know all too well from notions such as 'post-truth' or 'alternative facts' (Stenmark 2018). (On a quick side note, in 'Rick Potion #9', Rick himself explains to Morty that science is sometimes 'more art than science', right after he has compromised human DNA beyond repair.)

Back to Barbour's typology and *Rick and Morty*'s highly critical view of religion. It is interesting to note that Barbour defines two mutually exclusive positions in this conflict, both, just as the series seems to argue. On the one hand, we have scientific materialism, on the other biblical literalism. As Barbour (1990, 4) explains:

> Both seek knowledge with a sure foundation – that of logic and sense data, in the one case, that of infallible scripture, in the other. They both claim that science and theology make rival literal

statements about the same domain, the history of nature, so that one must choose between them.

Barbour makes the accusation that those who argue in favour of the exclusivism of science as the only epistemological means by which true knowledge can be attained have, in fact, a reductionist perception of the concept of religion and a philosophical and untenable trust in (empirical) science. As Barbour suggests, religion and science are not intrinsically opposed or mutually exclusive (giving three other possibilities for the two realms to interact: independence, dialogue and integration); neither can (empirical) science prove its own epistemological premises.

The other position Barbour describes under the notion of 'conflict' is biblical literalism, the idea – indeed upheld by several (fundamentalist) religious communities all around the world – that only the Bible, the Qur'an or some other Divine Revelation written down can give trustworthy information on the nature of things, and when science and the Bible are in conflict, the second should always prevail. Within the context of *Rick and Morty*, two things are noteworthy. First, this adherence to biblical literalism is by no means the only or even the most common attitude of Christian believers towards their sacred scripture. Secondly, *Rick and Morty* seems to frame *all* religion as biblical literalism in order to exclude its possible value in an uncomplicated way. The use of biblical quotes indicates – quite paradoxically – this framework.

Rick and Morty's complex intertextual relationship with the Christian Bible is both a conduit for the show's religion criticism, and an expression of the show's reductionist view of religious phenomena.

'Headism is a hit!': cults and religion as a coping mechanism

Rick and Morty also expresses its religion criticism by means of the exploration of the concept of 'cult', partly because of the notion's negative undertones in popular culture (Richardson 1993; Urban 2015). Over the four seasons of *Rick and Morty*, this concept is explicitly dealt with in two episodes: as a minor plot device in 'Close Rick-counters of the Rick Kind' (S1E10), and as a full-blown narrative in 'Get Schwifty' (S2E3).

In 'Close Rick-counters of the Rick Kind', Rick and Morty are held prisoner by some evil counterparts from another dimension. The 'evil Rick' hoards Mortys from different dimensions, since their specific brainwaves prevent him being found by the authorities. When this evil

Rick throws 'our' Morty into a cell, he meets dozens of other ones there. Most of the Mortys are trembling in fear of evil Rick's terror, but some have found another way to cope with their desperate situation.

These Mortys wear brown, monk-like habits and red paint on their faces. One of them says to 'our' Morty: 'There is no escape, my son. We will find our peace in the next world. ... We are giving in. To the power of the one true Morty. One day he will return.' All the Mortys pray in unison: 'Praise the one true Morty!' When Morty gives a passionate speech about Mortys' self-awareness, one of them says: 'This sounds like something the one true Morty might say. ... He is the one true Morty.'

The cult member offers Morty a booklet, depicting his face with a halo around his head, accompanied by the words 'The Good Morty'. On the back the words 'Only one way to Morty salvation' are printed. When Morty looks inside, it depicts a little cartoon, in which two Mortys are looking at a computer screen. The first says: 'Morty, take a look at this website', to which the second replies: 'Hmmm, I don't think we should be on a site like this.'

The whole scene is an ironic commentary on Christian pretensions concerning the way salvation is to be attained: only through faith in the one true God. The cartoon of the website is a joke about Christian sexual ethics, which is commonly associated with prudishness, modesty and contained sexuality (Ranke-Heinemann 1990).

The second, and longest, discussion of religion as cult is found in the episode 'Get Schwifty', in which the planet Earth is visited and abducted by the Cromulons, an alien race addicted to music-competition television series like *The Voice*. They appear as enormous heads in the sky, whose voices can be heard everywhere on the planet. The Cromulons force Earth into a galactic music competition in which the winning planet will be spared, while the rest are obliterated by a giant space laser beam. While Rick and Morty try to win the competition by performing their newly written hit 'Get Schwifty', the rest of humankind yields to a new religion called 'Headism'.

The episode revolves around the idea of a disconnection between cause and effect. On the one hand we have the Cromulons reacting to Rick and Morty's performances, while on the other hand the new devotees try to communicate with their new deities. When the Cromulons react to the performances, the devotees believe it is because of what *they* did, since they have no clue what is really happening. Only at the end of the episode is the true identity of the heads-in-the-sky revealed to all, stimulating Jerry to summarise: 'Yeah, it's possible that we may have been correlating some things that weren't actually related at all.'

For example, when the Cromulons appear for the first time, they cause major storms all over the world. People, gathered in the local church, try to reason what the true nature of the new phenomenon is. Morty's school principal rails against Father Bob, who sees the whole situation as an opportunity to get some donations for his church:

> I'm just gonna come out and make this pitch. The old gods are dead. Fuck all previous existing religions. All hail the one true god, the giant head in the sky. … I'm going out on the sidewalk and dropping to my knees and pledging my eternal soul to the thing that literally controls the fucking weather!

Then, the principal goes outside the church to pray to the heads in the sky:

> Giant head in the sky, please forgive all that we've done. We're sorry for increased levels of emissions and our racism. And of course, the amber alerts I keep ignoring on my phone. … Please be kind to us for we are but tiny things with entire bodies stuck to your ground.

At exactly the same time, Rick and Morty end their first performance in Area 51; the Cromulons are very pleased with it and they stop the bad weather instantly. This causes the principal and the other churchgoers, who have followed him outside, to reason that the heads have improved the weather because of their devotion and loyalty to their new gods. Within days, Headism develops into a full-blown cult, with its own creed and rituals like Ascension Day, its own priests pretending to interpret the will of the gods exclusively, and its own punishment in the form of sending heretics skywards tied to a massive quantity of balloons. The devotees believe that these 'unwantables' will be absorbed by the gods and sneezed out some time later in the form of newborn babies.

When Beth and Jerry decide to leave the new church, they are deemed unwantables too (see figure 3.2), and are to be sent skywards by a very enthusiastic Summer. At Area 51, Rick and Morty perform again, at first displeasing, but later humouring, the giant heads in the sky. The followers of Headism interpret these divine mood swings as caused by their actions, and a violent row starts between two factions within the cult, both claiming to know the true meaning of the divine signs in the sky. It is only after the heads reveal themselves to be the creators of a cosmic music competition in which Earth had to perform that they re-evaluate their reasonings, understanding that they saw cause and effect where there was actually none.

3.2 Summer (girl with balloon in hand) is all too eager to send her parents Beth and Jerry skywards to her newly adopted godheads, the 'giant heads in the sky'. Beside her, we see (left to right) Morty's and Summer's school principal and maths teacher. From 'Get Schwifty' (S2E3). *Rick and Morty* (2015). The Cartoon Network, Inc.

Even though *Rick and Morty*'s 'cultic' understanding of religion has many elements, I want to focus on two of them: religion as proto-science (Quadrio 2017, 101–2; Smith 2017, 211–12) and religion as coping mechanism (Hood et al. 2009, 435–76; Pargament 2001). Jerry, Beth and Summer are depicted as 'awed and terrified "primitives"' who tremble in the face of the 'opacities of nature and society' (Orsi 2016, 38), that is, in their case, the true meaning of the giant heads' appearance in the sky, and the influence, or rather the non-influence, that the Headists have on the unfolding of events. It is only at the end of the episode that the cultists understand the true, immanent meaning of the Cromulons' appearance, through which they 'switch' from a religious to a scientific perspective on the matter at hand, a transition that is looked upon favourably by the series.

The second qualification of religion *Rick and Morty* presents is one of providing a psychological mechanism by which people can cope in a meaningful way with experiences such as pain, suffering or loss of control. As Riesebrodt (2010, 172, 173) puts it,

> religious institutions ... uphold the ability to act in situations where people feel powerless and incapable of action. ... In this existential sense, religion is a way of coping with contingency. ... [It] maintains

people's ability to act in situations in which they run up against their own limits. … [R]eligion allows humans to continue to act even when overtaxed. Religious practices offer humans a structure in situations in which they might otherwise oscillate between panic and despair.

This is exactly what we see happening in both the episodes discussed above. The Cult of the One True Morty helps the imprisoned Mortys to cope with their captivity specifically, but even more with their own existence. All the captured Mortys are without their own Ricks, which leaves them not only without protection from the dangers of the universe, but also void of their primary and self-explanatory place in the universe, that is, beside a Rick as his sidekick. The Cult of the One True Morty tries to give the prisoners a new goal to live and to hope for, easing their suffering to tolerable levels.

Coping is also at the heart of the Cult of Headism in the second episode. When people are confronted by a literally awesome alien force, which (empirically) controls the weather on the whole planet, and to whose mercy all of humankind is abandoned, they have to choose between surrendering to the utter meaninglessness and uncontrollability of human life in the face of the uncaring universe, symbolised by the Cromulons, who sacrifice whole planets for their own petty entertainment, and reframing the fabric of their reality into a paradigm that fits the new situation in such a way that it gives (at least the impression of) control and purposefulness.

Rick and Morty's depiction of religion as a cult incorporates not only the traditional criticisms like inherent violence and blind obedience to the cult's leaders, but also the ideas of religion as a coping mechanism and a form of proto-science. Both qualities of religion are criticised throughout the series, because the lack of scientific insight into the 'true' nature of things pacifies the individual into a state of acceptance of the status quo, preventing him or her from rising to the occasion, taking matters into their own hands and trying to change the situation for the better.

If 'our' Morty hadn't risen to the occasion, to rebel against the 'evil' Rick's keeping the Mortys prisoner, and had been content with his new religiously interpreted status quo, the Mortys would never have escaped. And if Rick and Morty hadn't grasped the true nature of the Cromulons and acted accordingly, all the devotees of Headism would have been destroyed by the displeased heads in the sky all the same.

'There is no such a thing as hell': atheism and the existence of evil

Rick and Morty's religion criticism is perhaps most visible in its principal and consequently professed atheism. Even though Rick is identified by various characters, and frequently self-identifies, as a kind of 'living god' (S3E10 'The Rickchurian Mortydate'; see also the next section of this chapter), the series' universe appears to be void of any transcendent reality or divine entity. Beth may appear to be a goddess, and may even be identified as one by Jerry, but she is not a god in the traditional sense (S2E7 'Big Trouble in Little Sanchez'). And the Zeus-like figure who claims to be the father of Gaia's children (S4E9 'Childrick of Mort') is not a transcendent being either. Rick identifies and dismisses his competition as an 'off-brand Yahweh' and 'just a Zeus'.

Over the whole series, Rick's adage, formulated in the pilot episode – 'There is no God!' – echoes continuously. In two specific episodes, this theme of the denial of any transcendent being is discussed in more depth and quite explicitly: 'Rickmancing the Stone' (S3E2) and 'The Ricks Must Be' (S2E6). In the first of these, when Rick, Morty and Summer are visiting a post-apocalyptic version of Earth in another dimension in search of a very valuable but at the same time very imaginary kind of rock, identified as 'isotope 322', the violent raiders they meet appear to worship the substance as a kind of divine object.

The raiders' leader, Hemorrhage, explains its paradoxical meaning: 'That is our glowing rock. We carry it with us for desecration, to remind us there are no gods.' It is a reversal of the original meaning of a sacred object (relics, totems, idols and the like), which is typically revered because of its connection to the divine realm or because it symbolises or even manifests the divine itself (Hahn 2017, 18–47). Isotope 322 is, however, not a symbol of the divine–human connection, or of a connection between mortals and their gods, or a magic tool to manipulate the physical or the divine realm, but a symbol of the opposite, that there is no divine reality or deity to begin with.

Another possibility is the interpretation of the glowing rock as a form of 'material irreligion' (Chalfant 2020). Atheism has been regarded as an intellectual endeavour first and foremost; in contrast, scholars such as Matthew Engelke (2015) and Jacob Copeman and Johannes Quack (2015) argue that material culture is just as important for the non-religious as it is for traditional religions. The glowing rock of Hemorrhage could be considered to be such an object: significant, but in a non-religious way.

Hemorrhage's statement that they 'have no gods' is especially interesting if we take into account the apocalyptic context of his raider-clan, because it invokes the theological theme of theodicy and the series' constant criticism of this. The theodicy lies at the heart of three monotheistic religions and focuses on the ancient question about the existence of an omnipotent and good God vis-à-vis the existence of evil within this world (Bosman 2019, 127–30). A theodicy is an attempt to find a solution to the principal problem: how can one believe in a God who is both omnipotent and righteous, in the face of all the evil and suffering in the world? According to John Hick's famous typology (1966), the majority of these 'defences' either excuse evil and suffering itself – suggesting it serves a higher, yet undiscovered good – or excuse God by reframing the existence of (moral) evil as a necessary condition of the absolute freedom of the human will.

Isotope 322 symbolises both the question being asked – why did God not prevent the apocalypse in the afterdays of which Hemorrhage and his clan have to live? – and the ultimate, atheistic answer to that question – because there is no God in the first place. It is a reversed causality: *because* the suffering of the apocalypse happened, that is, was not prevented by a divine entity, the existence of that entity is nullified, or at least one's faith in such a divinity. It is a signpost of the series' atheist religion criticism: if God exists, why all the suffering?

Examples of the critical discussion of the theodicy in *Rick and Morty* can be found in at least three other instances. (1) In the pilot (S1E1), when Summer is confronted with her boy-crush being frozen by Rick and shattered to pieces, she cries out: 'What kind of God lets this happen?' (2) In 'Rick Potion #9' (S1E6), when Jerry fights off the human monsters created by Rick's failed manipulations and rescues Beth, she cries: 'Jerry! Thank God!' But Jerry disagrees: 'God? God is turning people into insect monsters, Beth! I am the one beating them to death. Thank me.' (3) In 'The Vat of Acid Episode' (S4E8), Rick confronts Morty with the consequences of his behaviour, which is killing thousands of Mortys from other dimensions, and his grandson cries in despair. Rick comments: 'It's over, Morty. Feel this. Take this in. This is God.' All these examples echo the same criticism of any religion: why the suffering?

Yet another train of thought, intended to underline the idea of the non-existence of any godhead whatsoever, is found in 'The Ricks Must Be' (S2E6). Inside the battery of Rick's spaceship, he had created a 'microverse' that includes intelligent life. Rick has visited this microverse earlier and introduced to it Goobleboxes, devices that generate electricity, which is partly rerouted to power Rick's battery. Inside the microverse, the scientist Zeep has created his own miniverse in which people operate a Flooble Crank to create electricity. Within the miniverse, another scientist, Kyle, is busy creating his own teenyverse, which includes another electricity-making device, called the Blooble Yank. In this episode, *Rick and Morty* evokes the idea of (earthly) life as the result of extraterrestrial interference (Feder 2002), leaving their memory distorted in the world's religions and mythologies, popularised by Erich von Däniken's bestseller *Chariots of the Gods?* (1969).

When Kyle realises his ontological status, he despairs: 'So he made a universe, and that guy is from that universe, and that guy made a universe, and that's the universe where I was born? Where my father died, and where I couldn't make time for his funeral because I was working on my universe.' Kyle smashes his spaceship into the rocks, killing himself in the process and blocking Rick, Morty and Zeep from returning to their respective universes. Zeep and Rick engage in a month-long conflict in which verbal cursing takes an important part, usually of an existential kind. For example, Rick says to Zeep: 'I made the stars that became the carbon in your mother's ovaries.' To which Zeep replies: 'I didn't ask to be born!' They even mock each other theologically. Zeep says: 'I hope your god is as big a dick as you.' To which Rick replies, true to his atheist inclinations: 'My god's the biggest dick that's never existed.'

The denial of any transcendent reality or divine being also has consequences for the existence of an afterlife, be it a good one (heaven), or a bad one (hell). Rick denounces both explicitly. In 'The Rickchurian Mortydate' (S3E10), Rick warns a security officer of the US president not to touch him: 'Son, you have a right to refuse his order, and I guarantee you're going to die if you touch me, and there's no afterlife. Everything just goes black.' And in 'Rest and Ricklaxation' (S3E6), a very evil version of Rick says the same: 'There is no such thing as hell.' The same applies to the afterlife the alien Tony arrives at in 'The Old Man and the Seat' (S4E2). It is only after he meets his deceased wife that Tony understands he is in a fake version of heaven, created by Rick, based on 'what he wants' and 'what he has'. The morality of this fake heaven is that every conception of the afterlife is not based on reality, but on the hopes and dreams of individuals (as a part of religion's quality of being a coping mechanism; see above).

It is, however, interesting to see that the series explicitly denies the existence of divine entities and an afterlife in some episodes, while at the same time it has no problem with depicting a very real hell, several demons and the devil in other ones. I will give three examples. In the first, in an extraterrestrial commercial, a leprechaun with an Irish accent, Tophat Jones, is slain by two children who empty the contents of his stomach in order to eat the cereal (called Smiggles) the creature has just devoured. When the apparently Roman Catholic (what else?) leprechaun dies, he weeps: 'Jesus Christ! It hurts! … Ah, Jesus Christ. Lord. Savior. And Spirit. Save me! Take me to the light. Oh, my God! I see demons. I see demons are coming.'

Of course, this is not the same as depicting an actual afterlife, since we have only Tophat's dying words to testify to it, and he is – after all – in a commercial. But we have other examples. In the second, in the earlier discussed parody of King's novel *Needful Things* (S1E9, see above), Lucius Needful, the self-identified devil, and Rick have a quarrel over the cursed objects in the store. Rick discovers a way to remove the curses, about which he comments: 'Does evil exist, and if so, can one detect and measure it? … The answer is yes, you just have to be a genius.'

The third example is from the anthology episode 'Morty's Mind Blowers' (S3E8), in which Rick and Morty revisit former adventures too painful for either of them to remember. In one of those memories, a Floop Floopian warlord, Zick Zack, asks Rick to kill him, since his people believe that such an honourable death will bring them everlasting happiness in the afterlife. When Rick goes to the bathroom, Morty and Zick Zack have a conversation on the afterlife.

> **Morty:** You know, I'm a little envious. Your species has an actual afterlife. That's gotta be nice.
> **Zick Zack:** What do you mean?
> **Morty:** Well, you know, here on Earth, we don't know what's going on. It must be nice for you guys to, you know, have that proof's in the pudding, you know, evidence.
> **Zick Zack:** Evidence? There's supposed to be evidence?
> **Morty:** Um, yeah, uh … otherwise, how do you know if it's true?

Zick Zack runs outside, very unsure about his former request, but is killed instantly by a passing car. Upon his death, dark figures, chanting in eerie voices, drag Zick Zack's soul downwards.

> **Zick Zack:** Oh, God, it's all real! Oh, it hurts! Oh, I shouldn't have doubted it! I shouldn't have let you make me doubt it! Aah! I blame you, I blame you!
> **Morty:** But he said there wasn't any evidence! That was a ton of evidence!
> **Rick:** Well, silver lining. Now I know their religion's real. They have a hell, and it does not look good.

From these examples, we see the interesting fact that, while there is an 'official' denial of any transcendent reality, deity or afterlife, hell seems to be a pretty real deal in *Rick and Morty*'s universe. In combination with the subtle hints about the theodicy issue I touched upon earlier, the series gives evidence of the struggle of postmodernity with the existence of suffering and evil in the world, exactly *because* there is no transcendent reality or entity that could be connected to these experiences (Bosman and Wieringen 2020).

The death of God extinguished the self-explanatory nature of God, an afterlife and the accompanying judgement between good and bad. It did not, however, extinguish the (experiences of) pain and suffering, nor the experienced need for a (final) judgement to reward what is good and punish what is evil. This results in the strange phenomenon whereby depicting hell is far more popular than depicting heaven, a tendency stretching from Dante's *Inferno* to animated sitcoms like *South Park* and *The Simpsons* (*Zocalo Public Square* 2012; Baird 2007). The reality of our world *not being* a very heavenly place 'produces' the need to 'expel' the evils from this world to another realm, at least in a collective cultural sense. This is why hell is very real in *Rick and Morty*, while every trace of heaven is eradicated.

'I am a goddamn god now!': Rick as a Nietzschean Übermensch

Connected to the concept of the death of god and the disappearance of an afterlife is the idea of the Übermensch. Nietzsche's superman has to work out, in the face of the vanishing of an external value-creating instance or entity, his own new goals, ideals and values (Loeb 2006; Fitzsimons 2007, 149–65). Rick answers to the description of the Nietzschean superhuman: (1) he is his own god, in the sense that he accepts no higher authority than his own, (2) he is constantly working towards self-realisation, sublimation and creativity, and (3) he fights a constant battle against ethical and teleological nihilism that is so intricately connected to Nietzsche's ideal (Abesamis 2019).

During most of the series, Rick seems perfectly able to operate (and incarnate) this Nietzschean philosophy to the fullest, including the accompanying nihilism:

To live is to risk it all. Otherwise you are just an inert chunk of randomly assembled molecules drifting wherever the universe blows you.

(S3E2 'Rickmancing the Stone')

I don't respect therapy, because I'm a scientist. Because I invent, transform, create and destroy for a living, and when I don't like something about the world, I change it.

(S3E3 'Pickle Rick')

Worse, you're smart. When you know nothing matters, the universe is yours. ... The universe is basically an animal. It grazes on the ordinary. It creates infinite idiots just to eat them.

(S3E9 'The ABCs of Beth')

Many times, indeed, Rick is identified as some kind of god; elsewhere, he claims to be a god himself. For example: 'the smartest thing in every conceivable universe, the Infinite Rick, a god', 'a demon' and 'a super fucked-up god' (S3E1 'The Rickshank Rickdemption'), 'if God exists, it's fucking me' (S3E6 'Rest and Ricklaxation'), 'a living God' (S3E10 'The Rickchurian Mortydate'), 'a goddamn god' (S4E1 'Edge of Tomorty'), a 'god of death' (S4E7 'Promortyus') and bigger than 'a Zeus' (S4E9 'Childrick of Mort').

The interesting part of Rick's portrayal as a Nietzschean Übermensch is not when he is successful, but rather when he fails and his superhuman properties are unveiled as masking an ultimately unsure, bitter and (most of all) lonely figure. Several moments spring directly to the mind of any fan of the series. The first example of the dissolving of Rick's self-proclaimed semi-divinity can be found in the episode 'Auto Erotic Assimilation' (S2E3). Rick reconnects with his former girlfriend Unity, a relatively small 'hive mind', a collective of individuals whose interconnected consciousnesses form one giant new entity. Rick and Unity plunge themselves into a planet-wide orgy, sprinkled with booze and drugs.

Eventually, Unity breaks up with Rick, not because she has stopped loving him, but because she realises that she will lose herself – even as a hive mind which has absorbed millions of individuals – because of her relation with the intellectually and psychologically stronger Rick. She writes: 'I lose who I am and become part of you. As in a strange way you're better at what I do without even trying.' When Rick returns home to his garage, he puts together a strange contraption. After having defrozen and gently caressed a strange, squeaking alien, he puts it in the machine, which – after a few seconds – kills the creature instantly. Rick, heavily drunk, also puts his own head in the death-ray contraption, but passes out before the machine can kill him.

Rick's depression is evidently due to lovesickness – he apparently really loved Unity – but also to the hive mind's comments on their breaking up. Unity seems to think Rick is already 'evolved' and 'whole' on a level she will never attain even if she unifies uncountable species. Rick, however, is of another and much more negative opinion concerning himself. His consciously chosen Nietzschean worldview, including his own self-realisation, prevents him from loving and being loved as a 'normal' person could. In 'Rick Potion #9' (S1E6), Rick has already listed his opinion on love, sex and marriage:

> Listen, I hate to break it to you, but what people call 'love' is just a chemical reaction that compels animals to breed. It is hard, Morty, then it slowly fades, leaving you stranded in a failing marriage. I did it. Your parents are gonna do it. Break the cycle. Rise above it. Focus on science.

This 'focus on science' has brought Rick two opposed things: the capability to live the life of a Nietzschean demigod *and* the incapability to connect to *Untermenschen*, who cannot follow in his footsteps. The same happens in the episode 'The Old Man and the Seat' (S4E2); Rick – shy pooper that he is – has built himself an artificial world for the sole purpose of taking a shit in private, but discovers that his royally positioned toilet is also used by another creature. After some investigation, Rick identifies the alien Tony – also a shy pooper – as the culprit. Instead of killing him right away, Rick goes to great lengths to prevent him from intruding ever again. Tony keeps coming, however, and eventually explains the situation to a furious Rick:

> You need the same thing I needed, Rick. You need someone to give you permission to live. … You know what shy pooping is, Rick? It's a pointless bid for control. You want to take the one part of life that you truly think is yours, and you want to protect it from a universe that takes whatever it wants. … We can spend our lives fighting that, or we can choose to be free.

When Tony eventually dies – which is unrelated to Rick's efforts – the scientist returns to his artificial world in order to grieve the death of his 'friend', silently being humiliated by the devices he had installed for Tony. As Unity was the symbol of Rick's incapability to connect to loved ones,

Tony is the symbol of his incapability to control the world around him in every detail, even with his superhuman intellect. Rick knows he is ultimately limited, but refuses to acknowledge this fact to himself, which results in the controlled environment and his shy pooping.

A third time, Rick fails to live up to his own Nietzschean standards. During the four seasons of the series, it becomes more than clear that Rick left Beth's mother early in his daughter's life, which led to great abandonment issues during her adulthood. When Beth struggles with her life choices, going back and forth between her bourgeois life with her family and a wild life on her own in the spirit of her father, Rick offers to create a perfect clone for her, giving her every opportunity to take decisions in life (S3E9 'The ABCs of Beth').

The viewer is left in the dark as to which path Beth chooses, until the fourth season's finale, 'Star Mort Rickturn of the Jerri' (S4E10). 'Wild' Beth returns home to find 'sensible' Beth running her household. Both daughters try to squeeze out of their father who is the clone and who is the real Beth. Eventually, Rick is forced to explain he doesn't know either, since he let a computer mix up the two at random. Both daughters walk away disgusted, leaving Rick to himself. Rick is visibly shocked by his own behaviour. He sighs and says: 'Holy shit. I'm a terrible father.'

Just as Unity exposed Rick's inability to connect to a loved one, and Tony showed Rick's incapacity to cope with his own contingency, the two Beths are incarnations of Rick's inability to take any form of long-term responsibility. The question the series poses towards the Nietzschean idea of the Übermensch, at least as it is popularly understood, is a tough one: is Rick insufficient to be a real superhuman or is the superhuman insufficient as a model for one's individual life?

Intriguingly enough, the series does not answer that question very clearly: *Rick and Morty* leaves the unanswered question 'hanging' above the series' arch. Rick is continually swung back and forth between succeeding and failing his Übermensch calling. In this respect, the series is criticising not only the 'old-fashioned' bourgeois and 'religious' worldview, as Nietzsche did himself by introducing his concept of the superhuman, but also the concept itself by illustrating the practical problems of maintaining such a status in one's life.

'My best friend and personal savior': religion as a bad story

Now, after having established Rick as a not unproblematic but still strong incarnation of the Nietzschean Übermensch, whose place is within a universe void of meaning and without any transcendent reality or supernatural deity, the series – again – makes a final U-turn. And it collides, precisely, with its own religion criticism.

In 'A Rickle in Time' (S2E1), Rick, Summer and Morty have managed to split time into multiple fractions of itself. Rick manages to produce a device which should restore order, but the device of one of the many Mortys involved across the different timelines is malfunctioning. The accompanying Rick gives Morty his own device, saving the grandchild but condemning the grandfather to certain death by the collapsing of the fractured time. When Rick accidentally finds the broken one, floating through space, he immediately navigates to it, trying desperately to fix it before it is too late.

During this short period, Rick fervently and feverishly prays to God: 'Oh, sweet Jesus, please let me live. Oh my God, I have to, I gotta fix this thing, please, God in heaven. Please, God, oh Lord, hear my prayers.' When he succeeds, as he inevitably does, he denounces his faith instantaneously: 'Yes, fuck you, God. Not today, bitch!' In the meantime, another Rick is on his knees praying too, hands folded, eyes closed: 'Please God, if there is a hell, please be merciful to me.' When he is saved (by the other Rick), he also renounces his faith immediately: 'Yes! I did it! There is no God! In your face!'

This episode is remarkable for containing the only moment in the series in which Rick seems to genuinely testify to his faith in a personal God, something that is in stark and blatant contrast to his usual denial of any deity or transcendental reality. Of course, one could dismiss this scene as a kind of temporary regression into a state of proto-scientific behaviour: in the face of immanent and seemingly unavoidable mortal danger, even a Nietzschean Übermensch like Rick is not immune to the comfort and hope faith can bring. But as soon as the emergency is overcome, Rick shows his true colours again.

This could indeed be so, but I want to suggest that the series runs deeper than this. In the already much-discussed and -quoted episode 'Childrick of Mort' (S4E9), Rick reassures Beth when he is confronting his competitor Zeus: 'Relax, it's just a Zeus. If this was the real God, it'd be a completely different story.' Again, this is a remarkable moment in the series, since it is one of the very few in which Rick seems to testify to his belief in the possibility of the existence of a 'real', that is transcendent, God.

The clue, so to speak, lies in the word 'story'. Of course, 'x is so and so, but y is another story' is a standard expression in the English language, but I want to argue in favour of a different interpretation. To do so convincingly, I have to discuss a scene from what is probably the most difficult and most discussed episode so far (Joest 2020; Di Placido 2020). 'Never Ricking Morty' (S4E6) is very 'meta' and self-referential, even by *Rick and Morty* standards, and declares itself to be 'non-canonical'. It revolves around the idea that Rick and Morty are aboard a literal 'story train', a materialisation of the series' creator's literary device which he calls 'story circle' (Walsh 2020).

This physical train is operated by a character called Story Lord, who actively wants to harness the narrative power of Rick and Morty to maximise narrative success. It is a reference to the series' publisher Adult Swim, which urges the series' creators to maximise the output of the *Rick and Morty* franchise in order to earn as much money as possible. The fact that the Story Train Rick and Morty are aboard appears to be a physical toy Morty bought for Rick increases the urgency of the capitalist criticism even more.

In the middle of this very complicated episode, Story Lord positions Rick and Morty against an overwhelming number of enemies (most of them have appeared in earlier episodes). Morty seems to have lost all hope, but Rick has one last trick up his sleeve. He bursts into a very out-of-character prayer in a style parodying that of evangelical or Pentecostal traditions, pledging his faith in the risen Lord Jesus Christ:

> You're right, Morty. Sometimes it does seem like there's no way out. Like it's hopeless. But remember, there's always someone there for us. Who? My best friend and personal savior, Jesus Christ. What?! You don't believe in God. But he believes in us, Morty. You know, I thought I was the inventor, but the greatest invention of all is the free gift of eternal life. … Oh, trust me, Morty. I've done plenty of effed-up stuff in my life. But it's never too late to accept Christ. Jesus is always knocking at the door. All we have to do is open it and let him into our hearts. How? I'm so glad you asked, Morty. Just close your eyes and go to him in prayer. Like this. Heavenly father. Heavenly father. Thank you for sending your only begotten son. Jesus, I accept you into my heart. Fill me with your spirit. Make me a shining city on a hill for you. Make me born again. In Jesus' name, we pray. Amen. Amen. Amen!

After this prayer, Rick and Morty are greeted by a number of cartoonish characters, all connected to (more fundamentalist forms of) Christianity (see figure 3.3): an anthropomorphised cross-with-thorny-crown, Psalty the Singing Songbook (an actual character from a series of Christian children's music albums), Denver the skating dinosaur (from the Christian cartoon series *Denver, the Last Dinosaur*), some of the talking vegetables (from the Christian cartoon series *VeggieTales*), a Care Bear wearing a sweater with a cross on it, and a goofy kid with a T-shirt reading 'I love Jesus'. Rick identifies what is happening as 'the greatest story ever told', a reference to the biblical film of that name (George Stevens, 1965). Then Jesus descends from the heavens, uncovering his ripped abs, and all kneel down to him. One character utters: 'My Lord and my God!', a reference to the words spoken by Thomas (the 'doubting' apostle) in John 20:28.

This religious turn in the story makes Story Lord very angry, since the narrative (and therefore commercial) quality of 'his' Rick and Morty story plummets very fast. But when Story Lord enters his own story, Rick traps him inside it and takes control of the Story Train. Morty asks what will happen to Story Lord, to which Rick replies: 'He gets to spend eternity

3.3 After their prayer, Rick and Morty are greeted by a number of cartoonish characters, all connected to the Christian fundamentalist subculture. From left to right, we see an anthropomorphised sheep with a Hitler moustache, a Care Bear with a cross on his sweater, Psalty the Singing Songbook, a goofy kid with a T-shirt reading 'I love Jesus', in front of him three of the *VeggieTales* characters, then an anthropomorphised cross-with-thorny-crown, Rick, Morty and Denver the skating dinosaur. From 'Never Ricking Morty' (S4E6). *Rick and Morty* (2020). The Cartoon Network, Inc.

in every writer's hell: the Bible.' Morty seems concerned – also a first in the series – that they might have offended religious viewers of the show: 'I don't know. Some people actually like that stuff. Seems kind of cynical. I just don't like taking cheap shots, you know?' Rick replies, offended: 'Cheap shots? Morty, we were literally saved by Jesus Christ. Tell me in any way how that's offensive.'

It is at this moment that Rick finds out that the Story Train he tries to operate is actually a child's toy, making up the story they were (and are) part of. The scene switches to another location, a beach. Story Lord and Jesus are having a theological discussion:

> **Jesus:** So you're saying my father and his kingdom …
> **Story Lord:** Well, yes … it's based on the fusion of a Sumerian God named 'ya' and a Mesopotamian God named 'way'.
> **Jesus:** And we're in a toy train?
> **Story Lord:** Yes. It's enough to really make you question all of existence, isn't it?

The intertextuality is overwhelming in this scene, which seems to be aimed at blatantly criticising evangelical America (New 2012), including its prayer practices, its 'merchandise' (Schultze and Woods 2009, 312–36), its supposed disqualification of historical exegesis, and its adherence to the biblical fundamentalism Barbour (1990) criticised earlier. So it would not be difficult to interpret this scene as yet another example of the series' religion criticism, adding an explicit punch in the face of those who could (and probably would) be offended by the series' depiction of religion. Yes, Rick prayed to Jesus, who saved him and his grandson from Story Lord, but no Christian will recognise this as a genuine expression of orthodox faith.

Yet I argue that the series does something more complex and interesting. It criticises religion not so much for its beliefs or practices – as it did abundantly elsewhere – but for 'being a bad story'. This criticism could be interpreted in two distinctly different ways: either religion in general and Christianity specifically are a 'bad story' in themselves – as the atheist will argue and the series has argued – or the faithful of the numerous (world) religions fail miserably at 'selling' their belief, both narratively and commercially.

Even though the Bible still inspires some film-makers to produce Hollywood blockbusters like *Exodus: Gods and Kings* (Ridley Scott, 2014), *Noah* (Darren Aronofsky, 2014) and the older, animated *Prince of Egypt* (1998), the golden age of cinematographic biblical epics, when films like

The Greatest Story Ever Told and *The Ten Commandments* (Cecil B. DeMille, 1956) were at the forefront of the medium's popularity, is definitely gone. And authentic 'Christian' films, series and games, produced by and for devout believers, are usually of a very low quality (Ambrosino 2016; S. Brown 2007). Examples of such below-par productions are *Super 3D Noah's Ark* (Wisdom Tree, 1994), *Left Behind: Eternal Forces* (Inspired Media Entertainment, 2006), and the aforementioned Psalty show (1980) and *VeggieTales* (Phil Vischer and Mike Nawrocki, 1993).

Rick and Morty do stimulate the faithful, whom they attack so fiercely over the series in general and in this episode specifically, to improve their own storytelling, in order to make it appeal to a broader public and make it less vulnerable to atheist criticism like that of the series itself. *Rick and Morty* does more than criticise the content of the Christian meta-narrative, it criticises the way Christians have told and are telling that story.

Final thoughts

Yes, *Rick and Morty*'s religion criticism is blatantly present in the series, but what does it *mean*? On the one hand, the series has its place among the other popular adult animated sitcoms and their religion criticism, like *The Simpsons*, *South Park*, *Futurama* and *Solar Opposites*, even though none of them formulate their criticism as sharply and as significantly as *Rick and Morty* does; on the other hand the series' stipulated connectedness between atheist religion criticism and teleological and ethical nihilism is surprising.

One of the most common forms of criticism of atheism, usually formulated from an apologetic point of view, is that this worldview inevitably leads to an existence without any cause or reason, and without any moral point of reference (Tartaglia and Llanera 2021, 13–24). Without a god or an afterlife, people would find it very hard, if not impossible, the argument goes, to find purpose in their life or a need to conform to any moral value other than egocentric self-interest. Of course, philosophers, whether atheist or not, have argued *against* this supposedly necessary connection between believing in a transcendent deity and living a full, happy and ethical life (Nielson 1990; Kurtz and Craig 2009, 25–48).

Nevertheless, *Rick and Morty* seems to suggest exactly that: faith in a supreme being, morality and purposefulness seem to coincide, just as their opposites, atheism, immorality and purposelessness, seem to. The causality between the two is ambiguous in the series: either the idea that no God exists causes the teleological and ethical nihilism, or the experience of an uncaring and seemingly purposeless universe, including pain and suffering, causes the denial of any transcendent reality.

If the second option is the case, the theme of theodicy re-emerges, but more profoundly. *Rick and Morty* may suggest that the experience of the conflict between the existence of an all-good and all-powerful being on the one hand, and the horrors and suffering so firmly attached to the human condition on the other, combine to form an important 'moment' for the adoption of an atheist worldview, at least in our time. And truly, this may be the most fundamental religion criticism the series offers its viewers. *Rick and Morty* is not doing the atheists a favour by linking them so readily to nihilism. It evokes the old apologetic paradigm in which religious positivists argued against atheism as a nihilist worldview.

Rick and Morty seems to be – in the end – a kind of philosophical thought experiment. The idea of a 'thought experiment' itself is very well known, and is described and used in philosophy from ancient Greece to postmodernity (Brown 1986). A good definition is the following (Gooding 1998): 'A thought experiment is an idealization which transcends the particularity and the accidents of worldly human activities in order to achieve the generality and rigour of a demonstrative procedure.'

The thought experiment of *Rick and Morty* is – in short – on the practical viability of Nietzsche-based atheism and nihilism, when – at the same time – a return to the old religious 'naivety' is in itself not viable any more. The series portrays (institutionalised) religion as having become obsolete, that is, untenable for the postmodern, Western individual, because of its (supposed) inherent (negative) qualities, which the series so adeptly features. The atheism and nihilism, that – according to the series – are mutually dependent and co-constructive feature as a kind of reaction to the experience of a godless universe.

However, the attaining and maintaining of the self-realised Nietzschean Übermensch, the series argues, is not viable either, especially in terms of practicality. Notwithstanding the whole corpus of non-religious efforts to disconnect atheism from nihilism and immorality (as quoted and discussed above), the series shows that even the god-man Rick, at the zenith of his atheist and nihilist realisation, falls prey to the intellectual and – even more pregnant – practical heaviness of his self-given task. Rick 'floats' somewhere – as the postmodern human – between a definite goodbye to traditional (institutionalised) religion or to religion altogether, and an emotional nostalgia for a universe that was intrinsically purposeful and meaningful, in the face of a new and irreversible realisation that such things have to be produced by humans now.

Rick and Morty does not want to 'go back' to the old days of self-explanatory religion, but neither does it close its eyes to what it believes is the inevitable consequence of this farewell: that every human being is personally responsible for finding and producing their own meaning and purpose, or to how difficult, and lonely, such a task may be.

References

Abesamis, Lester. 2019. 'Neither the hero you deserve nor the hero you need', in *Rick and Morty and Philosophy: In the beginning was the squanch*, Lester Abesamis and Wayne Yuen, eds, e-book. Chicago: Open Court.

Abesamis, Lester and Wayne Yuen. 2019. 'Scientifically, introductions are an idiot thing', in *Rick and Morty and Philosophy: In the beginning was the squanch*, Lester Abesamis and Wayne Yuen, eds, e-book. Chicago: Open Court.

Ambrosino, Brandon. 2016. 'Why are Christian movies so painfully bad?' *Vox*, 1 April. https://www.vox.com/2015/2/15/8038283/christian-movies-bad-old-fashioned-fifty-shades (accessed 28 May 2022).

Baird, Robert. 2007. 'Paradise lost: Why doesn't anyone read Dante's *Paradiso?*' *Slate*, 24 December. https://slate.com/culture/2007/12/why-doesn-t-anyone-read-dante-s-paradiso.html (accessed 28 May 2022).

Barbour, Ian. 1990. *Religion in an Age of Science*, The Gifford Lectures, 1989–1991, 1. London: SCM Press.

Bingham, John, 2015. 'The Ned Flanders effect: Why God just isn't sexy.' *Daily Telegraph*, 8 April. https://www.telegraph.co.uk/news/religion/11519923/The-Ned-Flanders-effect-why-God-just-isnt-sexy.html (accessed 28 May 2022).

Bisset, Jennifer. 2020. 'Rick and Morty is brilliant TV you need to give a second chance.' *Cnet.com*, 3 May. https://www.cnet.com/news/rick-and-morty-is-brilliant-tv-you-need-to-give-a-second-chance/ (accessed 28 May 2022).

Bosman, Frank. 2019. *Gaming and the Divine: A new systematic theology of video games*. London: Routledge.

Bosman, Frank and Archibald van Wieringen. 2020. 'COVID-19 and the secular theodicy: On social distancing, the death of God and the Book of Job', in *The New Common: How the COVID-19 pandemic is transforming society*, Emile Aarts, Hein Fleuren, Margriet Sitskoorn and Ton Wilthagen, eds, 59–62. Tilburg: Tilburg University.

Brown, James Robert. 1986. 'Thought experiments since the scientific revolution.' *International Studies in the Philosophy of Science* 1 (1): 1–15. https://doi.org/10.1080/02698598608573279.

Brown, Seth. 2007. 'PrayStation: The 6 most misguided Christian video games.' *Cracked*, 18 November. https://www.cracked.com/article_15672_praystation-6-most-misguided-christian-video-games.html (accessed 28 May 2022).

Carr, Bernard. 2007. 'Introduction and overview', in *Universe or Multiverse?*, Bernard Carr, ed., 3–29. Cambridge: Cambridge University Press.

Chalfant, Eric. 2020. 'Material irreligion: The role of media in atheist studies.' *Religion Compass* 14 (3). https://doi.org/10.1111/rec3.12349.

Chandler, Abigail. 2019. 'Twisted grandpas and toxic fans: How *Rick and Morty* became TV's most unlikely hit.' *The Guardian*, 23 November. https://www.theguardian.com/tv-and-radio/2019/nov/20/twisted-grandpas-and-toxic-fans-how-rick-and-morty-became-tvs-most-unlikely-hit (accessed 28 May 2022).

Cobb, Kayla. 2017. '"Rick and Morty" is better when it embraces its strong women.' *Decider.com*, 4 October. https://web.archive.org/web/20171224214013/https://decider.com/2017/10/04/rick-and-morty-is-better-with-strong-women/ (accessed 28 May 2022).

Copeman, Jacob and Johannes Quack. 2015. 'Godless people and dead bodies: Materiality and the morality of atheist materialism.' *Social Analysis* 59 (2): 40–61. https://doi.org/10.3167/sa.2015.590203.

Däniken, Erich von. 1969. *Chariots of the Gods? Unsolved mysteries of the past.* New York: Putnam.

Dinham, Adam and Matthew Francis. 2015. 'Religious literacy: Contesting an idea and practice', in *Religious Literacy in Policy and Practice*, Adam Dinham and Matthew Francis, eds, 3–26. Bristol: Policy Press.

Di Placido, Dani. 2020. '"Rick and Morty" season 4, episode 6 recap: "Never Ricking Morty" might just be the best episode ever.' *Forbes*, 6 May. https://www.forbes.com/sites/danidiplacido/2020/05/06/rick-and-morty-season-4-episode-6-recap-never-ricking-morty-might-just-be-the-best-episode-ever/ (accessed 28 May 2022).

Engelke, Matthew. 2015. 'The coffin question: Death and materiality in humanist funerals.' *Journal of Objects, Art and Belief* 11 (1): 26–48.

Feder, Kenneth. 2002. 'Ancient astronauts', in *The Skeptic Encyclopedia of Pseudoscience*, Michael Schermer, ed., volume 1, 17–22. Santa Barbara, CA: ABC-CLIO.

Fitzsimons, Peter. 2007. *Nietzsche, Ethics and Education: An account of differences*. Leiden: Brill.

Gooding, David C. 1998. 'Thought experiments', in *Routledge Encyclopedia of Philosophy*, Edward Craig, ed. London: Routledge. https://doi.org/10.4324/9780415249126-Q106-1.

Hahn, Cynthia. 2017. *The Reliquary Effect: Enshrining the sacred object*. London: Reaktion Books.

Hood, Ralph, Peter Hill and Bernard Spilka. 2009. *The Psychology of Religion: An empirical approach*. Fourth edition. New York: Guilford Press.

Hick, John. 1966. *Evil and the Love of God*. London: Macmillan.

Idel, Moshe. 1990. *Golem: Jewish magical and mystical traditions on the artificial anthropoid*. Albany: State University of New York Press.

Jacobs, Alan. 2008. *Original Sin: A cultural history*. New York: HarperCollins.

Joest, Mick. 2020. 'How Rick and Morty broke canon to give us something new.' *CinemaBlend*, 7 May. https://www.cinemablend.com/television/2495790/how-rick-and-morty-broke-canon-to-give-us-something-new (accessed 28 May 2022).

Kurtz, Paul and William Craig. 2009. 'The Kurtz/Craig debate: Is goodness without God good enough?', in *Is Goodness without God Good Enough? A debate on faith, secularism, and ethics*, Robert Garcia and Nathan King, eds, 25–46. Lanham, MD: Rowman & Littlefield.

Loeb, Paul. 2006. 'Finding the *Übermensch* in Nietzsche's *Genealogy of Morality*', in *Nietzsche's On the Genealogy of Morals: Critical essays*, Christa Davis Acampora, ed., 163–76. Lanham, MD: Rowman & Littlefield.

Magnus, Bernd. 1983. 'Perfectibility and attitude in Nietzsche's Übermensch.' *Review of Metaphysics* 36 (3): 633–59.

Marnell, Blair. 2017. 'Dan Harmon reveals the meaning of life in *Rick and Morty*.' *Nerdist.com*, 4 June, https://nerdist.com/article/dan-harmon-meaning-of-life-rick-and-morty/ (accessed 28 May 2022).

New, David. 2012. *Christian Fundamentalism in America: A cultural history*. Jefferson, NC: McFarland.

Nielsen, Kai. 1990. *Ethics without God*. Revised edition. Buffalo, NY: Prometheus Books.

Nielsen, Kai. 2021. 'Atheism', in *Encyclopedia Britannica*, https://www.britannica.com/topic/atheism (accessed 28 May 2022).

Orsi, Robert. 2016. *History and Presence*. London: Belknap Press of Harvard University Press.

Pargament, Kenneth. 2001. *The Psychology of Religion and Coping: Theory, research, practice*. New York: Guilford Press.

Philips, Ian. 2015. 'Why you should watch "Rick and Morty" – Adult Swim's brilliant twist on all things sci-fi.' *Business Insider*, 28 July. https://www.businessinsider.com/rick-and-morty-review-2015-7 (accessed 28 May 2022).

Quadrio, Philip. 2017. 'Collateral damage', in *New Atheism: Critical perspectives and contemporary debates*, Christopher Cotter, Philip Quadrio and Jonathan Tuckett, eds, 87–116. Cham: Springer.

Ranke-Heinemann, Uta. 1990. *Eunuchs for the Kingdom of Heaven: Women, sexuality, and the Catholic Church*. Trans. Peter Heinegg. New York: Doubleday.

Richardson, James. 1993. 'Definitions of cult: From sociological-technical to popular-negative.' *Review of Religious Research* 34 (4), 348–56. https://doi.org/10.2307/3511972.

Riesebrodt, Martin. 2010. *The Promise of Salvation: A theory of religion*. Trans. Steven Rendall. Chicago: University of Chicago Press.

Schultze, Quentin J. and Robert H. Woods, eds. 2009. *Understanding Evangelical Media: The changing face of Christian communication*. Westmont, IL: InterVarsity Press.

Sherwin, Byron L. 1985. *The Golem Legend: Origins and implications*. Lanham, MD: University Press of America.

Smith, Christian. 2017. *Religion: What it is, how it works, and why it matters.* Princeton, NJ: Princeton University Press.

Stenmark, Lisa. 2018. 'Modern political lying: Science and religion as critical discourse in a post-truth world', in *Navigating Post-Truth and Alternative Facts: Religion and science as political theology*, Jennifer Baldwin, ed., 3–18. Lanham, MD: Lexington Books.

Stiebert, Johanna. 2016. *First-Degree Incest and the Hebrew Bible: Sex in the family.* London: Bloomsbury/ T&T Clark.

Tartaglia, James and Tracy Llanera. 2021. *A Defence of Nihilism.* Abingdon: Routledge.

Urban, Hugh. 2015. *New Age, Neopagan, and New Religious Movements: Alternative spirituality in contemporary America.* Oakland: University of California Press.

Walsh, Michael. 2020. 'Dan Harmon on writing Rick and Morty with a story circle.' *Nerdist*, 16 June. https://nerdist.com/article/rick-and-morty-story-circle-dan-harmon/ (accessed 28 May 2022).

Weintraub, David. 2008. *Is Pluto a Planet? A historical journey through the solar system.* Princeton, NJ: Princeton University Press.

Wieringen, Archibald van. 2020. 'Methodological developments in biblical exegesis: Author – Text – Reader.' *Analecta of the UCU (Theology)* 7: 27–46. https://doi.org/10.47632/2075-4817-2020-7-27-46.

Zocalo Public Square. 2012. 'Heaven's nice, but hell's more fun to paint.' 26 July. https://www.zocalopublicsquare.org/2012/07/26/heavens-nice-but-hells-more-fun-to-paint/events/the-takeaway/ (accessed 28 May 2022).

4
Aesthetics of the secular
Stefan Binder

Introduction: the aesthetic production of being 'other-than-religious'

This chapter explores how an aesthetic approach developed in religious studies offers a way to examine hitherto neglected aspects of 'lived secularity' in the specific sense of claims to and practices of being 'other-than-religious.' As a first step, this chapter briefly reviews why a focus on aesthetics is crucial to enlarging the methodological setup of scholarship on the secular beyond normative accounts of secularity as based on disembodied reason. After engaging with existing literature on the aesthetics of non-religion, the final section demonstrates the potential of this approach in a case study of organised atheism in South India. It engages lived secularity as an aesthetic phenomenon by exploring a specific historical imaginary of 'Indian Atheism' in relation to material culture, rhetorical practices, emotional habitus and representational economies.

Since the 2000s, questions related to the secular have become a major theme across disciplines in the social sciences and humanities. A variety of academic disciplines with divergent research agendas and methodologies have been involved in this project of reappraising the relationship between the religious and the secular. As a result, the research field is highly diversified, and no consensus exists about definitions of even its most central categories. While several authors have attempted to produce taxonomical clarity for terms like secularism, secularity, secularisation or the post-secular (Casanova 1994; Taylor 2007; Gorski et al. 2012; Lee 2015), the disciplinary perspectives and actual themes of existing scholarship seem too diverse to allow for a single, authoritative vocabulary. This chapter limits itself to the secular as it appears in an emerging field in religious studies, sociology and anthropology that deals with people, discourses and practices that are marked or consider themselves as different from and often opposed to religion: atheism, secular humanism, rationalism, disbelief, religious indifference, etc. (Bullivant and Lee 2012; Quack 2014; Blanes and Oustinova-Stjepanovic 2015). In approaching the secular as other-than-religion, the intention is not to postulate an essential difference between the religious and the secular; rather, the aim is to explore how certain groups of people use aesthetic or sensorially perceptible means to constitute themselves and their ways of living as different from or not religious.

Researching the secular: from secular ideology to an aesthetics of lived secularity

It is not coincidental that the turn toward aesthetic approaches to studying religion is contemporaneous with a renewed interest in the secular after deconstructions of the modernist secularisation paradigm. A common theme in both developments has been the critique of a tendency to construe religions primarily as disembodied, intellectual and textual phenomena concerned above all with questions of meaning and belief. The aesthetic and material turns in religious studies have retraced the origins of this truncated understanding of religion to a specifically modern episteme and semiotic ideology of 'disembedding' (Giddens 1991, 21–9). Within this framework, the secular has been identified as the 'ontology' (Asad 2003, 21) and conceptual grammar that undergirds a 'moral narrative of modernity' (Keane 2013, 159) telling of the liberation and purification of human reason and agency from supposedly premodern entanglements with material, bodily, affective or social constrictions (see also Latour 1993; Connolly 1999).

While critical scholarship on the secular-modern remaking of religion has been immensely productive in uncovering the hitherto neglected aesthetic dimensions of lived religions, it has tended to equate the secular with its normative accounts of disembodied reason. As a result, scholarship on the secular has dealt with aesthetics predominantly as a question of how secular-modern epistemologies, legal structures and forms of governance have misconstrued, ignored or regulated the aesthetic dimensions of religion (Mahmood 2006; 2009; Keane 2007; Asad 2011). While there are important exceptions, to which I return below, the growing body of research on the secular has been largely unable to address the materiality and embodied nature of secularity as anything other than a contradiction of the secular's own normative insistence on disembeddedness, universality and autonomy from material, bodily or socio-cultural domains. Within this methodological setup, to describe the embodied and material dimensions of the secular is to describe what it is not – or what it claims not to be. However, even explicit disavowals of aesthetics or projects of anaesthetics (Verrips 2006; Yelle 2019) within certain secular and/or modern discourses do not foreclose the analysis of the aesthetic forms and strategies through which such disavowals are put forth and made sensible.

This replicates a problem well known from the study of religions, where the concept of religion was based to a large extent on the discourses of religious professionals while so-called 'popular' or 'lived' forms of religiosity were measured by the extent to which they conformed to theological normativity. This is more than a mere analogy, since theology – especially in its Protestant variant – has been identified as a major driving force of (secular) modernity (Keane 2007; Meyer 2010; Bate 2010; Yelle 2013). By equating the secular with its normative self-representation, the study of secularity has been circumscribed by a conceptual grid reconstructed almost entirely on the basis of early modern European intellectual history. This Eurocentric bias presents a serious methodological problem for studying secularity outside the ambit of European languages or narratives of European diffusion. It has prevented existing research on religious critique, doubt, scepticism or withdrawal in area studies from being integrated into a systematic comparative and postcolonial perspective on the secular (cf. Engelke 2015c). In this chapter, I seek to demonstrate how a focus on aesthetics can offer a way forward beyond normative accounts and European conceptual history (for an extended discussion of this argument, see Binder 2020a).

Aesthetics of science and politics

Precisely because the secular has been closely linked to discourses around rationality, the intellect and science, the aesthetic approach as developed in the study of religions is a particularly suitable epistemological and methodological framework. The 'aesthetics of religion' (Grieser and Johnston 2017) as an emerging field of research focuses centrally on how the body, the senses, figuration and material media are intrinsic to processes of intellectual reasoning and knowledge. From this perspective, an aesthetics of the secular overlaps with an aesthetics of science, which analyses how scientific claims to objectivity and rationality are not only represented but also constructed through rhetorical strategies, sensorial engagements, material assemblages, assumptions about the body and the senses, as well as aesthetic judgments inherent to culturally shaped and historically changing epistemologies (Harris 1997; Weibel and Latour 2002; Pauwels 2006; Grieser and Borrelli 2017). It is important to note, however, that the science/religion binary is historically related to but cannot be collapsed into the secular/religious binary, as aesthetic forms associated with religious traditions may very well be employed in scientific practices and vice versa (Grieser 2017).

Besides science, another core area of secular boundary work concerns the relationship between the state and religion, a major theme in debates on political secularism (Cannell 2010; Calhoun, Juergensmeyer and van Antwerpen 2011; Scherer 2011) and the post-secular (Vries and Sullivan 2006; Braidotti et al. 2014; Gorski et al. 2012; Mapril et al. 2017). While recent debates have tended to focus on how secular states condition or suppress aesthetic dimensions of religions, an earlier stream of scholarship in the tradition of the Frankfurt School examined the aesthetics of political regimes themselves. Critical theory has focused especially on how the confluence of changing technological and media environments in a capitalist 'culture industry' is linked with projects of totalitarian politics (Horkheimer and Adorno 2002, 94). Beyond descriptive collections of tropes and themes associated with specific historical regimes, this research has approached political and social formations of fascism and socialism as fundamentally aesthetic projects, grounded in what Walter Benjamin called the 'aestheticizing of politics' (2008, 42). While this implied a critical perspective on the reduction of politics to aesthetics – as opposed to democratic or parliamentarian process – more recent perspectives stress the inherently aesthetic character of politics (Rancière 2004).

A phenomenon like 'socialist realism,' for example, is of particular interest for an aesthetics of the secular, as it was understood less as a classificatory category of style or genre than an artistic-political program and aesthetic method meant to construct and usher in the communist future of Real Socialism – rather than merely representing it (Gutkin 1999; Cai Xiang 2016; for more general discussions of secularism in post-Soviet contexts, see McBrien and Pelkmans 2008; Luehrmann 2011). It is, however, precisely on the basis of such aspects of 'applied aesthetics' that fascism and socialism have been interpreted as pseudo, political, civil or secular religions, thus raising again the question of what exactly is secular about their aesthetics other than the rejection of historical religions. Anja Kirsch (2017) shows that such interpretations are grounded in normative distinctions of 'good' and 'bad' religion. In describing the difference of secular and religious aesthetics, she proposes instead to focus on formal aesthetic criteria, in her case narratological structures, which may occur in both secular and religious contexts of world making without being themselves either religious or secular. Aesthetic dimensions of socialism, and other phenomena perceived as secular, can thus be analysed in comparison to religion and further our analytical understanding of the aesthetic efficacy of the secular/religious binary itself. Thus, potentially normative concepts like political or civil religion can be reappraised for their analytical value with regard to the larger project of an aesthetics of religion *and* the secular (Koch 2017).

Is there a secular body?

One of the first attempts to explicitly tackle the task of bringing together the aesthetic turn and the secular turn within scholarship on religion is Charles Hirschkind's essay on the 'secular body,' which he proposed to approach as 'a particular configuration of the human sensorium – of sensibilities, affects, embodied dispositions – specific to secular subjects' (Hirschkind 2011, 633). Hirschkind addresses the problem that the mere absence of religion would inflate the category of the secular to such an extent that it loses its analytical specificity. His solution is a turn toward genealogy and narrative, as he proposes to conceptualise a secular sensorium as those bodily and sensorial dispositions that contribute to instituting and legitimising 'the secularist narrative of the progressive replacement of religious error by secular reason' (p. 641). Following Talal Asad, he calls this the 'triumphalist narrative of secularism' (ibid.). An important area of research takes this line of inquiry as a starting point to explore secular sensibilities with regard to bodily practices like veiling (Amir-Moazami 2016), gender and sexuality (Cady and Fessenden 2013; Wiering 2017) or affects and emotions (Scheer, Fadil and Johansen 2019). While this solution is elegant, Hirschkind's secular remains fundamentally marked by traces of absence, inasmuch as 'every secular practice is accompanied by a religious shadow, as it were' and, therefore, 'will always be subject to a certain indeterminacy or instability' (Hirschkind 2011, 643; see also Asad 2011; Engelke 2015b).

Based on his ethnographic work on North American immortalism, i.e., techno-scientific attempts at prolonging human life through cryonics, biogerontology and artificial intelligence, anthropologist Abou Farman (2020) emphasises the historicity of the secular and thus argues that the secular can emancipate itself from a relational dependence on the religious. Farman shows that materialist or rationalist worldviews, their initially oppositional stance toward religion notwithstanding, have by now established their own 'traditions' (2013, 738), which generate identifiably secular bodies and notions of personhood at the nexus of institutional, legal and technological discourses. Similarly, sociologists and anthropologists have described how self-declared non-religious people in contemporary Britain engage with ethical questions of pleasure (Engelke 2015a), the troubling presence of material objects (Engelke 2015d) or everyday practices of dress and food (Lee 2015, 70–105).

Materialist, humanist or rationalist worldviews emerge here as frameworks for secular ways of living that refuse to be defined solely in negative relation to religion. In simplified terms, these studies do not ask how the secular/religious binary has been created or enforced through various modern institutions or state apparatuses but what happens once it has been put in place and is actively appropriated by people in their everyday lives. As the following case study illustrates, such a pragmatic approach makes room for collecting empirical narratives and aesthetics beyond those of triumphalism, pseudo-religion or anaesthetics – and hence room for more complex and plural genealogies of the secular as well.

Case study: organised atheism in South India

In this case study, based on my ethnographic research on an atheist movement in the two mainly Telugu-speaking states of Andhra Pradesh and Telangana (Binder 2020a), I explore a specific narrative of Indian atheism prevalent in South India. I mainly focus on how this narrative and its social imaginary relate to practices of materialisation and verbal articulation in order to illustrate an aesthetic approach to what it 'feels like' to be secular in a given place and time. Despite some doctrinal differences and the absence of an overarching institutional structure, the members of this movement recognise a shared goal of their secular activism: the reconstruction of a moral, just and rational society through the eradication of what they call 'mental slavery' (*bhavadasyam*), a condition manifesting itself most directly – though not exclusively – in religious beliefs and practices. While some members of the movement prefer to label themselves as humanists or rationalists, I refer to this larger movement as capitalised Atheism due to the centrality of the term 'atheism' and its Telugu equivalent '*nastikatvam*' for its history.

Due to Orientalist and anti-colonial ideas about the supposedly religious nature of Indian civilisation (Inden 1990; King 1999), Atheists today are regularly confronted with allegations that their worldview is a product of European colonialism and therefore 'Westernised' or foreign to Indian culture and history (cf. Quack 2012a, 286–93). While the colonial history of Indian Atheism and the influence of European rationalist and imperial discourses is well documented (Quack 2012b), its pre-colonial roots are highly contested and difficult to historically reconstruct (Quack and Binder 2018). However, precisely the ancient and pre-historical roots of Indian Atheism are of crucial significance to contemporary Atheists, who primarily try to establish their 'indigeneity' and cultural belonging in India in two ways: first, by harking back to materialist, empiricist and sceptical schools within classical Indian philosophy (Chattopadhyaya 1959; Bhattacharya 2009; Gokhale 2015); and second, through recourse to the so-called Aryan migration theory (Bergunder 2004; Bryant and Patton 2005).

Based on linguistic evidence gathered by European Orientalists in collaboration with South Indian pundits (Trautmann 2006), the Aryan migration theory posits the origin of Hindu civilisation around the second millennium BCE, when so-called Aryan migrants from Central Asia brought Vedic culture and religion to India and encountered there an indigenous Dravidian civilisation. Many contemporary Atheists, especially those speaking Dravidian languages of Southern India, link themselves and their worldview genealogically to this presumed indigenous Dravidian culture, which they tend to describe as atheist, materialist, rationalist or proto-communist (Pandian 2007). In Atheist iterations of this theory, Aryans do not figure as migrants but as violent invaders, who wilfully and strategically destroyed the original Atheist culture of the subcontinent by importing not only Vedic religion but religion as such – what Atheists call 'mental slavery.'

It is crucial to stress that for many Atheists in India, the 'triumphalist' narrative of secular dominance mentioned above is spliced with, at times superseded by, a narrative of decadence, destruction and corruption. There are moreover concrete historical agents, namely Aryan invaders, who make this narrative of secular decadence tellable as an intentional, strategic and political process rather than a merely 'natural' historical process of devolution. From the perspective of an aesthetics of the secular, what is at stake are the sensorial, material and affective[1] aspects that transform this spliced narrative from a mere 'story' into a potent 'imaginary' and thereby condition what it feels like to be an Atheist in South India (cf. Johannsen and Kirsch 2019).

From narrative to material culture

To refer to Atheist retellings of the Aryan migration theory as an 'imaginary' is not a comment on its historical facticity but stresses the role of imagination in structuring the perceptions of those who seek to practically realise that theory by living Atheist lives in the present (Traut and Wilke 2015). Since one of the core features of this imaginary is the wilful destruction of Atheist culture and its material remains, it conditions how contemporary Atheists can experience the absence of 'traditional' forms of Atheist material culture, rituals or social institutions. It allows them to reconfigure 'absence' not as lack but as the source for Atheist acts of heroism and resilience, which consist in either reinventing Atheist traditions or bravely facing their absence by developing the strength to do without them; after all, most Atheists claim that it is precisely the inability to let go of 'tradition' that leads to mental slavery. A substantial part of Atheist activism therefore consists of re-materialising Atheism by, first of all, writing down and narrating its history of destruction, secondly, by reinterpreting and thus reappropriating certain parts of Indian cultural history – like folklore, art forms, moral principles or philosophical insights – as purloined achievements of original Atheism (for a famous example, see Ramasami 1972) and, finally, by reinventing Atheist culture in the form of songs, plays or commemorative festivals. Atheists have also constructed physical structures, ranging from educational institutions, to venues for Atheist gatherings, to commemorative sculptures of past and present Atheist luminaries (cf. Binder 2020b). Such material structures scaffold concrete 'spaces of imagination' (Hermann, Laack and Schüler 2015) that function as both 'messengers' and 'traces' for making the history of Atheism's absence present in and for a contemporary Atheist community (Binder 2020b, 239–40). By inquiring into the concrete history of the visual and narrative figurations at play in such attempts at cultural reconstruction, an aesthetics of the secular can carve out an 'aesthetic ideology' (Grieser 2017, 261–5) specific to Indian Atheism.

Another common form of Atheist activism consists in the re-enactment of alleged supernatural miracles performed by religious practitioners, like the spontaneous materialisation of objects or certain forms of bodily mortification, and their subsequent exposure as 'mere' conjuring tricks. Jacob Copeman and Johannes Quack have described such performances as an instance of secular material culture based on a semiotic 'retooling of sacred objects for non-religious purposes' (2015, 42; see also Binder 2019). In a similar way, Atheist practices and discourses around body and organ donation become sites for pedagogic realisations of public materialism, where the utilitarian 'gift' of one's own (dead) body for the sake of medical science becomes not only the authenticating climax of an Atheist biography but also a heroic act of civic virtue and enlightenment (Copeman and Reddy 2012). Besides actual material culture and concrete 'things,' the imaginary of Atheist destruction and heroic resilience may also be *enacted* in and through the aesthetics of speech.

A crucial site for this enactment is the ongoing controversy around the name of the movement as well as individual professions of Atheism. As mentioned above, there is no commonly agreed-upon label for the movement, with atheism (*nastikatvam*), rationalism (*hetuvadam*) and humanism (*manavavadam*) being the most widely discussed alternatives. Beyond the diversity of arguments for one or the other option, their common thread is a concern with the public efficacy of labels. The bone of contention is the term atheism and its standard Telugu translation: *nastikatvam*. While atheism/*nastikatvam* is considered a taken-for-granted philosophical foundation, it is not necessarily considered appropriate as a public label. Both terms have historically been used as exonyms and invectives for ideological adversaries and have therefore accumulated a powerful negative affective charge – to the point where they may evoke suspicion, contempt or even fear.

Some within the Atheist movement argue that this negative affective charge will prove detrimental to the overall aim of the movement, because it alienates 'ordinary people' and thus prevents the movement from widely spreading its socially transformative message. Others, however, contend that the power of those negative affects even among Atheists testifies to the continuing legacy of Aryan invasion, whose prime strategy of cultural warfare was to slander their opponents as atheists/*nastikulu*. Hence, to reappropriate and revalue that name is tantamount to heroically liberating oneself and others from 'mental slavery.' Some of my interlocutors have reported intense anxiety and severe social or familial repercussions after their open self-identification as atheists/*nastikulu,* yet they have also described feelings of pride and heroism as well as forms of recognition and praise by peers once they had taken that step (Binder 2020a, 50–67).

The debate around labels also extends to the realm of personal names, where especially committed Atheist activists change their or their children's names by including surnames with references to Atheism or by removing all elements that may evoke caste or religion. Jacob Copeman has analysed such 'secular onomastic experimentation' (Copeman 2015, para. 6) as speech acts 'designed to iteratively produce a particular kind of intersubjective sensibility' (para. 34). Thus, what is at stake here are not merely issues of terminology, definition or individuals' (dis)beliefs but the way in which names, or rather sociocultural categories, are able to encode and evoke an 'emotional habitus' (Trawick 1990, 154). Margaret Trawick coined this term to describe how the literal and figurative use of kinship categories can mobilise and manipulate a repertoire of emotions as well as their appropriate expression or suppression. Such repertoires are acquired through processes of socialisation and manifested, rehearsed and negotiated through cultural imaginaries transmitted in folklore, pop culture or formal and informal educational systems. Furthermore, the question of who can mobilise or appropriate a given imaginary in contemporary India – and for which effects – is conditioned by its colonial and postcolonial political history. An important task for an aesthetics of the secular is thus to describe and analyse the production, reproduction and transformation of such emotional habitus as well as their sensorial deployment and manipulation. Though a crucial aspect of Atheist activism appears to consist of toppling the affective implications of historically and culturally entrenched social categories, that activism must work on and with existing emotional habitus to get its message across and make its 'secular mark'.

Atheist propagation as an aesthetics of persuasion

Insofar as onomastic experimentations or practices of naming are speech acts intending an individual or social transformation, they are part of the main modus of Atheist activism: written and oratorical propagation. Atheists in India are known for giving speeches, to the point where some critics complain that they do nothing but talk. They are moreover frequently accused of being arrogant, haughty or condescending, as they relish in ridiculing religious scriptures and beliefs. Critics sometimes attribute this simply to a psychological personality trait of arrogance that Atheists are supposed to share. I propose instead to analyse it as an aesthetically produced affect and a counterpart to the affect of heroism involved in naming oneself an Atheist in the face of the absence of Atheist culture. I focus here on how this affect is produced in oratorical speech and how it is historically conditioned by concrete aesthetic criteria and rhetorical devices like fluency, hyperliteralism or decorum.

A common way to praise gifted and influential orators among Atheists is to say that their oratory is 'like a stream' (*pravahamlaga*).

Speakers are lauded if they are capable of spontaneously commanding knowledge about as vast an array of topics as possible. They should be able to speak continuously without having to search for words or arguments and, if possible, with a substantial number of verbatim citations from various sources – preferably in a classical language such as Sanskrit. Success or failure of Atheist speech acts is thus intimately connected to an aesthetic criterion of fluency, which can override questions of content or message: orators may be considered right, even bright, but nonetheless judged incapable of persuading others due to lacking skills of rhetorical delivery.

The art of memorisation is fundamental to this form of fluent, stream-like speech and has a long history in South Asian pedagogy. Most famous in this regard are traditions of Vedic recitation (Knipe 2015), which link forms of contemporary Atheist speech to a larger aesthetic dimension of sonality in South Asian and especially Hindu culture (Wilke and Moebus 2011). Atheist propagation has an ambivalent relationship to this sonal tradition, as Atheists commonly reject it as stale rote learning and mindless production of sound. It is important to note, however, that the fluent rejection of religious fluency is not just an argument about denotational content (or the lack thereof) but has itself an aesthetic form. Despite the great value placed on oratorical mastery in Indian culture and especially politics, scholarship of South Asian rhetoric beyond ritual speech in religious contexts is scarce (for an important exception, see Bate 2009).

Even in its most informal settings, Atheist oratory usually involves some sort of stage or dais which produces a frontal visual relationship between orator and audience and tends to corporeally immobilise the latter into seated positions. This can be physically demanding since oratorical events may stretch over a few days with individual speeches lasting up to several hours. Propagational events may occur indoors as well as outdoors, which further modulates the focus on the stage through different degrees of perceptual distraction or 'noise' (e.g., the largely unconscious humming of fans or air-conditioning in closed rooms versus the visual, olfactory and aural environment of an urban outdoor setting). Speeches tend to be amplified, often irrespective of the actual acoustic requirements for audibility in a given venue; in fact, excessive volume, overmodulation or audio feedback frequently impede audibility. A comprehensive analysis of Atheist oratory thus requires not only a historically sensitive and comparative contextualisation of aesthetic properties such as gestural repertoires, forms of staging, practices of rhetoric pedagogy or 'hearing cultures' (Erlmann 2004) but also an investigation into the cognitive, perceptual and physiological affordances and effects of material environments and technological infrastructures (architecture, seating arrangements, ambient sound, amplification, lighting, etc.).

In the following discussion, I focus on a specific rhetorical strategy of 'hyperliteralism' (Richman 1993, 190), where religious scriptures are interpreted in an extremely literal fashion so as to expose – or create – inconsistencies and absurd conclusions. This rhetorical-cum-hermeneutic strategy has historical antecedents in inter-religious polemics (Hudson 1995; Yelle 2013) and is inseparable from a larger shift from scribal to print culture in colonial India. Hyperliteral rhetoric has been enabled by printed texts, as an increasingly literate public could access scriptural material that had hitherto been restricted to and at times jealously guarded by circles of specialised readers/reciters trained in particular hermeneutic and exegetical technologies (Narayana Rao 2001). Hence, Atheist 'arrogance' is not merely a presumed psychological trait based on a conceit of intellectual superiority, but an affect that is aesthetically produced as Atheists literally 'arrogate' the social power that comes with the right to rhetorically appropriate, manipulate and reproduce (religious) knowledge as printed and thus publicly accessible 'text' (cf. Bauman and Briggs 1990 on politics of 'entextualization').

As Bernard Bate (2009) has shown for the case of Tamil oratory, modern technologies like print and language ideologies based on denotation have therefore not simply replaced existing notions of poetic efficacy. One example is the Sanskrit poetological concept of 'decorum' (*aucitya*), which grounds the efficacy of literary and ethical discourse in a careful balancing of content and form as well as performative social context (Prasad 2012, 168–77). Despite an emphatic commitment to the denotational dimensions of language, it is within the confines of historically entrenched and often implicit aesthetic criteria like decorum that Atheist orators deploy strategies such as fluency or hyperliteralism in order to produce secular difference within changing media environments. As Atheist rhetoric is firmly grounded in print culture and the physical co-presence of audiences, the expansion of satellite television and digital media since the early 2000s present entirely new challenges for both secular and non-secular oratorical aesthetics. In other words, the efficacy of Atheist verbal propagation is not exhausted by the intellectual or logical persuasiveness of arguments but also depends on the historically conditioned ways in which Atheists manage to produce secular difference by aesthetic means.

Conclusion: toward a comparative and postcolonial approach to secular difference

In this chapter, I proposed to approach the aesthetics of the secular by examining phenomena that are understood or declare themselves to be different from and possibly antagonistic toward religion. This is indeed meant as a starting point and an alternative to outright dismissals of such a project on the basis of an ideological self-representation of the secular as disembodied reason. The chapter's aim was to demonstrate that a focus on aesthetic themes may function as a heuristic that enables us to expand scholarship on the secular beyond the immediate ambit of the conceptual grid and genealogy of the secular/religious binary. The example of Indian Atheism sketched how a civilisational imaginary of Indian Atheism conditions the ways in which forms of and attitudes about material culture and rhetorically produced affects are constructed, enacted and contested within a larger, historically shaped 'representational economy' (Keane 2003, 410). Instead of circumscribing a priori what secularity refers to, for instance by postulating a singular secularist narrative of triumphal antagonism toward religion, an aesthetic approach attends to the historical and cultural plasticity of secularity as an aesthetic phenomenon, i.e., as a form of producing aesthetically mediated secular difference in specific social settings. The surplus of this approach consists of conceptualising secular difference also as a question of *aesthetic efficacies* rather than primarily a question of conceptual *classification* or semiotic *ideology*. Such an aesthetically grounded comparative approach to the secular can feed back into the analytical apparatus of the larger project of an aesthetics of religion, not by juxtaposing substantialist notions of secular and religious aesthetics but by making our analytical categories and conceptualisations of aesthetic strategies sensitive to a specific dimension of differentiation: secular difference.

Acknowledgement

This chapter is a slightly updated version of: Binder, Stefan. 2019. 'Aesthetics of the secular', in *Bloomsbury Handbook of the Cultural and Cognitive Aesthetics of Religion*, Anne Koch and Katharina Wilkens, eds, 263–72. London: Bloomsbury Academic. It is reprinted here with the permission of the previous publisher.

Notes

1 Although there is no commonly accepted definition of affect, an important theme in 'affect theory' (Gregg and Seigworth 2010) concerns the ways in which affects circulate between bodies and things and stimulate certain responses. I am using the term affect to stress this intersubjective and stimulating aspect.

References

Amir-Moazami, Schirin. 2016. 'The secular embodiments of face-veil controversies across Europe', in *Islam and Public Controversy in Europe*, Nilüfer Göle, ed. 83–98. London: Routledge.

Asad, Talal. 2003. *Formations of the Secular: Christianity, Islam, modernity.* Stanford, CA: Stanford University Press.

Asad, Talal. 2011. 'Thinking about the secular body, pain, and liberal politics.' *Cultural Anthropology* 26 (4): 657–75.

Bate, Bernard J. 2009. *Tamil Oratory and the Dravidian Aesthetic: Democratic practice in South India.* New York: Columbia University Press.

Bate, Bernard J. 2010. 'The ethics of textuality: The Protestant sermon and the Tamil public sphere', in *Ethical Life in South Asia*, Anand Pandian and Daud Ali, eds, 101–15. Bloomington: Indiana University Press.

Bauman, Richard and Charles L. Briggs. 1990. 'Poetics and performance as critical perspectives on language and social life.' *Annual Review of Anthropology* 19: 59–88.

Benjamin, Walter. 2008. *The Work of Art in the Age of Its Technological Reproducibility, and Other Writings on Media.* Edited by Michael W. Jennings. Translated by Edmund Jephcott. Cambridge, MA: Belknap Press of Harvard University Press.

Bergunder, Michael. 2004. 'Contested past: Anti-Brahmanical and Hindu nationalist reconstructions of Indian prehistory.' *Historiographia Linguistica* 31 (1): 59–104.

Bhattacharya, Ramkrishna. 2009. *Studies on the Cārvāka/Lokāyata.* Florence: Società Editrice Fiorentina.

Binder, Stefan. 2019. 'Magic is science: Atheist conjuring and the exposure of superstition in South India.' *HAU: Journal of Ethnographic Theory* 9 (2): 284–98.

Binder, Stefan. 2020a. *Total Atheism: Secular activism and the politics of difference in South India.* New York: Berghahn.

Binder, Stefan. 2020b. 'Storytelling and mediation: The aesthetics of a counter-narrative of atheism in South India,' in *Narrative Cultures and the Aesthetics of Religion*, Dirk Johannsen, Anja Kirsch and Jens Kreinath, eds, 219–45. Leiden: Brill.

Blanes, Ruy L. and Galina Oustinova-Stjepanovic, eds. 2015. 'Being Godless: Ethnographies of atheism and non-religion (Special Issue).' *Social Analysis* 59 (2): 1–145.

Braidotti, Rosi, Bolette Blaagaard, Tobijn de Graauw and Eva Midden, eds. 2014. *Transformations of Religion and the Public Sphere: Postsecular publics.* New York: Palgrave Macmillan.

Bryant, Edwin F. and Laurie L. Patton, eds. 2005. *The Indo-Aryan Controversy: Evidence and inference in Indian history.* London: Routledge.

Bullivant, Stephen and Lois Lee. 2012. 'Interdisciplinary studies of non-religion and secularity: The state of the union.' *Journal of Contemporary Religion* 27 (1): 19–27.

Cady, Linell E. and Tracy Fessenden, eds. 2013. *Religion, the Secular, and the Politics of Sexual Difference.* New York: Columbia University Press.

Cai Xiang. 2016. *Revolution and Its Narratives: China's socialist literary and cultural imaginaries, 1949–1966.* Translated by Rebecca E. Karl and Xueping Zhong. Durham, NC: Duke University Press.

Calhoun, Craig J., Mark Juergensmeyer and Jonathan van Antwerpen, eds. 2011. *Rethinking Secularism.* Oxford: Oxford University Press.

Cannell, Fenella. 2010. 'The anthropology of secularism.' *Annual Review of Anthropology* 39 (1): 85–100.

Casanova, José. 1994. *Public Religions in the Modern World.* Chicago: University of Chicago Press.

Chattopadhyaya, Debiprasad. 1959. *Lokāyata: A study in ancient Indian materialism*. New Delhi: People's Publishing House.

Connolly, William E. 1999. *Why I Am Not a Secularist*. Minneapolis: University of Minnesota Press.

Copeman, Jacob. 2015. 'Secularism's names: Commitment to confusion and the pedagogy of the name.' *South Asia Multidisciplinary Academic Journal* 12 (October). https://samaj.revues.org/4012.

Copeman, Jacob and Johannes Quack. 2015. 'Godless people and dead bodies: Materiality and the morality of atheist materialism.' *Social Analysis* 59 (2): 40–61.

Copeman, Jacob and Deepa S. Reddy. 2012. 'The didactic death: Publicity, instruction and body donation.' *HAU: Journal of Ethnographic Theory* 2 (2): 59–83.

Engelke, Matthew. 2015a. '"Good without God": Happiness and pleasure among the humanists.' *HAU: Journal of Ethnographic Theory* 5 (3): 69–91.

Engelke, Matthew. 2015b. 'On atheism and non-religion: An afterword.' *Social Analysis* 59 (2): 135–45.

Engelke, Matthew. 2015c. 'Secular shadows: African, immanent, post-colonial.' *Critical Research on Religion* 3 (1): 86–100.

Engelke, Matthew. 2015d. 'The coffin question: Death and materiality in humanist funerals.' *Material Religion* 11 (1): 26–48.

Erlmann, Veit, ed. 2004. *Hearing Cultures: Essays on sound, listening, and modernity*. Oxford: Berg.

Farman, Abou. 2013. 'Speculative matter: Secular bodies, minds, and persons.' *Cultural Anthropology* 28 (4): 737–59.

Farman, Abou. 2020. *On Not Dying: Secular immortality in the age of technoscience*. Minneapolis: University of Minnesota Press.

Giddens, Anthony. 1991. *The Consequences of Modernity*. Stanford, CA: Stanford University Press.

Gokhale, Pradeep P. 2015. *Lokāyata/Cārvāka: A philosophical inquiry*. New Delhi: Oxford University Press.

Gorski, Philip S., David Kyuman Kim, John Torpey and Jonathan van Antwerpen, eds. 2012. *The Post-Secular in Question: Religion in contemporary society*. New York: New York University Press.

Gregg, Melissa and Gregory J. Seigworth, eds. 2010. *The Affect Theory Reader*. Durham, NC: Duke University Press.

Grieser, Alexandra. 2017. 'Blue brains: Aesthetic ideologies and the formation of knowledge between religion and science', in *Aesthetics of Religion: A connective concept*, Alexandra Grieser and Jay Johnston, eds, 237–70. Berlin: De Gruyter.

Grieser, Alexandra and Arianna Borrelli. 2017. 'The "beauty fallacy": Religion, science, and the aesthetics of knowledge.' *Approaching Religion* 7 (2): 1–3.

Grieser, Alexandra and Jay Johnston, eds. 2017. *Aesthetics of Religion: A connective concept*. Berlin: De Gruyter.

Gutkin, Irina. 1999. *The Cultural Origins of the Socialist Realist Aesthetic, 1890–1934*. Evanston, IL: Northwestern University Press.

Harris, Randy A., ed. 1997. *Landmark Essays on the Rhetoric of Science: Case studies*. Mahwah, NJ: Hermagoras Press.

Hermann, Adrian, Isabel Laack and Sebastian Schüler. 2015. 'Imaginationsräume', in *Religion – Imagination – Ästhetik: Vorstellungs- und Sinneswelten in Religion und Kultur*, Lucia Traut and Annette Wilke, eds, 193–6. Göttingen: Vandenhoeck & Ruprecht.

Hirschkind, Charles. 2011. 'Is there a secular body?' *Cultural Anthropology* 26 (4): 633–47.

Horkheimer, Max and Theodor W. Adorno. 2002. *Dialectic of Enlightenment: Philosophical fragments*. Edited by Gunzelin Schmid Noerr. Translated by Edmund Jephcott. Stanford, CA: Stanford University Press.

Hudson, D. Dennis. 1995. 'Tamil Hindu responses to Protestants: Nineteenth-century literati in Jaffna and Tinnevelly.' In *Indigenous Responses to Western Christianity*, Steven Kaplan, ed., 95–123. New York: New York University Press.

Inden, Ronald B. 1990. *Imagining India*. Oxford: Blackwell.

Johannsen, Dirk and Anja Kirsch. 2019. 'Narrative strategies', in *The Bloomsbury Handbook of the Cultural and Cognitive Aesthetics of Religion*, Katharina Wilkens and Anne Koch, eds, 143–54. New York: Bloomsbury Academic.

Keane, Webb. 2003. 'Semiotics and the social analysis of material things.' *Language & Communication* 23 (3): 409–25.

Keane, Webb. 2007. *Christian Moderns: Freedom and fetish in the mission encounter*. Berkeley: University of California Press.

Keane, Webb. 2013. 'Secularism as a moral narrative of modernity.' *Transit: Europäische Revue* 43: 159–70.

King, Richard. 1999. *Orientalism and Religion: Postcolonial theory, India and 'the mystic East'*. London: Routledge.

Kirsch, Anja. 2017. 'Religious in form, socialist in content: Socialist narratives and the question of civil religion.' *Journal of Religion in Europe* 10 (1–2): 147–71.

Knipe, David M. 2015. *Vedic Voices: Intimate narratives of a living Andhra tradition*. Oxford: Oxford University Press.

Koch, Anne. 2017. 'Introduction: Revisiting civil religion from an aesthetic point of view.' *Journal of Religion in Europe* 10 (1–2): 1–15.

Latour, Bruno. 1993. *We Have Never Been Modern*. Translated by Catherine Porter. Cambridge, MA: Harvard University Press.

Lee, Lois. 2015. *Recognizing the Non-Religious: Reimagining the secular*. Oxford: Oxford University Press.

Luehrmann, Sonja. 2011. *Secularism Soviet Style: Teaching atheism and religion in a Volga republic*. Bloomington: Indiana University Press.

Mahmood, Saba. 2006. 'Secularism, hermeneutics, and empire: The politics of Islamic reformation.' *Public Culture* 18 (2): 323.

Mahmood, Saba. 2009. 'Religious reason and secular affect: An incommensurable divide?', in *Is Critique Secular? Blasphemy, injury, and free speech*, Talal Asad, Judith Butler and Saba Mahmood, eds, 64–100. Berkeley, CA: Doreen B. Townsend Center for the Humanities.

Mapril, José, Ruy Llera Blanes, Emerson Giumbelli and Erin K. Wilson, eds, 2017. *Secularisms in a Postsecular Age? Religiosities and subjectivities in comparative perspective*. Cham: Palgrave Macmillan.

McBrien, Julie and Mathijs Pelkmans. 2008. 'Turning Marx on his head: Missionaries, "extremists" and archaic secularists in post-Soviet Kyrgyzstan.' *Critique of Anthropology* 28 (1): 87–103.

Meyer, Birgit. 2010. '"There is a spirit in that image": Mass-produced Jesus pictures and Protestant-Pentecostal animation in Ghana.' *Comparative Studies in Society and History* 52 (1): 100–30.

Narayana Rao, Velcheru. 2001. 'The politics of Telugu Ramayanas: Colonialism, print culture, and literary movements.' In *Questioning Ramayanas: A South Asian tradition*, Paula Richman, ed., 159–85. Berkeley: University of California Press.

Pandian, M. S. S. 2007. *Brahmin and Non-Brahmin: Genealogies of the Tamil political present*. New Delhi: Permanent Black.

Pauwels, Luc, ed. 2006. *Visual Cultures of Science: Rethinking representational practices in knowledge building and science communication*. Hanover, NH: Dartmouth College Press.

Prasad, Leela. 2012. *Poetics of Conduct: Oral narrative and moral being in a South Indian town*. New York: Columbia University Press.

Quack, Johannes. 2012a. *Disenchanting India: Organized rationalism and criticism of religion in India*. New York: Oxford University Press.

Quack, Johannes. 2012b. 'Organised atheism in India: An overview.' *Journal of Contemporary Religion* 27 (1): 67–85.

Quack, Johannes. 2014. 'Outline of a relational approach to "nonreligion."' *Method & Theory in the Study of Religion* 26 (4–5): 439–69.

Quack, Johannes and Stefan Binder. 2018. 'Atheism and rationalism in Hinduism.' In *Oxford Bibliographies in Hinduism*, Tracy Coleman, ed. New York: Oxford University Press.

Ramasami, E.V. 1972. *The Ramayana: A true reading*. Tiruchirappalli: Periyar Self-Respect Propaganda Institution Publications.

Rancière, Jacques. 2004. *The Politics of Aesthetics: The distribution of the sensible*. London: Continuum.

Richman, Paula. 1993. 'E. V. Ramasami's reading of the *Ramayana*.' In *Many Rāmāyaṇas: The diversity of a narrative tradition in South Asia*, Paula Richman, ed., 175–201. Berkeley: University of California Press.

Scheer, Monique, Nadia Fadil and Birgitte Schepelern Johansen, eds, 2019. *Secular Bodies, Affects, and Emotions: European configurations*. London: Bloomsbury Academic.

Scherer, Matthew. 2011. 'Landmarks in the critical study of secularism.' *Cultural Anthropology* 26 (4): 621–32.

Taylor, Charles. 2007. *A Secular Age*. Cambridge, MA: Harvard University Press.

Traut, Lucia and Annette Wilke, eds, 2015. *Religion – Imagination – Ästhetik: Vorstellungs- und Sinneswelten in Religion und Kultur*. Göttingen: Vandenhoeck & Ruprecht.

Trautmann, Thomas R. 2006. *Languages and Nations: The Dravidian proof in colonial Madras*. Berkeley: University of California Press.

Trawick, Margaret. 1990. *Notes on Love in a Tamil Family*. Berkeley: University of California Press.

Verrips, Jojada. 2006. 'Aisthesis & an-aesthesia', in *Off the Edge: Experiments in cultural analysis*, Orvar Löfgren and Richard Wilk, eds, 29–36. Copenhagen: Museum Tusculanum Press.

Vries, Hendrik de and Lawrence Eugene Sullivan, eds, 2006. *Political Theologies: Public religions in a post-secular world*. New York: Fordham University Press.

Weibel, Peter and Bruno Latour, eds, 2002. *Iconoclash: Beyond the image wars in science, religion, and art*. Karlsruhe: ZKM, Center for Art and Media.

Wiering, Jelle. 2017. 'There is a sexular body: Introducing a material approach to the secular.' *Secularism and Nonreligion* 6. http://doi.org/10.5334/snr.78.

Wilke, Annette and Oliver Moebus. 2011. *Sound and Communication: An aesthetic cultural history of Sanskrit Hinduism*. Berlin: Walter de Gruyter.

Yelle, Robert A. 2013. *The Language of Disenchantment: Protestant literalism and colonial discourse in British India*. New York: Oxford University Press.

Yelle, Robert A. 2019. 'Protestant (an)aesthetics', in *The Bloomsbury Handbook of the Cultural and Cognitive Aesthetics of Religion*, Katharina Wilkens and Anne Koch, eds, 241–52. New York: Bloomsbury Academic.

5

Gender, affect and atheism in Arabic media

Natalie Khazaal

Introduction

The beginning of the 2011 uprisings was a watershed moment for the public appearance of atheists in the Arabic-speaking world. Since then, a bold generation of atheists has begun to announce their apostasy (leaving religion) publicly through various media like Facebook, Twitter and YouTube, managing to create a like-minded community. Their use of social and other media kicked off a new stage of atheist and irreligious publicity in the Arabic-speaking world, a stage intimately related to the media and the public sphere it affords contemporary societies. In this chapter, I explore how the new public atheists interact with the media and what role gender plays in their engagement with the media. This chapter contributes to the book's project – to conceptualise the relations between media and non-religion – by exploring the nexus of atheism, media and gender in Lebanon. Ultimately, the Lebanese case of what Jacob Copeman and Mascha Schulz call 'sceptical publics' helps reconceptualise the link between the secular and public spheres.

An explicit goal of this loose movement has been to normalise atheism. Normalisation for the movement means creating a safe space for a presently unknown but considerable number of secret atheists to come out in public and live their truth. It also means not being punished for their convictions, by forced veiling, being disowned by their family or fired from their job, for instance. Yet, many Lebanese and other Arab atheists remain anonymous or pseudonymous because creating a more hospitable environment has been difficult (Khazaal 2017). Legal systems often forebode danger for them. For example, the Lebanese constitution does not directly penalise apostasy or atheism, because it explicitly endorses freedom of conviction (§ 9). However, §§ 473–5 of the Penal Code criminalise blaspheming the name of god and insulting religious practices and punish the accused with up to three years of imprisonment.[1] This law has been used selectively to accuse musicians, journalists and activists of blasphemy (16 cases between 2018 and 2021), and then to silence the accused from social media under the pretence of preserving public safety, thus violating the Lebanese constitution and the Universal Declaration of Human Rights. In addition, personal status law on such matters as marriage, inheritance and custody is exclusively delegated to religious sectarian courts, which do not recognise apostasy or atheism. Many Lebanese, then, feel that they are religious subjects, not citizens, because the freedom of conviction guaranteed by the constitution is meaningless without actual freedom of expression.[2]

Despite Lebanon's status as a more liberal Arabic-speaking country, revealing that one is an atheist attracts stigmatisation even in more private, family settings there, and often carries serious consequences. According to a 2021 study about forms of abuse perpetrated against atheists in Lebanon, all 40 interviewees said that they had suffered serious abuse because they were atheists, such as forced veiling, psychological violence, threats of death or violence, physical violence, illegal detention, discrimination in employment, restricted access to education and social services, and restrictions on expressing personal beliefs (Harakeh, Ayat and Abdallah 2021). Of all the abuse, the most common was forced veiling. Of the 25 female interviewees, 22 were 'forced to wear the veil at some point during their lives, are currently forced to wear it, or are facing the consequences of refusing to wear it, from physical to emotional abuse' (Harakeh, Ayat and Abdallah 2021). As a socially imposed punishment for their atheism, two of the participants were arrested and charged with apostasy, two were fired from their jobs, two were abducted by a religious party and two took their lives: a 25-year-old woman who lost her custody battle and whose family disowned her (by Muslim personal status law, as practised in Lebanon, children belong to the father) and a 24-year-old man who was covertly held and tortured for months.

Why has there been relatively little progress, after a decade, towards normalising one's non-religious convictions in Lebanon and the

Arabic-speaking world, despite the opportunities for self-expression and community building offered by certain media? Why have atheists' stories not resonated with the general public? And, most importantly here, does the way women explain publicly (via the media) why they left religion differ from the way men frame their exit? If so, what can we learn from this? Finally, can region-specific insights about Arabic-speaking contexts shed light on broader global contexts?

The media strategies employed by Lebanese atheists who for activist reasons explicitly seek publicity take particular forms. Prominent among them are closed social media groups such as Facebook groups, as well as public spaces that are open to everyone, like YouTube channels and television talk shows reposted on the internet. Whereas closed Facebook groups involve conversations between self-proclaimed atheists or agnostics, YouTube channels address a broad audience rather than just other atheists, while television shows target mostly religious audiences. Entertainment and emotions seem to be prominent in the latter, in contrast to other media like intellectual-argumentative books on atheism as well as closed atheist Facebook groups.

To address the above questions, this chapter focuses on public atheists on YouTube and traditional Lebanese media. Since the total number of public Lebanese atheist–activists is perhaps only about 10–15,[3] by necessity my sample is also small: I selected four individuals, whom I divided into two groups. The first group consists of two women: journalist, writer, poet and rights activist Joumana Haddad, a well-known and respected Lebanese media personality with a long history in journalism and her own television show, and Pamela Ghanem, a Twitter activist and a YouTuber for 'Jumhuriyyat al-Ilhad' ('Atheist Republic'; see also Neelabh's chapter in this volume, which analyses Atheist Republic in India). The second group consists of two men: activist and Freethought Lebanon co-founder Mazen Abou Hamdan, and geology professor Ali Haydar. Although my sample is small, in the Conclusion I present four more cases from the Arab world, which confirm my analysis and suggest that when more Arab atheists come out publicly a statistically significant sample will be an option.

In the second section I describe the meanings which believers and non-believers attribute to faith and atheism and how such meanings are theorised in academic discourse; in the third, I examine the differences between the two groups of public Lebanese atheists. My textual analysis of their statements about their reasons for leaving religion contributes to our understanding of public atheism and its ties to the media by highlighting how affect, embodiment and aesthetic sentiments are central to creating a positive reception for atheist publicity. Although the chapter offers one of the first, and therefore provisional, deep dives into gendered sceptical publics in the Arabic-speaking world and beyond, as I point out later, it also aims to provide insights that transcend gender. The conclusion poses the question: what do these differences tell us about atheists' progress towards normalising apostasy in the Arabic-speaking world and the directions that may speed up normalisation? The answer helps explain how Lebanese sceptical publics engage with the media to address non-religion and non-religious identity.

Ideology versus affect as a vehicle for shared meaning

Lebanese atheists' appearances in the media shed light on their understanding of atheism and religion. Their concept of faith is at odds with that of Lebanese theists (believers), just as believers' concept of atheism is at odds with that of atheists. (Of course, I look at this disagreement in general terms, as individuals within the two groups disagree among themselves on the definition and utility of these terms.) But it is the difference in the meanings with which atheists and believers imbue non-religion and religion that sits at the core of current challenges to atheists' inclusion in the broader community.

New Atheism has influenced the ways in which many atheists around the world, including in Lebanese communities, see atheism and faith (Zenk 2012). New-wave atheists depict themselves as proponents of an evolutionary approach to scepticism, science, faith and religion (Kettell 2013; Taira 2012; LeDrew 2012). Assuming that religious claims should be subject to the same rules of argumentation and refutation as scientific claims, new-wave atheists juxtapose science with religion, doubt with belief and the modern with the pre-modern. This juxtaposition portrays atheism as the outcome of free inquiry, critical thinking and rigorous scrutiny, while religion is seen as a product of dogma, fallacious and irrational thinking and shallow analysis, and as stemming from fear or insecurity.

Some critics argue that the new movement does not have a concept of atheism beyond dismantling faith (Beha 2012). Others argue that it reduces religion to cognitive acts, leaving out substantive, functional and polythetic ways to define religion. For instance, Paul-François Tremlett and Fang-Long Shih show how belief and doubt could be used strategically as a form of practice rather than being simply delusional concepts about reality. According to them, in the Philippines belief and doubt are 'fundamentally about practice' rather than beliefs (2017, 88). When a group of believers asked a local goddess for a prediction on an important matter and got unfavourable results, they kept rephrasing their question until they got the answer they needed to back up their political claims. Belief and doubt, then, could be products of self-interest and experiential efficacy, rather than simply mental acts.

On the other hand, in a 2016 episode of 'Al-'Ayn bi-l-'Ayn' ('An eye for an eye') aired on the Lebanese television channel Jadeed, Lebanese Catholic priest Edgar al-Haybi (director of the Institute for Religious Studies at Saint Joseph University) frames faith as a personal experience for Lebanese believers, rather than as an idea that could be logically refuted (emphasis added):

> No matter how much we want to find in our mind logical arguments to say yes or no – there's a creator or there is not, the universe has a beginning and an end or it does not – I do not think that faith is a matter of physical, tangible evidence, of scientifically demonstrable proof. Faith is inside the mind, it's an act of the mind and not beyond the mind. However, it's *an act that we experience, that we live but cannot argue or demonstrate with tangible evidence, with logic.*[4]

Despite the variety of views on the nature of religion among Lebanese believers, al-Haybi's frame captures the common understanding of it as personal, emotional experience. The Maronite Christian show host Tony Khalife also emphasised the greater importance of the heart in comparison to the mind in his opening to this episode: '[Atheists say:] I'm an atheist because I use my brain, not my heart. ... This group's numbers are not small at all, and they say that their mind told them that there's no God.'[5]

As for atheism, conservative and many non-conservative Lebanese believers see atheism as a mental disease rather than an intellectual position, as we can see from a viewer poll on a 2019 episode of *Tawasul* ('Communication') aired on the Shi'ite-owned Manar television channel.[6] Furthermore, Lebanese religious communities see atheism as a rebellion against the rise of religious extremism (ISIS, al-Qa'eda), or as a desire to transgress religious prohibitions against alcohol, sex, etc.[7] In all these cases, atheism amounts to a deviation from religio-normativity: 'Every child is born with the innate knowledge that God Almighty is his creator. What drives people to deviate from this instinct and turn towards atheism?'[8]

Believers too are occasionally accused of failing to engage productively with atheists, especially as a type of religious minority (Eyadat 2013). Criticisms of the nature of atheist and theist publicity largely focus on the ideological aspects of non-religion and religion. I would like to assess here an additional aspect of that publicity: the role of affect and disposition. I will focus on affect in gendered visions of atheist publicity on the media. I chose affect because it was apparent to me that it played a major role in gendered atheist publicity and because of its shared significance for atheists and believers alike.

According to Samuli Schielke, non-believers in Egypt, including atheists, share with believers similar structures of affect brought about by similar 'underlying tensions and conflicts over the ways Egyptians experience their lives and the powers to which they are subjected' (2012, 304). As Raymond Williams explains, structures of affect or feelings are types of affective social experiences that cannot be boiled down to ideologies or convictions. This helps Schielke point out that questioning the minimal requirements of Muslim faith (belief in Allah and Muhammad) is an affective, rather than epistemic, issue. In other words, both atheism and religiosity carry a core affective aspect, even though the term religion is imbued with various aspects of morality, metaphysics, subjectivity, ritual, politics, etc. This core aspect is not negated by the different motivations for engagement with religion or the multiple reasons for disengagement from it. According to Schielke, this core is the affect of 'lifeworldly certainty', while each side has divergent ways of achieving it, the religious side through textual knowledge and renewed divine presence, and the non-religious side through turning 'the loss of divine presence into an accomplishment with the help of a trust in human agency and judgment' (2012, 317).

Moreover, doubt has social dimensions and is not exclusively a cognitive mechanism, as Ruy Llera Blanes and Galina Oustinova-Stjepanovic (2017) have argued (we can see this in cases when people distrust corrupt religious practitioners, for instance). Given these insights, I explore the role played by the appeals to affect made by atheists versus the role played by intellectual arguments and how they impact audiences. If affect is a major aspect of experience shared by atheists and believers, are Lebanese atheists who make their public admission of atheism on traditional and social media using affect strategically? Are there gender differences in their use of affect? And do their strategies resonate with the larger audiences of believers?

Gender and atheist publicity

Although academic interest in atheism and non-religion is growing fast, research projects on non-religion and the media are still few; some examples are studies of the secularist press in Victorian England (Nash 1995), the coverage of atheism and atheists in American and British newspapers (van der Veen and Bleich 2021), atheist publicity campaigns (Lee 2017; Knott, Poole and Taira 2013), atheist cartoon strips (Luehrmann 2011, 2015), the material culture of Indian atheism (Copeman and Quack 2015), secularist cyber-activism (Smith and Cimino 2012), atheism and Reddit (Lundmark and LeDrew 2019), gaming (Bosman 2019), apostate blogs (Rashid and Mohamad 2019) and online social groups in Indonesia (Duile 2021). There have been even fewer studies on non-religion and the media in the context of Arabic-speaking communities, such as on digital periodicals like the *Arab Atheist Magazine* (Khazaal 2017), on Arab Twitter (Al Hariri, Magdy and Wolters 2019) and on YouTube (Elsässer 2021).

Few scholars have explicitly engaged with gendered dynamics surrounding atheism. This is concerning, because gender is an important factor when it comes to professing atheism in public. Most public atheists in Lebanon and the Arabic-speaking world have been male. While exact statistics are hard to generate, the proportion of men versus women on the Facebook page 'Lebanese Atheists', for instance, is 71.5 per cent male and 28 female. Without claiming that there are 'female accounts' per se, this chapter nevertheless infers from the juxtaposition of the two female and two male cases that men and women articulate atheism differently. The chapter does not argue that 'female' accounts are structured around an 'affective defence' because women are emotional; on the contrary, it shows that female accounts incorporate both affective and intellectual defences but connect to audiences better by the strategic use of the affective defence. In this section, I draw on gender literature to situate my study in the wider literature on atheism beyond the Arabic-speaking world and reference other works that have highlighted the gendered dimensions of humanist, rationalist and atheist projects and publicity. Thus, I engage explicitly with how questions of the constructions of femininity and masculinity tend to be interlinked with notions of 'women as emotional' and 'men as intellectual/rational', which might result in gendered forms of atheist publicity.

For example, in her study exploring whether empathy is gendered, Claudia Strauss (2004) argues that women typically exhibit more empathy, but that gender difference varies across cultures. According to Yoshihisa Kashima et al. (1995), US women demonstrate noticeably greater emotional connectedness than US men, but the difference between Korean women and men is negligible. Various reasons have been postulated to explain differences in empathy, among them: higher expectations on women to behave empathetically because empathy is more important to women's identity (Davis 1996); the fact that women are typically the primary caregivers forces them to learn to control aggressiveness and mimic same-gender behaviour by the caregiver (Chodorow 1999); cultural devaluation of the affect of caregiving (Benjamin 1988); the impact of larger, rougher play groups for boys and smaller, more intimate ones for girls (Maccoby 1998); and typical economic and power differences between women and men (Miller 1986), which mean that those in subordinate positions need to be more skilled in decoding the thoughts and feelings of their superiors than vice versa.

Readers will notice that, while gender is a significant dimension, other factors also shape Lebanese atheists' dynamics of self-representation. This fact shows how important it is to apply an intersectional perspective in future analyses. The selected cases demonstrate, for instance, that class, social milieu, urbanity, established social status and, arguably, transnational interactions are very significant for a person's relative scope to engage effectively with atheist publicity, and for how the latter is perceived.

Female accounts: an affective defence of atheism

Joumana Haddad

Joumana Haddad is the single most influential open Lebanese atheist and the single most influential open female atheist in the twenty-first-century Arabic-speaking world. Her integrated identity as a writer, journalist and rights activist defines the horizons of her impact. Raised in a conservative family with a huge library and an avid interest in reading, Haddad began writing when she was ten. After a two-year affair with medical school to appease her parents, she embarked on an extraordinary career in journalism and literature. As a writer, she is famous for five poetry collections, a play, a novel and a trilogy of essays about women in the Arab world. During this time, she has also been a well-known journalist, the first woman to serve as the cultural editor of the most prestigious Lebanese daily, *Nahar*. In 2018, she began hosting the political-social show *Kalimat Haqq* ('Word of truth') on the US-operated Arabic-language television channel Hurra, in which she focuses on critical thinking and free speech regarding cases of human rights abuse, censorship and discrimination against disenfranchised groups in Arab countries. She has long been an activist for women's, LGBTQ+ and atheist rights, and in 2019 she founded the youth-centred, secular, independent human rights organisation the Joumana Haddad Freedoms Center.[9]

In the early days of her atheism, she used to debate with believers, pointing to the irrefutable evidence of contradictions in religious scripture and appealing to believers' quest for truth through logic. But after multiple failed attempts, she discovered that believers always find a way to explain away even the most hard-to-justify contradiction. This kind of activism has long ceased to attract her because she understood that every person has the right to believe in different things even if they were wrong. Now she favours a different type of atheist activism, what I call 'an affective defence of atheism'. I argue that her 'affective defence of atheism' has two main steps: disarming believers' fears and appealing to their sense of compassion.

On 23 March 2013, Haddad published a brave article in *Nahar* called 'Limadha Ana Mulhida' ('Why I'm an atheist', later (2014) republished as the preface to the Arabic edition of her popular book on patriarchy, *Superman Is an Arab: Why I'm an atheist*).[10] The title is in homage to Egyptian writer, critic and mathematician Dr Ismail Adham's famous 1937 manifesto of the same name. Adham has achieved a revered status in the Arabic-speaking atheist community for his bravery in openly revealing his atheism at the time. Notice how even Haddad's title marks step 1: breaking the atheist taboo and disarming the audience's fear of atheists (since she is a journalist whom readers have known and respected for a long time). In the body, she unambiguously affirms that she is an atheist, thwarting any attempts to explain her atheism as a metaphor or a phase: 'I do not feel that this essence [god] is part of me or of the essence of my existence. I now live without god inside me'; 'That is the reason I'm no longer a believer. That is why I'm an atheist.'

By 2012, Haddad had been in the public eye for long enough to become a beloved cultural and feminist icon. She had enemies too, which made her announcement of atheism risky, but not reckless because of the cultural cachet she had amassed and the connections with colleagues, supporters and friends she had made over the years. Her atheism was not the first thing to be known about her publicly. Her prior popularity as an iconoclast helped Lebanese audiences reappraise her atheism and consequently took away some of their fear. It also challenged a stereotype that there are no Arab women atheists in the Arabic-speaking world. Some bloggers commented how shocked they were to discover not only that there are Arab women atheists but also that Haddad was a worthy opponent with many positive qualities. Single-handedly, Haddad forced many to deal with atheism as a legitimate part of the Arabic-speaking socioscape.

In what I call step 2 – evoking believers' sense of compassion and justice – Haddad's article describes her atheism as simultaneously a result of an intellectual position in which god has become an unconvincing idea, and a feeling or lived experience: in other words, it is an 'intellectual and existential position':

> The issue is one of life that I live; and I do not feel that this life needs the essence (or 'crutch') I had been brought up believing in. I do not feel that this essence is part of me, or of the essence of my existence. I now live without god inside me. This is, in short, my intellectual and existential position on the question of faith. That is the reason I'm no longer a believer. That is why I'm an atheist. ... I believe in science, in its current breakthroughs (many of which decisively refute the idea of a god, or at least the 'need' for one to explain the existence of this universe) and in its future breakthroughs.
>
> (Haddad 2014, 12–13)

While Haddad acknowledges the intellectual roots of her atheism, she focuses her attention on its existential/affective roots. This focus closely parallels the signposts in al-Haybi's definition of faith; as she presents her convictions as 'an act that we experience, that we live', she reaches believers who might respond negatively to definitions focused on 'physical, tangible evidence, of scientifically demonstrable proof'. (She also communicates successfully with anyone interested in logical reasoning and intellectual positions by describing her atheism as an intellectual position.) By talking the language of believers Haddad conditions them to listen to her message and be more open to her ideas. Their listening allows (but does not compel) them to feel compassion for Haddad, the narrator, when she explains her atheism as an outcome of the deep schism between her morality and that of Abrahamic religions, as a consequence of the ways in which religions offend and oppress women: 'they are racist, misogynistic, homophobic, unforgiving, blood-stained, intolerant of difference, biased in their actions against humanity, freedoms and human rights' (Haddad 2014, 15). Or, in greater detail:

> Monotheistic religions offend me, in the first place as a woman. A woman with dignity. A woman who believes unequivocally that she

is equal to men and that she should enjoy the same rights and privileges that they do. How can I not reject religions that are inherently misogynistic and against gender equality, that compete with each other to apply patriarchal standards, from humiliating women to describing them as a kind of property owned by men, to oppressing them, to treating them as inferior? ... And then, monotheistic religions offend me, in the second place, because I believe my body is my property, yet religious hypocrisy about sex has no limit.

(Haddad 2014, 16–19)

Haddad's article stirred much public debate on the topics of her atheism and atheism in general when it was first published. One outcome was that in 2015 *Nahar*'s sister outlet, Nahar TV, enthusiastically accepted Haddad's proposal to make a series of short shows on controversial topics, including atheism. The purpose of each episode was to raise awareness in younger generations through an intellectual conversation between Haddad and an opponent chosen from her students at the Lebanese American University (LAU). Haddad created the series (especially the episodes on atheism and removing the veil, which provoked the most viewer interest) having in mind that religious faith is a tool which communities use to create a sense of belonging.[11] Haddad wanted to dislodge the links between religion and the sense of belonging and to show viewers that they have the freedom to choose the community they belong to. To achieve this, she wanted to leave them with 'earworms', or thoughts that challenge them to question their convictions. She conveyed this idea directly in the signature statement that ended each episode: 'My goal is not to persuade you or anyone else. My goal is that we respect each other and start thinking.'

In line with her strategy of atheist activism, the atheism episode focuses on morality, rather than on contradictions and logical fallacies in religious scripture. This is how Haddad described the reason why she chose morality as the episode's focus:

NK: Why did you choose to focus on morality in the episodes on atheism and the veil above anything else, for example contradictions in religious scripture?

JH: You know, there has been a lot of focus on contradictions in religious scripture. But if someone is a believer, they'll always find a justification and an excuse to explain away these contradictions. On the other hand, the question of morality has been an important one for me because believers see atheists as immoral people, as if religious belief were what defines human morality. For me it is extremely important to demonstrate that morality and humane values precede religion; and that a believer who prays to god could be either moral or immoral, and an atheist could also be either moral or immoral. That is why I chose this topic instead of dealing with 'Byzantine polemics', which has been done. I wanted to offer a view of atheists as moral people who are not deficient in comparison with believers, because morality is the standard by which we judge anyone.[12]

The discussion of the origins of morality could be framed by a discussion about how defining religious communities as the only moral communities contradicts historical evidence, and how the sense of belonging is a biologically hard-wired component of decision making and the moods of happiness in social animals (including humans). The debate format of the episode could also fit with a kind of atheist activism that focuses on exposing contradictions in religious scripture and discussing morality from an intellectual, philosophical point of view. Yet Haddad's implementation fuses this approach with her affective defence of atheism, which appeals to believers' sense of compassion and justice. If atheists can be moral persons, as the episode suggests, then is it moral for a religious community to rob them of some of their rights? Do not they deserve the same freedoms of expression and belonging as their religious counterparts?

Pamela Ghanem

Pamela Ghanem also uses an affective defence of atheism, but targets primarily atheists or believers with doubts. These considerations and her own experience have been key to the crystallisation of her message as an activist: if you are an atheist, you are not alone and you do not need to embrace society's traditions in order to belong.

Ghanem was born to a Roman Catholic family from Tripoli, Lebanon's second largest city, with a Muslim-majority population. She used to go to church every Sunday when she was younger, although her family was not strict and her father often criticised clerics. This relaxed atmosphere fostered her doubts about the possibility of a virgin birth and that eating the body of Christ and drinking his blood during Communion implies cannibalism. But she was truly frustrated with male priests' harassment of boys, nuns and others over whom they exerted power. She also deplored women's secondary position in the Church and in Christianity. Ghanem started using Twitter when she left for the US, and soon came across Twitter users like George Carlin, Ricky Gervais, Richard Dawkins, Neil deGrasse Tyson and Sam Harris who talked openly about evolution, a subject she was never taught at school. At the same time, she encountered on Twitter Joumana Haddad, who impressed her with the frankness and boldness with which she talked in Arabic about liberated female sexuality, atheism and women's rights. Haddad's model of activism inspired Ghanem to open up about her own doubts about religion and become a more passionate defender of women's rights. She befriended Haddad on Twitter and the two started talking. By 2012, Ghanem had left religion but still held on to some of its imagery; over the next year, she transitioned to scientific deism, then to agnosticism and finally to atheism.[13] Soon after, she contacted Armin Navabi, founder of the popular Atheist Republic online community, proposing that she should create an Arabic-language version of it on YouTube. Navabi accepted the proposal, and promoted the community before it launched in January 2019.

Ghanem's own experience of trying to find a new community to belong to – one that did not incur high costs such as forcing one to accept mythology or condone misogyny – created the framework from which she speaks about her own atheism in episode 2 of her series, titled 'Limadha ana mulhida' ('Why I'm an atheist'). The main message to viewers is that they are not alone. This is important to Ghanem because, by her own admission, she was unable to shake off her religious identity on her own, despite her scepticism, while she was in a deeply religious environment, that is, without a new community to embrace her. A major aspect of her affective defence of atheism, then, is to look beyond the transitional stage between faith and atheism, during which the discussion of contradictions in religion is essential. Instead, her focus is on the stage at which the atheist builds connections with a new community better aligned with their own identity. Achieving this goal has been difficult for many atheists in the Arabic-speaking world because of the enormous obstacles religious communities place in the way of members who are likely to defect. In other words, Ghanem places more weight on the harm done by religious rhetoric and the policing of likely defectors than on the contradictions in religious scripture. After all, an encounter with a more accepting environment with less communal policing has been paramount in her own defection.

Impact

The gender-based discrimination and abuse that many women in Arabic-speaking communities experience or witness lead women atheists there to talk about atheism from a more affective place. Even though Haddad and Ghanem have never been abused in the way some other women have, their commitment to four fundamental ways to fight discrimination and abuse – gender equality, secularism (including the rights of non-believers it guarantees), LGBTQ+ rights, and personal freedoms (sexual freedom, freedom of expression, etc.) – is undeniable.[14] In her first episode (January 2019), Ghanem announced that she would touch on the following important subjects on her channel: 1) women's rights, 2) LGBTQ+ rights, 3) religious freedoms and 4) freedoms outside of religion. Even if we ignore the ranking of these topics suggested by her mention of women's rights before those of atheists, we can still see how important women's rights are to the content and direction of Ghanem's tenure. Many of the episodes Ghanem posted on the channel focus on religious and patriarchal oppression of women and other minorities: 'Women in Saudi Arabia and atheist movements' (to which Ghanem invited the Saudi atheist Danah), 'Atheist women', 'God is a man', 'Homosexuality is not an illness, homophobia is', 'Political and religious repression during the COVID-19 pandemic', 'Shutting down the *Pamela 'alayha al-Salam* account', 'Brainwashing kids', 'Seeds of harassment', etc. In comparison, there is just one episode dedicated to science: 'I trust science'.

While the strategic effects of the affective defence of atheism are complex, and difficult to establish definitively, there is much evidence that it is worth considering seriously. For instance, Haddad's cumulative life efforts in atheist activism have led to some remarkable achievements. Her open admission of atheism has on the whole enhanced her success and broadened her influence rather than curtailing them. A case in point is the 2020 episode of her show *Word of Truth*, which focused on atheism and where Haddad featured Hamed Abd al-Samad – a famous Egyptian atheist activist residing in Germany – as a guest. As a joint study of the portrayal of atheists on Lebanese television demonstrates, atheists are depicted negatively and as second-rate guests, even though Lebanon boasts of being the most liberal Arabic-speaking country (Khazaal, Itani and Abdallah 2022). While their portrayal on Hurra, which hosts the show, is remarkably more positive than on other channels, this episode is historic because it is the first ever Arabic-language show to feature only open atheists – the show host and the guest. Furthermore, Haddad's open admission of atheism probably encouraged her wide recognition in and as part of the Arabic-speaking world, and certainly has not discouraged it. She made it into *Arabian Business* magazine's 100 most influential Arab women, as well as into *Apolitical*'s 100 most influential people in gender politics (2021). Her recognition in Lebanon is just as impressive. After a lengthy discussion of her atheism on the popular talk show *Ana Heyk* ('This is how I am') on Jadeed TV (aired in 2019), 23 out of 25 people in the audience voted that they would like to see Haddad as a member of parliament in the show's audience polling segment.[15] Indeed, on the night of the 2018 elections, Haddad went to bed an elected member of the Lebanese parliament after the media announced her victory, but she woke up having lost the election. The voting commission allegedly rigged the votes, but Haddad's lawsuit to force a recount was dismissed by the higher courts. Still, an enormous crowd marched in her support, proving her unwaning popularity.

As for Ghanem, although she does not have the public visibility and successful career of Haddad, her Twitter account had 30,000 followers before it was shut down.[16] Another indicator of the acceptance of her message is the number of closeted atheists – famous Lebanese journalists, singers, actors and regular citizens – who frequently contact her on social media to share that they agree with her but do not feel comfortable coming out in the current environment. According to her own testimony, these followers are thankful for the community she and others like her have created, where they can feel a sense of belonging and counter social isolation.

Male accounts: an intellectual defence of atheism

The two male accounts below present a different approach to explaining one's atheism, which I call an intellectual defence of atheism. The core of this defence is the idea that religious scripture and tenets are created around logical contradictions and fallacies, whose implications lead to atheism, or the denial of the existence of supernatural entities like gods.

Mazen Abou Hamdan

Mazen Abou Hamdan comes from a Druze family. In 2016, he co-founded Freethought Lebanon as a Facebook group and, after it reached 10,000 subscribers, created a website with the same name.[17] These platforms provide space to build a community of Lebanese and other atheists, but also target recent apostates going through an 'angry' phase. According to Abou Hamdan, anger is an unproductive response to the religious delusions one espoused before becoming atheist. The platforms help young atheists grow out of this phase by organising different events, such as debates and a showing of the documentary 'Dawkins on Darwin' in Masrah al-Madina, Beirut in 2012, by posting atheism-related articles, by participating in conferences such as the International Humanist Conference, and by appearing on a BBC show about Arab atheists. His goal is not to claim separate rights for atheists, but to build alliances with other rights movements to advance secular causes, like legitimising civil marriage in Lebanon. Out of three possible ways – submission, aggression and assertion – of advancing atheists' visibility and guaranteeing that they have the same rights as everyone else, he chooses the third.[18]

However, Abou Hamdan was not always as polished in the way he presents his ideas. In 2011, a news story on *Qadiyat al-yawm* ('The issue of the day', Jadeed TV) featured him in a segment titled 'Al-Mulhidin fi Lubnan' ('Atheists in Lebanon').[19] When I interviewed him, he shared that the audience did not respond warmly to this first television appearance of his. In the segment, Abou Hamdan explained the reasons for his atheism this way:

> I studied philosophical books for a long time; I read, dug deep into and thought about big existential questions. In the end, I discovered that the logical arguments against the existence of god were for me a lot more convincing than the arguments for god's existence. … I wish that you all would accept us and not kill us.

His explanation is an encapsulation of the intellectual defence strategy: it captures the intellectual growth of a critical thinker who takes the time to review and thoroughly analyse important sources on the given topic, and only then comes to reasoned conclusions. This process guarantees him complete freedom of inquiry, analysis and conclusion, and then opinion. It allows him to consider several opposing viewpoints and independently select one of them as the correct option. His time is well spent because the topic is germane to human life, signifying his ability to rank issues in terms of importance. His devotion to logic helps him identify and remove affective conclusions, and positions emotions outside of the mechanism of validation or refutation of any truth.

What is interesting is the brief appeal to the audience at the very end of Abou Hamdan's account. It is clearly the wish that he and most atheists hold most dear – that the religious community would accept them as legitimate community members and not harm them (or kill them). Notice that this plea is entirely based in feeling. It suggests a desire to be seen as one's true self without having to hide one's atheist thoughts and identity. It also suggests a desire to be considered equal to the rest of the members of the community, that is, the nation-state, despite how ineffective the state is in enforcing the equal rights laws on the books when it comes to atheists. Again, there is nothing fundamentally wrong with such a plea. The question is whether it resonates with the audience for whom it is meant: would this audience be convinced they need to change their feelings about atheists and consequently their behaviour? Why are their current feelings misguided? The entire rationale for the plea is missing, as the intellectual defence cannot provide one. Perhaps it was cut out during production and the editing team decided to substitute it with a brief statement by an attorney explaining how Lebanese law penalises those who blaspheme against god. In any case, Abou Hamdan's logic is not made explicit. It does not move the audience – not yet.

Ali Haydar

Ali Haydar also uses the intellectual defence strategy, speaking to a similar audience. His position as a geology professor at the American University of Beirut (AUB) endows him with the status of an expert in science. As a result, his main message is that scientific discoveries reveal the true nature of humans, life, death and the universe.

Haydar was born into a Shi'ite family and became an atheist in his teenage years. In 1991 he graduated from the University of Parma in Italy with a master's degree in science, and in 1997 he finished his doctorate at the Swiss Federal Institute of Technology in Zurich, specialising in nanofossil recognition and geochemistry. He taught at the University of Parma before joining AUB, where he continues to do research in palaeontology and geoscience.

In 2018, Jadeed TV featured Haydar as the second guest on the show *Ana Heyk* under the title 'The atheist in confrontation with the repentant debauchee'. When the host asked him how he became an atheist, Haydar answered:

> I'm always in a process of searching, even today that is still going on. When I grew up and was able to read whole books by myself – I mean, we are talking about when I was about 16 – I began reading the exegesis of the Qur'an by al-Tabarsi and finished all the volumes of Khalafi in one summer. I mean because my goal was not to decide if I was an atheist, my goal was to discover the truth. ... Science opened avenues of thought outside the religious ones.

Using the intellectual defence strategy like Abou Hamdan, Haydar carefully presented himself as an open-minded thinker who always re-evaluates his ideas, suggesting that ideas should not be set in stone, because new scientific discoveries constantly improve our knowledge of the world. He appeared as an independent thinker, who could not only read books by himself at age 16, as he literally said, but also, he implied, evaluate their claims independently. Critical, independent thinking, then, gave him strength, and confidence that he could understand the world around him. According to his account, he diligently and thoroughly reviewed multiple primary and secondary sources (al-Tabarsi's exegesis of the Qur'an, all Khalafi's volumes), so that he could evaluate some of the best existing religious evidence. The implication was that if he had been biased he would not have consulted theological sources, and therefore he could be trusted. The viewer could also infer his dedication to discovering the truth, since not many 16-year-old boys would rather spend the summer vacation reading twelfth-century religious exegeses than swimming with their friends at a beach on the Mediterranean, or chasing after some heartthrob (what parent would not delight in seeing their child spend a summer reading books!). His implied message to the audience was that his convictions, and his conclusion, are trustworthy. Only after he had established that did Haydar present his conclusion: science is a better route to truth than religion.

Before asking this question, the host, Nishan Derharoutyounian, had introduced Haydar as a guest who represented a 'secular' viewpoint based on secular sources 'incompatible with Abrahamic scripture'. It is clear from Haydar's answer that he made an effort to counter Nishan's frame. To appeal to the religious audience in the studio and at home, Haydar implied that his atheism should not be discredited, because it is an outcome of his engagement with famous religious exegeses, the very sources they deem most credible. Despite this effort, his intellectual defence appeared out of sync with the celebration of the power of faith that took place during the first part of the show.

The story of the first guest, Tony Frangieh, was dramatically different from Haydar's peaceful pursuits. Frangieh, a born-again Christian who had engaged in drug and alcohol abuse, gambling, theft and infidelity, had spent the better part of an hour relating in detail all the vice and debauchery from which he claimed his newfound faith in Christ had saved him. Again and again, Nishan came back to how alone, confused and weak Frangieh had been without god and how the world turned from a cold, heartless place to a source of strength and wisdom once he accepted Christ into his heart. The pain and shame of his previous life were still visible in his facial expressions, body language and tone. It might have appeared cruel for Nishan to probe relentlessly into Frangieh's earlier sins, but the more uncomfortable the guest appeared, the more it enabled him to play the role of the 'living proof' of the existence of god, who was called upon to move the audience to tears of joy. Nishan ended the segment by saying:

ND: Religions are hospitals for the soul. Hallelujah.
TF: Amen.

Frangieh called himself a 'haykal for the Holy Ghost' (temple, skeleton), whose infectious faith had saved from atheism and 11 suicide attempts a young woman he had brought with him into the studio. During Haydar's portion of the interview, Frangieh addressed the studio audience directly: 'Christianity is a strategy for salvation. I bring to you the good news of joy, the message of jubilation', and the host followed with, 'What science or philosophy can make you a new person [like] the divine power, just by a brief encounter with it?'

Compared to this direct message in simple Arabic, Haydar's response in English – which described Frangieh's experience as 'SICPT, or spiritually integrated cognitive processing therapy' – seemed esoteric. After the 'living proof' presented to the audience (Frangieh and the young woman), Haydar's foray into 'dead' proof – 'the fossil record', 'sediments' and skeletal 'remains' – to demonstrate that god did not exist seemed ineffective. So did his mention of *Australopithecus afarensis* – a recent prehuman ancestor – as a proof of evolution that 'we see with our eyes' and 'touch with our hand'. After all, the record was not in the studio. The audience could not see or touch *A. afarensis*, but they could see and touch Frangieh and the young woman. We cannot directly observe evolutionary changes that occur over millions of years. Understanding evolution requires abstract and logical thinking and at least nominal familiarity with the evidence. At one point, even Haydar became aware how esoteric his measured scientific explanations and references seemed to the other, religious, participants. This made him smile at his own answer as if to signal: 'Yes, I know how unbelievable it sounds.' It happened when host Nishan asked an affective question and seemed lost for words (emphasis added):

ND: When somebody dies, you go to the funeral, to the *mourning* ceremony and you see a sheikh who is *praying* or a Christian priest. How do you approach this topic, the topic of burial and *the greatest tragedy*, the tragedy of *separation*, bidding another person a *farewell*, burying him *under the ground*, covering him *with dirt* and *tears*, this *huge pain* that a person *feels* when they *lose* someone?

AH: We are not saying that the secular person's gotten rid of emotions. Tragedy is still tragedy, regardless if you are a believer or secular. Human relationships gain a deeper dimension if you are secular, that is what is expected in my opinion, because the secular person has no extra – spiritual – credible resources. That is why the human dimension deepens rather than shrinking for the secular person.

ND: Death gives Muslims the right to see the face of their merciful lord; for Christians, death is resurrection. What is death for you?

AH: The bacteria show up and eat us, that is all. [*Smiles*]

ND: That's it? Worms show up and eat us? We get disintegrated? That is the end?

Haydar's initial answer – that atheists have the normal range of feelings like other humans – answered the question. But the host did not let go until Haydar framed his perspective as a heartless, cold reality devoid of human feeling or memory. The audience could compare the two mediated frames – Frangieh's who had filled his heart with Christ and presented to them a world of love and strong bonds with the religious audiences and Haydar's – with the appalling image of bacteria and worms eating one's heart.

Impact

The male atheists in my sample present themselves as serious thinkers who carefully evaluate the evidence, letting it take them to the truth without any bias or preconceived expectations. All are careful not to offend believers. For instance, Haydar presented his atheism as born out of 'the questions of discussion between science and religion'; he clearly meant contradictions, but changed that word to 'questions' in the middle of his statement. He also declined to answer a provocative question about Christianity on the grounds that the Lebanese penal code does not allow him to answer such a question. What is the impact of this measured, rational and respectful way of presenting one's atheism in the Lebanese media?

Similarly to the women's case, the effectiveness of this common male strategy is difficult to establish. Yet some trends emerge. Joumana Haddad and Ali Haydar were guests on the same show, 'This is how I am', with host Nishan. Overall, Lebanese channels, like other channels in Arab countries, are biased against atheists. Yet there was a noticeable difference in the host's attitude towards the guests. While he introduced Haddad at the beginning of the show, Haydar appeared 63 minutes into the 87-minute show, or after 72 per cent of the duration of the episode had lapsed. The host's tone was almost favourable towards Haddad, but noticeably unfavourable towards Haydar, just as was the host's introduction of Haydar and his atheism. In the joint study (Khazaal, Itani and Abdallah 2022) of political bias against atheists on Lebanese talk shows, we found that the Haydar episode was strongly biased against atheists, scoring 17/18 on the overall bias scale, where 18 is the most biased. Most importantly, while 23 out of the 25 studio audience members voted in favour of Haddad becoming a member of parliament, not a single studio audience member voted in favour of Haydar, an unprecedented event in the history of the show, as the host commented. It is possible that Haddad's popularity as a writer and journalist versus Haydar's much less visible position as a university professor made a difference, or that the ethnically Armenian host felt an affinity with Haddad, whose grandmother was also Armenian, or that the polling question's wording biased the audience in opposite ways: 'Would you like to see Joumana Haddad as a member of parliament?' versus 'Are you like Tony Frangieh or like Ali Haydar?'

Yet I believe there is more to this, and it has to do with messaging. Why did the audience overwhelmingly vote against Haydar's main message, that science establishes what truth is and religious dogma contradicts science? Why did the born-again Frangieh's message of eternal joy find such support while Haydar's was stillborn? Why did Abou Hamdan's feedback suggest his message needed more work?

Conclusion

In this chapter, I have argued that the messaging male Lebanese atheists have used in traditional media like television reflects the tenor of the global wave of atheism in the twenty-first century that renders their atheism as an intellectual pursuit, implicitly framing religion as an irrational assumption. By contrast, female Lebanese atheists incorporate an additional affective defence of atheism that finds a more positive reception among the general public. The previously unexplored intersection of gender with the media and the public sphere that this investigation of atheism revealed helps reconceptualise the link between the secular and the public sphere. In particular, I have shown that different media like television and YouTube have a meaningful affective potential, not just an active role in circulating ideas and ideologies.

I also argue that these insights apply to the larger Arabic-speaking world, not just to a society like the Lebanese, typically seen as more liberal than the rest of the Arab world. Consider the following four examples described in the media. When the family of Moroccan student Siham, now an atheist, forced the veil on her at the age of ten, she asked why men did not have to hide their charms as well.[20] The traditional answer that women should not provoke male lust did not satisfy her. Trying to figure out which part of the female body was responsible, she explored her naked body in the mirror. But her family caught her and forced her to swear on the Qur'an that she would never do it again. This set her off on a quest to discover the meaning of life and religion. Years later, Siham's eyes fill with tears when she remembers how she silently gave in to wearing the veil, all the while crying on the inside. Religious TV channels like an-Nas played an important role in the life of another Moroccan woman, Rabab, who also later became an atheist. She was devoted to prayer and other Muslim rituals, owing her religious zeal to popular Islamic televangelist Muhammad Hassan, whom she greatly admired. But one day she heard about something called 'rada' al-kabir' (breastfeeding grown men) and ironically it was Hassan who confirmed that Islam condones it without a trace of embarrassment. 'That started my research into Islam, whereupon I was shocked by its fallacies and glaring contradictions.'[21]

Compare the above two accounts with two male accounts, also from the media. For Jabir – a Saudi man – the road to atheism started with his asking why music is haram (forbidden),[22] while for another man – Syrian YouTuber Kosay Betar – leaving religion began with his asking if non-Muslims can go to heaven. When Kosay was a child, people around him warned him that asking insistently who god was and where he came from was blaspheming. Kosay was intent on understanding his religion, but after years of study in a children's Qur'anic circle and in his religion class in regular school, his faith in Islam was shattered by the answer that even good non-Muslims go to hell:

> After years of reading and thinking, of asking and searching, I found myself forced to reject this silly story. The same story that was once the ultimate truth for me. At age 20, I reached the conclusion that, based on the sources we have today, Muhammad was not a prophet of god, the Qur'an was not written by the creator of the universe and Islam is no doubt a man-made religion.[23]

Siham's and Rabab's stories are common when women in the Arabic-speaking world talk about leaving religion. Logical contradictions in religion certainly stunned Siham and Rabab: however, a painful personal experience of misogyny and an encounter with an idea that demeans women were the keys to their apostasy. Girls often get their first taste of sex-based discrimination inside their own family when religious traditions allow their brothers freedoms prohibited to them and force on them duties their brothers are excused from. Many Muslim girls are powerless to resist their first experience of oppression or injustice, since it is typical that their freedom to choose the clothes they wear or to move around freely is taken from them at the age of 10 or younger. Siham's and Rabab's testimonies above show that even if religion was not based on myth and rife with contradictions, they would probably have left religion because their experience of it violated their rights and freedoms as women. In Rabab's words, 'How can a sane woman believe in a religion that buries her, kills her humanity and makes her men's slave?'[24]

In contrast, Jabir and Kosay frame their departure from religion as an outcome of an intellectual struggle sparked by contradictions in the religious texts, questions religion fails to answer or moral problems not related to them personally. Between March 2020 and April 2021, Kosay posted on his YouTube channel a 20-episode series titled 'Why I left Islam'.[25] Each episode exposes a contradiction or failure: for example, episode 1 is subtitled 'The failure of the story of the Creation', episode 3 'Fallacies and logical contradictions in the Qur'an', episode 4 'The scientific mistakes in the Qur'an', and episode 17 'Islamic superstitions'. Kosay's videos present him as a critical thinker with extraordinary curiosity about truth and the world: 'In this episode, I'll focus just on the problems I discovered in the Creation myth after I began using critical thinking.' In comparison, he paints religion as a set of irrational beliefs, accepted by uncritical thinkers who fail to apply reasonable standards for verification:

> The first step for me to leave Islam was recognising that this Creation myth, which I once thought was the ultimate truth, is just a joke … it is not good enough even to be a story. And I was not surprised that my family, those around them and the whole country still believed in it, because it turns out that, just like me, they were born into this story and believed it without any thinking whatsoever. They did nothing but copy and paste. It sounds like … a story written by ignorant people that lived 1,500 years ago with no real understanding of reality or the world around them, who were raised on myths by people even more ignorant than them albeit with a vivid imagination.[26]

So, can region-specific insights into Arabic-speaking contexts shed light on broader global contexts as well? I believe they can. How does the miscommunication between the typical male atheist story and the general religious audience affect the demands of atheist communities for equal rights, protection and positive visibility? According to one of the founders of cognitive science, George Lakoff (2010), proper messaging is of crucial importance for the success of any social movement or issue. He has demonstrated that we think through frames, that is, in terms of roles and the relationships between those who play these roles. Frames work through the circuitry of the brain, which is connected to the affective regions of the brain. As Lakoff (2010, 72) puts it, 'Without emotion, you would not know what to want, since like and not-like would be meaningless to you. When there is neither like or not-like, nor any judgment of the emotional reactions of others, you cannot make rational decisions.'

Religious communities have spent centuries building systems of frames, and other systems to communicate these frames quickly and parsimoniously. Atheists have not done so yet. Moreover, many in the audiences they address when they appear in the media have strong frames that contradict those of the atheists, or lead audiences to ignore the facts that matter. Just presenting new facts is unlikely to erase old frames. One needs to build background frames, so that audiences can understand the issue and what to do about it. This is a long game and atheists are not coming to a level playing field.

The consequences of the misalignment, then, are serious. That is why I argue that presenting atheism as an intellectual position is appropriate to targeting atheists or atheist-curious individuals, but unless atheists in Arabic-speaking communities and globally incorporate an affective defence of atheism, like the women in my sample, they will find a much steeper road ahead.

Notes

1   Freethought Lebanon, n.d. 'Legal report: Discrimination against atheists in Lebanon.' https://www.youtube.com/watch?v=28FCwXQnT2A (accessed 29 May 2022).
2   Freethought Lebanon, n.d. https://www.youtube.com/watch?v=28FCwXQnT2A (accessed 5 July 2022).
3   Many members of Facebook groups are not publicly visible as atheists or agnostics outside the group.
4   Al Jadeed. https://www.youtube.com/watch?v=v9tS5ZEaaGA (accessed 29 May 2022).
5   Al Jadeed. https://www.youtube.com/watch?v=v9tS5ZEaaGA (accessed 29 May 2022).
6   *Tawasul*, Manar, 2019. https://program.almanar.com.lb/episode/63241 (accessed 29 May 2022).
7   https://www.youtube.com/watch?v=yLOIO8rbwx8 (accessed 29 May 2022).
8   *Tawasul*, Manar, 2019. https://program.almanar.com.lb/episode/63241. See also David Eller's (2004) opposite view, arguing that every child is born an atheist.

9   Joumana Haddad Freedoms Center, 'We are the Lebanon of the future'. https://joumanahaddadfreedoms.org/ (accessed 29 May 2022).

10   The full text can be found at https://www.ahewar.org/debat/show.art.asp?aid=351886 (accessed 29 May 2022).

11   'W intou? with Joumana Haddad – Episode 8 – Faith and Atheism': https://www.youtube.com/watch?v=sJPNLZLFF8o (accessed 7 June 2022); 'W intou? with Joumana Haddad – Episode 4 – The veil': https://www.youtube.com/watch?v=TUoBTm6s4aA (accessed 7 June 2022).

12   Interview with author, Beirut, April 2021.

13   Interview with author, Beirut, May 2021.

14   'W intou? with Joumana Haddad – Episode 8 – Faith and Atheism.'

15   'Ana heyk ma' Nishan – al-katiba Joumana Haddad': https://www.youtube.com/watch?v=kPAKM-rl8Mk (accessed 7 June 2022).

16   For shutting down social media accounts of Arabic-speaking atheists, see Khazaal 2017.

17   https://www.freethoughtlebanon.net/ (accessed 7 June 2022).

18   Interview with author, Beirut, 2019.

19   'Al-mulhidin fi lubnan – Ramiz al-Qadi': https://www.youtube.com/watch?v=tQTqCrV3vZs (accessed 7 June 2022).

20   'Al-ilhad aw hikaya maghribiyya rafadna quyud al-mujtama' w-al-din'. https://tinyurl.com/svunzfu3 (from https://www.hespress.com) (accessed 7 June 2022).

21   'Al-ilhad aw hikaya maghribiyya rafadna quyud al-mujtama' w-al-din'. https://tinyurl.com/svunzfu3 (from https://www.hespress.com) (accessed 4 July 2022).

22   William Bauer, 'Interview with a Saudi atheist', *Your Middle East*, 12 November 2012.

23   'Limadha taraktu al-islam – al-halqat 1 - fashl qissat al-khalq': https://www.youtube.com/watch?v=fZMFZvKPjX4&t=2s (accessed 7 June 2022).

24   'Al-ilhad aw hikaya maghribiyya rafadna quyud al-mujtama' w-al-din.'

25   'Limadha taraktu al-islam – al-halqat 1 - fashl qissat al-khalq.'

26   'Limadha taraktu al-islam – al-halqat 1 - fashl qissat al-khalq.'.

References

Adham, Ismail. 1937. *Limadha Ana Mulhid* (Why I'm an atheist). Alexandria: Matba'at al-Ta'awun.

Al Hariri, Youssef, Walid Magdy and Maria Wolters. 2019. 'Arabs and atheism: Religious discussions in the Arab Twittersphere', in *Social Informatics: 11th International Conference, SocInfo 2019, Doha, Qatar, November 18–21, 2019, Proceedings,* Ingmar Weber, Kareem M. Darwish, Claudia Wagner, Emilio Zagheni, Laura Nelson, Samin Aref and Fabian Flöck, eds, 18–34. Cham: Springer.

Beha, Christopher. 2012. 'Reason for living: The good life without God.' *Harper's Magazine* 325 (1946): 73–8.

Benjamin, Jessica. 1988. *The Bonds of Love: Psychoanalysis, feminism, and the problem of domination*. New York: Pantheon Books.

Blanes, Ruy Llera and Galina Oustinova-Stjepanovic. 2017. 'Godless people, doubt, and atheism', in *Being Godless: Ethnographies of atheism and non-religion*, Ruy Llera Blanes and Galina Oustinova-Stjepanovic, eds, 1–19. New York: Berghahn.

Bosman, Frank. 2019. *Gaming and the Divine: A new systematic theology of video games*. Abingdon: Routledge.

Chodorow, Nancy. 1999. *The Reproduction of Mothering: Psychoanalysis and the sociology of gender*. Berkeley: University of California Press.

Copeman, Jacob and Johannes Quack. 2015. 'Godless people and dead bodies: Materiality and the morality of atheist materialism.' *Social Analysis* 59 (2): 40–61. https://doi.org/10.3167/sa.2015.590203.

Davis, Mark. 1996. *Empathy: A social-psychological approach*. Boulder, CO: Westview Press.

Duile, Timo. 2021. 'Social media in research on a marginalized identity: The case of atheism in Indonesia.' *Österreichische Zeitschrift für Südostasienwissenschaften* 14 (1): 121–8. https://doi.org/10.14764/10.ASEAS-0049.

Eller, David. 2004. *Natural Atheism*. Cranford, NJ: American Atheist Press.

Elsässer, Sebastian. 2021. 'Arab non-believers and freethinkers on YouTube: Re-negotiating intellectual and social boundaries.' *Religions* 12 (2): art. no. 106, 1–18. https://doi.org/10.3390/rel12020106.

Eyadat, Zaid. 2013. 'Fiqh al-Aqalliyyat and the Arab Spring: Modern Islamic theorizing.' *Philosophy and Social Criticism* 39 (8): 733–53. https://doi.org/10.1177/0191453713494970.

Haddad, Joumana. 2013. 'Limadha Ana Mulhida' ('Why I'm an atheist'). *An-Nahar*, 23 March.

Haddad, Joumana. 2014. *Superman 'Arabi: Limadha Ana Mulhida* (Why I'm an atheist). Beirut: Dar al-Saqi.

Harakeh, Sarah, Ayat A. and Sami Abdallah. 2021. 'Atheists in Lebanon: Human rights violations report. Case studies.' Beirut: Freethought Lebanon.

Kashima, Yoshihisa, S. Yamaguchi, U. Kim, S.-C. Choi, M. J. Gelfand and M. Yuki. 1995. 'Culture, gender, and self: A perspective from individualism-collectivism research.' *Journal of Personality and Social Psychology* 69 (5): 925–37. https://doi.org/10.1037/0022-3514.69.5.925.

Kettell, Steven. 2013. 'Faithless: The politics of new atheism.' *Secularism and Nonreligion* 2: 61–72. http://doi.org/10.5334/snr.al.

Khazaal, Natalie. 2017. 'The cultural politics of religious defiance in Islam: How pseudonyms and media can destigmatize.' *Communication and Critical/Cultural Studies* 14 (3): 271–87. https://doi.org/10.1080/14791420.2017.1296170.

Khazaal, Natalie, Moustapha Itani and Sami Abdallah. 2022. 'Political bias against atheists: Talk shows targeting Arabic speaking audiences.' *Religions* 13 (7).

Knott, Kim, Elizabeth Poole and Teemu Taira. 2013. *Media Portrayals of Religion and the Secular Sacred*. Abingdon and New York: Routledge.

Lakoff, George. 2010. 'Why it matters how we frame the environment.' *Environmental Communication* 4 (1): 70–81. https://doi.org/10.1080/17524030903529749.

LeDrew, Stephen. 2012. 'The evolution of atheism: Scientific and humanistic approaches.' *History of the Human Sciences* 25 (3): 70–87. https://doi.org/10.1177/0952695112441301.

Lee, Lois. 2017. 'Vehicles of new atheism: The atheist bus campaign, non-religious representations and material culture', in *New Atheism: Critical perspectives and contemporary debates*, Christopher Cotter, Philip Quadrio and Jonathan Tuckett, eds, 69–86. Cham: Springer.

Luehrmann, Sonja. 2011. *Secularism Soviet Style: Teaching atheism and religion in a Volga republic*. Bloomington: Indiana University Press.

Luehrmann, Sonja. 2015. *Religion in Secular Archives: Soviet atheism and historical knowledge*. New York: Oxford University Press.

Lundmark, Evelina and Stephen LeDrew. 2019. 'Unorganized atheism and the secular movement: Reddit as a site for studying "lived atheism".' *Social Compass* 66 (1): 112–29. https://doi.org/10.1177/0037768618816096.

Maccoby, Eleanor. 1998. *The Two Sexes: Growing up apart, coming together*. Cambridge, MA: Belknap Press of Harvard University Press.

Miller, Jean. 1986. *Toward a New Psychology of Women*, 2nd edn. Boston, MA: Beacon Press.

Nash, David. 1995. 'Blasphemy in Victorian Britain? Foote and the freethinker.' *History Today* 45 (10): 13–19.

Rashid, Radzuwan Ab and Azweed Mohamad. 2019. *New Media Narratives and Cultural Influence in Malaysia: The strategic construction of blog rhetoric by an apostate*. Singapore: Springer.

Schielke, Samuli. 2012. 'Being a nonbeliever in the time of Islamic revival: Trajectories of doubt and certainty in contemporary Egypt.' *International Journal of Middle East Studies* 44 (2): 301–20. https://doi.org/10.1017/S0020743812000062.

Smith, Christopher and Richard Cimino. 2012. 'Atheisms unbound: The role of the new media in the formation of a secularist identity.' *Secularism & Nonreligion* 1: 17–31. http://doi.org/10.5334/snr.ab.

Strauss, Claudia. 2004. 'Is empathy gendered and, if so, why? An approach from feminist psychological anthropology.' *Ethos* 32 (4): 432–57. https://doi.org/10.1525/eth.2004.32.4.432.

Taira, Teemu. 2012. 'New atheism as identity politics', in *Religion and Knowledge: Sociological perspectives*, Mathew Guest and Elisabeth Arweck, eds, 97–114. Farnham: Ashgate.

Tremlett, Paul-François and Fang-Long Shih. 2017. 'Forget Dawkins: Notes toward a social ethnography of religious belief and doubt.' *Social Analysis* 59 (2): 81–96. https://doi.org/10.3167/sa.2015.590205.

van der Veen, A. Maurits and Erik Bleich. 2021. 'Atheism in US and UK newspapers: Negativity about non-belief and non-believers.' *Religions* 12 (5): 291–311. https://doi.org/10.3390/rel12050291.

Zenk, Thomas. 2012. '"Neuer Atheismus": "New Atheism" in Germany.' *Approaching Religion* 2 (1): 36–51. https://doi.org/10.30664/ar.67490.

II

Mediated scepticism: historical and contemporary trajectories

6

'Apostates': a new secularising public in the United Kingdom

John Hagström

In this chapter, I argue that self-described 'apostates' have become an influential public whose impact has led to broad shifts in the sensibilities and practices of non-religious individuals and organisations in the United Kingdom. As national rates of disbelief and non-religiosity have increased, the need for a legitimising atheist politics of visibility has decreased. The relative ease with which many people can arrive at explicit and public non-religious identities and labels is substantiated by both social survey reports and anthropological studies. As a result of the gradual absence of obstacles to disbelief, however, the need for an *apostate* politics of visibility has increased, since the experiences of those for whom leaving religion is a tumultuous process marred by hardships and upheavals ('apostates') have been obscured. This chapter is informed by ethnographic research on atheist and humanist refugees, apostate spokespersons and awareness organisations, and their impact on non-religious groups. I also describe and analyse relevant portable media forms and content on a digital education platform.

Apostasy and asylum

Conway Hall, a renowned centre of ethical culture, freethought and humanism, is located a convenient 15-minute walk from King's Cross railway station in London. As members or patrons, anthropologists frequented Conway Hall throughout the discipline's history in the twentieth century. For instance, A. C. Haddon gave the Conway Memorial Lecture in 1921 and Edmund Leach in 1972 (during his presidency of the British Humanist Association; the organisation was renamed Humanists UK in 2017), followed by Ernest Gellner in 1974. Since at least the early 2010s, however, anthropologists have been turning up in growing numbers, not necessarily as supporters or contributors but as researchers who study atheism, humanism and other varieties of non-religion. For the expanding range of students as well as junior and senior anthropologists with such research aims in the United Kingdom – not to mention those working in closely related social sciences – Conway Hall is something of an obligatory port of call even if one's research is not situated in London, given its bustling schedule of relevant talks, discussions and socials. A significant number of humanist interlocutors whom I first met in cities like Liverpool, Manchester and Edinburgh had visited Conway Hall to attend this or that notable event. The spokespersons and officers of Humanists UK[1] – as distinct from the dozen or so affiliated but 'local' humanist groups in the Greater London area – hold the majority of their events at Conway Hall, attracting visitors not just from humanist groups in London and beyond but also from the wider bricolage of the city's atheist, sceptic and freethought scene.

A few months into my fieldwork in early 2019, I attended an evening panel discussion at Conway Hall titled 'Apostasy and asylum'. It was organised by Faith to Faithless, an apostasy awareness and support organisation founded by two ex-Muslim atheists in 2015 and incorporated into Humanists UK in 2017. In keeping with the norm for this type of event, the panel was hosted in the Brockway Room. In a conference space large enough to seat nearly 80 people, less than half the chairs were full that evening. Humanists International's red retractable cassette banner contrasted with the uniformly white walls of the room.[2] A slanted skylight – one of the Brockway Room's selling points as a venue for hire – spanned the perimeter of the ceiling. I knew the invited speakers, having met them on previous occasions. As the result of a thorough networking effort, I also knew most of the three dozen audience members in attendance. I had long since, and on numerous occasions, obtained permission to place a digital voice recorder on the front table during events like this one, but as a matter of courtesy – and for a bit of small talk, since I arrived early – I repeated the process, before taking a seat with the rest of the audience.

The panel comprised four invited speakers. The first to be introduced was Hamza bin Walayat, a humanist from Pakistan who was infamously denied asylum in 2017 on the basis of his inability to identify Plato and Aristotle as signal contributors to 'humanist' thought. In response, non-religious and secularist organisations mobilised to recriminate against the Home Office, the ministerial department responsible for immigration. A published letter of support signed by 120 philosophers and academics declared, 'There is no scholarly basis to think that Plato and Aristotle were humanist thinkers' (Sherwood 2018). This debacle, in conjunction with media attention to related cases unfolding elsewhere at the time, contributed to the establishment of the topic of apostasy and the predicaments of apostate refugees as novel concerns for atheist, humanist and other non-religious groups and movements in the United Kingdom. Hamza has become a singularly well-known humanist refugee *cause célèbre*, and the legal implications of his case were already the subject of academic inquiry by the time I started my own fieldwork (e.g., Nixon 2018). Also on the panel was Rasel,[3] a Bangladeshi atheist, LGBTIQ+ activist and writer who was in the process of applying for asylum, and Maria, an immigration solicitor with over a decade's worth of experience of assisting non-religious asylum seekers. The fourth invited panellist, a Home Office agent involved in the training of asylum assessors, was unexpectedly absent. Amelia, one of Humanists UK's campaigns officers, started the discussion with an introductory talk, striking a confident tone despite the somewhat sparse attendance:

> We set ourselves three big campaigning aims as part of our 'Save Hamza' campaign. The first of those was to overturn his refusal decision. The second was to ensure new training is introduced for all asylum assessors so that they are fully conversant with non-religious beliefs – what humanism or atheism means and how you interview claimants on those grounds. And thirdly, it needed to be made crystal-clear in all training that non-religious claimants should be given equal treatment to religious claimants and religious converts, since there seems to be a huge disparity of treatment. ... The non-religious were just not included in the Home Office's thinking at all. It was as if a whole group of people did not exist and their beliefs didn't count. Those were our three main aims that we set ourselves in January of 2018 and as of last week we have now achieved all three of them.

Humanists UK's monthly newsletter had been issued the week before the Conway Hall panel and its headline read: 'Our members helped save Hamza's life!' Andrew Copson, chief executive of the organisation and one of its most prolific spokespersons, shared an additional – and every bit as celebratory – e-mail, largely restating the newsletter's message:

Last year, we brought national attention to the plight of humanist asylum seeker Hamza bin Walayat, who was told by the Home Office that he would be deported to Pakistan, where humanists can be executed, on the grounds that he couldn't identify Plato and Aristotle. It was an absurd and barbaric decision. Thousands of you agreed. Over 12,000 people like you signed a petition to the Home Secretary. … Hamza's fresh claim for asylum has just been granted. … It is all thanks to supporters like you. This shows the power of our work together – changing Home Office policies on asylum. Saving lives.

Ever since Humanists UK began providing Hamza with support in 2017, there had been regular updates on his case in the monthly newsletter. But, significantly, since early 2018 the newsletter has featured at least one article on the subject of apostasy – unrelated to Hamza's case – nearly every month. The specific topics have included an update on Humanists UK's efforts to contribute to proposed changes to the Domestic Abuse Bill in mid-2019 in order to call attention to 'domestic abuse against apostates'. The headline of that issue read: 'Humanists UK and Faith to Faithless to call for stronger laws to protect apostates'. Another newsletter featured an interview with Ste Richardsson, an ex-Jehovah's Witness and vice chair of Faith to Faithless. He described the organisation's ongoing work to 'support apostates on a personal and emotional basis', and he also mentioned the need to 'identify and tackle the systemic societal issues that lead to apostates slipping through the cracks' (Richardsson 2019).

By calling attention to 'seemingly mundane media products such as … monthly newsletters', I take a cue from Omri Elisha's emphasis on how their 'material and social functionality is a big part of the *story* they tell' (2016, 1064, my emphasis); in the case of her research, the stories are about persecuted Christians in non-Western contexts. But, more specifically, I describe these newsletters here in order to attend, following Ashley Lebner, to 'published/public texts (scholarly, political, etc.), because secular *concepts* … have most clearly developed therein' (2019, 129, my emphasis). And rather than stories, it is precisely the concept of 'apostasy' and its related forms (e.g., 'apostate,' 'apostatise') that these newsletters popularise and promote. Connectedly, all the speakers on the Conway Hall panel used the words 'apostasy' and 'apostate' – and they did so unhesitatingly, without pausing to expound on definitions or meanings. This might seem like a trivial observation, but my aim is to underscore the regularity of these concepts, that is, to highlight the significant extent to which they are discursively well established. Amelia described an ongoing effort to 'build a network of stakeholders – lawyers, academics and supporters – who are able to provide the assistance we need, equivalent to what – if you were a Christian convert – you could expect from your church. … We are raising awareness and building a network to rally round apostates.' As mentioned, by the time of this 2019 discussion, two years had passed since the debacle surrounding Hamza's case, and in that time these concepts and terms had entered the mainstream. Below, I include examples of contexts where they still find explicit definition and elaboration.

At the discussion, Rasel described social and political hardships facing secular, liberal and LGBTIQ+ minorities in Bangladesh. In key respects, he fitted the mould of the 'Bangladeshi atheist blogger', an iconic figure known to humanist and other non-religious audiences throughout the West in part because of intensive media coverage of the murders of activists, writers and publishers, such as Ahmed Rajib Haider, Avijit Roy, Ananta Bijoy Das, Niloy Chatterjee and Faisal Arefin Dipan, between 2013 and 2016 (see Schulz 2021 for a critical assessment of Euro-American press coverage of these killings and related attacks). In the course of my fieldwork, I met scores of humanist interlocutors who were familiar with the 'atheist bloggers' in Bangladesh, a metonym regularly used in lieu of the names of specific individuals. In contrast, while Hamza spoke briefly about laws, religion and conservative social mores in Pakistan, he spent more time giving a personal account of his gradual – and often traumatic – route to disbelief and humanism. Critically, the substance of what Rasel and Hamza had to say about their countries of origin resonated quite strongly with the content of reports by the United Nations Human Rights Council (e.g., United Nations 2017, 2014) and Humanists International's own Freedom of Thought Report (e.g., 2018, 2017a). These are reports that international humanist organisations have either publicised or called attention to for nearly a decade. In 2017, Dr Ahmed Shaheed, the UN Special Rapporteur on Freedom of Religion or Belief – speaking at a Humanists International conference – restated what nearly all of his predecessors had said when he claimed, 'in my observations, humanists – when they are attacked – they are attacked far more viciously and brutally than I think in other cases' (Humanists International 2017b; McAdam 2018). What distinguished the Conway Hall panel discussion – and other events like it in 2019, and more recent occasions, for instance Humanists UK's first Apostasy Conference in 2021 – is that persecuted non-religious people are now present and visible, speaking directly to allied and sympathetic audiences. It is this presence that partly accounts for the considerable extent to which – from 2017 – the plight of maltreated atheists and humanists both abroad and in the United Kingdom has become a central organisational concern of Humanists UK. Two months after the panel discussion at Conway Hall, Hamza spoke on a different stage: the 2019 Humanists UK Conference, held in Leicester. There he was elected to the organisation's board of trustees.

A different kind of secularising public

In this chapter, I argue that apostates constitute a novel secularising public that has been a key driver behind several widely felt shifts in the campaigns, practices and sensibilities of non-religious individuals and groups in the United Kingdom. My analysis here is primarily fixed on organised humanism in urban contexts throughout England; however, I also allude to the more far-reaching ramifications of these shifts. Lebner has argued that 'secularisation' is an undeservedly neglected concept in the anthropology of secularism (2019, 127), and to resolve this impasse she recommends that analysts depart from the concept's prevailing connotations, such as state secularism, structural differentiation and the government regulation of politics and religion: 'I contend that, historically, new conceptual-practical distinctions from religion – secularizing practices – were first developed and engaged with prior to and beyond the state' (p. 126). In other words, Lebner suggests that researchers foreground the multiple and chequered attempts of individuals, groups, movements and publics to establish 'conceptual-cum-practical domain[s] distinguished from religion'. She gives two examples of secularising publics. The first is historical: in nineteenth-century Brazil, 'Enlightenment ideas gained influence with the Brazilian elite, especially the positivist writings of Auguste Comte. [...] This call for science, order, and progress motivated Brazilian elites to agitate against the church's claim on power and knowledge as they vied for a Republic' (p. 132). The second example, set in the present day, is the Landless Workers' Movement (MST), a Marxist agrarian movement and a focus of Lebner's fieldwork in Brazil.

In order to delineate my argument, I want to underscore that Lebner places descriptive emphasis on how these two publics target religion. In other words, they are depicted as outward-oriented: the nineteenth-century positivists agitated 'for an autonomous political domain *distinct from religion*', while the Marxists claim the ability to 'know and transform reality, a reality *not reliant on God*', and promote a pedagogy that 'focuses on the development of autonomous human consciousness, *distinct from the divine*' (pp. 132, 139, my emphases). The activities of these two publics exemplify the tenuous establishment of contestable 'difference[s] between religion and the secular' (p. 142). I take Lebner's approach in a different direction here by shifting attention to a public that is primarily inward-oriented, less concerned with distinctions between religion and the secular than with the betterment of an existing secular domain.[4] In their capacity as a secularising public, apostates direct their efforts mainly at audiences that are already atheist, humanist or non-religious, and at a wider society that is understood to be secular, yet which exhibits 'systemic societal issues that lead to apostates slipping through the cracks', as the vice chair of Faith to Faithless put it (Richardsson 2019).

The 2019 British Social Attitudes Survey, published by the National Centre for Social Research, estimated that 52 per cent of adults in Britain have 'no religion', a number that is expected to increase since, on average, '[t]wo non-religious parents successfully transmit their lack of religion. Two religious parents have a 50/50 chance of passing on the faith. ... To borrow the terminology of radioactive decay, institutional religion in Britain now has a half-life of one generation' (Voas and Bruce 2019, 21). Unsurprisingly, Humanists UK capitalised on this report and produced shareable graphics that amplify key points from the survey (e.g., Humanists UK 2019). There is one significant fact that the organisation did not call attention to, however, and it concerns the nature of the 52 per cent: '[M]ost were simply not brought up with a religion, with a smaller minority having lost a childhood faith' (Voas and Bruce 2019, 18). In other words, large numbers of non-religious people in Britain have paid no cost – or a relatively low social cost – for leaving their former religion. For such individuals, the type of atheist politics of visibility that Eric Chalfant describes in the first part of his contribution to this volume is not required, although there exist several historical parallels in the United Kingdom. My research indicates that, in part because of this general absence of obstacles to disbelief, a specifically *apostate* politics of visibility has become necessary. In their capacity as a secularising public, apostates call attention to and publicise the kinds of experiences, ambiguities and hardships that 'closeted' atheists, including ex-Jews (e.g., Fader 2017, 2020), ex-Muslims (e.g., Cottee 2015) and ex-Mormons (e.g., Brooks 2018), discuss in anonymous digital spaces (as Chalfant describes in the second part of his chapter). At stake here is not a call for such individuals to 'come out' en masse. The efforts of this public are intended to educate comparatively fortunate non-religious peers, so that they can understand the upheavals and costs attached to the disclosure of disbelief, with the aim of building capabilities for solidarity and support, both within non-religious movements and in society at large.

If apostate spokespersons and awareness organisations comprise an inward-oriented secularising public that is more concerned with the ameliorative improvement of secular knowledges than with the targeting of religious premises, there is still a key sense in which they are defined by a 'negative relation' to religion, to echo Matthew Engelke's remarks on a common analytical approach to secular and non-religious phenomena: 'when we highlight the quality of secularity, what we are highlighting is another kind of negation: a not-religiousness. So often … to be secular is to be not religious' (2019, 203).[5] While it is not possible to theorise apostasy without recognising it as a kind of 'not-religiousness', in this chapter I emphasise the ways in which apostates shed light on the matter of forming *positive* relations to *non-religion*, which for many of them is a protracted and traumatic process. In other words, apostates – as a secularising public – not only aim to disseminate sympathetic understandings of the difficulties involved in leaving religion behind, they also call attention to the problem of non-existent or inadequate secular communities of support.

The normalisation and 'realisation' of apostasy

In mid-2019, Humanists UK launched a Massive Open Online Course (MOOC) on the digital education platform FutureLearn. The course, titled 'Humanist lives', is designed to run for six consecutive weeks, each week featuring between five and seven thematic segments comprising short videos and texts, and accompanied by question prompts for attendees to discuss. The introductory course overview states: 'On this course you'll meet individual humanists from around the world. From their stories, you'll learn what motivates them, and how they express their humanism. You'll learn about the questions, choices, challenges, and joys found in a humanist approach to life' (FutureLearn 2021). This is perhaps an optimistic summary for a course that deals with a number of arguably difficult topics, as expressed by some of the thematic headings, such as 'Leaving religion, losing community' and 'Humanists in danger', the first of which I give particular attention here. 'Leaving religion, losing community' contains an introduction to Faith to Faithless, which is described as 'a programme of Humanists UK working to reduce the stigma faced by people leaving religion (apostates)'. Aliyah Saleem and Imtiaz Shams, the two co-founders, are featured in a short video in which they interweave personal accounts of apostatising from Islam with descriptions of the organisation's activities: 'It raises awareness about the prejudice and discrimination that they [apostates] face. It offers training and it also creates social groups or social events that people can go to so they can meet like-minded individuals who are going through very similar experiences to them', Aliyah says, before she relates these activities to her own background:

> I grew up in a traditional Muslim family and I went to religious schools, so I had a thorough religious education – an Islamic one. And then as I reached towards my twenties, I started to have doubts. At first, I was, I would suppose – I felt very anxious about my doubt. I felt like I was doing something very wrong, so I felt very guilty and ashamed to speak to other people about it, so, I thought, I made myself quite isolated. … And then when people around me did find out – so, when friends found out, I lost a lot of my Muslim friends, which was very difficult for me. And my family found out as well. And, you know, it didn't go down well. So, it was difficult and it's taken a lot of time, a lot of support from people around me, a lot of healing to get to a place where I'm quite comfortable and happy with myself and my beliefs.

Aliyah's experiences are not uncommon, as studies of ex-Muslims attest (e.g., Cottee 2015), while research on disaffiliates from other religious groups (e.g. ex-Mormons, Brooks 2020) likewise demonstrates that there exist significant experiential overlaps. Indeed, towards the end of an autobiographical text not featured in the MOOC, Aliyah reflects on her work with Faith to Faithless and calls attention to shared experiences of hardship, upheaval and loneliness:

> We work with apostates, people who have left religions and cults, from all backgrounds, not only people who have left Islam. This experience has taught me that the discrimination which affects ex-Muslims also affects people from other groups such as in the case of former Jehovah's Witnesses who can face excommunication and shunning. Last year I visited Plymouth Humanists and a woman cried during my talk. I spoke to her later and she had left a Christian denomination and had lost her family and friends because of it. She spoke about how lonely she has felt and that she was glad to have met someone who understood what she was dealing with.
>
> (Saleem 2018, 59)

This excerpt is telling, since it is implied that the ex-Christian she met was a member of the humanist group in Plymouth, which suggests, even if it is not Aliyah's intention to make this point, a lack of understanding of apostasy by non-religious peers. In a different part of the MOOC video, Shams describes the organisation's apostasy-awareness efforts directed at social institutions: 'We will train the police, we'll train the NHS [National Health Service], in how to properly recognise apostasy, how to help apostates better, and how to make sure that we are taken care of properly, like anyone else going through their institutions.' This training does not only target institutions, however. The other main target audience is members of non-religious groups and movements, as I demonstrate in the next section. Shams concludes the video by describing his hopes for the organisation's work: 'I really think, and I really believe, that in the next couple of years, apostasy will become much more understood as a normalised form of discrimination, rather than, right now, where no one even knows what we go through.' In the discussion section below Aliyah and Shams's video, an attendee named David R. Freke[6] expressed a kind of recognition – or realisation – that bore a strong resemblance to statements made by my humanist interlocutors, some of whom had taken the course during my fieldwork: 'I feel fortunate in that I don't have to face the issues faced by leavers of full-on sects/faith, and am sympathetic to their situations.'

In Engelke's research on British humanists – based on fieldwork he carried out in 2010–11, several years before apostasy became a major concern for Humanists UK – he labels some of his interlocutors 'realization humanists' (e.g., 2014, 297). The label refers to individuals who, through a variety of trajectories, came to understand – to 'realise' – that there exists a label ('humanist') for ideas and values that they held before ever hearing the word: '[they] only recognize[d] themselves as humanists after reading about it or talking to someone else who is' (p. 296). It is important to note that the realisation narratives described by Engelke are sometimes lackadaisical, occasionally enthusiastic, and always light-hearted in nature: 'It's nice to have found a label', as one humanist put it, while another recalled the day on which a friend suggested that she might in fact be a humanist (p. 296). He adds that 'this particular framing is not the only one in play' and becoming a humanist can of course involve a great deal more than this. But it is this type of 'realisation' that underscores the need for an apostate politics of visibility. To 'stumble' across a label and recognise that one holds the values attached to it is an experience that is strikingly different from the stories recounted in studies of apostasy; Aliyah's own story, while brief, is a case in point. For many apostates, the gradual and tumultuous process of becoming aware that it is even possible to be 'not religious' – an awareness or recognition that is still worlds away from an explicit self-identification as 'atheist' or 'humanist' – is marred by social, moral and cosmological upheavals. As a secularising public, apostate spokespersons have aimed to compel their non-religious peers to have a different kind of 'realisation' from the type Engelke identified: a realisation of one's comparative ease of access to non-religious affordances and public labels, and the concomitant realisation that capabilities for understanding, solidarity and support are required.

Awareness, education and the 'apostate' label

I first visited Liverpool to attend a roving training course given by Faith to Faithless, titled 'Apostasy awareness and safeguarding training'. I had already attended one of these sessions in Sheffield some weeks before. The local Liverpool humanist group and the University of Liverpool humanist society co-hosted the meeting, enabling the use of a spacious conference room on the second floor of the university's Guild of Students complex. The iconic circular Liverpool Metropolitan Cathedral, located not quite directly across the street, was visible through the windows. In contrast to the digital newsletters and the MOOC I described above, where the frequent use of apostasy and related terms was rarely unpacked in any comprehensive manner, the training sessions provided by Faith to Faithless are sites of more in-depth conceptual explication. 'It's an old-fashioned word, one that we're sort of trying to reclaim,' said Asma Salehi, the course instructor. Asma was an ex-Muslim atheist and humanist in her mid-thirties, born in London into a devout Sunni Muslim immigrant family from Pakistan. She apostatised from Islam in her late teens and had been a key member of Faith to Faithless since the organisation was founded in 2015. We were given course trainee handbooks, the first page of which read: 'The term apostasy is derived from the ancient Greek word (apostátis), meaning rebellious.' Asma did not read at length from the handbook, however. She knew that the course participants in Liverpool were humanists and that the group included two apostate refugees (one from Afghanistan and one from Iran, both men). It was also her first time teaching the course, as she would later tell me. In contrast, the Sheffield session was attended by a mixed group that included teachers and charity workers, and a smaller number of humanists. In Sheffield, the instructor read directly from the definition given in the handbook:

> Apostasy is the disaffiliation from, or renunciation of, a religion or cult. This applies to someone who leaves a religion to join another religion (or who leaves one sect to join another), or someone who has

gone from following a religion to expressing a lack of belief in any religious tenet. The term 'apostate' may be used by religious groups as a derogatory label to identify someone perceived as no longer following the traditions of that religion or cult to their expected standard. The term may also be used as an insult or admonishment, even if the individual does not self-identify with the label.

The course participants at the two different sessions I attended – one in Liverpool and the other in Sheffield – exemplify two main audiences that Faith to Faithless is trying to influence. As the organisation's website puts it, echoing the description given by Shams in the MOOC video, the apostasy awareness course is intended to benefit '[l]ocal authorities, [p]olice, social services, NHS workers, homeless shelters, teachers, university staff and charities' (Faith to Faithless 2021). Printed and digital advertisements for the course almost always include the following review: 'The Faith to Faithless training event was some of the best training I have ever received, in 29 years of service', attributed to an anonymous 'Constable Detective, London Metropolitan Police' (Faith to Faithless 2021). But the impact that Faith to Faithless has on, for example, legal and medical domains has been beyond the scope of my research. Although I briefly reference the Sheffield session here for the purpose of contrastive description, my concentrated research focus has been on the other – smaller and more manageable from a research standpoint – target group that Faith to Faithless is attempting to impact: non-religious people and groups in the United Kingdom. The course participants at the Liverpool session were part of that landscape.

Asma did not have to 'start from scratch', as the instructor in Sheffield did. There existed an undeclared background of common knowledge. As I mentioned, the humanist group in Liverpool included two apostate refugees who were at different stages of applying for asylum. But, to restate one of my earlier points, apostates had become increasingly visible and the topic of apostasy had been receiving concentrated attention for several years at this point. Throughout the course of my fieldwork, it was rare for me to meet anyone in a humanist context who was unfamiliar with at least one key problem or topic, even if this only extended to a cursory familiarity with a *cause célèbre* like Hamza – or in even vaguer terms: the 'humanist from Pakistan who was denied asylum'. For local humanist groups like the one in Liverpool – or the group in Manchester, where Hamza was based – Faith to Faithless provide experienced and authoritative guides who can educate the wider membership of a group or help it expand its accumulated knowledge.

The definition of apostasy provided in the course handbook, parts of which were read aloud by the instructor in Sheffield, does not comprehensively represent the use of the apostate label in my research context. For instance, it does not express what Asma meant when she spoke of 'reclaiming' the label. Her view – a widespread view, as I discovered in the course of my fieldwork – is that the label is used, or ought to be used, in the service of subversion and normalisation, and to raise awareness. This view maps closely onto the terminological approach that Simon Cottee selected for his study of ex-Muslims in Britain:

> It does not use insipid or opaque sociological terms like 'exiter', 'disaffiliate' or 'leave-taker', opting instead for the term 'apostate'. This is primarily because 'apostate' is the more readily understandable term and conveys not merely loss of faith, but its active rejection. I recognize of course that the term may carry a negative connotation, but this depends entirely on how it is used. Indeed many ex-Muslims I have met and interviewed referred to themselves as 'apostates'. Their objection wasn't to the term itself, but to the moral condemnation of their apostasy by others, especially loved ones.
>
> (2015, 9–10)

This use of the apostate label coheres with Marshall Brooks's study of ex-Mormons in the United States, and is evocative of the sensibilities he found among his interlocutors:

> Normalizing, and even embracing the term apostate, has thus become among some newly nonreligious people an effective strategy for combatting and overturning the negative stigmas attached to it. Invoking the literal definition of apostate as someone who rejects religion yet otherwise stays 'normal' has enabled the term to be appropriated as a 'badge of honor' to be worn proudly by many ex-Mormons aiming to make their rejection of religious dogma an identity to rally under.
>
> (2018, 179–80)

Brooks writes that the apostate label is 'harnessed as a basis of struggle, effectively creating a foundation of temporary solidarity on which social action can occur' (p. 181), an assessment that is portable enough to apply quite well to the use of the label in my own research context. But there are also a number of striking differences that, when properly highlighted, shed additional expository light on the distinctiveness of apostates as a secularising public in the United Kingdom. Cottee's study contains thorough descriptions of how ex-Muslims engage anonymously with online self-help communities, sites on which descriptors like 'ex-Muslim' and 'apostate' are popularised. Likewise, Brooks examines at greater length those forms of organised sociality, both digital and physical, that ex-Mormon apostates engage in for self-help and community. Faith to Faithless and its allies are similarly engaged in the provision of such forms of support, guidance and sociality for apostates, but their efforts extend in equal measure to the education of secular others: atheists, humanists and other non-religious people who have experienced fewer difficulties, or no difficulties at all, in embracing these labels and self-understandings.

It is conceivable, and perhaps even likely, that apostate spokespersons like ex-Muslim Aliyah Saleem, ex-Jehovah's Witness Ste Richardsson, ex-Christian Audrey Simmons and ex-Jew Izzy Posen have contributed to advancing existing critiques of the multiple religious traditions and groups that they indirectly target by publicising their experiences and by calling attention to apostasy.[7] Although such a research focus would not be unmerited, I argue that it would obscure their more significant impact. As an inward-oriented secularising public, apostates have been more consequential in their educational outreach efforts and in building capabilities for support. In other words, one would be ill advised to focus on what apostates bring to the table in terms of enabling new kinds of criticisms of religion. It is 'apostasy' itself, for itself, that is their primary focus, as a concept that ought to be entered into an existing secular vocabulary. I expand on this point by recourse to a brief example before moving on to the conclusion of this chapter.

The word 'cult' is mentioned in the trainee course handbook, Shams used it in the MOOC video, and Aliyah used it in her writing, but it was not otherwise a common term in my research context. 'High-control religion', however, was a ubiquitous concept. As I understand it, on the basis of my encounters with its use, it is a catch-all term intended to evoke the high degree of social encapsulation associated with a 'cult' while including mainstream religious traditions to which that label is not typically appended, such as Islam. Rather than a definition of this term, however, the handbook presented 15 examples of experiences that fall under the intended use of the concept. In Liverpool, Asma asked us to break into groups of three and consider the list:

From a young age, my sister and I were made to wear very modest clothing whenever we went out in public. My mother insulted me and hit me when I said I didn't like the clothes.

I was not allowed to touch any men other than close family members – not even a handshake.

I wanted to go to college and university, but my parents forbade it because they wanted me to focus on my religious studies.

I only had close friends from within my religious community and wasn't allowed to socialise with any non-believers.

In religious education lessons we were taught that contraception was morally wrong and a sin, and that we would go to hell if we used it.

When I broke a church rule, my parents locked me in my bedroom for a whole weekend and told me to pray for forgiveness.

I wasn't allowed to play with any of the children from my school because my parents didn't want me to mix with people outside our religion.

When I came out as gay, my family took me to gay conversion therapy.

We were constantly told not to trust people from outside our faith, as their thoughts were guided by Satan and they didn't know the truth.

When I was a little girl my family arranged for me to undergo 'female circumcision'. My genitals were mutilated and it was only later that I found out that I won't be able to enjoy sex when I'm older.

My parents didn't allow us to use the internet or go to the local library, because they were worried about what we would learn.

As a teenager I was forced to take part in fasts, even when I didn't want to.

When I was on my period, I wasn't allowed to touch any men, including my husband. They said I was impure at those times.

When my brother left the religion, we were required to treat him as if he had died. We carried out the formal mourning ritual for him.

At eighteen I ran away from home in the middle of the night. I am fourth-generation British, but I didn't speak any English or have any meaningful education to speak of outside of my religious community.

Two main elements characterise the majority of these examples: they implicitly refer to practices belonging to specific religious traditions or groups but do not explicitly name any, and they foreground experiences of suffering. I want to underscore the emphasis at stake in these examples: the hardships of apostates. At none of the training sessions I attended was the focus of attendees ever directed to a more distinctly critical register evocative of common objections to specific religions. To be sure, there are attendees who might use their newfound knowledge of apostasy to entrench and fortify their existing qualms about 'religion' at large, or a specific religious tradition in particular. But efforts by Faith to Faithless course instructors and other apostate spokespersons to educate atheists, humanists and other non-religious people about the kinds of experiences that apostates go through should not be written off as a veiled conduit for critique. Strikingly, the educational aim at stake here recurs in studies of apostasy. For instance, Brooks, a medical anthropologist, has leveraged the findings of his research on ex-Mormons in the United States to call for 'greater competency in matters of religious disenchantment', since existing guidelines risk rendering clinicians 'grossly unprepared to ... treat former believers seeking help, thus contributing to new forms of misdiagnosis and perpetuating the lack of support for those leaving such all-encompassing faith traditions' (2020, 208). Although his academic background probably helped him reach these conclusions, they are also assessments he arrived at as a result of acquiring fieldwork-based insights about a prevailing lack of understanding of the forms of distress and disintegration that are characteristic of detachment from a religious group. In the epilogue to his study of ex-Muslims, Cottee writes that a crucial policy issue is 'how to provide better support for wavering and ex-Muslims in moral jeopardy', and he specifically mentions the need to properly train 'social workers and mental health care professionals not only about the intricacies of the Islamic faith but also the difficulties and dilemmas involved in leaving it' (2015, 212). He advances these suggestions precisely because several of his ex-Muslim interlocutors expressed disappointment at a lack of understanding of apostasy (pp. 164–5).

Conclusion

A number of the contributions to this volume contain descriptions and analyses of how atheist strategies and technologies are enlisted in the service of a politics of visibility. But in Lena Richter's and Natalie Khazaal's chapters, such efforts unfold in national and regional contexts that are marked by a high prevalence of religious sensibilities, institutions and authorities. In the United Kingdom, however, a range of explicit and public non-religious positions and labels – including 'atheist' and 'humanist' – have reached unprecedented levels of social normalisation. As a consequence of how this normalisation has occurred – as a gradual, generational 'decay' of religious identities rather than their abrupt rejection – the experiences of those who leave tightly knit religious communities or religious contexts characterised by high degrees of social encapsulation and pietistic devotion ('apostates') have faded from view, becoming invisible or misunderstood by a secular society and the non-religious movements in it. As a result, since 2017 apostate spokespersons and their organisations have embarked on campaigns that seek to realise a specifically apostate politics of visibility. As a secularising public, such apostates have not only worked to develop and provide forms of community, solidarity and self-help to those who need it, but also aimed to educate non-religious peers: those atheists and humanists who have arrived at their non-religious self-understandings without great difficulty.

Ruy Blanes and Galina Oustinova-Stjepanovic have remarked that 'not every context creates enabling conditions for an unequivocal break away from one's religious tradition' (2015, 3), an observation that apostate self-help groups would probably affirm. I have shown that the presence of highly visible non-religious movements in a society that is reportedly secular can impair rather than provide the enabling conditions required for apostasy. Indeed, non-religious organisations may generate enabling conditions only for those forms of religious detachment that are already familiar, such as the 'realisation' humanist. I should note that apostate spokespersons and awareness groups do not claim to have resolved the situation that Cottee identified: there is still no reliable 'post-apostasy script', no definitive guide for 'knowing what to do in the face of the myriad dilemmas and difficulties which befall the person who renounces' (2015, 173). The difference made by the years separating Cottee's fieldwork and my own is that this observation is now more widely recognised. While Faith to Faithless does not offer a ready-made post-apostasy therapeutics, it does offer space and support for those who share that lack of guides and scripts.

I close this chapter with a few brief remarks on the relationship between an anthropology of non-religion that is no longer 'hypothetical'[8] and a fledgling anthropology of apostasy. The two are no doubt related, and while the latter could be viewed as a specialisation that falls under the broader thematic jurisdiction of the former, I wonder if this emphasis on complementarity risks devaluing the antagonistic potential of an anthropology of apostasy to correct as well as complement its parent field. This corrective potential, and a critical recursion of emic and etic dimensions, can be gleaned from my chapter. I noted how, in Engelke's work, the 'realisation' humanist takes centre stage, shaping our understanding of how people in certain places arrive at or adopt a 'humanist' label. As my research indicates and as studies of apostasy richly demonstrate, however, 'realisation' is a distinctly privileged narrative. This is the same essential problem that apostate spokespersons and awareness organisations are dealing with on the emic level. In other words, one of the reasons apostates are relevant and interesting – to us, as analysts, and as a secularising public – is not their capacity to upset or expand what an 'atheist' or 'humanist' label signifies, but their provocative potential to enrich understanding of the variegated routes and hazardous trajectories that can precede the adoption of such labels.

Notes

1 Humanists UK is the largest charity working on behalf of non-religious people in the United Kingdom: 'We're committed to putting humanism into practice. Through our ceremonies, pastoral support, education services, and campaigning work, we advance free thinking and freedom of choice so everyone can live in a fair and equal society' (Humanists UK 2021).

2 In London, the staff of Humanists UK and Humanists International overlap to a degree, so it was not uncommon to see banners and other promotional materials from the latter at events hosted by the former. Humanists International, formerly the International Humanist and Ethical Union (IHEU), was founded in 1952: 'We are the global representative body of the humanist movement, uniting a diversity of non-religious organisations and individuals. ... We work to build, support and represent the global humanist movement, defending human rights, particularly those of non-religious people, and promoting humanist values world-wide' (Humanists International n.d.).

3 The names in this chapter are pseudonyms, with the exception of well-known and high-profile individuals.

4 Copeman and Hagström (this volume) similarly emphasise the outward-oriented campaigns of Indian rationalist activists: as a secularising public, they target superstitious/supernatural beliefs and practices. I am not suggesting that the MST, or the Indian rationalists – as secularising publics – do not exhibit what I refer to here as 'inward-oriented' dimensions. As a consequence of the specific examples that Lebner uses to dust off the concept of secularisation, however, the religion-facing or 'outward-oriented' aspects of such publics take centre stage. My argument should be considered a complementary expansion of her approach, rather than a critique.

5   Importantly, Engelke goes on to express scepticism about a scholarly insistence on 'the impossibility of the secular as a substantially independent entity' (Scheer, Johansen and Fadil 2019, 3) and he argues – drawing on Abou Farman's work (e.g., 2013, 2020) – that 'we do see secular ontologies and epistemologies emerging on their own terms, putting forward specific combinations of values, emotional sensibilities and affective registers' (2019, 205). I am broadly sympathetic to this approach, and, in a different text, I have sought to contribute to a move beyond a relational view of secularity and non-religion (Hagström and Copeman, forthcoming).

6   FutureLearn allows course attendees to be as anonymous as they wish, but a majority of those who participated in the discussions in this specific course appeared to be using real names, profile pictures and personal biographies.

7   As mentioned in this chapter, Aliyah Saleem is a co-founder of Faith to Faithless and Ste Richardsson is vice chair. Izzy Posen and Audrey Simmons are affiliated with the organisation and have spoken at several events.

8   As Blanes and Oustinova-Stjepanovic put it (2015, 2).

References

Blanes, Ruy and Galina Oustinova-Stjepanovic. 2015. 'Introduction: Godless people, doubt, and atheism.' *Social Analysis* 59 (2): 1–19. https://doi.org/10.2307/j.ctvw048p3.3.

Brooks, E. Marshall. 2018. *Disenchanted Lives: Apostasy and ex-Mormonism among the Latter-day Saints*. New Brunswick, NJ: Rutgers University Press.

Brooks, E. Marshall. 2020. 'The disenchanted self: Anthropological notes on existential distress and ontological insecurity among ex-Mormons in Utah.' *Culture, Medicine, and Psychiatry* 44 (2): 193–213. https://doi.org/10.1007/s11013-019-09646-5.

Cottee, Simon. 2015. *The Apostates: When Muslims leave Islam*. London: Hurst & Company.

Elisha, Omri. 2016. 'Saved by a martyr: Evangelical mediation, sanctification, and the "persecuted church".' *Journal of the American Academy of Religion* 84 (4): 1056–80. https://doi.org/10.1093/jaarel/lfw016.

Engelke, Matthew. 2014. 'Christianity and the anthropology of secular humanism.' *Current Anthropology* 55 (S10): S292–S301. https://doi.org/10.1086/677738.

Engelke, Matthew. 2019. 'Afterword: Getting hold of the secular', in *Secular Bodies, Affects and Emotions: European configurations*, Monique Scheer, Nadia Fadil and Birgitte Schepelern Johansen, eds, 199–207. London: Bloomsbury Academic.

Fader, Ayala. 2017. 'Ultra-Orthodox Jewish interiority, the Internet, and the crisis of faith.' *HAU: Journal of Ethnographic Theory* 7 (1): 185–206. https://doi.org/10.14318/hau7.1.016.

Fader, Ayala. 2020. *Hidden Heretics: Jewish doubt in the digital age*. Princeton, NJ: Princeton University Press.

Faith to Faithless. 2021. 'Safeguarding training.' https://www.faithtofaithless.com/training/ (accessed 8 June 2022).

Farman, Abou. 2013. 'Speculative matter: Secular bodies, minds, and persons.' *Cultural Anthropology* 28 (4): 737–59. https://doi.org/10.1111/cuan.12035.

Farman, Abou. 2020. *On Not Dying: Secular immortality in the age of technoscience*. Minneapolis: University of Minnesota Press.

FutureLearn. 2021. 'Humanist lives, with Alice Roberts.' https://www.futurelearn.com/courses/humanist-lives (accessed 8 June 2022).

Hagström, John and Jacob Copeman. Forthcoming 2023. 'Clarification and disposal as key concepts in the anthropology of non-religion.' *Religion and Society*.

Humanists International. n.d. 'About.' https://humanists.international/about/ (accessed 8 June 2022).

Humanists UK. 2019. 'Latest British Social Attitudes survey shows continuing rise of the non-religious.' 11 July. https://humanists.uk/2019/07/11/latest-british-social-attitudes-survey-shows-continuing-rise-of-the-non-religious/ (accessed 8 June 2022).

Humanists UK. 2021. 'About us.' https://humanists.uk/about/ (accessed 8 June 2022).

International Humanist and Ethical Union. 2017a. *The Freedom of Thought Report 2017: Key countries edition*. https://www.uvh.nl/uvh/nl/up/ZcdbjmuJcD_FOT17_Key_Countries_edition.pdf (accessed 29 August 2022).

International Humanist and Ethical Union. 2017b. 'Tears and joy at IHEU General Assembly 2017.' https://humanists.international/2017/08/tears-joy-iheu-general-assembly-2017/ (accessed 8 June 2022).

International Humanist and Ethical Union. 2018. *The Freedom of Thought Report 2018: Key countries edition.* https://drive.google.com/uc?export=download&id=1ChqeM59-jyB5wE2_72d8XKcTmgyq3MOB (accessed 8 June 2022).

Lebner, Ashley. 2019. 'On secularity: Marxism, reality, and the Messiah in Brazil.' *Journal of the Royal Anthropological Institute* 25 (1): 123–47. https://doi.org/10.1111/1467-9655.13000.

McAdam, Marika. 2018. *Freedom from Religion and Human Rights Law: Strengthening the right to freedom of religion and belief for non-religious and atheist rights-holders.* Abingdon: Routledge.

Nixon, Alan G. 2018. 'The case of non-religious asylum seekers.' *Journal for the Academic Study of Religion* 31 (2): 113–48. https://doi.org/10.1558/jasr.36227.

Richardsson, Ste. 2019. 'Faith to freedom: Ste Richardsson discusses apostasy and humanist peer support.' 4 June. https://humanists.uk/2019/06/04/faith-to-freedom-an-interview-with-ste-richardsson-vice-chair-faith-to-faithless/ (accessed 8 June 2022).

Saleem, Aliyah. 2018. 'Breaking the silence', in *Leaving Faith Behind: The journeys and perspectives of people who have chosen to leave Islam,* Fiyaz Mughal and Aliyah Saleem, eds, 38–60. London: Darton, Longman and Todd.

Scheer, Monique, Birgitte Schepelern Johansen and Nadia Fadil. 2019. 'Secular embodiments: Mapping an emergent field', in *Secular Bodies, Affects and Emotions: European configurations,* Monique Scheer, Nadia Fadil and Birgitte Schepelern Johansen, 1–14. London: Bloomsbury Academic.

Schulz, Mascha. 2021. 'Convoluted convictions, partial positionings: Non-religion, secularism, and party politics in Sylhet, Bangladesh.' PhD thesis, University of Zurich.

Sherwood, Harriet. 2018. 'Philosophers urge rethink of Pakistani humanist's asylum.' *The Guardian,* 26 January. https://www.theguardian.com/uk-news/2018/jan/26/philosophers-urge-rethink-of-pakistani-humanist-hamza-bin-walayat-asylum (accessed 8 June 2022).

United Nations. 2014. A/HRC/28/66. 'Report of the Special Rapporteur on freedom of religion or belief, Heiner Bielefeldt.' https://digitallibrary.un.org/record/793599?ln=en (accessed 8 June 2022).

United Nations. 2017. A/HRC/34/50. 'Report of the Special Rapporteur on freedom of religion or belief.' https://documents-dds-ny.un.org/doc/UNDOC/GEN/G17/008/79/PDF/G1700879.pdf?OpenElement (accessed 29 August 3022).

Voas, David and Steve Bruce. 2019. 'Religion: Identity, behaviour and belief over two decades', in *British Social Attitudes 36,* John Curtice, Elizabeth Clery, Jane Perry, Miranda Phillips and Nilufer Rahmin, eds, 17–44. London: National Centre for Social Research.

7
Satan, sex and an Islamist zombie apocalypse: religion-sceptical publicity and blasphemy in Turkish cartoons and comic books

Pierre Hecker

Turkey has a long and richly diverse history of cartoons and comic books that traces its roots to the late Ottoman and the early Republican era (Küper-Büsch and Rona 2008; Cantek 2014; Demirkol 2016). Cartoons and comic art have always provided a popular space for humour, satire and entertainment, but also for religion-sceptical publicity. The history of cartoons and comic books in Turkey has been closely linked to the ascendancy of Turkish secularist modernity and is thus situated within a much broader, contentious debate on religion and secularism that dominates Turkish politics to the present day. This chapter provides a contextual, though incomplete, history of religious scepticism and blasphemy in Turkish comic books and cartoons. It investigates how Turkish comic artists challenge religious norms and narratives, by mocking and criticising, and appropriating and rewriting them.

Comic books and cartoons have been prominent vehicles for religious scepticism in Turkey. They have helped to establish a non-religious, sceptical counterpublic and defend it against the encroachments of political Islam. Turkey's comic artists have been vehement critics of the incumbent President of the Republic Recep Tayyip Erdoğan and his government's attempt to educate a new pious generation (*dindar nesil*) and de-secularise the state and society.[1] The discourse about religion-sceptical publicity in Turkish cartoons and comic books also relates to more recent debates on the representation of atheism, deism and non-religion in the public sphere (Hecker 2021, 2022; Tayfur 2022). Against this backdrop, this study examines the potentially blasphemous representations and metaphoric implications of religious concepts (Satan, Adam and Eve, female rebellion and sexuality, etc.) in the works of the comic artists Bahadır Baruter, Ramize Erer, Kenan Yarar and Suat Gönülay.

The chapter begins with a few remarks on the troubled relationship between contemporary art and political Islam in Turkey. It thereby also touches briefly upon the phenomenon of 'lynching culture' and the anger of the provoked public. In doing so, this study seeks to contribute to a wider debate on the popular mobilisation of outraged communities in predominantly Muslim societies (see Blom and Jaoul 2008). The investigation subsequently delves into the intricacies of the legal discussion of Article 216/3 of the Turkish Penal Code ('the denigration of religious values') and the right to freedom of (artistic) expression. The legal discussion provides the background for an analysis of the works of these comic book artists that forms the main body of the present investigation. The chapter ends with a reflection on the role Turkey's comic book subculture has played in the formation, expansion and preservation of a non-religious, sceptical counterpublic in Turkey.

Contemporary art and political Islam: a troubled relationship

Turkey's secularism from above has never gone uncontested and, in recent years, has come under increased pressure from Turkish political Islam, as represented by President Erdoğan's Justice and Development Party (Adalet ve Kalkınma Partisi, AKP). Turkish secularist modernity is rooted in the reform efforts of the early Turkish Republic founded on 29 October 1923. Under the leadership of Mustafa Kemal (Atatürk), Turkey's new state elite initiated a cultural revolution from above that sought to establish a modern secularist nation state.[2] The republican state also promoted European-style forms of artistic expression that were meant to signify and consolidate the advent of secularist modernity in Turkey. The foundation of state-run cultural institutions (museums, theatres, conservatoires, opera houses, etc.) sought to establish a Turkish national culture that was based on modern forms of music, dance, literature, theatre and painting.

The advent of modern and contemporary art in Turkey therefore also represented a rupture with religious traditions. The Republic no longer supported the condemnation of figure representation and, consequently, paved the way for the emergence of contemporary art and, subsequently, the rise of satirical magazines and comic books. Figural representations in painting and other arts are, usually, no longer seen as religiously offensive. However, contemporary art is still often accused of denigrating religious values and thus being a source of blasphemy.

The issue of blasphemy in Turkey is a rather complex one. Turkish law does not operate on religious concepts and therefore does not recognise blasphemy as a legal concept. This, however, does not mean that Turkish citizens have been given carte blanche to blaspheme, as explained later in this chapter. Public scepticism towards 'religious truths' has been a characteristic phenomenon of Turkish secularist modernity but has never become the norm in society. The concept of blasphemy (and apostasy) continues to play a vital role in significant parts of society.

Blasphemy, as David Nash so aptly summarised it in the introduction to his book *Blasphemy in the Christian World*, is 'the attacking, wounding, and damaging of religious belief' (2007, 1). Nash's clear and simple definition should not, of course, obscure the fact that blasphemy is by no means a universal and homogeneous concept. The English term blasphemy, derived from the Greek *blasphēmía* ('abusive speech', 'personal mockery') (Kittel and Friedrich 1985, 107), only partially resonates with an Islamic tradition. What comes closest to the concept of blasphemy in a Muslim religious context is the Arabic term *sabb* ('abuse', 'insult', 'slander').[3] Medieval Muslim jurists developed the related concepts of *sabb al-allāh* (insulting God), *sabb al-rasūl* (insulting the Messenger) and *sabb al-ṣaḥāba* (insulting the Companions of the Prophet) (Wiederholt 1997, 40–7; Saeed and Saeed 2004, 37–9; Saeed 2021), according to which the mocking, ridiculing or criticising of God, his Messengers or the Companions of the Prophet Muhammad not only constitutes an act of blasphemy but, if committed by a Muslim, also apostasy (Saeed 2021, 18–19). This is also why the Islamic idea of blasphemy (*sabb*) has been linked to a much wider theological debate on *ridda* or *irtidād* ('renunciation', 'apostasy'), *kufr* ('denial', 'unbelief'), *nifāq* ('hypocrisy'), *zandaqa* ('heresy') and *shirk* ('idolatry') (see, for instance, Saeed and Saeed 2004, 35–50). Contemporary Muslim jurists predominantly view blasphemy as an attack on the religious concepts and symbols of Islam (Saeed 2021, 18–19). This very broad understanding of blasphemy makes it a dangerously volatile concept. Basically, every act of criticising religious concepts or personalities venerated by Muslim believers might be included in this category.

Turkish public opinion still appears to be dominated by the view that it is incumbent upon Muslim believers to protect and defend Islam against any form of critique, ridicule or mocking. This accompanies a national identity politics that supports the myth of the Muslim nature of the Turkish nation. Non-religion, apostasy and blasphemy, therefore, have the potential to represent not only a grave sin to the believer but also an act of treason against the state and nation. What is deemed blasphemous is not so much a matter of religious doctrine and theological debate but the present government's politics of 'us' and 'them' and the logic of public outrage.

The outrage of the provoked public represents a constant threat to sceptical artists and intellectuals. Criticism of religion and, moreover, the ruling bloc's political agenda can easily draw the anger of ordinary people who have been incited by public hate speech. Turkey's pious conservative government has more than once drawn on the support of the provoked public in recent years. Encouraging ordinary citizens to act on behalf of the nation and punish those who deviate from societal norms has somehow become popular in Turkish politics. Tanıl Bora comprehensively describes these politics of public outrage in his book *Türkiye'nin Linç Rejimi* ('Turkey's lynching regime', 2014). The term 'lynching culture' (*linç kültürü*) denotes a state of public outrage and mobilisation that seeks to restore the dignity of the nation and cleanse society from national shame and disgrace. In particular, right-wing politicians like Nihal Atsız, the father of Turkish fascism, and Devlet Bahçeli, at the time of writing Erdoğan's ultra-nationalist junior partner in Turkey's coalition government, have publicly acknowledged lynching as an appropriate means of defending the nation (Bora 2014, 12, 34). On several occasions, even President Erdoğan himself has threatened to call upon his supporters and unleash the 'will of the people' (*milli irade*) upon those who will not comply with his political agenda. More than once this 'national anger' (*milli öfkesi*) has targeted Turkey's non-religious, sceptical public.

Probably the best-known example of public lynching in Turkey is the so-called Sivas Massacre (Madımak Katliamı) on 2 July 1993 (*see* Çavdar 2020). During the event, which pre-dates Erdoğan's rule, an agitated Islamist mob set fire to a hotel and burned 37, mostly Alevi, artists and intellectuals alive (see Çavdar 2020). Video footage of the event shows some of the perpetrators calling the members of the Alevi religious community 'atheists' and 'unbelievers'.[4] The attack was directed not only at the members of the Alevi community who had gathered to celebrate the annual Pir Sultan Abdal Festival, but also at Aziz Nesin, a well-known atheist intellectual who had translated parts of Salman Rushdie's *Satanic*

Verses into Turkish. While the Islamist mob prevented the trapped intellectuals from escaping the burning building, the police, the military and the fire brigade stood idly by and watched. A more recent incident involved the Turkish fashion designer Barbaros Şansal, who barely escaped a lynching attempt upon his arrival at Istanbul Airport in early January 2017. Şansal, a professed atheist and homosexual, had dared to openly criticise the government and the Turkish nation (Şansal 2017).

Wine and virgins: a legal debate

The Turkish Constitution acknowledges secularism as a permanent and unalterable principle of the state (Article 4) and guarantees the right to freedom *of* and *from* religion (Article 24). Religious scepticism is thus not directly punishable under Turkish law; neither are apostasy, atheism and blasphemy. This does not mean, however, that a person who publicly criticises or pokes fun at religion, religious groups or religious values necessarily goes unpunished. Article 216/3 of the Turkish Penal Code stipulates that 'any person who publicly denigrates the religious values embraced by a part of the population', and, through this, commits an 'act liable to disturb public peace'[5] shall be punished with imprisonment from six months to one year (Artuk and Alşahin 2014, 993). Essentially, this provision aims to protect the right to freedom of religion and to combat hate speech and racism directed towards individuals and groups for their religious beliefs (Yıldırım 2012; Şirin 2014, 76). Recently, however, it has also been applied to prosecute criticism of religion and religious values, and thus create a legal battlefield where the complementary human rights of freedom of expression and freedom of religion collide. It is here that the current shift in the judicial interpretation of statutory law under AKP rule becomes most obvious, especially when particular verdicts and publications of Turkish jurists are considered.

Mehmet Emin Artuk and Mehmet Emin Alşahin, for instance, reassessed the legal applicability of Article 216/3 after examining previous court verdicts. Against the backdrop of these verdicts, they sought to clarify the legal meaning of the terms 'denigration' (*aşağılama*), 'in public' (*alenen*) and 'religious values' (*dini değerleri*). According to their findings, 'denigration' does not even require a direct insult towards religious values. An act of denigration can already be constituted by a lack of respect or simply any act that publicly undermines people's feelings of respect and trust in religious values (Artuk and Alşahin 2014, 994–6). The act of denigration itself needs to be witnessed by a large number of people (that is, it must be 'in public') to be considered a crime under Article 216/3. In practical terms, this means it must be in a public space such as 'the street', 'a coffee house', 'a mosque' or 'a police station' (pp. 995–6). Artuk and Alşahin further suggest that this also applies to the realm of social media, given that the potential insult can be perceived by a wider public (for example through a public post on Twitter). However, the denigration of religious values cannot be punished if posted confidentially within a circle of friends or, for instance, in a closed group on Facebook (p. 1002).

Artuk and Alşahin also address the question of how to define 'religious values' in legal terms: 'Religious values should be understood as anything that represents [a particular] faith or is of religious value for the believers, such as a belief system, senior religious figures or places and forms of worship'(p. 997). For Islam, these values include religious practices such as fasting during Ramadan, the ritual sacrifice of animals during the annual Eid al-Adha celebrations or the pilgrimage to Islam's holy sites in Mecca (p. 997). Any public mockery of these practices falls within the scope of Article 216/3. To summarise Artuk's and Alşahin's legal conception of Article 216/3, the 'crime of denigrating religious values' can be literally anything that a particular group of believers considers an act of denigration of whatever 'thing' they consider sacred or representative of their religion. The vagueness of these concepts entitles Turkish courts to utilise a broad scope of interpretation and implementation, thereby increasing the potential threat of judicial arbitrariness and political abuse. Artuk and Alşahin further promote the view that Article 216/3 does not apply to insults directed against the beliefs and ideas of non-religious individuals (p. 998). Against this backdrop, it is difficult to escape the conclusion that Article 216/3 functions as a legal instrument to curb religious scepticism and protect dominant religious belief systems.

Tolga Şirin, a human rights expert from Marmara University, suggested that in recent years 'the limits of tolerance for critiques towards Islam (not to other religions) have been enormously narrowed' (2014, 76). This becomes evident when considering the increasing number of cases opened by public prosecutors against individuals who express scepticism towards religious truths and teachings or advocate atheist positions in public. The most prominent case of this kind was the indictment of the classical composer and jazz pianist Fazıl Say over several Twitter posts in 2012. Say had not only publicly proclaimed himself an atheist, but also shared a poem by the medieval mathematician and philosopher Omar Khayyam (1048–1131) which reads as follows:

You say rivers of wine flow in heaven,
Is heaven a tavern to you?
You say two beautiful virgins [*houris*] await each believer there,
Is heaven a brothel to you?

In another Tweet cited in the indictment, Say had jokingly commented on a muezzin's all too hasty delivery of the call to prayers, implying that he must have been in a rush either to meet his sweetheart or have a drink with friends ('Man, the muezzin read the evening call to prayer in only 22 seconds. Prestissimo con fuoco!! Why the haste? A girlfriend? A *rakı* table?' *Yeni Şafak* 2012). The public prosecutor at a local criminal court in Istanbul argued that Say's joke about the muezzin's alleged lack of personal religious conviction did not fall within the scope of the right to freedom of expression, but instead constituted a threat to public peace, 'considering the reaction and complaints from a huge number of individuals and non-governmental organisations from various parts of society' (*Bianet* 2015). The pianist was eventually found guilty of purposely mocking and insulting religious concepts ('paradise') and practices ('prayer') considered sacred in Islam, Christianity and Judaism and, as a result, sentenced to 10 months in prison (Altıparmak 2013; *Bianet* 2015). Following an appeal by his lawyers, Turkey's Supreme Court of Appeals finally overturned the initial verdict, stating that Say's Tweets do indeed fall within the scope of the right to freedom of thought and expression.

Notwithstanding Say's acquittal, the initial verdict delivered by a local criminal court in Istanbul can be interpreted as an attempt to prioritise religious principles (and not freedom of religion) over basic human rights, namely the right to freedom of expression, and, moreover, to let the outraged public decide who is to be indicted under Article 216/3. In his analysis of the initial verdict, Kerem Altıparmak of the Ankara-based School of Human Rights (İnsan Hakları Okulu) pointed out an important detail. While human rights law only approves restrictions on freedom of expression if the individual rights and freedoms of others are at stake, it does not accept any restrictions for the sake of protecting religion or religious values (Altıparmak 2013). This, however, is exactly what the initial verdict in the Say trial came down to.

What also needs to be mentioned about the Fazıl Say case is the fact that the pianist was not the only person, nor even the first, to share Omar Khayyam's poem via Twitter. Arne Lichtenberg (2012), a correspondent for the *Deutsche Welle*, reported that Say was one of 166 Twitter users who circulated the quote but the only one to be prosecuted. This underlines the volatility and unpredictability of the situation Turkish artists and intellectuals are confronted with. It has become unclear on what grounds and at what point public prosecutors will take action against such artists. Looking at the various cases opened against Turkish citizens under Article 216/3 in recent years, it would seem that legal action is linked to popularity: the better known the work, the higher the chance of prosecution (for example, the case against the Turkish publisher of Richard Dawkins's *The God Delusion*, and the case against the Turkish-Armenian writer Sevan Nişanyan). This pattern of legal action points towards a strategy of intimidation that has the potential to pressure people into self-censorship. Legal action against popular artists and intellectuals serves as a warning that criticism of religion or religious concepts can (and will) be prosecuted.

Şevket Kazan, Lord of the Jungle

It was the controversy over the sculpture of a naked woman that, in 1974, plunged Turkey's newly formed coalition government into serious crisis. National elections had failed to produce a clear parliamentary majority, and, after months of political negotiation, a fragile, and in the end short-lived, alliance between two improbable partners was formed: Bülent Ecevit's (1925–2006) centre-left Republican People's Party (Cumhuriyet Halk Partisi, CHP) and Necmettin Erbakan's (1926–2011) National Salvation Party (Milli Selamet Partisi, MSP), an openly Islamist movement and the political predecessor of today's AKP. The sculpture, with the title 'Beautiful Istanbul', had been commissioned by the Istanbul Metropolitan Municipality in 1973 to celebrate the 50th anniversary of the foundation of the Republic of Turkey. Its creator, Gürdal Duyar (1935–2004), a graduate of the State Fine Arts Academy in Istanbul and student of the expressionist sculptor Rudolf Edwin Belling,[6] explained that the naked female body is meant to represent the natural beauty of Istanbul (Antmen 2009, 367). The deputy prime minister, Erbakan, certainly did not share the artist's views: he described Duyar's artwork as obscene and a 'statue of shame' that was an insult to the 'Turkish mother' (Antmen 2009, 369–70). His demand to have the sculpture removed resulted in an open political confrontation with his coalition partners from the CHP.

Nudity in art is where ideologies collide, especially in connection with religion and the female body. Public nudity has always been a political statement in Turkey, whether intended or not. This is closely related to the fact that the female body has been credited with considerable symbolic significance in Turkish national culture. Kemalism has always sought to represent the modern Turkish nation in the image of the unveiled, enlightened woman, while political Islam contrasted this image with its own conception of the female. The practice of Islamic veiling is central to the identity of Turkish political Islam, which, as a political movement, has put the veiled, and therefore pious, woman at the forefront of resistance to secularist modernity in the public sphere. The exposure of the naked female body in modern and contemporary art can thus only be considered un-Islamic and contrary to religious values and morality. Nudity therefore still constitutes an object of moral outrage, as it is perceived as a challenge to Islam itself. In 1974, the conflict between the CHP and MSP coalition partners was (temporarily) settled by relocating the 'Beautiful Istanbul' sculpture from the busy Karaköy Square to the more remote Yıldız Park in Istanbul's Beşiktaş neighbourhood. However, in 2017, the sculpture caused new controversy when the AKP authorities ordered that the sculpture's nudity be concealed by planting a fence of saplings around it. Following a protest from local residents, the 'fence' was removed (*Diken* 2017).

The 'Beautiful Istanbul' incident is related to Turkish comic art because erotic cartoons and comic strips had become quite popular at the time. Turkish satirical magazines had been able to enhance circulation by increasingly depicting sexualised nudity. The eroticisation of the female body has been a common feature of Turkish comic books and magazines since the early 1970s. Şevket Kazan (1933–2020), minister of justice for the Islamist MSP, consequently took up the fight against these 'obscene publications' (*müstehcen neşriyat*), which he blamed for the decline of moral values in Turkish society. As a result, he ordered several newspapers and magazines to be confiscated (Demirkol 2018, 66–71). However, Turkish caricaturists did not back down and resisted by depicting and mocking the minister himself.

The satirical magazine *Gırgır*'s Mehmet Polat (1929–81), for instance, portrayed Kazan as 'Ormanlar Hakimi' ('The Lord of the Jungle') in reference to Edgar Rice Burroughs's Tarzan novels. In Polat's comic strip, Kazan discovers that obscenity – in the form of nudity – has come to the jungle. He forces all the animals to get dressed. Satisfied with his work, he leaves the scene, saying: 'Now, you look like animals!' (Demirkol 2018, 67–8).[7] Swinging on a liana through the trees, Kazan lets out a jungle call similar to Tarzan's famous trademark yell. In Kazan's case, however, the yell resembles the Islamic Basmala: 'Ya bismillaaa ... AAA ... aaa' ('In the name of God ...'). The artist apparently intended to make fun of a political figure who had attempted to restrict freedom of artistic expression. From today's perspective, the religious reference in the cartoon – even though obviously used for the purpose of ridiculing politics – might be considered an act of denigration of religious values according to Article 216/3. However, when the cartoon was published in 1974, the artist went unpunished. Today, the situation seems different.

A telephone conversation with God

Article 216/3 has also been used against Turkish cartoonists. Following a complaint by the Directorate of Religious Affairs (Diyanet İşleri Başkanlığı)[8] and several concerned individuals, the Chief Public Prosecutor's Office in Istanbul opened a case against Bahadır Baruter (b. 1963) over a cartoon published in *Penguen* on 10 February 2011. Baruter is a cartoonist, painter and sculptor well known for his biting criticism of society and politics. Since the mid-1990s, he has worked for many of Turkey's most prestigious satirical magazines, such as *Pişmiş Kelle, Penguen, Kemik, Lombak* and *L-Manyak*.

The cartoon illustration under investigation depicts the interior of a mosque, signified by a minbar (pulpit), chandeliers hanging from the ceiling, carpets on the floor, and a line of middle-aged men with skullcaps (*namaz takkesi*) kneeling in prayer. In front of the praying men is an imam who can be easily recognised by his white turban-like headgear, the *sarık*. Directly behind them, another man – also kneeling, also wearing a skullcap – discreetly speaks into his mobile phone. The man, who is depicted side-on, averts his eyes from the rest of the group as he apparently seeks to conceal his inappropriate behaviour. However, his telephone conversation does not go unnoticed and, with an expression of shock, the other men turn towards him. The shocked expression on their faces does not derive from his supposedly impious behaviour of talking on the phone during prayer but from the fact that he is apparently speaking to the Almighty himself: 'Dear God, do you mind if I skip the last part of the prayer? I have work to attend to.' After a pause (indicated by '...' in a speech bubble), he continues: 'Thank you very much, God! Have a nice day.'

Baruter's God at the other end of the line appears to be gracious and kind. He seems neither to take himself (and the need to be worshipped) too seriously, nor to want to keep the worshipper from pursuing more urgent business. However, from a believer's perspective, the cartoon might also signify a denigration of religious values. The act of prayer is indeed one of the Five Pillars of Islam (*arkān al-Islām*), that is, the five obligatory acts of worship in Islam, and is thus a fundamental manifestation of the Muslim faith. Baruter's humorous depiction of the prayer scene at the mosque might therefore be interpreted as an expression of contempt for the commands of God. A small detail in the background of the cartoon certainly strengthens this impression. Almost hidden from the viewer, an inscription on the wall of the fictional mosque reads: 'Allah yok din yalan' ('There is no God. Religion is a lie').

The artist's outright denial of God's existence triggered outrage among Muslim believers, especially on social media (*Internet Haber* 2011). *Penguen* and Baruter were accused of advocating atheist ideas and sowing hatred against Muslims. Amid growing criticism, *Penguen* felt compelled to respond and released a public apology stating that the magazine did not mean to be disrespectful to the faithful. They said that the cartoon only represented the personal opinion of the artist. However, *Penguen*'s editors emphasised their conviction that the right to freedom of expression needs to be protected from the outraged public.

Baruter explained to *Radikal* newspaper that he felt as if a lynching campaign had been unleashed upon him on social media (*Radikal* 2011). Despite widespread opposition to his cartoon and obvious attempts at intimidation, reactions to the cartoon were not entirely negative. Many readers of *Penguen* expressed their support for the cartoonist. The well-known columnist and writer Ayşe Arman interviewed Baruter for *Hürriyet* and asked whether he was afraid of the public threats and insults. Baruter said that he felt more disgusted than afraid, disgusted by the many insults of ordinary people towards his alleged family (mother, sister, wife): 'I shuddered only once, when they said: "Don't send your kids to school. Be careful, they might not return!" This kind of threat. Luckily, I don't have children. If I did, I would have left the country a long time ago' (Arman 2015).

'Fun' and taboos

The heyday of satirical magazines is indelibly linked to one name: *Gırgır* ('fun', 'josh'). Formed in August 1972 under the leadership of the famous cartoonist Oğuz Aral (1936–2004), *Gırgır* soon became one of the bestselling satirical magazines in the world (Tunç 2001; Cantek 2014, 211–21; Demirkol 2018). Starting with a modest circulation of 40,000 copies weekly, *Gırgır* ended up selling as many as half a million copies per week in the late 1980s (Demirkol 2018, 105).[9] For a whole generation of youngsters who grew up in the 1970s and 1980s, *Gırgır* became an integral part of collective memory and nostalgia (Marcella 2021). *Gırgır's* success was certainly linked to the fact that the Turkish state had not given up its national broadcasting monopoly, which happened in the early 1990s.[10] Radio and TV were state-controlled, the days of satellite TV and the internet were still to come, and the sources of entertainment and critical inspiration were seriously limited. In the end, the magazine's popularity resulted from a combination of factors, but mostly from its transgressive character and ability to entertain. *Gırgır* provided both a welcome source of light-hearted fun and laughter, and a rare outlet for addressing societal and political taboos.

One of these taboos was sexuality. The depiction of sexualised nudity and the eroticisation of the female body attracted a wide (male) readership. Demirkol argues that it would be wrong to claim that *Gırgır* used sexuality solely for the purpose of boosting sales (2018, 71–2). Even so, the editorial board was predominantly male, and the cartoons were dominated by a male gaze. It is certainly questionable whether the use of sexist depictions of the female body is a suitable means for challenging society's conservative moral values. However, *Gırgır* always insisted that the depiction of sex and nudity also represented an attempt to promote liberal worldviews and criticise sexism and misogyny in Turkish society. Many of the cartoons published in *Gırgır* did indeed reflect critically on heteronormative gender roles and went beyond stereotypical depictions of sexuality (for example, Oğuz Aral's well-known cartoon classic *Avanak Avni*).

Demirkol (2018, 7, 46–9) stresses the close relationship between cartoons and everyday life. Not only did the artists use everyday language and depict scenes from ordinary life in their cartoons, they also drew inspiration from real-life encounters. Abdülkadir Elçioğlu, the author of the once very popular cartoon series *Grup Perişan*,[11] for instance, claims that his cartoon narratives were often directly influenced by his and his friends' personal experiences (such as being harassed in the streets for their long hair, earrings and supposedly non-Turkish behaviour), which he depicted in an exaggerated, ironic way in *Grup Perişan*.[12] That being said, many of the societal conflicts portrayed in *Gırgır* were not purely fictional but representative of the *Zeitgeist* of a particular period in Turkish modern history.

Gırgır also actively brought in talented young cartoonists from among its readership (Tunç 2001, 247; Marcella 2021). Readers were encouraged to send in their own drawings, on which they would receive personal feedback from the editors. The best cartoons would be published in the magazine. Some of the 'apprentice cartoonists' eventually became part of *Gırgır's* permanent staff. This made it possible for the magazine to recruit aspiring young cartoonists early on and become Turkey's unofficial 'school of cartoon'. Over the years, *Gırgır* produced numerous successful artists who would either establish their own satirical magazines (e.g. *Limon*, *Hıbır*) or turn into professional comic book authors and graphic designers. Even today, Turkey's (cartoon) art scene still benefits from *Gırgır*'s early efforts in the 1970s and 1980s. One of the most prominent representatives of *Gırgır*'s 'school of cartoon' is Ramize Erer, who is often described as Turkey's first feminist cartoonist.

'Bad Girl'

Ramize Erer invented the cartoon character Kötü Kız (Bad Girl). She rose to fame as a cartoonist only when she depicted a young girl masturbating in front of her parents. Following the publication of the cartoon, Erer was heavily criticised for the supposedly pornographic nature of her work. The girl in her cartoon, somewhat confused or delirious, declares that her hymen has been broken, but also claims that she has protected her hymen from being broken. Turning to her father, she tells him that, with her virginity intact, so are his reputation and his bank account. The girl's obviously shocked mother, seated on a sofa next to her husband, whispers to her husband: 'Pssst … we shouldn't have put so much pressure on her. Our little girl has lost her mind!' The cartoon clearly represents a critique of patriarchal society, a traditionalist society that expects its members to preserve the sexual integrity of the female body (*namus*) as a precondition of the father's as well as the girl's social reputation (*şeref*).

Erer's cartoon also contains several visual references to religion. While the girl's mother wears a rural-style Islamic headscarf, her father feeds a string of prayer beads (*tesbih*) through his fingers. On the wall behind the girl's parents, a painting (or maybe a carpet) depicts Islam's holiest site, the Kaaba in Mecca. The combination of these three signifiers marks the family as most likely poor and uneducated pious believers. Through this correlation of religious and patriarchal references, Erer appears to suggest a causal relationship between religion and patriarchy.

Similar meaningful connections appear in many of Erer's cartoons. In a more recent drawing for the feminist magazine *Bayan Yanı*, for instance, she portrays a young couple on a park bench. The male character has put his arm around the woman's shoulders. In a partly flirtatious, partly condescending, mansplaining way, he seeks to persuade his girlfriend (or wife) to start wearing the (Islamic) headscarf, suggesting that if she does not the wind will ruffle her hair in a 'very seductive way'.

In another, more drastic, cartoon, Erer depicts a young woman vomiting on the floor, while shouting 'Enough. Oooh, enoughhh' ('Yeter yaaa yeterrr'). Her vomit contains several dwarfish men complaining about women's supposedly immoral behaviour. By their attire (prayer beads, beards, skullcaps, etc.) they can be recognised as pious conservatives or representatives of political Islam.

Erer's cartoons advocate for female emancipation and sexual freedom. Her critique of patriarchal society certainly establishes a connection between patriarchy and religion. But it does not seem to represent an attack on religion itself. The target of her criticism is primarily men, traditionalist men who make use of religion and religious values to sustain their dominant position in society. Erer's 'Bad Girl' represents the prototype of the rebel girl who criticises religious tradition as a source of patriarchy in Turkey's society.[13] Yet it was not until the mid-1990s that a colleague of Ramize Erer, Kenan Yarar, invented an even more terrifying bad girl: Hilal.

'And God created Hilal'

Hilal first appeared in a serialised short story with the title 'The most beautiful girl in the class' ('Sınıfın en güzel kızı'), whose first episode was published in *H.B.R. Maymun* on 14 September 1995.[14] The character of Hilal had been inspired by one of Kenan Yarar's former classmates, who was of the same name.[15] The artist initially conceptualised Hilal only as a supporting character that the main protagonist of the story, a shy and ugly nerd with an enormous nose and glasses, had a crush on. But it was Hilal who stood out from the rest of the story, not so much for being young and sexy but for possessing genuinely devilish traits that made her murder the school's headmistress when she slaps Hilal in the face for wearing too short a skirt. The reader does not see the actual murder and only learns from a sequence of content panels that the headmistress has died from falling down a stairwell. But it is this insidious, secretive smile on Hilal's face that conveys a sense of cheerfulness and thus implies to the reader that she has taken deadly revenge on the choleric schoolteacher. However, at the very end of the story, it is Hilal herself who dies in a gruesome traffic accident. Driven by jealousy and unrequited love, the school nerd manipulates the brakes on the motorcycle of Hilal's lover and thus accidentally kills the girl he adores.

The story of Hilal could have been that brief and simple if it hadn't been for Ergün Gündüz, *H.B.R. Maymun*'s editor-in-chief, who also fell in love with the uncompromising heroine.[16] According to Kenan Yarar, it was Gündüz who talked him into developing a cartoon based on the adventures of his short-lived devilish blonde. Eventually, Hilal came back from the dead with her own cartoon series, this time entitled 'The devil in school' (*Okuldaki Şeytan*). A few years later, this evolved into the 'Hilal' comic strips that were eventually published in the form of three comic books in 2016, 2017 and 2018. The narrative structure of this cartoon revolves around Hilal's relationship with the Devil, whom she meets in her sleep or when she is caught up in a daydream. The line between dream and reality is frequently blurred, especially when Hilal wakes up to a reality that is worse than any nightmare. Yarar creates a dark, dystopian atmosphere full of human ugliness, violent perversion and repulsive characters. He does not stint on sex, faeces, decay and violence. In the midst of this apocalyptic chaos he places Hilal, the young, lean and sexy blonde with a lust for life and a sharp mind. The beautiful young woman stands in sharp contrast to the ugliness and dreariness that surround her. But the beauty and purity of Hilal's features only obscure the fact that she shows no mercy to those who do her harm, killing and rampaging her way through the story. The author skilfully plays with the psychotic atmosphere he creates, and sometimes it is no longer clear if Lucifer is just an appearance in Hilal's dreams or if Hilal is herself the Devil.

Yarar's *Hilal* is part of a whole genre of dystopian comic books from Turkey. Galip Tekin's *Tuhaf Öyküleri* ('Weird stories'), Suat Gönülay's *Vakur Barut*, Ersin Karabulut's *Yeraltı Öyküleri* ('Underground stories') and the various works of Nuri Kurtcebe all appear to represent a surrealist intervention into Turkish modernity, embodying the dark, psychotic fantasies of their authors. The fictional worlds depicted in these comic books are transgressive in that they contest dominant norms in Turkish society. *Hilal*, for instance, is replete with depictions of sex, nudity and violence, redefinitions of gender roles and explicit language (similar to many works of the aforementioned comic artists). On top of that, *Hilal* contains various recurring references to religious mythologies. These become adapted and modified within the surrealist, fictional world created by Yarar. Hilal's personal relationship to religion remains rather obscure and open to interpretation. Yarar himself describes it in the following way:

> I can't tell if Hilal has a religious belief or not. I can't say she is an atheist. But I also can't say that she is outright religious either. Is she a deist? I am also not sure about that. First and foremost, she is a very young girl at the beginning of her life [who] explores herself,

the world and her body. ... In some scenes, Hilal angrily shouts at an invisible entity because of the personal, inner rage she experiences. In return, she is punished in various ways, for instance by being struck on the head by lightning. Sometimes, she enters into an inner dialogue with this invisible creator and quarrels and fights [with him]. ... It is obvious that Hilal does not live in accordance with common religious rules. [But] none of this makes her either a non-religious atheist or a pious believer.[17]

The metaphorical implications of the various religious references in the *Hilal* comic books are certainly a matter of interpretation and cannot necessarily be read as religious scepticism or, as related to the legal discussion above, as an act of blasphemy. For this reason, the analysis below must be seen as what it is: the present author's interpretation and not the artist's intention.

In the opening chapter of the second comic book in the series, 'And God created Hilal ...' ('Ve Tanrı Hilal'i Yarattı...'), Yarar appears to reverse the Islamic (and Judaeo-Christian) creation myth. His way of storytelling adheres to a form that is common to many comic books. Visual images combined with text (speech bubbles, captions) are arranged in separate panels of varying size and divided by gutters (white spaces between the panels). The caption of the first panel of the story of Hilal's creation tells the reader the location ('heaven') and date ('minus zero' – before the beginning of time) of the depicted setting. The author begins his story by picturing an almost idyllic scene. A young, naked woman, who is in the centre of the picture, is skipping. She is surrounded by exotic plants and fantastic animals that, at first glance, appear to coexist in peace and harmony. What gives the scene a somehow dystopian, demonic touch are the dot-like greenish eyes of the animals, which stand out on the blackness of their demon-like empty eye sockets. It almost seems as if the author is trying to warn the reader of the darkness and evils in heaven.

The following panel zooms in on the skipping Hilal who sings a song and whose private parts are covered only by a single leaf. Still, the setting of the story looks pure and innocent. But then Adam appears on the scene. As announced in one of the captions, he had been created by God only after Hilal ('ve ardından de Adem'i ...'). Adam, as depicted by Yarar, looks nothing like Hilal. He is fat and hairy, a middle-aged man with a huge moustache, wrinkled skin and eyes that resemble those of the other heavenly creatures (bluish dots on blackened eye sockets). When he sees Hilal, he utters a dirty laugh and twists the ends of his moustache. In his left hand, he holds a toffee apple on a stick, with which he approaches

Hilal from behind. He offers it to her by addressing her in an awkward, clumsy, inarticulate way: 'Yoo-hoo … Excuse me, little lady. Would you like to eat a toffee apple? Would you? Very nice … very sweet … do you want it? Eh?' (Yarar 2017, 3). When Hilal reaches out for the apple, Adam stops her (from touching the forbidden fruit) and wags an admonishing finger at her. He will only give her the apple if she agrees to come with him to the nearby bushes. As he explains this to her, he calls her 'my little bird'. From Adam's demeanour and the angry look on Hilal's face, it is obvious that he intends to lure her into the bushes to sexually abuse and rape her. Nevertheless, Hilal follows him towards a huge tree. When the imaginary camera zooms out again, the reader can only see the tree, from under which a loud sound of something breaking and a muffled voice can be heard. Animals can be seen fleeing in panic. In the next panel, it is Hilal who can be spotted running away from the tree. In her right hand, she is triumphantly holding the apple. With a broad smile on her face, she is looking back at the tree, laughing, while Adam is hanging, dead, from a branch of the tree.

This is the moment an alarm clock rudely rouses Hilal from sleep. Angry, she smashes the device with her fist and falls back into a slumber, masturbating. Back in her dream, she begins excitedly licking the toffee apple she stole from Adam, and then, all of a sudden, as if summoned by her desire, Satan appears in front of her. With his massive horns, goat face, hooves and beard, glowing eyes and long tail, Yarar's depiction of the Devil embodies all the clichés. The two characters enter into a discussion, during which the Devil seeks to persuade Hilal to accompany him to hell and give her virginity to him. Hilal is very annoyed, and with an obscene gesture ('fuck you!') she sends the Devil back to hell. Only later in the story will she have sex with the Devil, driven by her own lust.

The metaphorical implications of this narrative are numerous, as this reversal of the Islamic creation myth encompasses various layers. According to Islamic tradition, Adam is the father of mankind, created by God from soil and clay. He may not be identified as such in the Qur'an but de facto he holds the status of a prophet in Islam and is therefore considered impeccable (Bolay 1988, 358–9; Tottoli 2008). The Islamic creation myth shows many similarities to Jewish and Christian traditions, despite some differences. Eve, for instance, is not given a name in the Qur'an but only referred to as Adam's wife, created by God to be his companion. Only in other Islamic sources is she mentioned as Eve. Islamic exegetical tradition (*tafsīr*) also seizes on the Judaeo-Christian narrative, according to which Eve was created from one of Adam's ribs while he was asleep (Tottoli 2017). The narrative of the expulsion of Adam and Eve from Paradise, which in the Christian tradition is commonly referred to as the Fall, is also broadly similar to the Judaeo-Christian narrative. Adam and Eve were allowed by God to dwell in the Garden of Paradise 'and eat thereof as freely as [they] please' (Qur'an 2:35); only one particular tree in Paradise was taboo, and they were not allowed to approach it (Qur'an 2:35–6, 7:20–4; see also Bolay 1988, 361–2). This tree, which in Judaeo-Christian tradition is known as the 'tree of knowledge' or the 'tree of knowledge of good and evil', has no name in the Qur'an. However, in Islamic theology, it is referred to against the backdrop of God's previous revelations (the Torah, the Psalms and the Gospels), in which the expression 'tree of knowledge' (*bilgi ağacı*) is not uncommon (see Bolay 1988, 361). When Adam and Eve succumb to the temptation of Satan and eat from the tree, they are expelled from the Garden of Paradise and sent to earth to live in strife with each other. Roberto Tottoli (2017) points out that post-Qur'anic traditions tend to downplay Adam's responsibility and put the blame for sin on Eve instead.

In Yarar's portrayal of events, the connotative meanings of religious signifiers are renegotiated and reversed. Hilal appears to represent Eve. So when Yarar places Hilal's creation before that of Adam, he challenges not only the alleged truth of a particular religious narrative but also the hierarchical order between the sexes that it implies. In Islamic tradition, Adam is not only considered impeccable but also depicted as a tall and formidable man (Bolay 1988; Tottoli 2008). Yarar's Adam is a fat and ugly rapist. The way he looks, talks and behaves signifies that he is the prototype of the *maganda*. The invention of this term is often attributed to Nuri Kurtcebe, one of *Gırgır*'s earliest cartoonists. The character of the *maganda* represents the stereotype of the rude and brutal, uneducated guy from rural Anatolia whose only outlet is to sexually harass young women. He is depicted in the cartoons and comics of countless artists, such as the works of Ramize Erer and Abdülkadir Elçioğlu. Depicting an alleged Islamic prophet as a *maganda* certainly holds potential for conflict.

If Hilal represents Eve in this story, then the toffee apple represents the forbidden fruit from the Garden of Paradise and the tree from which Adam has been hanged the tree of knowledge. Likewise, it is Adam who seeks to seduce Hilal into sin (that is, to eat the apple and have sex with him under the tree of knowledge), not the other way round. This represents another reversal of gender roles, similar to Yarar's reinvention of the creation myth (Hilal first, Adam second). What the series of events comes down to is this: Hilal hangs Adam from the tree of knowledge after he tries to rape her, and runs away with the apple, which functions as a symbol of her own sexual fantasies when her desire for the forbidden fruit appears to conjure up the Devil, who tries to seduce her. Can this be seen as an act of female revenge on patriarchy or an act of female self-empowerment narrated by a male author? Or should the story of Hilal rather be seen as an act of blasphemy that intends to make fun of religious mythologies and, consequently, the people who believe them to be true? Yarar himself denies having any intention of blasphemy in his works:

> As for the religious references in Hilal, although these references seem to represent Islam ... these themes were not written and drawn to target, praise or vilify Islam directly. It might seem obvious but I have no such intention. ... Personally, I respect all kinds of religious belief or irreligion. It's not my place to interfere with people's beliefs or disbelief or to express my opinion and to praise or criticise [them]. I only react to issues such as bigotry, emotional abuse, suppressing people's free will or targeting their thoughts, as any democratic individual should do; and I convey this with my art and stories in my own way. ... After all, I produce adult comics. I cannot write these kinds of underground stories and fully abide by moral, religious and societal rules. There has to be some anomaly, tantrum and contradiction so that the work is entertaining and interesting to read.[18]

Yarar denies any intention to blaspheme or denigrate Islam. Instead he points towards the artist's legitimate right to address social issues of moral corruption ('bigotry, emotional abuse, suppressing people's free will') and, on a different note, to entertain his readers. The artist has no obligation to abide by moral, religious and societal norms but does have the right to freedom of expression and creative activity. Freedom of artistic expression is an integral part of the right to freedom of expression more broadly, and thus a fundamental human right as covered by the European Convention on Human Rights and the United Nations Universal Declaration of Human Rights, to both of which the Republic of Turkey is a signatory. So even if Yarar's comic books pose a challenge to a normative order shaped by religious narratives they can hardly be classified as a deliberate act of denigrating religious values. Still, Yarar admits that his artistic creativity is 'always' affected by 'a self-censoring mechanism' at the back of his mind:

> There are very few countries and people in this world that tolerate artists whose works criticise religion or satirically engage with religious themes. Considering that many of my international colleagues have

been ruthlessly murdered for fanatic reasons ... I am concerned about the misinterpretation of my works. It breaks my heart that today veteran artists are lynched and their works torn down when [for instance] a word in a song has an anti-religious meaning.[19]

An Islamist zombie apocalypse

Adam and Eve, the tree of knowledge, the Garden of Paradise, Satan and the serpent, the forbidden fruit and the reversal of good and evil are recurring themes in the *Hilal* comic books. In a different story Hilal imagines Adam as a young and sexy lover. She angrily tells the serpent to shove the offered apple up its arse, as it is interrupting her flirtatious encounter with Adam. In the end, it is the sexy, young Adam who turns into a fat and shapeless mass of man and finally explodes after eating all the apples on the tree of knowledge (Yarar 2017, 65–6). In another chapter of the story, Hilal is expelled from heaven and dragged into hell after complaining about how boring heaven is (Yarar 2016, 18). Other religious references are rare. In the second chapter of the first volume (Yarar 2016, 6) the reader finds Hilal sitting at the centre of a prison-like structure. Apparently, she is in a state of repentance. This is signified by the word *tövbe* ('repentance'), which echoes through the first couple of pictures of the story. Dressed in a black chador (a full-length garment that covers the head and the whole body), which only reveals her eyes, Hilal reads from the Qur'an, only to be distracted by a butterfly. It is the butterfly and the sound of music that finally guide her towards a hole in the wall, through which she escapes and enters into a beautiful garden, where she throws off all her clothes.

The theme of Adam and Eve appears in various other Turkish cartoons and comic books, such as Suat Gönülay's *Halkım İstesin Hemen* ('My people want it now'). Gönülay's story is also situated in a dystopian urban environment. In contrast to Yarar's *Hilal*, Gönülay's story is designed to convey a political message to its readers. The comic book is dedicated to 'the Republic' ('Cumhuriyet'e'), which identifies the author as a representative of what has been described earlier as Turkish secularist modernity. Adam and Eve are represented by the story's main characters, Tonguç and Tomris, a young, intellectual couple who share a flat in a nameless, faceless city. Their attire (denim jeans, glasses, unkempt hair) and several references to the Turkish socialist movement (such as DEV-YOL, the Marxist-Leninist 'revolutionary path') mark them out as sympathisers of a Turkish socialist revolution. Another marker that functions as an indicator of the author's political orientation is the names Tonguç and Tomris. They hold a connotative meaning in that they do not derive from the Qur'an, or other religious sources, but date back to pre-Islamic times.

The narrative of the comic begins with a monologue by Tonguç. His eyes wide open, he romanticises about the Turkish people: 'Oh, my people, my love. … One day, I will tell them to come and stand up. … Come, my people. Come. Shoulder to shoulder. Back to back. … May the time come soon, when I gather my people behind me. Come on, march on. Close your ranks. … Hey! Hey! … Oh, I would give my life for these people, Tomris ….' (Gönülay 2013, unpaginated). Tomris listens attentively and tries to calm him down ('Alright, sweetheart. Your people are my people too'), when suddenly a massive crowd appears in the streets in front of their house and calls out Tonguç's name. When Tonguç looks out of the window, excitement grips him again: 'Ah … This is my worker, my peasant, my civil servant …. Oh, look at my people. … They have come for me. HELLO, HELLO! HEY, HEEEEY … HELLOO!' (Gönülay 2013, unpaginated). However, the crowd responds by shouting 'Get out of here', and starts to throw stones through the windows of the couple's flat. Eventually, the crowd breaks through their door and attacks them. Gönülay depicts the attackers as almost completely dehumanised creatures: naked males with long arms and erect penises. Shocked, Tonguç identifies them as 'randy *maganda*'. When the creatures begin to tear off Tonguç's trousers with the apparent intent of raping him, Tomris takes out a gun that lies hidden on a bookshelf and shoots them. After the *maganda*, several more waves of attackers hit the building, each of them representative of a section of Turkish society: the workers, the police and, finally, the Islamists, in Tonguç's words, those who are 'inclined to radical religion'. The story repeats itself when the zombie-like mass of turbaned, bearded men scale the walls of the apartment building, and Tomris holds them off by firing her gun at them at close range. Only at the last moment do the couple escape to the rooftop of the building.

To make a long and confusing story short, Tonguç and Tomris end up naked under the tree of knowledge where the Devil forces Tomris to feed the forbidden fruit, again in the form of an apple, to Tonguç. At this point, Tonguç is still unable to process what has happened and laments that his people have forsaken him. He seems panic-stricken and confused, unable to digest what has happened to him. It is Tomris who keeps a clear head and saves them from being killed.

The metaphorical implications of Gönülay's comic book can be interpreted in a number of ways. For instance, it could be seen as an anti-religious polemic, but it could also be seen as the ultimate disillusion with the dream of a socialist revolution in Turkey. Within the framework of this chapter, it constitutes a final example of how religious narratives are being adapted and reversed by Turkish artists, and how these depictions pose a challenge to dominant religious norms in Turkey's society. What Gönülay's story has in common with that of Yarar is the character of the strong, sexualised, smart and violent heroine who challenges the moral boundaries set up for her by society. Both comic books might furthermore be seen as an expression of feminist revenge on the stereotyped Islamist male and religious concepts that legitimate societal patriarchy. Within Turkey's political context, these comics and cartoons constitute a popular medium for the proliferation of religious scepticism, and might even be interpreted as an act of resistance towards the de-secularisation of state and society by the encroaching forces of pious conservatism.

Conclusion

This chapter has sought to provide a contextual, though incomplete, history of religious scepticism and blasphemy in Turkish comic books and cartoons. It has also intended to investigate how Turkish comic artists challenge religious norms and narratives, by mocking and criticising, and appropriating and rewriting them. The investigation will conclude with a brief discussion on comic books as a means of cultural resistance and a way of promoting alternative narratives within the narrow frames of an authoritarian political system. The history of cartoons and comic books is situated within a contentious debate on religion and secularism that polarises Turkish society to the present day. President Erdoğan's Justice and Development Party (AKP), which has been in power since November 2002, has been following an agenda of authoritarian populism that puts religion at the centre of national identity politics. The idea of the Muslim nature of the Turkish nation provides the basis for a politics of 'us' versus 'them' that has been the main source of the growing marginalisation of the secularist, and therefore allegedly non-religious, other in society (see, for instance, Özyürek 2006; Toprak et al. 2009). The transformation of Turkey's political system from a parliamentary democracy to an authoritarian presidential system that has ceased to operate on a functional separation of powers has furthermore contributed to a systematic dismantling of the rule of law and a successive loss of democratic rights and freedoms (Tahiroğlu 2020). The earlier discussion of Article 216/3 of the Turkish Penal Code points towards an ideology-induced change in legal interpretation that also marks the impending decline of Turkish secularist modernity. Article 216/3 has de facto been turned into a powerful tool to protect and maintain the supremacy of Islam in Turkish society. Public blasphemy or, more precisely, the denigration of religious values in public is now seen as transgressive behaviour that needs to be criminalised for the sake of protecting religion and religious belief itself. Public prosecutors increasingly appear to follow a logic of dominance and subordination in which religious belief enjoys supremacy over non-religion, and the individual right to freedom of (artistic) expression is not sufficiently protected.

The potentially blasphemous representations of religious concepts in the works of the artists discussed here appear to make cartoon and comic art the natural adversary of political Islam. Cartoons and comic books do indeed provide space for religious scepticism, and one might argue that Turkey's cartoonists and comic artists have helped to reinforce Turkish secularist modernity. Today, however, cartoons and comic books address only a very limited public. In recent years, Turkey's conservative government has systematically taken legal action against political cartoonists and satirical magazines. As Valentina Marcella (2022) and others have pointed out, most satirical magazines have ceased publication, because of political pressure and falling sales. Consequently, most cartoonists have lost their public platform and their economic livelihood. Comic books are still available from local comic book shops and the internet, and they certainly have a cult following among younger readers, but their outreach appears to be increasingly limited. It is therefore difficult to assess what cultural impact Turkey's comic book subculture has on the wider public. Public hate speech and the potential outrage of the provoked public create a volatile situation and probably contribute to the fact that many religion-sceptical artists and intellectuals prefer to keep a low profile. Nonetheless, cartoons and comic books continue to facilitate the existence of a religion-sceptical counterpublic that offers a challenge to the power of religion in Turkey's society.

Notes

1   Erdoğan's announcement that his government would prioritise the education of a new pious generation amplified the fear of a forced Islamisation of Turkish society from above. Indeed, several studies, such as Iren Özgür's *Islamic Schools in Modern Turkey* (2012), Ceren Lord's *Religious Politics in Turkey* (2018) and Elif Gençkal Eroler's *Dindar Nesil Yetiştirmek* ('Raising a religious generation'; 2019), provide detailed insight into the ruling elite's comprehensive efforts to strengthen religious discourse in the field of education.

2   In the course of building a modern, Europe-oriented nation-state, Turkish reformers under the leadership of Mustafa Kemal (Atatürk) enacted a bundle of wide-ranging reforms. In addition to abolishing the Sultanate (1 November 1922) and the Caliphate (3 March 1924), removing the constitutional provision designating Islam as the state religion (9 April 1928), replacing the Arabic alphabet with the Latin one (1 November 1928), and granting equal civil rights to male and female citizens (17 February 1926), the reformers adopted a secular legal system based on the Swiss Civil Code (17 February 1926) and the Italian Criminal Code (1 March 1926).

3   Lutz Wiederhold (1997, 40) mentions several other terms that are used to denote acts of blasphemy in Arabic (e.g. *shatm*, *la'n*, *ta'n* and *īdhā*). In Sunni legal literature, the debate on blasphemy does, however, centre on the term *sabb*.

4   Markus Dressler (2013, xii) wrote that 'Alevism constitutes an intrinsic part of Anatolian and Turkish culture'. The Alevis of Turkey represent approximately 10–15 per cent of the population. Alevism can be described as a religious community at the margins of the Islamic tradition. It differs from Sunni Islam in its heterodoxy and syncretism and exhibits a certain closeness to Shia Islam. Turkish Sunni supremacists commonly characterise Alevis as heretics and unbelievers (Akyıldız 2022), and even some Alevi diaspora organisations insist that Alevism is an autonomous religion distinct from Islam.

5   All quotes, unless stated otherwise, have been translated by the author from Turkish into English.

6   Rudolf Edwin Belling (1886–1972) was a German expressionist sculptor who spent almost 30 years in exile in Turkey after his works had been classified as 'degenerate art' (*entartete Kunst*) in Nazi Germany.

7   The cartoon was originally published in *Gırgır* magazine on 23 June 1974 (see Demirkol 2018, 67).

8   The Directorate of Religious Affairs is a state institution responsible for administering religious affairs in Turkey. It was established under article 136 of the Turkish Constitution and is the state's key instrument for placing religious affairs under state control.

9   Aslı Tunç puts the numbers even higher and mentions a weekly circulation of 750,000 copies (Tunç 2001, 243). Demirkol's figures are far more detailed; therefore they appear to be more reliable (2018, 61, 88, 105).

10 The first private TV channels began operating in 1990, followed by private radio broadcasters in 1992.

11 *Grup Perişan* ('Group of losers') was published in the satirical magazine *Hıbır* from 1989 to 1995. It depicted the lives of three young men in Istanbul, one of them an uncompromising rocker and metalhead. *Grup Perişan* played a huge part in the dissemination of rock and metal culture among Turkey's youth.

12 Personal interview with Abdülkadir Elçioğlu conducted in Istanbul on 24 December 2003.

13 Ramize Erer's equally famous cartoon characters Eşi Nadide and Bir Bıyıksız follow the same lines.

14 *H.B.R. Maymun* (originally *Hıbır*) was founded by a group of cartoonists who broke away from *Gırgır* in the late 1980s. The early *Hilal* comic strips were published weekly in autumn 1995 (issues 67 to 73, 14 September 1995 to 26 October 1995).

15 The name Hilal means 'crescent moon' in Turkish. The crescent moon is historically known to symbolise Islam. It can be found on coins, flags and stamps, on top of domes and minarets and, more recently, on religious lifestyle products (clothes, food, etc.). Yarar stresses that he did not choose the name Hilal for its religious meaning but in tribute to his classmate of the same name from middle school. He thus does not intend to poke fun at Islam (Kenan Yarar, e-mail to author, 11 April 2022).

16 According to Kenan Yarar in an interview with Meltem Şahbaz for *Habertürk* (Şahbaz 2018).

17 Kenan Yarar, e-mail to author, 11 April 2022 (translated by the author from Turkish to English).

18 Kenan Yarar, e-mail to author, 11 April 2022 (translated by the author from Turkish to English).

19 Kenan Yarar, e-mail to author, 11 April 2022 (translated by the author from Turkish to English).

References

Akyıldız, Kaya. 2022. 'The affirmation of Sunni supremacism in Erdoğan's "New Turkey"', in *The Politics of Culture in Contemporary Turkey*, Pierre Hecker, Ivo Furman and Kaya Akyıldız, eds, 277–91. Edinburgh: Edinburgh University Press.

Altıparmak, Kerem. 2013. 'Fazıl Say'ın Tweetleri ve doğru sandığınız yedi yanlıs.' *Bianet*, 19 April. https://bianet.org/bianet/siyaset/146003-fazil-say-in-tweetleri-ve-dogru-sandiginiz-yedi-yanlis (accessed 10 June 2021).

Antmen, Ahu. 2009. 'Türk kültüründe beden ve "Güzel İstanbul" olayı.' *Elektronik Sosyal Bilimler Dergisi* 8 (30): 366–75.

Arman, Ayşe. 2015. 'Çocuğum olsaydı iltica ederdim.' *Hürriyet*, 29 March. https://www.hurriyet.com.tr/yazarlar/ayse-arman/cocugum-olsaydi-iltica-ederdim-28585618?sessionid=7 (accessed 10 June 2022).

Artuk, Mehmet Emin and Mehmet Emin Alşahin. 2014. 'Dini değerleri aşağılama suçu (TCK m. 216/3).' *Marmara Üniversitesi Hukuk Fakültesi Hukuk Araştırmaları Dergisi* 20 (1): 989–1012. https://doi.org/10.33433/maruhad.607165.

Bianet. 2015. 'Yargıtay Fazıl Say hakkındaki kararı bozdu.' 26 October. https://m.bianet.org/bianet/insan-haklari/168642-yargitay-fazil-say-hakkindaki-karari-bozdu (accessed 10 June 2022).

Blom, Amélie and Nicolas Jaoul, eds. 2008. 'Outraged communities: Comparative perspectives on the politicization of emotions in South Asia'. *South Asia Multidisciplinary Academic Journal*. https://doi.org/10.4000/samaj.234.

Bolay, Süleyman Hayri. 1988. 'Adem', in *TDV İslam Ansiklopedisi*, TDV İslam Araştırmaları Merkezi, ed., 358–63. Ankara: Diyanet Vakfı Yayınları.

Bora, Tanıl. 2014. *Türkiye'nin Linç Rejimi*. Istanbul: İletişim.

Cantek, Levent. 2014. *Türkiye'de Çizgi Roman*. Istanbul: İletişim.

Çavdar, Ozan. 2020. *Sivas Katliamı: Yes ve bellek*. Istanbul: İletişim.

David, Isabel and Kumru Toktamış, eds. 2015. *'Everywhere Taksim': Sowing the seeds for a new Turkey at Gezi*. Amsterdam: Amsterdam University Press.

Demirkol, Gökhan. 2016. 'Türkiye'nin ilk Türkçe mizah dergisi: Terakki.' *Akademik Bakış* 10 (19): 141–60.

Demirkol, Gökhan. 2018. *Gırgır: Bir mizah dergisinde gündelik hayatın dönüşümü (1972–1989)*. Istanbul: İletişim.

Diken. 2017. '1974'ten bugüne: Güzel İstanbul'un etrafındaki fidanlar tepkiler sonrası kaldırıldı'.28 October. https://www.diken.com.tr/1974ten-bugune-guzel-istanbulun-etrafindaki-fidanlar-tepkiler-sonrasi-kaldirildi/ (accessed 10 June 2022).

Dressler, Markus. 2013. *Writing Religion: The making of Turkish Alevi Islam*. Oxford and New York: Oxford University Press.

Gençkal Eroler, Elif. 2019. *Dindar Nesil Yetiştirmek: Türkiye'nin eğitim politikalarında ulus ve vatandaş inşası*. Istanbul: İletişim.

Gönülay, Suat. 2013. *Halkım İstesin Hemen*. Istanbul: Mürekkep.

Hecker, Pierre. 2021. 'İslam'ı terk etmek, ateizmi tercih etmek.' *Pasajlar: Sosyal Bilimler Dergisi* 3 (8): 101–27.

Hecker, Pierre. 2022. 'Tired of religion: Atheism and non-belief in "New Turkey"', in *The Politics of Culture in Contemporary Turkey*, Pierre Hecker, Ivo Furman and Kaya Akyıldız, eds, 68–88. Edinburgh: Edinburgh University Press.

Internet Haber. 2011. 'Penguen'den İslam'a ağır hakaret.' *Internet Haber*, 14 February. https://www.internethaber.com/penguenden-islama-agir-hakaret-327949h.htm (accessed 10 June 2022).

Kittel, Gerhard and Gerhard Friedrich, eds. 1985. *Theological Dictionary of the New Testament*, translated and abridged in one volume by Geoffrey W. Bromiley. Grand Rapids, MI: Eerdmans.

Küper-Büsch, Sabine and Nigar Rona. 2008. *Die Nase des Sultans: Karikaturen aus der Türkei*. Berlin: Dağyeli.

Lichtenberg, Arne. 2012. 'Turkish pianist faces trial for joking on Twitter.' *Deutsche Welle*, 9 June. https://www.dw.com/en/turkish-pianist-faces-trial-for-joking-on-twitter/a-16011575 (accessed 10 June 2022).

Lord, Ceren. 2018. *Religious Politics in Turkey: From the birth of the Republic to the AKP*. Cambridge and New York: Cambridge University Press.

Marcella, Valentina. 2021. 'A satirical magazine in its own way: Politicisation and dissent in Gırgır (1972–1983).' *DIYÂR* 2 (2): 329–48. https://doi.org/10.5771/2625-9842-2021-2-329.

Marcella, Valentina. 2022. 'Between resistance and surrender: Counter-hegemonic discourses in Turkish satirical magazines', in *The Politics of Culture in Contemporary Turkey*, Pierre Hecker, Ivo Furman and Kaya Akyıldız, eds, 130–50. Edinburgh: Edinburgh University Press.

Nash, David. 2007. *Blasphemy in the Christian World: A history*. Oxford and New York: Oxford University Press.

Özgür, İren. 2012. *Islamic Schools in Modern Turkey: Faith, politics, and education*. Cambridge and New York: Cambridge University Press.

Özyürek, Esra. 2006. *Nostalgia for the Modern: State secularism and everyday politics in Turkey*. Durham, NC and London: Duke University Press.

Radikal. 2011. 'Bahadır Baruter'in karikatürü tartışma yarattı.' 14 February. http://www.radikal.com.tr/turkiye/bahadir-baruterin-karikaturu-tartisma-yaratti-1039956/ (accessed 11 June 2022).

Saeed, Abdullah. 2021. 'Blasphemy laws in Islam: Towards a rethinking?', in *Freedom of Expression in Islam: Challenging apostasy and blasphemy laws*, Muhammad Khalid Masud, Kari Vogt, Lena Larsen and Christian Moe, eds, 17–31. London and New York: I.B. Tauris.

Saeed, Abdullah and Hassan Saeed. 2004. *Freedom of Religion, Apostasy and Islam*. Farnham: Ashgate.

Şahbaz, Meltem. 2018. 'Dünyaca ünlü çizgi roman Barbarella'nın 50. yılına özel çizimleri Kenan Yarar'dan'. *Habertürk*, 3 January. https://www.haberturk.com/hilal-ve-psikoz-oykuleriyle-tanidigimiz-kenan-yarar-barbarella-nin-cizgi-romanini-ciziyor-1778607 (accessed 11 June 2022).

Şansal, Barbaros. 2017. *Makam Odası Linç*. Istanbul: Destek.

Şirin, Tolga. 2014. 'Freedom from religion in Turkey', in *Freedom of Religion and Belief in Turkey*, Özgür Heval Çınar and Mine Yıldırım, eds, 59–88. Newcastle upon Tyne: Cambridge Scholars Publishing.

Tahiroğlu, Merve. 2020. 'How Turkey's leaders dismantled the rule of law.' *The Fletcher Forum of World Affairs* 44 (1): 67–96.

Tayfur, Hamdi. 2022. 'Eski İslamcılar yeni dinsizler anketi.' *Bilim ve Gelecek: Aylık Bilim, Kültür, Politika Dergisi* 215: 4–9.

Toprak, Binnaz, İrfan Bozan, Tan Morgül and Nedim Şener. 2009. *Being Different in Turkey: Religion, conservatism and otherization: Research report on neighbourhood pressure*. Istanbul: Boğaziçi University.

Tottoli, Roberto. 2008. 'Adam', in *Encyclopaedia of Islam*, 3rd edn, Kate Fleet, Gudrun Krämer, Denis Matringe, John Nawas and Everett Rowson, eds, 64–9. Leiden: Brill.

Tottoli, Roberto. 2017. 'Eve', in *Encyclopaedia of Islam*, 3rd edn, Kate Fleet, Gudrun Krämer, Denis Matringe, John Nawas and Everett Rowson, eds, 42–4. Leiden: Brill.

Tunç, Aslı. 2001. 'Gırgır as a sociological phenomenon in Turkey: The transformation of a humor magazine.' *Humor* 14 (3): 243–54. https://doi.org/10.1515/humr.2001.002.

Wiederhold, Lutz. 1997. 'Blasphemy against the Prophet Muhammad and his Companions (*sabb al-rasūl, sabb al-ṣaḥābah*): The introduction of the topic into Shāfiʿī legal literature and its relevance for legal practice under Mamluk rule.' *Journal of Semitic Studies* 42 (1): 39–70.

Yarar, Kenan. 2016. *Hilal 1. Kitap*. Istanbul: Marmara Çizgi.

Yarar, Kenan. 2017. *Hilal 2. Kitap*. Istanbul: Marmara Çizgi.

Yarar, Kenan. 2018. *Hilal 3. Kitap*. Istanbul: Marmara Çizgi.

Yeni Şafak. 2012. 'Fazıl Say İslam dinine hakaret etti!' 6 April. https://www.yenisafak.com/gundem/fazil-say-islam-dinine-hakaret-etti!-376639 (accessed 11 June 2022).

Yıldırım, Mine. 2012. 'Turkey: "Denigrating religious values" – A way to silence critics of religion?' *F18News*, 15 February. https://www.refworld.org/pdfid/4f3e5a402.pdf (accessed 11 June 2022).

8

From campaign and dispute to 'public service broad/narrowcasting': secularist and atheist media strategies in Britain and America – a contextual history

David Nash

This chapter investigates the long and varied history of atheists and freethinkers in Britain and America and their attempts to communicate amongst themselves and to a wider world. This history is traced through the development of this phenomenon within the British and American contexts, stretching roughly from the French Revolution to the present. In doing so it focuses upon atheist and secularist forms of resistance to organised Christianity and uses exclusively English-language sources.

Commencing with the philosophies developed as a result of Enlightenment ideals – which cultivated freedom of speech and expression – the chapter investigates how these ideas were put into practice, from the first few generations of nineteenth-century campaigners right through to contemporary atheist/freethinking use of media. It analyses their adoption of new media technologies (from pamphlets and, subsequently, newspapers and books, to multiple and various online presences) and of changing styles and narratives. Many of these technologies have been related to specific tactics as well as to the confrontation of perceived evils and ills, whilst some have been replies to the specific 'provocation' of opponents and authority. These narratives have also been determined to showcase the exposure of error and 'gullibility', creating and disseminating alternative viewpoints. What emerges from this study is that the various analyses which see digital communication as a sea change in both approach and opportunity for atheist/freethinkers/secularists significantly overstate the case. In elaborating a long-term history of one particular context for atheism and communications strategies it is hoped to provide opportunities for comparison with different contexts, histories and possibilities.

The chapter assesses the relative successes and failures of different media strategies by emphasising the tensions that came with them for atheists and freethinkers. How did atheists resolve the tensions between the private quietism of some unbelievers and the urge to proselytise and create public controversy, alongside the personalities who inspired both approaches? When was it appropriate to convert and when was it appropriate to speak to the converted? How did media aid or hinder these objectives? How were media utilised in the different strategies of work on single issues and, alternatively, the broad front of undermining religion's control of state, cultural and social institutions? Lastly, how did the use of media alter around discussions about whether atheism would overturn religion, or widen its constituency to colonise a 'market share' of belief/ unbelief? Fundamentally, resolving such tensions often came down to less than obvious choices about whether atheists should be broadcasting or narrowcasting. Whilst these strategies were always in debate, the wider assertion of rights and identities resembles the 'talking back to power' described by Richter in this volume.

Such a contextual history is necessary because too many writers on contemporary atheism and its strategies view the problems and possibilities created by new media as a novelty that possesses no prehistory. Too often they fail to look beyond the arrival of the modern cyber age and its technological breakthroughs and forms. This outlook has a tendency to cite the contemporary world as having foisted a sudden and unwilling engagement with communications technology for the first time upon atheist and secularist groups. Cimino and Smith, for example, described contemporary atheists in America as 'creating an alternative ethos and discourse, using social media to "talk back" to society whilst "speaking with" one another' (Cimino and Smith 2014, 2). The medium's tools and mechanisms have even, by these same analysts, been seen as moulding and shaping the nature of unbelief itself (Smith and Cimino 2012).

Tracing the very existence of what we would now call atheists, agnostics and freethinkers becomes more fraught with difficulty for historians the further back they go. Their visibility scarcely breaks the surface for a host of reasons. Such a gap and silence meant that Lucien Febvre was persuaded that religious culture was so all-encompassing and pervasive that medieval and early modern atheism was actually impossible (Febvre 1985).

Such a conclusion seems scarcely credible, and it is not the purpose of this chapter to probe this particular historical conundrum any further. However, the current existence of this absence of visibility is pertinent to our investigation of atheist communications strategies. Historians are still uncovering hidden religious congregations that function under the radar when the prevailing religious regime is unfavourable to their cause, such as the previously unknown continuation of the émigré 'Stranger' Church in Marian London (MacCulloch 1999, 182). Even religious congregations that surface when the situation is favourable are often found to have had an 'illegal' prehistory. With atheists and freethinkers such a situation is impossible to replicate. Congregations, groups, families and even perhaps the concept of 'like-minded individuals' do not exist for atheists until modernity. The evidence we have is of what we might call 'opinion'. This is portrayed as something at least semi-private, and conspicuous to the individual consciousness only of those who hold such opinions (Royle 1974, 12–16). We might here think about how this privacy is replicated elsewhere in this volume, where there are some very different examples of how dissident opinions are deliberately hidden from scrutiny as a protective measure. This can be simple self-defence, or the careful protection and possible nurturing of dissident opinion still at an early stage of development.

The solitariness of those individuals is reinforced partly by the history and historiography of unorthodox belief and unbelief. Carlo Ginzburg's investigation of an early modern Friulian miller emphasised his sustained learning and outlook, the creation of a strange heterodox universe deduced from the collision of reading, observation and sustained thinking (Ginzburg 2013). Yet this individual stepped out of the darkness into the historical record when made to speak through court records. Such appearances before the law are probably our most important evidence of religious dissent. For the medieval and early modern period this has been crucial for detecting such opinions, ranging from heresy to what later becomes nonconformity. It is also significant because it highlights the importance of blasphemy and blasphemy cases, demonstrating places where the orthodox objected to the behaviour and speech acts of others (Bradlaugh Bonner 1934). Although blasphemy was for much of the time unwitting, it sometimes emerges from these episodes, especially from the seventeenth century onwards, as a deliberate method of communication.

What, for obvious reasons, is left hanging is the question of how representative Ginzburg's miller and his desire to build his own intellectual universe may have been in practice. Were there others out there whose self-imposed sceptical quietism left no trace in the historical record? Similarly, the episodic appearance of a work of biblical criticism, or critique of organised religion, might break the surface much later, in the later seventeenth or early eighteenth century. But our history tells us of the author whose prosecution or pariah status further emphasised their isolation, both to contemporaries and to subsequent historians. Such individuals are plucked from their time, recorded and returned to it as individualistic milestones in the history of unbelief (Bradlaugh Bonner 1934, 33–8).

It is not the purpose of this chapter to investigate this lacuna/dark figure, but this prehistory of unbelief makes a fundamentally important point about the vitality of communications for unbelievers themselves, and for historians trying to uncover their history. Unbelievers only leave significant traces of themselves when they interact through communication that often bridges significant distances. Until the nineteenth century there was almost no interactive communal life that could remotely have resembled the congregations of their Christian counterparts. All communication between atheists was via the spoken word and through written communication, often constructed as material to reach an unknown or imagined audience, something Lundmark and Khazaal have both noted in this volume in relation to atheism's contemporary history. Thus communication has historically been central to the identity of unbelievers since 1800, and we must be aware of how, for historians, this creates a slightly lopsided story. Such a narrative probably tells us too readily about places where the vocal and articulate predominate at the expense of the silent and the silences. The latter emphatically may not represent assent to any belief system, religious or otherwise, and certainly do not represent an empty space. However, this visibility of 'speaking out' within unbelieving circles has itself influenced an ongoing desire to reach out to the 'imagined audience'. This 'imagined audience' for atheist, freethinking and humanist ideas has been a driving force behind many initiatives and activities. It has also been defined and redefined at significant moments in unbelief's past. This driving force has also, at times, created a tension between outward-looking proselytising, informing and campaigning and the desire to fortify existing unbelievers against a world often ranged against them.

Forging the imagined audience

The Deism- and Enlightenment-inspired critiques of religion were quite often shaped to appeal to an 'imagined audience'. Thomas Paine's own prose style was testament to his desire to popularise critiques of established religion, which became eminently quotable to his immediate contemporaries. His writings also became accessibly readable and memorable through the republication of his central text (*The Age of Reason*); subsequent editions made conversions to unbelief even after the Second World War. In the 1820s a generation led by Richard Carlile was prosecuted for blasphemy and sedition for republishing Paine's works, amongst other texts (Carlile 1821). The principle at stake for Carlile, and for other defendants such as Susannah Wright, was the power of free speech to transform society. In court they saw the attempts to censor and silence their opinions as an affront and an assault upon reason and the Enlightenment ideal of free and unfettered discussion (Carlile 1825). This combination fused the unbelievers' enduring link with arguments for free speech. Carlile and his acolytes believed that publishing their writings on monarchy, the clergy and biblical criticism was self-evidently a social good. Hence preventing the publication was harmfully repressive. In many courtroom defences they stated that if the government and its supporters could clearly demonstrate that their writings and opinions were causing widespread harm they would immediately desist from publishing them (Carlile 1822, 11–12). This was not a rhetorical question, since it was an appeal to their imagined audience, which would encounter such opinions, defendants believed, simply because they had been made available.

Such beliefs were also put into action in the behaviour of these defendants in the courtroom, with the elaborately stage-managed reading of defences that involved lengthy extracts, and attempts to read whole texts that were central to accusations against them. These disseminated such opinions to the court's public gallery, and those present were entertained by rebukes aimed at prosecuting counsel and the presiding judge. Such verbal 'republication' of these opinions and arguments from texts reached beyond the courtroom, since they fished for further 'republication' in court reports that found their way into some newspapers. This determination to communicate was further enhanced by Carlile's own publishing venture, which republished the reports of court cases in pamphlet form (Carlile 1821, 1822, 1825; Nash 1999, 84–8). These cases were sometimes published together, whilst others were singled out for individual publication when an especially important rhetorical point had to be made. Although these publications reached out to the 'imagined audience', the number of individuals prepared to face prosecution for publishing and selling Carlile's numerous works indicated that there was a significant community of the like-minded.

These like-minded, as we have discovered, initially appeared, in the eighteenth century, to be scattered and dispersed. Although the isolated atheist was an archetype that would continue into the early twentieth century, in the nineteenth century some different common characteristics began to emerge. Unbelievers, not surprisingly, consumed print culture avidly, and sometimes it is possible to believe that some unbelievers were drawn into this cultural world specifically through their consumption of texts. This perhaps explains why we encounter, in equal measure, sudden conversion from Christianity and a more long-term 'falling away'. Many working-class unbelievers were thus part of an autodidact world in which the possession and consumption of texts became a central aspect of unbelieving culture. Ensuring the ready availability and distribution of such texts became something of an enduring preoccupation within the wider movement (Royle 1980, 131–2).

By the third quarter of the nineteenth century unbelief had fused into more sophisticated ideological positions, notably the ideology of secularism, which offered degrees of protection to its adherents by creating an ideology which appeared to outside observers to be like modern agnosticism (Rectenwald 2018). This ideology was able to create a movement culture that craved lectures and expositions of new ideological developments. These could be in such areas as biblical criticism, biology, politics and the emerging social sciences. In counterpoint to this was a more metropolitan and visible campaigning culture centred on the person of Charles Bradlaugh and his various crusades to gain citizenship rights for unbelievers (Royle 1980, 12–18, 23–8, 263–71). For this branch of the movement communications focused upon the speeches and on their republication in various forms. Where the pamphlet form was used this genre owed a great deal to the lecturing format, with a plethora of rhetorical questions and assured assertiveness about the arguments and their presentation. Both sides of this divide would frequently come together in both the capital and provincial contexts to involve themselves in disputing the truth of the Bible with Christian debaters (Royle 1980, 150–5). These events were immensely popular; they could straddle several nights of speech and counter-speech, and attract considerable attention and surprisingly large crowds. Through the medium of questions from the floor, and audience engagement with the speeches, individuals were invited to 'use' the fruits of atheist culture communicated to them as a method of repelling attacks upon their identity. Such events could be contests of moral superiority in which speakers like Bradlaugh were forced to defend individuals like Carlile and Paine from accusations of immorality, and from accusations that their doctrines were the clear source of crime within society (Bradlaugh Bonner 1894, 158–60).

This period also saw the growth of a mature secularist press that had titles to reflect the philosophical and thoughtful end of the movement, such as *The Secular Review* and the *Agnostic*, as well as the more politically hard-edged campaigning periodicals such as the *National Reformer*. Each could be counted on to display a range of sensibilities in asking and seeking to answer religion's central questions. For example, discussions of the historical Jesus and his resurrection could range from outright denial of these events to a more moderate discussion of their precise importance. Beyond such philosophical discussions, a niche market in lampoon and scurrility would also, episodically, serve the individual purposes of the movement and the agenda of specific editors. This press presence was a further appeal to the 'imagined audience' through communication to the isolated, living, perhaps covertly, in an otherwise Christian and believing landscape. Such newspapers would contain news of the national movement as well as records of poorly behaved clergy, or instances where it detected that Christianity was found wanting in its stewardship of everyday life. Letters pages carried echoes back from that audience, often with similar stories. Many communications displayed isolated atheists reaching out to a national movement when sickness drove them to create final statements of their enduring unbelief. These statements were portrayed as courageous attempts to thwart spurious deathbed conversion stories (Nash 1995).

Occasionally, papers like the *Freethinker*, the *Jerusalem Star* and in the Edwardian period the *Truthseeker*, adopted genres of writing and illustration that were designed to push free speech onto a collision course with prosecution in the form of blasphemy (discussed below). These episodes saw communication as a means of creating offence in those believers who experienced a casual encounter with such material. There is evidence that comic lampoons of Christianity and its beliefs were fleetingly amusing to some unbelievers whilst creating discomfort in others. In genres like this the Freethought movement confronted the dilemma of whether communications media should be used to enrich the lives of adherents, or whether to submerge this aspect in favour of their potentially campaigning impact (Nash 1999, 107–17).

Publishing why and how? The world of the cheap edition

By the end of the nineteenth century the metropolitan secular organisations had become especially keen to promote published editions of important works. This keenness was a tacit admission that the days of the lecture platform were largely over, and that very cheap consumption of the printed word and its messages was a real alternative. By this time lecture audiences had fused into the committed unfaithful, meaning that casual engagement with others and the possibility of conversion had become less likely. Again, this development seems to reflect the passing of attractive and strident personalities with high-profile campaigns and visible agendas. This campaigning competed (again) with a more quietist agenda that sought dissent and criticism which was more considered, whilst providing content and comfort to the stable membership. To a large extent such publishing had to replace the aspirations of the lecture platform, which always entertained the idea of reaching a wider audience, whether in oral or printed form. The quest for sustained cheap publishing seemed a logical next step which might yet offer the desirable possibility of pleasing both constituencies.

In Britain one outcome of this quest was the Rationalist Press Association (RPA), which ambitiously hoped to be an important means of projecting secular and rational ideas into the wider community. Whilst this was an innovation, it sought to shape reading habits by focusing on the human sciences, echoing the message that Paine and Carlile had advanced in the first quarter of the nineteenth century. In the latter part of the same century, a concentration on these subjects appeared valid. This was because they had seemingly been in the forefront of the erosion of Christianity's authority as an objective truth, alongside critiques of its authority over the governance of behaviour. The time also felt right because such a concentration could capitalise on the impact of Christianity's own 'fifth column', those who had produced English translations of David Friedrich Strauss's *Life of Jesus*, *Essays and Reviews* and *Lux Mundi*. The RPA's publishing initiatives actively wanted not just to inform but also to create a predisposition to distrust beliefs and embrace reason (Whyte 1949, vii). The human sciences offered the chance to benefit the whole of society, both on their own terms and as the most potent weapon against religion's claims. These strategic goals assisted the movement's desire to move from 'guerrilla warfare to a full scale campaign' (Whyte 1949, 2).

The RPA readily utilised the publishing experience and skills of those who remained from the heyday of secularist newspaper publishing, chiefly Charles A. Watts (1858–1946), the former editor of Charles Bradlaugh's *National Reformer*. Watts was also responsible for the creation of a highbrow newspaper, *Watts' Literary Guide*, which was designed to reach the opinion-forming classes, and eventually morphed into the modern magazine *New Humanist*. A changed emphasis on new subjects also vied with repolishing and republishing elements of the past, almost in an attempt to create an alternative history and canon. So human sciences competed for attention, to an extent, with biographies of past great thinkers in a secular and humanist tradition. These latter publications would be leavened with the occasional individual publishing success story, such as John Mackinnon Robertson's *Christianity and Mythology*, which (trading on his wider reputation) went through several editions.

The RPA, at least for a while, relied on word of mouth, unofficial forms of promotion, and casual encounter with its contents for its success. To all intents and purposes the organisation had become a 'book club', financed by modest sales and Association subscriptions. The aspiration to reach the wider world came when the RPA was able to publish jointly with Macmillan when they released a reprint of T. H. Huxley's *Essays and Lectures*. It quickly became a success story, selling out a first edition and a hasty second reprint (over 40,000 copies). To some extent this desire to publish popular works became a wider trend in 1928 when the RPA embarked upon the ambitious venture of producing the particularly eye-catching concept of the 'Thinker's Library'. It showcased what the RPA considered to be 'classics of rationalism' from such writers as J. S. Mill, Herbert Spencer, H. G. Wells, Charles Darwin and T. H. Huxley. These editions carefully trod the line between being distinctively stylish and being cheap, and were sold from an attractive, bespoke display cabinet which could be purchased by enterprising booksellers. The series offered a renewed opportunity to revisit the autodidact complete education of Secularism's forebears, and allowed for pick-and-mix reading habits or chance discovery. Eventually the effort put into these initiatives meant that Christianity itself, in the interwar period, often bemoaned the fact that, for the layperson seeking to educate themselves, the best introductions to many of the sciences were penned by atheists. This left the Church lagging behind in its potential explanatory power over the modern world. For this reason atheist publication strategies in the first third of the twentieth century had some degree of ideological success.

Nonetheless, as a business proposition the RPA was occasionally a liability and to many seemed stuck in a time warp, repeating the publication of Victorian and Edwardian material that was unable to speak to the modern generation in their twenties, an audience which the secular and later humanist movement sorely needed.

The Open Society unfolded

The interwar period saw humanism in Britain interact with the ideas of Karl Popper and his concept of the 'Open Society'. The BHA later expressed this fundamental principle in the following terms:

> The Open Society is the name given to a society which respects all viewpoints and traditions present in it and in which the ideas of democracy are extended to include a much expanded participation of individuals in decision making and the conduct of affairs. It is the antithesis of the authoritarian society.
>
> (British Humanist Association 1972)

This ideology was ostensibly formed in response to the episodic success of tyrannical regimes in the 1930 and 1940s, and appeared to be a tacit admission that societies 'closed' to debate and progressive ideas had fallen into totalitarianism. Popper's 'Open Society' was thus an attempt to enrich debate and actively encourage the spread of the participatory element within politics and other decision-making processes. Moral education was to be an important tool and would be shaped to create an expectation that institutions would be 'shared' by all, rather than dominated by specific interests. The secular humanist movement in Britain only fully adopted the 'Open Society' manifesto meaningfully in the 1960s. For those who embraced these ideas communications media seemed to have a crucial role in furthering this cause. Moreover, the 'Open Society's' belief in what had been surrendered to tyranny made communications media almost into a commodity, something to be possessed, or at least not surrendered so readily to malevolent forces.

The 'Open Society' concept did create a belief that access to the media would enable a sharing of this common good, whilst also safeguarding its appropriate use. This belief became a de facto commitment to a strategy of seeking the right to 'broadcast' alongside other denominations and religious positions. Judged on these terms the secular and humanist movements were always likely to come away disappointed. In the immediate post-war period humanists who did manage to enter the media (such as Jacob Bronowski, Bernard Williams and Bertrand Russell) did so largely on the strength of their reputations in other spheres. When in the media spotlight they were closely chaperoned and were refused the right to speak openly on secularist or humanist matters. The summing up in such programmes also had a supervised and invariably Christian bias. In 1959 a Humanist Broadcasting Council was formed to discuss permitting secular and humanist issues to be debated on public service broadcasting. Debate was all that ensued except for isolated programming victories. To this day humanist viewpoints are absent from BBC Radio 4's *Thought for the Day*. Likewise, equality would not come from elbowing aside the practitioners of religious broadcasting in the hope of 'sharing' this important institution. Instead the collapse of enthusiasm for sabbatarian restrictions on Sunday broadcasting and the waning interest in religious broadcasting would turn it into a niche interest, one to be catered for alongside others as though it were a minority rather than a priority. Whilst the power and influence within public service broadcasting was narrowly held in a few hands, and the audience for its products was significantly captive, the quest for equality appeared to make clear and obvious sense. When eventually this situation became democratised by technological change, and its falling cost, new strategies and priorities would emerge.

Cyber scepticism: embracing the community *and* campaigning

Investigating atheist online presence in the late 1990s, I could see the gradual adoption of the new technology and its possibilities in the United States (Nash 2002). What was striking about this situation was its mirroring of the situation and problems of the nineteenth-century atheist movement in Britain. The Secular Web acted as a repository of many classic and standard atheistical texts which could be downloaded and printed, providing the possible apotheosis of the 'cheap edition' concept which the Rationalist Press Association struggled for so long to get right. The campaigning impetus was catered for with web links to the main freethought periodicals. Whereas in the nineteenth century the decision to purchase a newspaper may have had both monetary and ideological opportunity cost for some, the web links approach of the internet encouraged diversity of potential contact with related issues. This contact could occur through the simple inclusion of extra links as places the freethinker might wish to roam intellectually. Such roaming could be eclectic but not without controversy, or indeed inherent humour. One debate surrounding the apparent desirability of affiliation concerned who to 'include'. This could reach into unknown territory, as potential fellow travellers in unbelief asked whether links to groups involved in satanism were desirable. One side of the argument saw satanists as legitimate individuals circumscribed unjustly by Christianity and its cultural attitudes. Therefore they should be treated as potential allies because of their polar opposition to the Christian narrative. The dissenters from this view, which eventually won the argument, strenuously suggested that this was unacceptable because satanists were theists! Nonetheless, this outward desire to be 'inclusive' has been noted by some commentators as indicating a potential splintering of effort and ideological will, which essentially means that atheist groups are not competing with Christianity or other religions but rather with themselves (Laughlin 2016, 317–19).

What does emerge from this period is that many who eventually arrived at secularism did so through varieties of 'seeking' which saw them, however briefly, embrace forms of Buddhism and Wicca. This perhaps further raises a question about the precise active role of the internet itself in the creation of atheists. 'Seeking' around secularism and freethought is scarcely new; however, the ability and ease with which some could tap into a previously unknown subculture was suggestive even in the 1990s (Nash 2002). Many of the formative experiences of 1990s American secularists mirrored those of their nineteenth-century British counterparts and, in a vastly different religious context, the modern Moroccan non-believers described by Richter in this volume. Observing the moral hypocrisy of Christian neighbours, and undergoing the enforced nature of 1990s American religious culture within the social and political spheres, were formative experiences that had British nineteenth-century echoes. Feelings of isolation would also surface, in some cases alongside a strategy that avoided conflict with the wider community – a strategy observed by Gupta in this volume in surveying contemporary India.

Thus, as was the case in the 1990s, new media of communications were lauded as doing something different in creating a safe haven or space in which secularists could contemplate their ideological world and, for a time, escape theism-laden culture. The impetus to create such a haven has been noticed by Lundmark (this volume) in a description of atheism as seeking to 'think rationally' rather than pursue the idea of forming a wider movement. From the safety of physical distance (and anonymity, which has echoes in Gupta's chapter in this volume) secularists had started to use electronic discussion lists to debate with Christians and

Muslims. This recalled the set-piece discussion nights of their mid- to late-nineteenth-century British counterparts, albeit with significant advantages. Individuals expressed hope that this form of debate would transcend the limits of print media and return to a supposed prehistory of healthy organic discussion (Nash 2002, 263). This optimism, however, pre-dated the arrival of antagonistic responses in the form of flame wars and trolling. A consideration of the emergence of this new media may suggest that the optimism about a free trade in ideas asserted by nineteenth-century secularists was echoed in the aspirations of their American mid-1990s counterparts. The idea of the internet being uncensorable spoke to the highly regulated media landscape of 1990s America, and sustained optimism that the online world would remain a form of commons unsullied by vested interests.

The capacity for culture wars to limit freedom of speech was also contemplated by atheists, since the creation of new media meant the transmission of older culture into this media could be limited. Neglect, or cynical and partisan choice about what was moved into this new media, or even about what was moved into it first, had potential repercussions. The apparently laudable aims of Project Gutenberg were slightly tainted by its nomenclature, which signalled the centrality of Christianity to learning and enlightenment (Nash 2002, 284). Objectors to this argued that other unhelpful biases, concerning class, race and gender, would be an issue created around this new canon in its transfer from old to new formats. Whether the effect was anticipated or not, the change to a new form of media meant questions arose about whether the work of Voltaire could more readily be made available than that of street orators. Likewise, would the work of the Enlightenment's aged white males be privileged above that of other gender, race and demographic groups?

Blasphemy: the ambivalent communication

Blasphemy is obviously a transgression, but it is also a form of communication, however unwelcome encounters with it may be. As we have heard, historians rely on its existence as evidence of dissident views. However, some individuals embarked, and still embark, upon blasphemy as a communication strategy to fortify their unbelief, or as result of their repugnance towards or dislike of specific religious doctrines. Blasphemy's existence has thus been a source of ambivalence, or even problematic thoughts, for secularists. We have seen how blasphemous writing, and legal cases around blasphemy, were a vehicle for Richard Carlile's free-speech campaigns, but secularism's relationship to blasphemy has not always been so clear-cut.

When blasphemy was perpetrated by individuals outside the milieu of secularism in the nineteenth and early twentieth centuries, the secularists themselves could effectively stand aloof from subsequent events and choose their stance on the matter. Defending individuals against forces ranged against them by a vengeful Christian world was popular inside the movement, and involved forms of support which could be offered without ideological cost. It became easy to call into question laws that could be used to prosecute, maltreat and imprison those suffering from mental impairment (Toohey 1987). Likewise, class narratives could be enlisted as an attack on blasphemy prosecutions, if street-corner orators could be liable to imprisonment whilst academic works largely escaped such censure (Nash 1999, 181–2). In the late twentieth and early twenty-first centuries blasphemy accusations and prosecutions could be actively useful to secularist groups. These were opportunities to raise issues such as the unjustness of curbs on free speech, the discriminatory nature of the law and the shortcomings of religious explanations of the universe. Thus, commenting upon blasphemy cases headed for prosecution showed that religious progress was a situation of uneven development (Nash 2020, 163–88; Gubo 2015, 102–24).

In the West such 'progress' could be met with grassroots religious initiatives that sought to re-evangelise a world potentially lost to Christianity. In these instances blasphemy accusations and prosecutions were valuable warnings that the preservation of Enlightenment ideals was a work in progress that required renewed vigilance. In instances such as the Salman Rushdie affair secularists could easily reach out to other groups, such as writers and artists, to demonstrate how multiculturalism was potentially asking too much of the Western traditions of free speech and tolerance. In demanding the equalisation of blasphemy laws to protect religions other than Christianity, the presence and the potential power of religion in the modern world attracted attention, unwittingly on behalf of the secularist cause. When modern states beyond the West began to readopt blasphemy laws and define them anew, the accusation that they had ridden roughshod over Western liberal preconceptions and desires was easily made. In cases against Westerners who transgressed poorly understood cultural and religious prohibitions, the secular enlightenment flag could easily be waved. Indigenous individuals who made their own statements against their former faith very easily became lightning-rod causes that seamlessly fed campaigns against blasphemy laws in the West.

The situation became a little more complicated when the blasphemy was perpetrated from within the ranks of secularism itself. Blasphemy in this context does appear as a form of perceived legitimate expression which had a critical message for those who consumed it. What emerged from the survey of atheist attitudes in America in the mid- to late 1990s was that the First Amendment offered the freedom to be scurrilous in criticising Christianity. This perhaps enhanced the idea that pervasive religious landscapes instinctively create their own culture of resistance. Whether this is true or not, there was evidence that blasphemous postings were popular amongst rank-and-file atheists, potentially fortifying them for their lives in a pervasive Christian culture. Whilst not necessarily constituting a community that adhered to an alternative belief system, they could nonetheless rely on First Amendment protection. Moreover, the intended audience of the like-minded was meant to be a safe space into which the theistic world should not intrude, or in which it should at least keep silent, preventing the disruption of a blasphemy prosecution, whereas other contexts would welcome one. Chalfant describes the creation of such phenomena in this volume as a species of 'coming in' to digital spaces (as opposed to the proselytisation of 'coming out' or seeking to offend). Chalfant also saw this as an issue about the choice to be visible or otherwise. The status of such spaces was emphasised by a regime of warning screens to deflect the merely curious or religious from being offended (Nash 2002, 285–6).

Blasphemous expression as the most extreme communications media has been used by those within the movement at specific times to advance various causes; it could even be an accusation against what atheists and secularists considered mainstream educative material (see below). In 1880s England G. W. Foote's *Freethinker* deliberately published blasphemous cartoons in imitation of Bible scenes and stories. They turned religion into a series of narratives that could be considered bizarre or silly, inviting derision. This echoes the contemporary experiences of some Saudis, described in this volume by Khazaal, who found themselves confronting sacred narratives that emerged as 'silly' after serious scrutiny. Foote saw his action here as an adjunct and supportive action in aid of attempts to prosecute England's leading atheist of the late nineteenth century, Charles Bradlaugh. If his cartoons drew further attention to the attitudes of secularists and atheists, this attention was seen as valuable in highlighting Bradlaugh's plight and that of all who shared his unbelief (Nash 1999, 110–11). Not all agreed with this, and those who saw atheist communication and publishing as a way to promote movement culture and support for far-flung atheists in the provinces were embarrassed by the antics of a high-profile metropolitan campaign. Even this judgement could seem ambiguous when the resulting court case triggered petitions from all over liberal Britain against high-handed government action (Nash 1999, 148). In the end Foote had several days in court, and his imprisonment, though uncomfortable, ensured that he would attain the leadership of secularism when Charles Bradlaugh died.

The renewal, revisiting or construction anew of blasphemy laws themselves could similarly galvanise quasi-blasphemous action in defiance of them. Importantly, with electronic media this could be done swiftly and effectively. In 2009 the campaigning group Atheist Ireland were aghast to discover that Ireland's recently passed Defamation Act contained provisions that made blasphemous utterances and publication an illegal act. In response, at the start of 2010 the organisation published on its website a page entitled '25 blasphemous quotes'. It contained texts from the New Testament and the Hadith of Bukhari, and quotes from Mark Twain, Frank Zappa, Salman Rushdie, Björk, Amanda Donohoe, the Rev. Ian Paisley and Conor Cruise O'Brien.[1] It was later expanded with further lists, which fell into a range of common themes. The action of publishing this list was a modern equivalent of Foote's published biblical cartoons and comic life of Christ, since it challenged the government to institute a prosecution and affirm the supposed viability of the law (Nash 1999, 118–30). The difference was that, unlike Foote's publication, which had a narrower distribution, this material was so easily available on the internet that the casual reader could far more readily interact with the quotations' web page. As a strategy it may also have been more effective in Ireland, because the quotations had been available in the public domain in many guises. Displaying them in this form was intended to demonstrate their inherent rationality and reasonableness. They were also manifestly less offensive than the Foote cartoons.

Blasphemy laws and debates about them had only been portrayed as anachronistic when the prosecution of activists was contemplated and executed by authority. In the twenty-first-century world it is the arrival of new laws that has prompted concern and action. Communications media's relationship with celebrity, in some instances, exposed the problems inherent in blasphemy laws and potential prosecutions. The Salman Rushdie affair had proved that media coverage and the publicity it produced around a well-known individual writer were capable of galvanising public opinion on both sides. Nonetheless, celebrity involvement in other blasphemous incidents could, through media coverage, mean that individual high-profile causes could sustain a momentum of their own, providing immense publicity and critique of the legal situation.

This happened in Ireland, where a regular chat show host, Gay Byrne, interviewed Stephen Fry in 2015 on the long-running confessional television programme *The Meaning of Life*. As a parting question Fry was asked what he would say to God were he to meet him. Fry retorted with a rant against a creator who would visit bone cancer upon defenceless children. This was a classic 'problem of evil' statement which ought to have been familiar to all those who debate the nature of religious belief. However, within the context of Ireland's defamation laws Fry's statement was potentially blasphemous.[2] Within a short time an anonymous complaint had been laid at a Garda station in Dublin requesting that the law be used against Fry. The actions of the Garda (or rather their long-time inaction, since they merely filed the complaint, and finally resolved to take no action) further contributed to the anomalous situation of Ireland's blasphemy law.[3] What was significant was that when blasphemy laws could be made to appear untenable, the broadcast media would occasionally create situations that did the atheist and humanist groups' campaigning for them.

Atheist Ireland's campaign to remove the law of blasphemy in Ireland demonstrates what can be achieved through the astute use of communications media, and a recognition that a local or national issue can be made into an international one. Campaigning could be professional and slick, since the cost and availability of cheap technology and places to host its productions brought national or even international campaigning into the realm of even small-scale groups. This democratisation of technology made podcasting and the creation of professional-looking videos both important and increasingly expected. Technology, and proficiency in using it, could respond to campaigning successes, give immediate reports on discussion with government agencies, and broadcast reports and speeches from international meetings of supranational bodies.[4] The last of these was significant, since highlighting how the Irish law provided a precedent for other countries to pursue and retain blasphemy laws was crucial in marshalling hostile international opinion about what the Irish government had instigated without due care. This mistaken course of action could be made to assume the proportions of an international embarrassment (Cox 2019). Ireland's blasphemy law was abolished in 2018 (Nash 2020, 181–6).

In Ireland blasphemy served as a vehicle for accelerating change in the context of a country that was grappling with a liberalisation of its religious outlook. Suddenly its moral outlook adapted, with changes to laws allowing same-sex marriage and abortion. The only note of caution that could be advanced was the consideration that such liberalisation was quite often the result of urban Ireland conversing with itself. The votes cast in these referenda indicated a clear majority in favour of liberalisation in urban centres, with a 'burst circle' effect that spread into neighbouring counties, and enthusiasm for this stance waning in more isolated communities. Both broadcast and social media and the causes they espoused could have real effects, but they could not stretch everywhere on every occasion.

Conclusion: the reappearance of the older dilemmas, and their consequences for contemporary atheism

As we have noted, the tension between reaching out to new publics and consoling and comforting a constituency of adherents has been constant. It has appeared regularly in a considerable number of atheists' interactions on both sides of the Atlantic, since the rise of a recognisably modern movement in the first half of the nineteenth century. In the contemporary world this tension has to an extent continued, but the nature of this continuity deserves exploration. How does this perennial issue explain the situation of modern atheists on both sides of the Atlantic and the landscape they find in front of them? We might obviously consider that the rise and prominence of New Atheism and New Atheists appear to signal a more strident approach to proselytising and an (at least temporary) end to the culture of assimilation, compromise and cooperation. This had pervaded local relationships between atheists and humanists and those of other faiths. It was also the case that secular rhetoric conveyed a latent fear that the Enlightenment was somewhat 'in danger' from the resurgence of religious faith but also, and perhaps more importantly, from the blurring of the distinction between rationality and spirituality, a distinction New Atheists were anxious to preserve.

The problem then became that atheism and humanism continued to assume that all who came to them were seekers who had reached the end of their spiritual road. As such, they still carried the religious baggage and detritus from their journey. In another guise this analysis would appear in the regularly gathered statistics about waning religious belief and belonging, so long a valuable touchstone for atheist and humanist advocacy of their beliefs. Both sides of the Atlantic have seen humanist and atheist groups speak about, some have argued fixate on, these statistics in their communications to the public sphere. Statistics which show adherence to religion waning significantly can superficially be used to argue that countries on both sides of the Atlantic are becoming progressively more secular. Figures may not lie about waning religious belief, but the leeching away of religious adherence by no means equals a recourse to secularist alternatives.

Both religious and secular worldviews have had to confront the phenomenon of the rise of the 'nones', those not schooled or brought up with religion and who potentially have no need to embrace it or reject it (Quack and Schuh 2017). Modes of address and communicating with such people have the capacity to reshape communications agendas. Some commentators have noticed, with a strange amount of glee, just how much this is likely to affect the outlook of atheist humanists and their apparent demands for rationalism, and their distaste for vague spiritual and mystical trappings (Laughlin 2016). But this is to demand of secularists and humanists a degree of ideological purity of outlook and motive that Christianity in the West has long since forsaken and actively traded in. But it is possible to consider that secularism, humanism and atheism are undergoing, or experiencing, a Dietrich Bonhoeffer moment. This is a situation in which the sum of Bonhoeffer's message to Western Protestantism was that it should forsake the idea that religious belief and practice were central to the lives of Western men and women. Such ideas reached the popular mainstream in a number of influential books and pamphlets. The entrance of such ideas into the mainstream has been seen by one historian to have influenced a particular 'moment' at which British society had actively convinced that it had secularised itself to completion, whether or not this was true (Brewitt-Taylor 2013).

Atheism has arguably still to fully realise that its message does not carry the weight of moral indignation and sect-like self-preservation that it once did. Therefore it is having to respond to this constituency of 'nones' and follow them in both their tastes and their modes of communication. We can see some of this in action in relation to the former in, for example, Conway Hall's South Place Sunday Concerts (in London), which offer the regularity of a Sunday 'service' without any other commitment, either religious or secular.[5] What patrons individually gain from this is not clear but, as in post-Bonhoeffer Christianity, their attendance is perhaps all that can be hoped for and their willingness to simply attend has become the entire point. For the modern waning of moral indignation we might consider the message of the 2009 'bus campaign', which did not speak to the intense moral outrage of previous times. Instead it offered the reassurance of diffuse, and even unspoken, doubt (Kettell 2016). Its message that there was probably 'no god' and that individuals should thus simply strive to 'enjoy their life' reached out to 'nones', who were invited to become fellow travellers.

We might also speculate about the conclusions individuals might reach from seeing atheist and humanist organisations widen their appeal through some systematic use of the phenomenon of modern celebrity. Patrons and presidents of the British Humanist Association have come from the world of popular comedy, but also from amongst individuals who cross bridges that link academic subject advocacy and understanding with factual television presenting. Thus, within the history of atheist and secularist communications media a new episode had arrived in which organisations would once again have to cross their fingers about the level of commitment they could expect from individuals who became even partly sympathetic to their views and outlook. Whereas, once, lecture audiences could be counted and book sales calculated, modern media cannot assess commitment from lurking and the occasional comment. Whilst this may look like a difficult position, it is possible to see areas in which modern communications strategies link with consumer demand.

It is arguably the case that many who contact atheist and humanists groups are in search of the rites of passage that these organisations can perform. This also highlights that religious or non-religious affiliation might coalesce around 'moments' that speak to individuals in a post-Bonhoeffer style of requiring only specific needs to be satisfied. This is an area in which humanism itself has tailored its offer to outperform that of conventional religions in some specific ways. A non-invasive means of communicating the worldview of humanists is through the range of funeral provision now available. Humanism in Britain has been quick to prepare publications about secular funerals, which have gone through a significant number of editions and have shown a cycle of development. These publications, interestingly, have been geared to being inclusive and to cornering an increasing market that wants something different from prescribed and off-the-peg religious burial services (Wilson 1989, 1990, 1992, 1995, 1998, 2006, 2014). Humanists have been quick to state within these works that the emphasis in secular funerals, at least the ones portrayed in this literature, is on choice. This emphasis increasingly enables a degree of personalisation that pleases individuals contemplating their own funeral, or those close to them who are choosing something they deem to be appropriate. These publications also contain templates for a variety of circumstances pertaining to the manner of the individual's death, or indeed their age and gender (Mountain 2000). Choice and flexibility are the watchwords for this provision (Nash 2017).

If we seek to draw links between some current atheist and humanist publishing provision, 'worship' provision and rites of passage provision, there is perhaps a common thread. Alongside the 'no religion' declarers, and the 'nones' with no trace of religious culture, atheist organisations might be dealing with and assisting some people we might once again describe as deist. These are people who may have a sense of spirituality and a vague sense of a supreme being but want nothing to do with religion. Instead, these individuals seek to 'shop' for religiosity from a prepared list of needs (Stolz et al. 2016, 194). The creation of messages about dissatisfaction with religious practices, and, more interestingly, dissatisfaction with their prescriptiveness in an era of choice, means that atheist communications strategies in their role of reaching out to society adopt different stances. They thus use a mixture of 'popping up' in front of people in a variety of media, and publicising the possibility of open-ended provision when it comes to rites of passage. Although this can sound as though it contains elements of the story we started with, atheist organisations and their communications strategies have contributed to ensuring that plurality and freedom of speech, however challenged and incomplete, are here to stay.

Notes

1   Atheist Ireland 2010.
2   McSorley 2018.
3   Collins 2017.
4   See, for example: 'Atheist Ireland responds to abortion law questions at Irish parliamentary hearing', https://www.youtube.com/watch?v=VLrKNmocTNQ; 'Does God exist? Michael Nugent v William Lane Craig debate', https://www.youtube.com/watch?v=wmlcmVye4hM; 'You have rights, your beliefs do not: Michael Nugent of Atheist Ireland at OSCE meeting in Poland', https://www.youtube.com/watch?v=msJ8HWvTNCc; 'Does society need religious faith? Michael Nugent in debate with John Waters', https://www.youtube.com/watch?v=fPV1l_ZyztU; 'Can you believe in both science and religion? Michael Nugent debating at UCC', https://www.youtube.com/watch?v=KY2Sv25SrYs (all accessed 5 July 2022).
5   https://conwayhall.org.uk/sunday-concerts/history-archive/ (accessed 17 April 2022).

References

Atheist Ireland. 2010. '15 blasphemous quotes.' 2 January. https://atheist.ie/2010/01/25-blasphemous-quotations/ (accessed 12 June 2022).

Bradlaugh Bonner, Hypatia. 1894. *Charles Bradlaugh: A record of his life and work*, 2 vols. London: T. Fisher Unwin.

Bradlaugh Bonner, Hypatia. 1934. *Penalties upon Opinion; or, Some Records of the Laws of Heresy and Blasphemy*, 3rd edn, revised and enlarged by F. W. Read. London: Watts and Company.

Brewitt-Taylor, Sam. 2013. 'The invention of a "secular society"? Christianity and the sudden appearance of secularization discourses in the British national media, 1961–4.' *Twentieth Century British History* 24 (3); 327–50. https://doi.org/10.1093/tcbh/hwt012.

British Humanist Association. 1972. *Education for the Open Society*. London: British Humanist Association.

Carlile, Richard. 1821. *Suppressed Defence: The defence of Mary-Anne Carlile, to the Vice Society's indictment, against the appendix to the theological works of Thomas Paine*. London: R. Carlile.

Carlile, Richard. 1822. *Report of the Trial of Mrs Susannah Wright, for publishing, in his shop, the writings and correspondence of R. Carlile, before Chief Justice Abbott, and a special jury, in the Court of King's Bench, Guildhall, London, on Monday, July 8, 1822: Indictment at the instance of the Society for the Suppression of Vice*. London: R. Carlile.

Carlile, Richard. 1825. *Report of the Trial of Mrs Carlile on the Attorney General's Ex-Officio Information for the Protection of Tyrants*. London: Richard Carlile.

Cimino, Richard P. and Christopher Smith. 2014. 'How the media got secularism – with a little help from the New Atheists'. Oxford Handbooks Online. https://www.oxfordhandbooks.com/view/10.1093/oxfordhb/9780199935420.001.0001/oxfordhb-9780199935420-e-15?print=pdf (accessed 12 June 2022). https://doi.org/10.1093/oxfordhb/9780199935420.013.15.

Collins, Pádraig. 2017. 'Stephen Fry investigated by Irish police for alleged blasphemy.' *The Guardian*, 7 May. https://www.theguardian.com/culture/2017/may/07/stephen-fry-investigated-by-irish-police-for-alleged-blasphemy (accessed 12 June 2022).

Cox, Neville. 2019. 'Stephen Fry, the meaning of life and the problem with Irish blasphemy law.' *Oxford Journal of Law and Religion* 8 (2): 247–69. https://doi.org/10.1093/ojlr/rwz019.

Febvre, Lucien. 1985. *The Problem of Unbelief in the Sixteenth Century: The religion of Rabelais*. Trans. Beatrice Gottlieb. Cambridge, MA: Harvard University Press.

Ginzburg, Carlo. 2013. *The Cheese and the Worms: The cosmos of a sixteenth-century miller*. Trans. John Tedeschi and Anne C. Tedeschi. Baltimore, MD: Johns Hopkins University Press.

Gubo, Darara Timotewos. 2015. *Blasphemy and Defamation of Religions in a Polarized World: How religious fundamentalism is challenging fundamental human rights*. London: Lexington Books.

Kettell, Steven. 2016. 'What's really new about New Atheism?' *Palgrave Communications* 2, art. no. 16099. https: //doi.org/10.1057/palcomms.2016.99.

Laughlin, Jack C. 2016. 'Varieties of an atheist public in a digital age: The politics of recognition and the recognition of politics.' *Journal of Religion, Media and Digital Culture* 5 (2): 315–38. https://doi.org/10.1163/21659214-90000084.

MacCulloch, Diarmaid, 1999. *Tudor Church Militant: Edward VI and the Protestant Reformation*. London: Allen Lane.

McSorley, Christina. 2018. 'Blasphemy, Stephen Fry and referendum in Ireland'. BBC News, 20 October. https://www.bbc.co.uk/news/world-europe-45903094 (accessed 10 November 2022).

Mountain, Carole. 2000. *Circumstances out of the Ordinary: Ceremonies where the circumstances are unusual or tragic*. London: British Humanist Association.

Nash, David S. 1995. '"Look in her face and lose thy dread of dying": The ideological importance of death to the secularist community in nineteenth-century Britain.' *Journal of Religious History* 19 (2): 158–80. https://doi.org/10.1111/j.1467-9809.1995.tb00254.x.

Nash, David S. 1999. *Blasphemy in Modern Britain: 1789 to the present*. Aldershot: Ashgate.

Nash, David S. 2002. 'Religious sensibilities in the age of the internet: Freethought culture and the historical context of communication media', in *Practicing Religion in the Age of the Media: Explorations in media, religion, and culture*, Stewart M. Hoover and Lynn Schofield Clark, eds, 276–90. New York: Columbia University Press.

Nash, David S. 2017. 'Negotiating the marketplace of comfort: Secularists confront new paradigms of death and dying in twentieth-century Britain.' *Revue belge de Philologie et d'Histoire* 95 (4): 963–88.

Nash, David S. 2020. *Acts against God: A short history of blasphemy*. London: Reaktion Books.

Quack, Johannes and Cora Schuh, eds. 2017. *Religious Indifference: New perspectives from studies on secularization and nonreligion*. Cham: Springer.

Rectenwald, Michael. 2018. *Nineteenth-Century British Secularism: Science, religion, and literature*. Basingstoke: Palgrave Macmillan.

Royle, Edward. 1974. *Victorian Infidels: The origins of the British secularist movement, 1791–1866*. Manchester: Manchester University Press, and Totowa, NJ: Rowman and Littlefield.

Royle, Edward. 1980. *Radicals, Secularists and Republicans: Popular freethought in Britain, 1866–1915*. Manchester: Manchester University Press, and Totowa, NJ: Rowman and Littlefield.

Smith, Christopher and Richard P. Cimino. 2012. 'Atheisms unbound: The role of the new media in the formation of a secularist identity.' *Secularism and Nonreligion* 1: 17–31. https://doi.org/10.5334/snr.ab.

Stolz, Jörg, Judith Könemann, Mallory Schneuwly Purdie, Thomas Englberger and Michael Krüggeler. 2016. *(Un)Believing in Modern Society: Religion, spirituality, and religious-secular competition*. Abingdon: Routledge.

Toohey, Timothy. 1987. 'Blasphemy in nineteenth-century England: The Pooley case and its background.' *Victorian Studies* 30 (3): 315–33.

Whyte, A. Gowans. 1949. *The Story of the RPA: 1899–1949*. London: Watts and Company.

Wilson, Jane Wynne. 1989, 1990, 1992, 1995, 1998, 2006, 2014. *Funerals without God: A practical guide to non-religious funerals*. London: British Humanist Association.

III
Atheism and scepticism in a digital age

9
Intimate deconversions: digital atheist counterpublics on Reddit
Eric Chalfant

Introduction: publics and counterpublics

The term 'counterpublic' emerged in response to a wave of criticisms of Habermas, Lennox and Lennox's conception of the public sphere, which Nancy Fraser (1990, 62) neatly identifies as *'bourgeois masculinist'*. Among these criticisms is the recognition that the public sphere, being wrought by implicit and explicit exclusions that belie its ideally inclusive nature, is better understood as a plurality of competing public spheres (Fraser 1990, 61). This awareness gives rise to a description of 'counterpublics' as competing publics designed to resist or expose the ideological biases that define appropriate modes of publicity. Fraser describes counterpublics as publics that 'contested the exclusionary norms of the bourgeois public, elaborating alternative styles of political behavior and alternative norms of public speech' (1990, 61). Counterpublics, or more properly 'subaltern counterpublics' as Fraser elaborates (1990, 68), have a dual character: 'On the one hand, they function as spaces of withdrawal and regroupment; on the other hand, they also function as bases and training grounds for agitational activities directed toward wider publics. ... This dialectic enables subaltern counterpublics partially to offset, although not wholly to eradicate, the unjust participatory privileges enjoyed by members of dominant social groups in stratified societies.'

In the wake of Fraser's articulation of subaltern counterpublics, Michael Warner's *Publics and Counterpublics* (2005) asks whether subordinated status and idiomatic discourse are enough to constitute a public as a counterpublic. Warner begins by outlining the idea of *a* public as distinct both from *the public* (as an idealised social totality) and from concrete audiences assembled in visible space, as in a concert hall or sports event. *A* public, in this third sense articulated by Warner, comes into being only in relation to texts and their circulation; it is fundamentally a reading public – a collection of strangers self-organised around a text or other representational object, existing in relationship only by virtue of being addressed by that object and giving that object their attention and recirculating discourse around it.

A counterpublic, then, is first and foremost *a* public, already in a position distinct from *the public* in the totalising, bourgeois conception. Like any public, a counterpublic reshapes 'the most intimate dimensions of subjectivity around co-membership with indefinite persons in a context of routine action' (Warner 2005, 76). At the same time, since all publics are self-organised around an object to be read, all publics 'differ markedly in one way or another from the premises that allow the dominant culture to understand itself as a public' (Warner 2005, 113). How, then, can we preserve the category of counterpublic as different from any alternative public, subpublic or specialised public? Warner gives the example of the public of *Field & Stream,* a readership defined largely by a shared interest in hunting and fishing. This public is not a counterpublic, in Warner's eyes, since 'nothing in the mode of address or in the projected horizon of this subculture requires its participants to cease for a moment to think of themselves as members of the general public; indeed, they might well consider themselves its most representative members' (Warner 2005, 117). A public which, on the other hand, marks itself off unmistakably from the dominant public more closely approaches a useful understanding of counterpublic. This is roughly in line with Fraser's conception of a counterpublic, but Warner suggests that it is not enough that a public's oppositional character follow only from its content; this would better be understood merely as a subpublic. Instead, Warner seeks a 'difference of kind, or of formal mediation, or of discourse pragmatics, between counterpublics and any other publics' (2005, 118). Here, Warner is perhaps unfair to Fraser, whose insistence that counterpublics articulate 'alternative styles of political behavior and alternative norms of public speech' (Fraser 1990, 61) sounds little different from Warner's extension of the conflict between counterpublics and the dominant public to 'speech genres and modes of address' (2005, 119). Nonetheless, Warner's counterpublics circulate forms of discourse that 'in other contexts would be regarded with hostility or with a sense of indecorousness' (2005, 119).

There is a final facet of counterpublics that needs to be fleshed out before we turn to our case study, and that is the particular ways in which counterpublics marry intimacy with impersonality. As reading publics, counterpublics consist of people who, while self-organised around some shared interest or subordinated subject-position, nonetheless remain strangers to one another. To the extent that the public frees its members from the restrictions that would prevent identification with one another in public (for example, the requirement to remain closeted in dominant culture is lifted in a queer public), those freedoms remain bounded by a reflexivity that acknowledges the subaltern status of the public. And so counterpublic discourse tends to embrace a kind of performative poesis around identity, in which members 'fashion their own subjectivities around the requirements of public circulation and stranger sociability' (Warner 2005, 121). In other words, counterpublics enable and require a particular relationship between intimacy and publicity. Standing in a position of subordination to a dominant culture, the members of a counterpublic find themselves free to embrace forms of address 'laden with intimate affect', while simultaneously aware that those forms of address 'must also be extended impersonally, available for co-membership on the basis of mere attention' (Warner 2005, 121). Thus, Warner summarises, 'Counterpublics are "counter" to the extent that they try to supply different ways of imagining stranger sociability and its reflexivity; as publics, they remain oriented to stranger circulation in a way that is not just strategic but constitutive of membership and its affects' (2005, 121–2).

Here, then, we are ready to turn to our case study. I want to suggest that Reddit's atheists – members of a reading public self-organised around the r/atheism subreddit and its affiliates – constitute a counterpublic to the extent that they frame pseudonymity as a preferable and more intimate alternative to dominant forms of public identification. They seize upon a particular affordance of Reddit's interface – the pseudonymous nature of user profiles – as a way of cultivating a particular affect of stranger intimacy that serves not as a vehicle or platform for integration into the dominant public sphere, but as a counterpublic that provides an alternative space for the performance of (non-)religious identity as neither fully public nor fully private.

It is important to note at this point that the analysis that follows is not intended to generate sweeping generalisations about different media forms and their compatibility with particular political strategies, technologies of subject-formation or forms of collective organisation. I turn next to Madalyn Murray O'Hair as emblematic of one form of atheist politics and one understanding of the role of media (specifically broadcast media), in order to juxtapose that understanding with the kind of discourse frequently articulated by atheists on Reddit. This is my attempt to generate a contrast, not a typology or historical narrative. It would be reductive to overlook the diverse history of atheism in North America as a collection of social movements, particularly as they intersect with media forms. There have been diverse forms of print media aimed both at closed groups and at *the public* writ large. There have been radio and television broadcasts appealing to the 'subaltern' status of atheists rather than urging them to make themselves visible. There have been digital platforms geared towards the promotion of identity-based activism and publicity campaigns. And of course, there is ample disagreement among Reddit's atheist users about how to understand their relationship to a wider religious culture. The argument that follows is meant to draw out a particular understanding of digital atheist identity on a particular digital platform with particular affordances.[1] It must also be noted that my analysis here is limited in geographic and cultural scope. My argument about the relationship between atheism and visibility fits into the larger history of atheism in the United States and depends in large part on the unique character of American secularism as shaped by Protestant Christianity. And while Reddit is an internationally accessible digital platform, Americans account for the largest chunk of its user base by far, and so its content largely reflects American culture(s). Despite these caveats and qualifications, it is my hope that this case study may add some substance to the ongoing scholarly discussion about the relationship between atheist identity, the public sphere and the role of media in the formation of both.

Coming out: Madalyn Murray O'Hair and the politics of visibility

The first thing to do when thinking about atheist publics is to distinguish the strict materialism or rational scepticism of 'Atheism' (noted for emphasis here with the capital 'A'), that only exists in philosophical treatises and dictionary entries, from the diverse and frustratingly complex human beings who identify their own subject-positions according to much more nebulous and common understandings of 'atheism'. Most people find it relatively easy to understand Atheism as, roughly speaking, strict disbelief in personal deities and a more or less rigorous commitment to scientific empiricism. What is more difficult is wrapping one's head, in any satisfying way, round what it means or how it feels to *be* an atheist. For the sake of argumentative clarity, this chapter will begin with an oversimplification: atheism has been, from its emergence as a self-identity around three hundred years ago,[2] inextricably linked to the politics of visibility. Unpacking what exactly this politics of visibility entails is one of the primary aims of what follows, but for now I will claim that the primary social or political ambition of atheists in the West has long been to render atheism visible to a wider religious public.

The ambition to render atheism visible is an intuitive response to atheism's marginalised status in a religious society. The image of the atheist – immoral, licentious and philosophically confused – long preceded those who identified as atheists themselves; it was first a chimera created by theologians and religious leaders to conflate and denigrate various forms of heterodoxy. To identify as an atheist, then, long meant to inhabit an already visible (if imaginatively non-viable) subject-position and to attempt to recuperate it by making it viable – by giving it a coherent and defensible re-presentation.

The emphasis on rendering atheism visible reached its zenith in the mid- to late twentieth century with the work of American atheist Madalyn Murray O'Hair, founder and president of American Atheists and self-appointed representative of atheist identity writ large. Made famous by her involvement in the 1963 Supreme Court decision that prohibited mandatory prayer in public schools, *School District of Abington Township, Pennsylvania, et al. v. Edward Schempp, et al.; Murray, et al. v. Curlett, et al., Constituting the Board of School Commissioners of Baltimore City*, O'Hair arguably had as her overarching career ambition simultaneously to take control of her own public image as 'the most hated woman in America' (Howard 1964) and to force a Christian society to confront the figure of the atheist. While O'Hair's primary political tactic was legal, her larger ambition was to create a coherent and highly visible atheist subject-position with which religious sceptics could identify. O'Hair was singularly concerned with visibility. She took every opportunity to represent atheism on broadcast media, appearing on television shows like 'The Tonight Show' with Johnny Carson and 'The Donahue Show' with Phil Donahue. Her aim throughout her career was primarily to conjure into being the figure of the outspoken atheist:

> She did expend great effort to desensitize the nation to the 'A-word'. She used the words 'Atheist' and 'Atheism' – capitalized, no less – over and over in every possible venue. Before Madalyn, most

Atheists were afraid to use the word other than in whispers. Things are much different now, thanks to her, although I can't say the desensitization of society as a whole is yet complete. Nevertheless, Madalyn made it much safer – and much more natural – to call oneself an Atheist.

(Zindler 2013, 28)

O'Hair's preferred medium was radio, where she could present herself on her own terms without the interference of television hosts or formats (O'Hair 1968a). She founded and operated the *American Atheist Radio Series* out of KTBC Austin from 1968 to 1977 as a platform from which to elaborate her plea for atheism to render itself as visible as possible to the American public. The quest for equal rights for atheists, in O'Hair's descriptions, was predicated on the articulation of an identity as explicitly visible as ethnicity: 'We seek ethnic identity and the right to be free *from* religion in our cultural milieu, a right now specifically denied us by law' (O'Hair 1972a). O'Hair situated the political ambitions of atheists firmly among other countercultural movements of the time that were finding increased acceptance (O'Hair 1971).

The goal of developing a coherent definition of atheism that encapsulated and unified historical variants of religious scepticism was inextricably linked in her mind to the goal of rendering atheism visible to the wider public: 'The biggest underground in America is Atheism. This group has never been organised before to have our voices heard and that is what we are trying to do now. ... You are not alone, not anymore' (O'Hair 1968b). O'Hair's goal in 1968 was 'to have people who are Atheists admit this and to announce to the world that they are Atheists, for we have much to offer the American culture' (O'Hair 1968c). Visibility was power, and by 1983 O'Hair had distilled her goals down to a motto: 'Unity today, power tomorrow' (Murray 1988, 7).

To return for a moment to the language of publics and counterpublics, O'Hair's articulation of atheist identity politics as a means of integrating (albeit without assimilating) atheists into the larger public sphere complicates attempts to conceive her listening public as a counterpublic, in Fraser's and Warner's senses of the term. Fraser notes (1990, 59), for example, drawing on the work of scholars like Joan Landes, Mary Ryan and Geoff Eley, that alternative publics are typically situated in tension with the exclusions that constitute the official public sphere, even while the public sphere is idealised as universally accessible. In this sense, O'Hair clearly understands herself and her listeners as members of just such a public excluded from the public sphere writ large. If counterpublics, in Fraser's (1990, 64) sense, attempt in various ways to expose the mythical nature of the public sphere as a space of 'zero degree culture, so utterly bereft of any specific ethos as to accommodate with perfect neutrality and equal ease interventions expressive of any and every cultural ethos', then O'Hair's project is easily read in this light as an attempt to highlight the fiction of American secularism as a true bracketing or privatisation of religious belief. When O'Hair broadcasts in 1971 her claim that 'the need for complete assimilation into the dominant culture is no longer recognised as being absolutely essential to being a "good American"', she may very well be emphatically rejecting the influential logic of Will Herberg's *Protestant, Catholic, Jew: An essay in American religious sociology* (1955), which married American citizenship with religious identity. In other words, O'Hair's form of identity politics can be read as an attempt to expose the fiction that the public sphere is neutral towards public declarations of religious belief and disbelief. Where the idealised bourgeois public sphere purports to restrict religion to the private sphere, O'Hair wants to show that this restriction is only applied in practice to those who hold heterodox religious views. The important question here, however, is Warner's: do the discursive forms of this subpublic work towards eradicating this fiction and gaining access to the public sphere, or do they work instead towards maintaining a subordinate position in which to carry out an alternative poesis of identity? In the case of O'Hair, the goal seems to be to gain access to the public sphere, to reshape the public sphere so that it no longer excludes atheists. And for this reason, her public is not quite a counterpublic, for rather than 'keeping the counterpublic horizon salient' (Warner 2005, 120), it seeks the elimination of the implicit exclusions that would regard atheist identity as indecorous or incompatible with public speech. O'Hair's discourse does not 'supply different ways of imagining stranger sociability and its reflexivity' (Warner 2005, 121–2), instead aiming only to hold the public sphere to its own ideals: her public's poesis is not transformative, but merely replicative (Warner 2005, 122).

Coming in: deconversion online

In comparison with the emphasis on visibility and traditional identity politics espoused by Madalyn Murray O'Hair and others in the twentieth century, Reddit's atheist community expresses a much more ambivalent approach to the question of atheist identity in the process of coming out.[3] This is evident from r/atheism's front page. A link at the top of the page asks, 'Thinking about telling your parents? Read this first.' The link directs users to a page devoted to offering advice to those who wonder 'Should I come out to my parents as being an atheist?' and 'The short answer', the page emphasises, 'is **No**.' Given the risk for young people still living at home that their parents might evict them from the home, 'r/atheism will almost invariably respond that you should wait'. Such advice, it seems, is in response to 'the constant flow of submissions from people who discovered their parents were not nearly as understanding as they imagined', some 100 examples of which are then hyperlinked ('Comingout – Atheism', n.d.). Thus, a scepticism about the value of coming out is endorsed by the official face of r/atheism. This scepticism is reflected in the most substantial subreddit devoted to the collection of coming-out stories, r/atheismcomingout, the majority of which describe feelings of being misunderstood, ostracised or disowned.

If 'coming out' was one of the primary objectives of O'Hair's atheist identity politics in the twentieth century, it has here begun to give way to an emphasis on what I call 'coming in' to digital media spaces. A number of scholars have deployed the term 'coming in' in various and productive ways. For example, Hammoud-Beckett (2007) describes 'coming in' as the process of reversing the direction of disclosure of sexual orientation and selectively inviting personal relations into one's intimate identity rather than vice versa. Wilson (2008) describes 'coming in' as the process by which some Two-Spirit people recognise the interdependence (rather than declaring the independence) of sexual difference. And Rosenberg (2018) describes 'coming in' as the process of accepting one's sexuality while eschewing society's emphasis on social visibility and disclosure.

In this chapter, 'coming in' refers first and foremost to a dynamic of mediation, in which digital media constitutes a form of public that reconfigures the relationships between visibility, identity and intimacy. Coming out privileges the visibility of identity at the expense of intimacy, for the unity that comes with shared identity at least implicitly involves the dissolution of individuality on which intimacy is predicated. Coming in, on the other hand, involves a form of visibility that is circumscribed both by the fact of digital media's relative seclusion from the traditional public sphere and by the pseudonymous nature of participation in some digital platforms. Pseudonymity refers to a particular affordance of media in which a user's digital activity is connected not to that user's offline identity but instead to a more or less stable pseudonym.[4] Not every digital platform is pseudonymous, though many are. Facebook has made headlines for explicitly rejecting pseudonymity, insisting instead that each profile should correspond to exactly one 'authentic identity'

(Facebook Transparency Center n.d.). Reddit, on the other hand, is pseudonymous. Users may have as many pseudonyms – in the form of usernames – as they want, and Redditors frequently employ multiple usernames for different contexts and burn through new usernames as a means of clearing their history. It is important also to distinguish pseudonymity from anonymity. Reddit usernames are stable by virtue of being subscribed to individual subreddits and by being attached to a viewable history of posts, comments and comment replies. Thus, in comparison to anonymity, pseudonymity allows users to cultivate relatively stable relationships with other users as well as media-specific forms of personal memory and collective history.

Users of digital media are able, more than in most other media forms, to control the relationship between the visibility of their participation and the facets of their own identity that they find salient in different contexts. In the context of the pseudonymous space of Reddit, then, atheists can render their atheism highly visible online (and in a relatively durable sense) and still invisible offline, while at the same time rendering their 'real' identity invisible to the online world. Importantly for our consideration of whether Reddit's atheists constitute a counterpublic, the reconfiguration of the relationship between visibility and identity deployed in the process of 'coming in' allows digital media users to develop new forms and formations of intimacy.

A growing body of scholarship has begun to unpack the myriad personal circumstances and justifications that precede and precipitate an individual's decision to identify – either internally or to others – as an atheist (Barbour 1994; Bullivant 2008; Fazzino 2014; Hood and Chen 2013; Jacobs 1987; Perez and Vallières 2019; Smith 2011; Starr, Waldo and Kauffman 2019; Streib et al. 2009). Like any scholarship that takes human experience as its data, this body of work covers a broad range of approaches to the relationship between the processes of 'deconversion' and the 'deprivatization of disbelief' (Ribberink, Achterberg and Houtman 2013). Though they are often conflated, deconversion and 'coming out' or the 'deprivatization of disbelief' are not synonymous: the former refers to a basic internal self-understanding as reported in individual testimony, while the latter refers to a public declaration of one's identity. A deconversion narrative is a story that describes how one came to identify oneself as an atheist, more to oneself than to others, while 'coming out' is typically a process by which one reveals a pre-existing atheist identity to another person. Deconversion narratives primarily describe moments of realisation, while 'coming out' stories primarily describe moments of revelation. There is ample room for scholarly interpretation, however, in theorising the relationship between the two. For example, scholars vary in the extent to which they regard deconversion narratives as accurate enough recountings of experiences to constitute useful sociological data or as texts to be interpreted as discourse, literature or performance. And if there is a slippage between the two ideas – deconversion and coming out – it depends in part where one theorises the line between public and private.

Thus, in the analysis that follows, stories of deconversion offer an interface between atheists' purely interior understandings of self-identity on the one hand, and a performative deprivatisation of disbelief circumscribed by digital media on the other. While r/atheism tends to discourage its users from publicising their atheism too broadly, subreddits like r/thegreatproject actively encourage and celebrate the sharing of deconversion narratives. The difference between these two facets of atheist identification – deconversion and coming out – I argue, gets to the heart of an important ability of pseudonymous digital interfaces to alter traditional understandings of the relationships between public and private. The general celebration of deconversion narratives in conjunction with the scepticism concerning public acts of coming out points to a conceptualisation of the digital space as the proper site of the deprivatisation of disbelief. Traditional notions of 'coming out' are then replaced with a kind of 'coming in' in which the digital arena constitutes the truly public – now a kind of pseudonymous publicity – and the traditionally public sphere becomes a realm of enforced privatisation. For many atheist users of Reddit, in other words, the digital provides a more authentic form of publicity than the 'real world', suggesting a performative poesis of identity productively understood through the lens of counterpublics.

Digital deconversion: the complication of agency

The reorientation of the public/private divide that takes place in pseudonymous digital arenas like Reddit goes hand in hand with a complication of individual agency best understood through recourse to an analysis of the digital interface. In part because algorithmic culture obfuscates simple attributions of agency, rendering invisible and porous the processes that interpellate subjects, users tend to express a preoccupation with the question of agency. Put differently, as it becomes increasingly difficult in the digital arena to determine whether one's identity is freely chosen or determined by machinations outside the self, digital atheists express increasingly complex understandings of their own agency in relation to their identity as atheists.

We can take one striking moment from Madalyn Murray O'Hair's radio broadcasts as our point of departure. On 31 March 1969, O'Hair interviewed an atheist named Bill, eventually revealed to be her son William J. Murray III, on her weekly radio programme. At a certain point in the conversation, O'Hair sets Bill up to outline his deconversion story, asking, 'What kind of background would you say that you come from, that you have accepted the overall philosophy of life – Atheist thinking … in order to improve the condition of human beings and therefore of yourself, I suppose, in living?' (O'Hair 1972b, 230). Bill's response immediately pushes back against O'Hair's use of the term 'accept' in a way that foregrounds individual agency:

> First we have to realize that an Atheist does not accept. An Atheist critically examines a situation and then does what he feels is right. So, I do not feel that I have accepted anything. I feel that I have come to an intellectual decision as to what my ideas are as to working in the society, and what I should do. I think that with myself, as with any Atheist, these things are completely individualistic and do not reflect acceptable or non-acceptable 'anything', really.
>
> (O'Hair 1972b, 230)

Bill's ardent defence of his own agency, though obviously anecdotal, serves as a jumping-off point from which to analyse the rhetoric common to deconversion narratives on the internet. Deconversion narratives are examples of what Colin Campbell (1971) calls 'irreligious experience'. Campbell's 'irreligion', a departure from the intellectualist language of atheism or secularism, draws attention to the subcultural ethical and emotional underpinnings of non-religious identity. The focus on experience implicitly draws attention to those moments in a story of deconversion when the subject is unable or unwilling to distinguish between immanent and transcendent, force and agent, and passivity and activity. Using terminology more popular today, one might say that 'irreligious experiences' occur in an affective register, referring more to the blurry arena of felt experience than to that of clearly defined epistemology.

This affective quality explains, then, the ambivalent rhetoric that saturates accounts of deconversion, as individuals struggle to articulate an irreligious experience using inadequate terminology. Digital deconversion narratives often exhibit language that celebrates individual agency while simultaneously expressing countervailing disavowals of agency that are lacking in Bill's broadcast narrative. It is not uncommon to see, in stories of deconversion online, the very language of 'acceptance' that Bill rejects. A number of popular threads on Reddit emphasise a feeling that there is little agency at play in becoming an atheist.

In a popular thread called '[Does anyone else] think being atheist is not a choice', user u/secme (2011) writes, 'This is how it is with me at least, I don't think I could even chose to be religious ever again'. The most popular comments echo this sentiment: 'Atheist is simply the default operating system every human is born with before the virus of religion is implanted' (u/ALIENSMACK 2011). 'Belief is not subject to the will. You're either confronted with evidence that obligates belief, or you're forced to reject it as unsupported'(u/Painordelight 2011). 'I do not think one can choose to (not) believe something. It is a response' (u/dembones01 2011). Other strongly upvoted threads and popular comments replicate similar discussions: 'People do not choose to be atheists; they realize they are' (u/emblemparade 2015). 'Atheism is not a "choice"' (u/Humanst 2011). These explicit disavowals of agency are accompanied by more implicit linguistic tropes common to deconversion narratives on the internet.

One recurring trope in deconversion narratives is an account of a precise and instantaneous moment in which the deconvert was transformed into an atheist (Bullivant 2008; Chalfant 2011; Chalfant 2016). The trope of conversion as a kind of sudden gestalt shift or irreversible transmutation often implies a sense of passivity in relation to individual agency. In many cases, the instantaneousness of deconversion is connected to spiritual or quasi-spiritual language. Instant epiphanies, Damascene conversions and bolts from the blue mark deconversions as events visited upon passive individuals. Terms like 'epiphany' maintain pseudo-religious trappings of 'the time when the hand of the divine is most plainly visible … in which the individual feels guided, or coerced, or enraptured by a divine presence' (Buckser and Glazier 2003, xii). The claim is often that deconversion 'happened' according to its own inertia and that the individual undergoing deconversion did little to consciously enact the transformation.

Deconversion narratives also tend to highlight the social and emotional upheaval which follows 'coming out' (Bullivant 2008). These descriptions of deconversion as a moment of crisis imply that it is a process which happens whether the subject wants it to or not (Chalfant 2011, 2016). This is best understood as a reaction to a particular understanding of religion as a kind of ideology that preys on the agency of individuals. Because religion is constructed as wish-fulfilment – a corruption of agency in which normally rational individuals are coerced into believing what they want to believe – the claim that deconversion occurs against the individual's desires serves to establish an understanding of atheism as somehow more true than religious identification. Truth is positioned in an inverse relationship to desire and, accordingly, agency.

One might interpret the linguistic conventions of deconversion narratives in Foucauldian terms as confessional technologies of the self aimed at reinforcing the sovereignty of atheist subjectivity. Michel Foucault's discussions of confessional practices in *The History of Sexuality: Volume 1* (1978), as well as 'Technologies of the self' (1988), consider the ways in which truth is inscribed at the heart of the individual subject. For Foucault, confession is one of most potent means by which individual truths are objectified, by being placed deep in the body of the individual where they are purportedly out of reach of historical contamination:

> The obligation to confess is now relayed through so many different points, is so deeply ingrained in us, that we no longer perceive it as the effect of a power that constrains us; on the contrary, it seems to us that truth, lodged in our most secret nature, 'demands' only to surface; that if it fails to do so, this is because a constraint holds it in place, the violence of a power weighs it down, and it can finally be articulated only at the price of a kind of liberation.
>
> (Foucault 1978, 60)

Confession thus constitutes, for Foucault, a disciplinary power which strips truth from sovereignty, attributing its obfuscation to repressive force. Foucault's work on confession suggests that deconversion narratives may serve to insulate truth from relations of power by removing the individual agent – the vehicle of cultural construction – from the technology by which atheist subjectivity is constructed. In those tropes in which deconversion strikes an unwitting and passive individual like a bolt from the blue, truth is positioned as something external to the individual, who is understood as the locus for all of those desires that contribute to religious ideology. The emphasis on truth as originating from an external reality or as emerging suddenly from somewhere deep within the subconscious of the confessing subject serves to mask that 'its production is thoroughly imbued with relations of power' (Foucault 1978, 60).

Of course, the disavowals of agency common to digital deconversion narratives are complicated by discourse which celebrates individuality and choice against the oppressive conformity imposed by religion. One area in which r/atheism's users celebrate agency revolves around frequent discussions of LGBT identity. Given the popular embrace of the rhetoric of 'coming out', it is perhaps no surprise that atheists on the internet often find affinity with the queer community. But while it might seem intuitive that digital atheists would embrace wholesale the popular discourse that emphasises the naturalness of queer identity in response to critics who regard sexual non-normativity as a choice, instead one finds atheists rejecting disavowals of agency. Consider the following: user u/Cleev (2012) started a thread called 'Being gay is a choice', in which they caricaturise the conservative understanding of homosexuality as a choice: 'What is the gay agenda? Recruitment. Since no one is born gay, gay people have to try and indoctrinate and recruit the rest of us at an early age, before we have the wherewithal to figure out for ourselves that the gay agenda is a lie' (u/Cleev 2012). u/Cleev then asks readers to substitute the word 'Christian' for the word 'gay', implying that it is precisely the issue of agency that renders religion problematic and divorces atheism from the realm of ideology. This replicates, then, a familiar logic in which it is only that which cannot be chosen (in this case, queerness or atheism) that is immune from criticism.

But the responses to u/Cleev's post are hardly universally positive. The most popular serious comment isolates the issue of choice as a distraction: 'What I want to know is … Who really cares if it is a choice or not? What difference would it make if it was a choice? Are we not free men and women living in a free country with a guaranteed right to pursue happiness?' (u/Demaestro 2012). In another thread, a similar conversation transpires when user u/dperr117 links to an image of comedian David Cross overlaid with the text of a quote from Cross, in which he argues for an exclusively genetic understanding of homosexuality ('David Cross …' 2012). For Cross, we read, the humour lies in the absurdity of pretending that someone would choose to adopt an identity that made them the target of bigotry and hatred. Again, the most popular comments are highly critical: 'So fucking what if it's a choice. Why is that a reason to hate someone. Go about your life and don't say or do mean shit to people' (u/Wasmyfault 2012). 'Even if it was a choice, so what?' (u/Msheno 2012). In other words, while r/atheism's users often shun choice when it is said to underlie atheist identity, one sees simultaneous attempts to reclaim agency from those who would downplay it in the formation of identity. To account for this confused or paradoxical understanding of agency, we have to consider again the material specificity of the interface.

The invisible hand of the interface

One of the themes that course through the history of media is the extent to which particular anxieties provoked by particular media partially shape the notions of identity articulated there. For Madalyn Murray O'Hair – a broadcast media native – the primary anxiety around atheist identity had to do with visibility. Radio, her preferred medium, trafficked in invisibilities – of the material substrate of transmission, of the experience of listening, of the presence of the consuming audience. Thus, there is a constitutive resonance between the politics of visibility advocated by O'Hair and the affective contours of the media form through which she operated.

With the pseudonymous digital interface, the play of visibility and invisibility remains, but it is now relocated so that the digital becomes the primary site of visibility, and the anxiety concerning visibility becomes more than ever inflected by the question of control. This is one of the questions that theorists of 'algorithmic culture' (Chun 2013; Striphas 2015) attempt to isolate: is it possible any longer to differentiate between the free choice of the individual user and the determining machinations of invisible algorithms and aggregate data? On a pseudo-anonymous and highly algorithmic interface like Reddit, a traditional understanding of agency as free will appears hopelessly simplistic.

Thus, it is not adequate to theorise deconversion narratives on the internet as simply confessional technologies of the self aimed at establishing the sovereign subject. Instead, the interface, as a mediator between the visible and the invisible, aims at 'the resurgence of the *seemingly* sovereign individual, the subject driven to know, driven to map, to zoom in and out, to manipulate, and to act' (Chun 2013, 8). To an extent, neoliberal subjectivity has always relied on this interplay of the visible and the invisible. The freedom of the subject is always circumscribed and enabled by invisible forces (economic, genetic, cultural, ideological) that determine it.

Foucault's discussion of the economic subject, *homo oeconomicus*, provides a more useful means to understand a conception of truth which removes truth from the reach of sovereignty. In *The Birth of Biopolitics*, Foucault engages in an unconventional reading of Adam Smith's 'invisible hand' metaphor for describing economic rationality. In Foucault's reading, the invisible hand operates in a space in which the forces that constitute subjects are invisible to the eye of the sovereign:

> *Homo oeconomicus* is someone who can say to the juridical sovereign, to the sovereign possessor of rights and founder of positive law on the basis of the natural right of individuals: You must not. But he does not say: You must not, because I have rights and you must not touch them. ... You must not because you cannot. And you cannot in the sense that 'you are powerless'. And why are you powerless, why can't you? You cannot because you do not know, and you do not know because you cannot know.
>
> (Foucault 2010, 282)

This radical unknowability in the face of sovereignty is what, for Foucault, makes economics an 'atheistic discipline; ... a discipline without God; ... without totality' (2010, 282). It is also what allows us to ask the inverse question: whether atheism as it is constructed in these deconversion narratives has affinities with a kind of economic view of truth. This would be a response to sovereignty in which truth is not simply objectified or historicised, but obscured.

By analogy, when deconversion narratives undermine traditional notions of agency, what is rendered invisible is not the economic mechanisms that produce a collective good, but the very personal forces that constitute (a)religious identity. One cannot help what one believes because this facet of identity is mysterious and invisible, with its origins in the dark recesses of biology and the subconscious and rupturing the surface of consciousness in one brilliant moment. The denial of agency then produces an 'indispensable' (Foucault 2010, 280) form of invisibility which prevents an association between atheism and sovereign subjectivity while maintaining some notion of truth. In the same way that economic rationality is 'founded on the unknowability of the totality of the process' (Foucault 2010, 282), the atheist subject-position in these narratives is founded on the irrationality of atheist identity, which is partially synonymous with its truth.

Extending Foucault's insightful divorce between the sovereign subject and impersonal truth, Wendy Hui Kyong Chun (2013) has framed digital media as providing a metaphor and arena with which to play out their relationship: 'The linking of rationality with mysticism, knowability with what is unknown, makes it a powerful fetish that offers its programmers and users alike a sense of empowerment, of sovereign subjectivity, that covers over – barely – a sense of profound ignorance' (Chun 2013, 18). In the context of atheism, what the digital offers is an explicit recognition of the relationship of 'rationality with mysticism, knowability with what is unknown'. That is to say, despite atheists' frequent appeals to pure rationality, there has always been an element of mysticism to the question of subjectivity, wherein the self is simultaneously and paradoxically a free willing agent and a determined body. This is the paradox that Campbell's (1971) 'irreligion' is meant to illuminate: that the experience of becoming an atheist tends to exceed the language available to describe it. The digital provides the perfect interface for articulating this confusion of agency that simultaneously extends and undermines the sovereign subject. As Chun puts it:

> [The] paradoxical combination of visibility and invisibility, of rational causality and profound ignorance, grounds the computer as an attractive model for the 'real' world. Interfaces have become functional analogs to ideology and its critique – from ideology as false consciousness to ideology as fetishistic logic, interfaces seem to concretize our relation to invisible (or barely visible) 'sources' and substructures.
>
> (Chun 2013, 59)

The digital interface, by explicitly executing the power of the invisible, enables a more explicit engagement between traditional understandings of sovereign subjectivity and the invisible determining forces on which that subjectivity is founded. Hence, the confused understanding of agency articulated on r/atheism represents an accurate response to a 'postmodern/neoliberal confusion' (Chun 2006, 59) in which subjectivity is perpetually determined by invisible forces. In this regard, the digital arena offers 'a simpler, more reassuring analog of power, one in which the user takes the place of the sovereign executive "source", code becomes law, and mapping produces the subject' (Chun 2006, 59). The atheist online, then, is caught in a paradox enabled by the digital interface – simultaneously more insistent than ever that her identity is absolutely true and more aware than ever that this identity is merely a result of a mapping operation executed by inhuman forces – and simultaneously abstractly convinced that she is a free willing agent and specifically aware that her identity has been selected and imposed from a range of predetermined options.

How, then, can we consider the question of algorithmic culture in the context of counterpublics? Warner's discussion of counterpublics considers agency in primarily collective terms – that is, whether publics have agency in relationship to the state – but does offer resources to draw out the relationship between agency and the performance or narration of identity. Warner notes, for example, that publics with an uncomplicated sense of agency often deploy verbs of private reading that can be transposed upward to the aggregate of readers. Publics as well as their individual members are said to scrutinise, reject, decide, judge, etc. Counterpublics, on the other hand, 'tend to be those in which this ideology of reading does not have the same privilege' (Warner 2005, 123). And thus, counterpublics tend to conceive of agency in alternative terms. What then, can we make of a public that expresses a heavy scepticism of agency in general in the face of the determining effects of algorithms? In the first instance, it must be said that this interrogation of agency reflects a friction with dominant culture, in which the ideal neoliberal individual is a self-determining subject. That most atheists on Reddit enthusiastically embrace individualism even while some express scepticism about self-determination suggests a particular source of that friction. I would suggest that atheists frequently aim to expose a hypocrisy among their religious counterparts in that the religious *think* they are self-determining, while being in actuality religiously indoctrinated. And so, the scepticism about agency is easily understood as a distrust of any subject-position that can be freely chosen, for such a subject-position would be vulnerable to emotional manipulation (that is, wish-fulfilment, delusion).

Another fruitful line of reasoning has to do with Warner's emphasis on a counterpublic's performative character. According to Warner (2005, 114), every public deploys discourse performatively in that it necessarily attempts, through a variety of techniques, to specify in advance 'the lifeworld of its circulation'. Put differently, a public tends to negotiate the tension between being open to any stranger and yet generating sociability by deploying poetic-expressive discourse that situates the addressee or reader in idiomatic ways. Doing so creates a sense that one can trust a potential reader to understand your intention (Warner 2005, 116). However, this performative dimension of public discourse, Warner (2005, 114) writes, is routinely misrecognised when publics imagine, by analogy with *the* public, that their discourse is culturally neutral. Implicit in Warner's analysis is that this misrecognition succeeds or fails in obscuring the performative dimension of a public's discourse to the extent that the analogy between *a* public and the dominant culture feels appropriate or frictionless. If a public's members are able to imagine themselves as emblematic members of *the* public, they will have little problem overlooking the role of poetic-expressive discourse in the formation of their lifeworld. Here again, the question of stranger sociability is paramount. The ability to navigate and understand (albeit below the level of consciousness) the relationship between *a* public and *the* public depends in large part on being able to conceive, at least in theory, of the imaginary borders of a public, for the difference between being in and out of a public depends not on personality or affiliation but only on attention.

How can we theorise the specificity of stranger sociability within a public when the boundaries that circumscribe its self-organisation are determined largely by algorithmic processes? Crucially, for Warner (2005, 123), counterpublics share the tendency that they embrace their own performative poesis when they, for myriad reasons, have difficulty finding counterparts in public articulations of agency. Counterpublics embrace performativity because the misrecognition of that performativity is hindered by friction with the dominant public sphere. I am suggesting here, then, that the highly algorithmic affordances of Reddit's interface generate that friction. If subreddits can be thought of as publics, the processes that bring individual users in and out of those publics by way of manipulating and directing attention as well as the circulation of discourse are algorithmic, and thus both relatively unpredictable and invisible. This is to suggest that digital algorithms are uniquely capable of encouraging the kinds of poetic lifeworlds that constitute counterpublics by virtue of the fact that they explode the simple notions of affiliation or voluntary association that often render subpublics compatible with the dominant culture.

Intimate digital counterpublics

The question of intimacy lies at the heart of the intersection between public sphere and media studies. Diverse forms of intimacy central to personal and impersonal relationships alike pose a challenge to neat dichotomies between public and private spheres. Berlant and Warner's influential 'Sex in public' (1998) offers the touchstone for thinking about the relationship between intimacy and the formation of counterpublics. Berlant and Warner's provocative elaboration of the relationship between queer culture and sites of counter-intimacies provides a useful lens with which to understand r/atheism and r/thegreatproject. For Berlant and Warner (1998, 553), heterosexuality as a property of subjectivity is a myth to be replaced with the notion of heterosexual culture, which 'achieves much of its metacultural intelligibility through the ideologics and institutions of intimacy'. Specifically, heteronormative conventions of intimacy 'conjure a mirage: a home base of prepolitical humanity from which citizens are thought to come into political discourse and to which they are expected to return in the (always imaginary) future after political conflict' (Berlant and Warner 1998, 553). One of the goals of queer politics, then, is to generate new spaces of intimacy which are neither public nor private in the ways articulated by heterosexual culture: 'Making a queer world has required the development of kinds of intimacy that bear no necessary relation to domestic space, to kinship, to the couple form, to property, or to the nation' (Berlant and Warner 1998, 558).

I do not wish to argue that digital atheism is queer in any substantial sense. While many atheists articulate a number of affinities between atheist identity and queer identity, the overwhelmingly white, male and heterosexual make-up of the American atheist population along with a chequered history of problematic and exclusivist language necessitates restraint in taking these affinities too seriously. At the same time, there are noteworthy lines of connection between Berlant and Warner's aims and my own. One of my research projects has been to demonstrate that atheism, as an attribute possessed by subjects, is an illusion best replaced with the notion of atheist culture. And this culture, like queer culture or any other, 'indexes a virtual social world, in ways that range from a repertoire of styles and speech genres to referential metaculture' (Berlant and Warner 1998, 558). And as in the queer world-making project articulated by Berlant and Warner, there is an extent to which the users of r/atheism and r/thegreatproject are engaged in the creation of forms of counter-intimacy.

Indeed, many deconversion narratives published on r/thegreatproject exhibit a form of intimacy perhaps unique to pseudonymous media. Sharing a personal account of a momentous transformation in one's identity is already a deeply intimate act. But this sense of intimacy is heightened by the ambivalence of Reddit when it comes to personal encounter: that is, any contribution to Reddit might be immediately lost in a sea of impersonal information or it might speak directly to another individual user. This, of course, is one of the fundamental principles of reading publics, in which reaching strangers is the public's primary orientation (Warner 2005, 74). It is not uncommon for popular deconversion stories to end with appeals to this duality. One of the most popular deconversion narratives, an account by user u/makinwaffles (2012a), ends 'Thanks r/atheism, for listening, and even if you didn't (since this is way too long), thanks for existing. Its [sic] more than can be said for God.' Other stories end in a similar fashion, by facing up to the possibility that no one is paying attention or that any reaction will be negative: 'Feel free to ignore this or downvote to oblivion, too. I just had to put it somewhere' (u/Lunamanar 2012).

The invisibility of the audience is not unique to digital media, having been a defining problem of broadcast media (Lacey 2013), and yet the pseudonymous digital interface offers the audience a more direct avenue of response and a heightened visibility to any lack of response. Given the ease of voting and responding, it would be fairly obvious if a thread received no traffic; the audience in this case is not invisible but virtual, in that there is for any digital content a simultaneous potential to go completely unnoticed or to go viral and catapult a profile into high visibility. Again, this is true of all reading publics, according to Warner's description. The more interesting line of thought, in terms of the question of media, is how particular publics utilise the duality between the impersonal and the personal addressee to generate intimacy and 'how they make stranger relationality normative' (Warner 2005, 76). Reddit users can respond to an original poster's thread in public, or they can send them a private message, but the fact of that response takes on a significance proportional to the virtual size of the digital mediascape. If posting on Reddit is something like whispering into a cacophonous roar of other voices, there is always the potential that your whisper might fall precisely on the ears of someone receptive to it. Thus, when u/makinwaffles' thread receives supportive replies, their response (2012b) is very intimate:

> When I posted this, I did it so that I could have a chance to write out my story in solid form and express what it meant to me. I did tell some friends in junior high, but didn't include that in the original post since their reactions were just more of the same shit. After all that, I have a really hard time saying any of this out loud, and I figured I'd take a shot in the dark on a relevant anonymous forum to get some of it off my chest. I hardly expected such a supportive response, and I don't know that people will begin to understand how much it means to me.

Here, u/makinwaffles posits the digital space as providing more intimacy than their offline friendships. What's more, this intimacy is connected in part to the very pseudonymity characteristic of the digital arena: the fact that the original post constituted a 'shot in the dark' makes it that much more significant that the message was positively received.

If we recognise r/atheism and its affiliated subreddits as sites for the production of counterpublics, we must ask how the notions of intimacy generated there differ from those common to contemporary religion or to atheist engagements with other media forms. I am suggesting here that one key to this differentiation lies in the role of pseudonymity. The internet, more than other media, is capable of generating a close association between anonymity and intimacy, an association that lends digital atheism some degree of uniqueness. Where religious intimacy is commonly predicated on identity – of God, of the individual believer – atheist intimacy here is predicated on anonymity or pseudo-anonymity. Rather than being tied vertically to a mass-media broadcaster, intimacy in digital spaces is tied horizontally between users, who are themselves imbricated in complex algorithmic networks.

If, as Warner (2005, 120) argues, 'friction against the dominant public forces the poetic-expressive character of counterpublic discourse to become salient to consciousness', then Reddit's atheist public is predicated on pseudonymity. The poetic-expressive character of this atheist counterpublic is the awareness that one must, by virtue of one's subordinated position with relation to dominant culture, tell their most intimate story – the story of their own self-fashioning – in the most impersonal of ways. Writing a deconversion narrative on Reddit is like sending a message in a bottle. It might drift endlessly and never be read, or it might float into the hands of someone for whom it has tremendous meaning. Warner (2005, 113) reminds us that all public discourse 'abandons the security of its positive, given audience' and yet must, at the same time, perform the all-important function of 'poetic world making' by specifying the lifeworld of its own circulation (Warner 2005, 114). If Reddit's atheist public performatively conjures its own character, then this character is defined by these two necessary features of its medium: first, by virtue of pseudonymity, intimacy is inextricably tied to impersonality; second, by virtue of its algorithmic constitution, the generation of intimacy as an affective glue cementing the formation of the public is dictated largely by an invisible process more akin to chance than to individual agency, and so the self-fashioning of subjectivity is a process more of narrative performativity than of actual agential autochthony. Their embrace of these forms of poesis in the face of dominant culture's emphases on authentic identity and self-determination are what enable us to read Reddit's atheists as a counterpublic.

Notes

1   I use the term 'affordances', following Donald Norman's (1988) co-option of James J. Gibson's (1979) coinage, to refer to the properties of an object – in this case a media artefact – that determine its possible uses.
2   I am taking Jean Meslier's (d. 1729) *Testament: Memoir of the Thoughts and Sentiments of Jean Meslier* (2009) as the first significant public self-identification with atheism in the West.
3   Despite her preoccupation with atheist visibility, O'Hair only infrequently used the specific rhetoric of 'coming out of the closet' (see for example O'Hair 1990). Nonetheless, 'coming out' has today become the most common shorthand for public declarations of atheist identity.
4   Pseudonymity should not be confused with 'pseudo-anonymity', which I take to refer to media platforms that appear anonymous to users while nonetheless collecting personal information for network managers, developers, moderators, etc.

References

Barbour, John. 1994. *Versions of Deconversion: Autobiography and the Loss of Faith*. Charlottesville: University Press of Virginia.

Berlant, Lauren and Michael Warner. 1998. 'Sex in public.' *Critical Inquiry* 24 (2): 547–66.

Buckser, Andrew and Stephen D. Glazier. 2003. *The Anthropology of Religious Conversion*. Lanham, MD: Rowman & Littlefield.

Bullivant, Stephen. 2008. 'Introducing irreligious experiences.' *Implicit Religion* 11 (1): 7–24. https://doi.org/10.1558/imre.v11i1.7.

Campbell, Colin. 1971. *Toward a Sociology of Irreligion*. London: Macmillan.

Chalfant, Eric. 2011. 'Thank God I'm an atheist: Deconversion narratives on the internet.' MA thesis, Wake Forest University. http://wakespace.lib.wfu.edu/jspui/handle/10339/33473 (accessed 21 June 2022).

Chalfant, Eric. 2016 'Taylor-made: Immanent transcendence in a secular age.' *Implicit Religion* 19 (2): 203–24.

Chun, Wendy Hui Kyong. 2006. 'Introduction: Did somebody say new media?', in *New Media, Old Media: A history and theory reader*, Wendy Hui Kyong Chun and Thomas Keenan, eds, 1–10. Abingdon: Routledge.

Chun, Wendy Hui Kyong. 2013. *Programmed Visions: Software and memory*. Cambridge, MA: MIT Press.

'Comingout – Atheism.' n.d. https://www.reddit.com/r/atheism/wiki/comingout (accessed 27 April 2021).

'David Cross on homosexuality and choice: Atheism.' 2012. https://www.reddit.com/r/atheism/comments/q0dgx/david_cross_on_homosexuality_and_choice/ (accessed 27 April 2021).

Facebook Transparency Center. n.d. 'Account integrity and authentic identity.' https://transparency.fb.com/policies/community-standards/account-integrity-and-authentic-identity/ (accessed 21 June 2022).

Fazzino, Lori. 2014. 'Leaving the church behind: Applying a deconversion perspective to Evangelical exit narratives.' *Journal of Contemporary Religion* 29 (2): 249–66. https://doi.org/10.1080/13537903.2014.903664.

Foucault, Michel. 1978. *The History of Sexuality, Volume 1: An Introduction* (trans. Robert Hurley). New York: Pantheon Books.

Foucault, Michel. 1988. 'Technologies of the self', in *Technologies of the Self: A seminar with Michel Foucault*, 16–49. Amherst: University of Massachusetts Press.

Foucault, Michel. 2010. *The Birth of Biopolitics: Lectures at the Collège de France, 1978–1979* (ed. Michel Senellart, trans. Graham Burchell). London: Picador.

Fraser, Nancy. 1990. 'Rethinking the public sphere: A contribution to the critique of actually existing democracy.' *Social Text* 25/26: 56–80.

Gibson, James. 1979. *The Ecological Approach to Visual Perception*. Boston, MA: Houghton Mifflin.

Habermas, Jürgen, Sara Lennox and Frank Lennox. 1974. 'The public sphere: An encyclopedia article (1964).' *New German Critique* 3: 49–55.

Hammoud-Beckett, Sekneh. 2007. 'Azima ila hayati – An invitation in to my life: Narrative conversations about sexual identity.' *International Journal of Narrative Therapy and Community Work* 1: 29–39.

Herberg, Will. 1955. *Protestant, Catholic, Jew: An essay in American religious sociology*. Garden City, NY: Doubleday.

Hood, Ralph, Jr and Zhuo Chen. 2013. 'Conversion and deconversion', in *The Oxford Handbook of Atheism*, Stephen Bullivant and Michael Ruse, eds, 537–50. Oxford: Oxford University Press.

Howard, Jane. 1964. 'Madalyn Murray: The most hated woman in America.' *Life* 56 (25): 91–4.

Jacobs, Janet. 1987. 'Deconversion from religious movements: An analysis of charismatic bonding and spiritual commitment.' *Journal for the Scientific Study of Religion* 26 (3): 294–308.

Lacey, Kate. 2013. *Listening Publics: The politics and experience of listening in the media age*. Cambridge: Polity.

Meslier, Jean. 2009 *Testament: Memoir of the thoughts and sentiments of Jean Meslier* (trans. Michael Shreve). Amherst, NY: Prometheus Books.

Murray, Jon. 1988. 'Silver jubilee atheist-style.' *American Atheist*, June.

Norman, Donald. 1988. *The Psychology of Everyday Things*. New York: Basic Books.

O'Hair, Madalyn Murray. 1968a. 'History of atheists' fight for radio time.' *American Atheist Radio Series (Austin, TX: KTBC, June 3, 1968)* in *What on Earth is an Atheist!*, 1–5. Austin, TX: American Atheist Press.

O'Hair, Madalyn Murray. 1968b. 'Statistics on church members and atheists.' *American Atheist Radio Series (Austin, TC: KTBC, July 15, 1968)*, in *What on Earth is an Atheist!*, 32–7. Austin, TX: American Atheist Press.

O'Hair, Madalyn Murray. 1968c. 'Religion and morality.' *American Atheist Radio Series (Austin, TX: KTBC, December 16, 1968)*, in *What on Earth is an Atheist!*, 150–4. Austin, TX: American Atheist Press.

O'Hair, Madalyn Murray. 1971. 'American Atheist Radio Series.' *American Atheist Radio Series (Austin, TX: KTBC, August 2, 1971; October 25, 1971)*, in *American Atheist Radio Series Transcripts, Vol. IV*, housed at Charles E. Stevens American Atheist Library and Archive.

O'Hair, Madalyn Murray. 1972a. 'Roman Catholic-Humanist dialogue.' *American Atheist Radio Series (Austin, TX: KTBC, May 27, 1972*, in *American Atheist Radio Series Transcripts, Vol. IV*, housed at Charles E. Stevens American Atheist Library and Archive.

O'Hair, Madalyn Murray. 1972b. *What on Earth is an Atheist!* New York: Arno Press.

O'Hair, Madalyn Murray. 1990. 'Atheists: The last minority.' Speech at the Twentieth Annual National Convention of American Atheists. St Petersburg, FL, 14 April.

Perez, Sergio and Frédérique Vallières. 2019. 'How do religious people become atheists? Applying a grounded theory approach to propose a model of deconversion.' *Secularism and Nonreligion* 8 (3): 1–14.

Ribberink, Egbert, Peter Achterberg and Dick Houtman. 2013. 'Deprivatization of disbelief? Non-religiosity and anti-religiosity in 14 Western European countries.' *Politics and Religion* 6 (1): 101–20.

Rosenberg, Shoshana. 2018. 'Coming in: Queer narratives of sexual self-discovery.' *Journal of Homosexuality* 65 (13): 1788–1816. https://doi.org/10.1080/00918369.2017.1390811.

School District of Abington Township, Pennsylvania, et al. v. Edward Schempp, et al.; Murray, et al. v. Curlett, et al., Constituting the Board of School Commissioners of Baltimore City. 1963. 374 U.S. 203.

Smith, Jesse M. 2011. 'Becoming an atheist in America: Constructing identity and meaning from the rejection of theism.' *Sociology of Religion* 72 (2): 215–37. https://doi.org/10.1093/socrel/srq082.

Starr, Chelsea, Kristin Waldo and Matthew Kauffman. 2019. 'Digital irreligion: Christian deconversion in an online community.' *Journal for the Scientific Study of Religion* 58 (2): 494–512.

Streib, Heinz, Ralph W. Hood, Barbara Keller, Rosina-Martha Csöff and Christopher F. Silver. 2009. *Deconversion: Qualitative and quantitative results from cross-cultural research in Germany and the United States of America.* Göttingen: Vandenhoeck & Ruprecht.

Striphas, Ted. 2015. 'Algorithmic culture.' *European Journal of Cultural Studies* 18 (4–5): 395–412.

u/ALIENSMACK. 2011. Comment on 'DAE think being atheist is not a choice.' /r/atheism. https://www.reddit.com/r/atheism/comments/gr75q/dae_think_being_atheist_is_not_a_choice/c1po33v (accessed 22 June 2022).

u/Cleev. 2012. 'Being gay is a choice.' /r/atheism. https://www.reddit.com/r/atheism/comments/tilyc/being_gay_is_a_choice/ (accessed 22 June 2022).

u/Demaestro. 2012. Comment on 'Being gay is a choice.' /r/atheism. https://www.reddit.com/r/atheism/comments/tilyc/being_gay_is_a_choice/c4mzesy (accessed 22 June 2022).

u/dembones01. 2011. Comment on 'DAE think being atheist is not a choice.' /r/atheism. https://www.reddit.com/r/atheism/comments/gr75q/dae_think_being_atheist_is_not_a_choice/c1pny8h (accessed 22 June 2022).

u/emblemparade. 2015. ''People do not choose to be atheists; they realize they are.' /r/atheism. https://www.reddit.com/r/atheism/comments/3m04fe/people_do_not_choose_to_be_atheists_they_realize/ (accessed 22 June 2022).

u/Humanst. 2011. 'Atheism is not a "choice".' /r/atheism. https://www.reddit.com/r/atheism/comments/kd06k/atheism_is_not_a_choice/ (accessed 22 June 2022).

u/Lunamanar. 2012. 'I am "the worst thing that could ever happen" to my mother. [x-Post from /r/atheism].' https://www.reddit.com/r/thegreatproject/comments/yp3m4/i_am_the_worst_thing_that_could_ever_happen_to_my/ (accessed 22 June 2022).

u/makinwaffles. 2012a. 'Too fucked up to care anymore (x-post from r/atheism).' https://www.reddit.com/r/thegreatproject/comments/on45g/too_fucked_up_to_care_anymore_xpost_from_ratheism/ (accessed 22 June 2022).

u/makinwaffles. 2012b. Comment on 'Too fucked up to care anymore (x-post from r/atheism)'. https://www.reddit.com/r/thegreatproject/comments/on45g/too_fucked_up_to_care_anymore_xpost_from_ratheism/c3iqcrgs (accessed 22 June 2022).

u/Msheno. 2012. Comment on 'David Cross on homosexuality and choice'. r/atheism. https://www.reddit.com/r/atheism/comments/q0dgx/david_cross_on_homosexuality_and_choice/c3tqtuh (accessed 22 June 2022).

u/Painordelight. 2011. Comment on 'DAE think being atheist is not a choice'. /r/atheism. https://www.reddit.com/r/atheism/comments/gr75q/dae_think_being_atheist_is_not_a_choice/c1po0y7 (accessed 22 June 2022).

u/secme. 2011. 'DAE think being atheist is not a choice.' /r/atheism. https://www.reddit.com/r/atheism/comments/gr75q/dae_think_being_atheist_is_not_a_choice (accessed 22 June 2022).

u/Wasmyfault. 2012. Comment on 'David Cross on homosexuality and choice' r/Atheism. https://www.reddit.com/r/atheism/comments/q0dgx/david_cross_on_homosexuality_and_choice/c3tqwyj (accessed 22 June 2022).

Warner, Michael. 2005. *Publics and Counterpublics*. New York: Zone Books.

Wilson, Alex. 2008. 'N'tacimowin inna nah': Our coming in stories.' *Canadian Woman Studies/Les cahiers de la femme* 26 (3–4): 193–9.

Zindler, Frank R. 2013. 'Remembering Madalyn Murray O'Hair: April 13, 1919–September 1995.' *American Atheist* (Second Quarter): 24–9.

10
Pumpkins at the centre of Mars and circlejerks: do atheists find community online?

Evelina Lundmark

This volume prompts us to ask what forms of sceptical publicity atheists, sceptics and the religiously indifferent engage in, and what types of media encourage community formation or facilitate different expressions of religious scepticism in public. It thus allows us to consider the diversity of 'sceptical publics', which also obliges us to think about what publicness is in relation to the non-religious. Kate Nash has argued that '"Public" is a kind of placeholder to allow consideration of the moral dimension of democratic politics' (Nash 2014, 1). This allows us to explore the notion of publicness beyond the idea of the *polis*, beyond definitions of the public as a social totality. Michael Warner's (2005) work has also been influential in this respect, specifically in his attempt to define the public beyond external organisation, instead focusing on it as a space co-effected by the circulation of texts. Thus, one can argue that publicness broadly can be construed as a set of heterogeneous interlinking or opposing discourses centring on moral considerations or ideals related to issues of social organisation and 'desirable' identities. Similarly, a microcosm of minority discourse – such as discourse focusing on atheism – is no less heterogeneous, and thus necessitates reflection on this diversity, and on what characterises different discursive formations in this space. The aim of this chapter is thus to explore the role of conflict in atheist community formation, looking at how anti-religious sentiments should be conceived vis-à-vis atheist community formation online, the purpose of which is to bring nuance to if and how practices of engaging with atheist content online – or of '"reading with" like-minded strangers' (Cimino and Smith 2011, 33) – should be conceived of as participation in or formation of diffused communities.

Building on ideas of atheism potentially being experienced and expressed as imagined community in online spaces, I have previously analysed discourses on /r/atheism, a subforum of reddit.com populated mainly by US users,[1] finding that atheism was conceptualised by /r/atheism users as 'merely' a way of thinking rationally, as opposed to being a movement or an identity (Lundmark and LeDrew 2018).[2] In this chapter I consider the insights from this work in relation to findings from another study focusing on atheist vloggers on YouTube, specifically the comment section of one of Ana Kasparian's videos (the co-host and producer of *The Young Turks*, a progressive news and commentary channel on YouTube; Lundmark 2019).[3] The comment section of Kasparian's video stood out from the rest of the material in the study because of the strong focus commenters put on the lack of an atheist community and the lack of an atheist message in their critique of Kasparian's video. As these key themes, which dominated Kasparian's comment section, appeared to cohere with the hegemonic discursive formation of /r/atheism I had previously studied, the analysis presented here considers more deeply what appears to be a paradox observable in both data sets, a community forming around the notion that there cannot be an atheist community. Using the framework of antagonism and agonism posited by Chantal Mouffe (2013), the analysis in this chapter reflects on atheist community formation, and the role of conflict in atheist discourse, and asks if these types of online practices should be conceived as diffused or imagined communities, or as recursive echo chambers embodying atheist frustration.

Atheist community?

Atheism experienced a surge in visibility in the mid-2000s, something that has in part been attributed to the greater visibility enabled by the internet and social media technologies in general (Laughlin 2016; Smith and Cimino 2012). Research on atheist communities forming online (e.g. Starr, Waldo and Kauffman 2019), on the use of online resources by existing communities (e.g. Fader 2017), or following broader swathes of atheist discourses enacted on various platforms (e.g. Smith and Cimino 2012;

Cimino and Smith 2011; Laughlin 2016) shows that online resources form an important part in the deconversion and coming-out processes of some atheists. For example, Chelsea Starr, Kristin Waldo and Matthew Kauffman show that their respondents 'depended on the [studied forum] to process their intellectual, emotional, and social changes' (Starr, Waldo and Kauffman 2019, 508). In this case the online forum functioned as a type of community, providing respondents with a safe space for coming to terms with and handling the fallout of their atheist convictions. Previous research has indicated that, for atheists, being involved in atheist groups or feeling connected to other atheists is associated with higher well-being (Abbott and Mollen 2018; Brewster et al. 2020). However, it is important to note that, despite this, atheists do not tend to join organisations (Altemeyer 2010; Bullivant 2008; Manning 2010). Thus, atheists in the US have been posited to relate to a form of imagined community at the cross-section of atheist spokesmen, the reading of their texts and various social media platforms (Cimino and Smith 2011). This imagined community is thought to exist in tension with the religious majority, and to provide feelings of legitimisation, as well as exacerbating feelings of exclusion (Cimino and Smith 2011; Edgell, Gerteis and Hartmann 2006). The characteristics and diversity of this imagined community are less clear, but the heterogeneity of the group is recognised (e.g. LeDrew 2016).

Jack Laughlin (2016), opposing the idea that atheism forms a coherent community, has explored a particular type of atheist discourse he labels as 'progressive', which he describes as standing in opposition to 'dictionary atheism'. Laughlin describes how such progressive atheist discourse foregrounds social responsibility, thereby disavowing the dictionary definition of atheism as being not a comprehensive system of thought but simply and exclusively referring to God's non-existence (Laughlin 2016, 329–30). In this chapter I focus on the second type of atheism Laughlin describes, the dictionary atheist discourse which argues that atheism is simply the disavowal of a certain type of belief, and not an identity, community or worldview. As previous research has not tended to distinguish between different types of atheist discourse, some of the general characteristics attributed to atheists may refer mainly to this formation, such as a perceived tendency in atheist discourse to construct atheist identity as existing in opposition to religious others (Guenther 2014; Guenther, Mulligan and Papp 2013; J. M. Smith 2011). Atheist identity can in such cases be understood to be deployed in order to signal a set of antagonistic presuppositions about religion – as inherently fundamentalist and a threat to science – which in turn is thought to empower atheists in their disbelief (Taira 2012; Lüchau 2010). Other characteristics include scientism, epistemic dogmatism, a reduction of religion to the status of a primitive science and a general disdain for both fundamentalist and moderate religious practitioners (Asad 1993, 2003; Gorski 1990; Kaden and Schmidt-Lux 2016; Kidd 2017; Lundmark and LeDrew 2018; Martin 2014; Olson 2008; Stenmark 1997; Zenk 2014).

Social media dynamics

The data sets analysed here came from Reddit and YouTube, which calls for some reflection on the particular affordances of both technologies. To begin with, YouTube is a subsidiary of Google and the second most visited website in the world (Wikipedia 2021), and variously functions as a tool for the dissemination or uploading of hyperlinkable video content, as a public space and as a social networking site. Reddit also functions as a tool for dissemination of hyperlinkable content but is much more centred on discussion. It is a hubforum, and subreddits like /r/atheism focus on niche topics or areas of interest, and are generally moderated by users. Both platforms rely on user interaction, and function by ranking systems – likes and interactions on YouTube, up- and downvotes on Reddit – which to a large degree affect what the average user of either site is likely to see. While YouTube relies on users producing and publishing video content, Reddit works through its users submitting a broader range of content – links to news articles, memes, stories from their lives, questions, and so on – to particular subreddits, where users can vote on it. Content that receives many upvotes appears on the front page of any given subreddit, and if popular enough on the front page of Reddit itself. Thus, Reddit is particularly dependent on user interaction, which was especially true for /r/atheism at the time of the study as it was largely unmoderated. Reddit has thus been argued to function variously as a news aggregator and as a space for virtual community, both as a public forum and as a 'safe space' (Darwin 2017; Jürgens and Stark 2017; Robards 2018). Both sites function with a certain amount of anonymity and allow users to access content and comments or forum discussions without registering an account. Moreover, even users with accounts are afforded relative anonymity on both sites, an important thing to note since relative anonymity has been found to foster less cordial debate online, which tends towards hostility (Halpern and Gibbs 2013, looking specifically at YouTube).

The anonymity afforded by Reddit is identified as one of the key affordances of the site in recent work by Naveena Prakasam and Louisa Huxtable-Thomas (2021). They further highlight credibility, echoing and creating membership. The first of these refers to the way authority is created and maintained by users on Reddit via the karma system; users who receive up- and downvotes from others when they comment or post content receive 'karma', which gives credibility to their activities on the site. In addition, users are restrained by the rules established by each subreddit. Prakasam and Huxtable-Thomas argue that this brings about an echo-chamber effect, as moderators are able to delete any posts or comments which they feel do not adhere to the rules. Prakasam and Huxtable-Thomas also point out that in-group membership is established via particular jargon, and suggest that the 'material aspects of anonymity, upvoting, karma and the rules of each subreddit provide ways in which Users can create a "safe" space to air their views, use convincing language and narrative to recruit others and to reward those that share the same attitudes whilst excluding alternative views' (Prakasam and Huxtable-Thomas 2021, 24). In stark contrast to Reddit, most YouTube content focuses on specific people: vloggers. However, as noted by Stuart Cunningham and David Craig (2017), this type of content is still highly interactive, as it is centred on the relationship between vlogger and audience. Cunningham and Craig argue that key affordances of such vlogs include authenticity and community, and that the authenticity vloggers seek to establish exists in relation to the perceived artificiality of traditional media formats. Vloggers are thus able to forge authority in relation to their audiences, characterised by authenticity, connection and vulnerability (Lövheim and Lundmark 2019). While this vulnerability is often a strength for vloggers, the example of Kasparian analysed in this chapter shows that this emphasis on connection and authenticity also opens up vloggers to harsh personal attacks and critique (Lundmark 2019).

Articulating atheism

The analysis presented here builds on discourse theory, a methodology developed by Ernesto Laclau and Chantal Mouffe (1985), which posits that as meaning cannot be ultimately fixed there exists a constant struggle between different discursive formations for the fixation of the hegemonic. This struggle takes place via articulations, the linguistic acts that seek to establish a relationship between elements (any unarticulated difference), thus fixing them as moments (fixations of meaning; Laclau and Mouffe 1985). Looking at the shape of hegemonic discourse on /r/atheism, important moments include religious people, religion and atheism. User articulations of atheism suggest a different relation: 'Atheism is not and will never have a "word" or "message" to spread … We do the opposite of that, try to show critical thinking to people so they can reason for them selves what is and isn't real' (/r/atheism thread). Such an articulation is indicative of users' broader attempts to empty the concept of 'atheist' of meaning. Users almost never say 'atheism is …', but rather focus on what it is *not*; in this case it is articulated as not having a message. Within this discourse the element of 'atheist' is articulated as a moment in a way that indicates that it is neutral, without value, a natural state of the mind. This way of articulating atheism was in line with the /r/atheism FAQ at the time, which defined atheism as 'nothing more and nothing less than a lack of belief in any god or gods', and further stated that a 'person can be both atheist and religious, provided that he or she believes in a religion that does not have any deities', and that the 'word "atheism" is not a proper noun (we do not worship the All Powerful Atheismo), so there is no need to capitalize it'. Moreover, the FAQ clarified the relationship between atheism and agnosticism, stating that the two are not mutually exclusive and that calling yourself an agnostic is 'completely uninformative, and does not make you "not an atheist"'. These articulations proliferated on the forum, and were also the issue around which Kasparian's video and comment section circled.

In her video, Kasparian opened by introducing the issue: she had labelled herself as agnostic when asked about her beliefs during an interview. After this she describes having received negative feedback from atheists, which had prompted her to respond to these concerns in a video addressing the 'atheist community'.[4] To begin with, she inserts a clip of herself from the interview in which she says: 'I just feel really uncomfortable calling myself an atheist and pretending as though I know without a shadow of a doubt that there is no higher being. The truth is I don't know, and no one really knows' (Kasparian's video). She follows this by inserting a clip from a video response she received, in which another YouTuber outlines the difference between atheism and agnosticism:

> The two [presumably Kasparian and the interviewer, Dave Rubin] seem to want to put agnosticism between atheism and theism but agnosticism is about knowledge: it is the idea that we can never know whether or not a God exists, while atheism and theism is about belief. So, for example, I'm an agnostic atheist – I'm both an agnostic and an atheist. Also, Christians are gnostic theists, so to say 'I'm not atheist, I'm an agnostic' doesn't make any sense. It's like saying 'I'm not a liberal, I'm a vegetarian.' They're not on the same line of ideology. But what's worse is Ana is claiming that all atheists are completely gnostic about God – they know with one hundred

per cent certainty that God does not exist and in fact I've tried to criticise atheists who act in this way. I think it's wrong and I think it's not within the ideology of atheism. I think at the centre of atheism is scepticism – the idea that we only accept claims when there's sufficient evidence for them.

(Kasparian's video)

This particular way of articulating atheism and agnosticism is most likely familiar to many. It is often accompanied by an image illustrating the differing 'lines of ideology' referred to. Variations of it exist, but it is essentially a chart that on one axis measures belief (labelled atheism versus theism), and on the other measures claims to knowledge (labelled agnosticism versus gnosticism).[5] Thus, someone like Kasparian, who does not know but does not believe that God exists would, according to this understanding, be an agnostic atheist – which perhaps is why she receives responses like 'Atheism is NOT a claim to knowledge. Its an absence of belief in a deity. Simple,' and 'You dont believe in a god, you are unconvinced that there is one. BY DEFINITION YOU ARE AN ATHEIST also you are a pathetic coward unwilling to acknowledge reality' (Kasparian's comment section).

In this discursive formation, atheism is articulated as a statement – of knowledge of belief – that lacks substance in and of itself, which is not conceived as a 'proper noun', suggesting that it is not understood as an identity or community that one can inhabit or take part in. These types of articulations claim that 'Atheism is not an ideology' (Kasparian's comment section), and reject the notion that there is such a thing as an atheist community:

I don't like how people say 'the atheist community'. I believe that you belong to the 'catholic community' if you subscribe to that religion, same with 'muslim community' and 'anglican community'. Atheists are people who lack religious faith, they are a negative. It's like splitting hundreds of different coloured marbles into a red group and a green group, and then labelling the remaining as 'rainbow'. They lack a set group.

(Kasparian's comment section)

Instead, atheism is articulated as referring to people who – unlike religious people – simply are reasonable: 'I don't like to be labeled an Athiest, I label myself a Normal person who just doesn't believe in God, Santa Claus, The Devil, the Tooth Fairy or any other fairies!!!!' (Kasparian's comment section). This type of articulation divides the discursive field into two opposite, antagonistic poles. As one of Kasparian's commenters puts it: 'you think agnosticism is a middleground between theism and atheism, theism and atheism are BINARY positions there IS NO MIDDLE GROUND'. This antagonistic binary explains why Kasparian, who states several times that she does not believe in God, still receives these types of comment: 'Don't be weak minded. You are smart enough to know that goofy god is a bad joke on the idiot masses' and 'I wanna bang the Jesus out of Ana ... Oh wait ... we don't know if he really exists' (Kasparian's comment section). As she does not clearly identify herself as an atheist (and thus reasonable), she is perceived by some to be irrational, or simply wrong: 'It ain't that complicated, Ana. If there is no evidence for the objective existence of God(s) – and rationalism dictates that existence is illogical and astronomically improbable, then why waffle? You're an atheist' (Kasparian's comment section). These types of antagonistic articulations should be understood as attempts to maintain the coherence of a particular discursive formation. This is achieved by repeating that articulating atheism in any other way simply does not make sense. Kasparian's comment section is thus filled with suggestions that her calling herself agnostic is absurd – 'Are you agnostic about there being a pumpkin in the centre of Mars, Ana?' – or simply wrong:

> Do people ever research their beliefs before spouting out convictional ignorance??? It's really sad that we live in a digital age where knowledge is spread throughout the world instantly and yet people don't have a clue of how to properly identify and represent their beliefs!
>
> (Kasparian's comment section)

While the hegemonic discourse apparent on /r/atheism similarly divides the discursive field into a binary, there the binary is one in which primarily religious people are othered as irrational. The religious moderate was perceived as particularly problematic for trying to combine 'actual' rationality with religion, which was apparent in comments like 'Please state your beliefs. I'll be happy to explain to you why they are either silly and/or rediculous or, alternatively, why you shouldn't be calling yourself a Christian' (thread on /r/atheism). In contrast, in Kasparian's comment section the irrational other is the agnostic, but as should be apparent from the examples taken from the /r/atheism FAQ, claiming to be agnostic as opposed to atheist was similarly articulated as absurd on /r/atheism. Thus, the coherence of this discursive formation was maintained by arguing that anyone who disagrees is irrational, that atheism is a neutral, natural position, and those who claim not to be atheists like Kasparian do not know their own minds: 'Agnostics are the Atheists without balls' (Kasparian's comment section).

> It is not unreasonable for me to criticise the atheist community in the sense that there are gradations and I think that there are different interpretations, so there definitely are atheists without question that say 'Hey, you know what, God does not exist without a shadow of a doubt.' Now, I don't know what percentage of atheists that is, but there are some people.
>
> (Kasparian, video)

This is said by Kasparian in response to the video she cites, explaining why she prefers the term agnostic. This claim – that different people interpret atheism differently – appears to be threatening to the coherence of the discursive formation I am focusing on here. Within this discursive formation, which attempts to empty atheism of meaning by defining it as the natural state of mind, the idea of an atheist community is rejected. Ideas of atheism being a neutral position, and atheism not being a community or a positive claim of any kind, are related: 'Atheism makes no claim about the existence or non existence of gods. It is simply the lack of belief in gods. Nothing more, nothing less. It makes no positive claim. Assigning meaning because of positive claims by some atheists is disingenuous' (Kasparian's comment section). Moreover, some commenters go further and claim that there is no such thing as an atheist who expresses absolute certainty about the non-existence of God:

> I know very few atheists, in fact none, that would declare that there is absolutely no god or higher power. Instead we just have no reason to believe there is a god or higher power. The universe could have been created by the Flying Spaghetti Monster, but I have no evidence that points to that possibility so there is no reason to believe that it was created by FSM. However I am completely sure there is no Christian god because of the overwhelming evidence that in my opinion is so great that I cannot even consider the possibility
>
> (Kasparian's comment section)

This articulation affirms that atheism is not a positive claim and is a natural state of mind by maintaining that no atheist would declare that there is no God, while simultaneously emphasising that there is no way they themselves would consider the possibility there could be (at least a Christian) one.

Kasparian's choice to label herself as agnostic comes to be contentious, as it suggests that in maintaining definite disbelief, atheism may not always be entirely rational. She thus receives many comments restating the definition of agnostic atheism she cited in her video, coupled with the wish that the internet 'was a dictionary alone rather than a forum that allows misconceptions to perpetuate themselves' (Kasparian's comment section).

This type of atheistic discourse, which was hegemonic on /r/atheism at the time, and which proliferated in Kasparian's comment section, is far from being the only form of atheist discourse. Kasparian herself is an example of this: in response to the video she cites she says that while she could consider herself an agnostic atheist under this definition, there are atheists who appear certain that there is no God and that was what she was distancing herself from in calling herself agnostic. She thus articulates agnostic in opposition to atheism, as referring to someone who does not believe in God, but recognises that 'we don't have any evidence disapproving the possibility that there could be a god' (Kasparian's video). She did also receive comments either agreeing with her definition, or defending it in various ways:

> For every who wants to tell us what an atheist really is – atheism has two definitions. Both are correct. This is from Dictionary.com:
> 1. the doctrine or belief that there is no God.
> 2. disbelief in the existence of a supreme being or beings.
> (Kasparian's comment section)

The comments section of her video is thus an example of clashing discourses, a struggle over different definitions of atheism: one that is highly antagonistic in its division of the discursive field into rational/ irrational, where atheism is conceived as natural and neutral, and all attempts at bringing any sort of nuance to the understanding of that concept are articulated as absurd. On the other hand, we have other discursive formations that appear less clear, but do imply a more agonistic acceptance of differences in definitions, and a willingness to make concessions. Kasparian herself readily admits to being an 'agnostic atheist' under the given definition; she just does not think that this is the only definition. As a commenter puts it: 'I can't believe people have spent this much time wailing about her use of terms on whether or not she calls herself an atheist or agnostic. She clearly doesn't have a belief in theism, and that's really all that matters' (Kasparian's comment section).

Atheist discourses in the wild: community or circlejerk?

Emphasising the role of conflict in discursive formations, Laclau and Mouffe (1985) understand the limit of every objectivity as antagonism, which reveals objectivity as a partial and precarious objectification. Antagonism is thus the experience of the limit of all objectivity, a relation which shows the limit of every objectivity. It occurs when the alternative meanings a particular discourse has excluded threaten to undermine the fixity of meaning in the discourse and therefore the integrity or very existence of that discourse. Antagonism is thus not the same as conflict, but rather the undermining of fixity, the constant threat of modification or subversion (Laclau and Mouffe 1985). In the analysis above I have shown the ways in which one discursive formation, which defines atheism as simple negation, attempts to defend itself against being undermined by a perceived threat that renders atheism as sometimes less than perfectly rational. Mouffe (2013) has refined the notion of antagonism in her later work as conflicts between non-negotiable values and struggles between enemies who wish to destroy each other, contrasted with agonism, which she defines as a struggle between opponents that is based on a mutual recognition that differences in perspective are important, and that leads to discussions that improve democracy. To further distinguish antagonism and agonism, Nico Carpentier (2018) has presented a typology which identifies antagonistic discourse as discourse characterised by radical othering, as a discourse which seeks to eliminate the other, attempts to establish total differentiation and distance from the other, and thus produces a homogenisation of the self. The antagonistic discourse centres on articulations of us and them, sometimes resulting in the complete dehumanisation of the other, but at the very least predicated on the establishment of a hierarchy in which the other is articulated as inferior. These types of articulations are often expressed as if they were common-sense, neutral statements. As a result, the 'us', or the self, is united against the other as its antithesis – not via articulations of positive qualities, but as the negation of the perceived qualities of the other (Carpentier 2018). This is very much in line with the analysis above, which identifies articulations of atheism that assert that it is not a positive claim, an identity or an inhabitable worldview, but a natural state of mind.

/r/atheism users themselves identify the discussion on the forum as characterised by a 'circlejerk', a metaphor for recursive discourse that does not lead anywhere. In the case of /r/atheism, the circlejerk consists of the continuous othering of religious people, mainly for comedic purposes, but also as a way to vent frustration. The different ways users articulate the circlejerk reveal a tension in the perceived purpose of /r/atheism as being either primarily a space meant to foster rational thinking, in which atheists can hone their argumentation skills in order to deploy them against religious others, or primarily a space for atheist entertainment or venting, and thus for finding confirmation of one's minority identity (Lundmark and LeDrew 2018). /r/atheism was in either case predominantly characterised by antagonistic articulations of religious people as the prime example of an irrational other, who existed in opposition to the rational atheist. Following Carpentier's typology (2018), this discourse was marked by radical othering, seeking to eliminate the irrationality of others and to sustain a total differentiation between the two. This is apparent in articulations meant to police how other users argued for their atheism: 'You need to realize that when you argue these things you are in a sense using circular reasoning to say "our situation is different because we are right", and that is virtually the exact same rationale they use' (/r/atheism thread). 'They' in this case refers to religious people. Much as Carpentier (2018) argues, this line of reasoning appears to be predicated on a view of the radically othered – religious people – as inferior to atheists, as they are articulated as having given up their inherent rationality ('They neatly fold up their reason and skepticism and put it in a locked box. Then they chuck it in the nearest canal with a hearty cry "Well, reality's not for me after all"', /r/atheism thread). Moreover, the atheist self that is established is articulated through opposition; that is, it is explicitly articulated as not having any positive content, but simply as being a negation of the irrational, religious other. This particular way of arguing for the atheist self as neutral and objective is in line with Charles Taylor's (2007) concept of the secular self as buffered; articulations of the atheist self as neutral, factual, rational and reasonable are thus in line with those articulations of the secular self that have marked political discourse in Western states (Asad 2003; Scheer, Fadil and Schepelern Johansen 2019; see also Binder in this volume).

A very similar antagonistic discursive formation is present in Kasparian's comment section. Again, we see the explicit articulation of atheism as lacking any form of positive content. This is an attempt to articulate atheism as a moment defined as common sense, rational and inherent, again in line with Taylor's (2007) notion of the buffered self. Atheism is articulated as not referring to a community, but to people who are simply reasonable or normal. While the othering of agnostics was less common on /r/atheism, it was central to the discursive formation in Kasparian's comment section. However, these processes of radical othering appear to follow similar logics. In this process the presented definition (via the atheist compass) is not introduced as the best or most useful definition of atheism or agnosticism; rather, it is presented as objective and as the only possible definition. This articulation divides the discursive field into two opposite, antagonistic poles. As one commenter articulates it, there can be no middle ground between these 'BINARY positions' (Kasparian's comment section). Claiming to be agnostic is articulated as absurd and irrational, and Kasparian is associated with religion and faith in God despite explicitly stating that she does not believe in God and that she is against organised religion. The type of vitriolic responses Kasparian receives can be perceived as attempts to maintain the coherence of this discursive formation: they are instances of antagonism which expose how the alternative meanings this discourse has excluded threaten to subvert its fixity of meaning, and thus undermine its integrity. Thus, users argue both that there is no such thing as a 'gnostic atheist', despite what Kasparian may claim, and that there is no way they themselves could entertain the idea of God existing. This of course functions to establish them as rational (by articulating their inability to believe in God), while solving the threat of Kasparian's statement and identification (by maintaining that no proper atheist would claim that God does not exist, for certain).

The wish to erase the radically othered is clear in the responses, apparent in the way Kasparian is told either that she does not know her own mind (reasserting the atheist compass as the only possible definition of atheism), or that her refusal to assert an atheist identity means that she is 'a pathetic coward unwilling to acknowledge reality' (Kasparian's comment section). The radical other in both discursive formations is the irrational human, the human who refuses to acknowledge the objective reality presented by the atheist; in other words, the radical other is the projected unbuffered self. The radically other is neither religious nor agnostic, but irrational; the coherence of the discursive formation is maintained by arguing that anyone who disagrees is irrational and that atheism is a neutral, natural position lacking positive content, and by repeating that articulating atheism in any other way simply does not make sense. The characteristics of the discursive formation I have outlined are thus in line with previous research that shows that atheists construct atheist identity in opposition to religious others (Guenther 2014; J. M. Smith 2011). That is, within this discursive formation atheist identity is deployed to signal a set of antagonistic presuppositions about not just the religious other (Taira 2012; Lüchau 2010), but anyone who disagrees. Thus, if atheists go online to imagine themselves as part of a community of any kind (Cimino and Smith 2011; Smth and Cimino 2012), these communities might be described as forming through processes of antagonistic othering and the projection of the undesirable (Ahmed 2014; Carpentier 2018; Chun 2016) – in this case irrationality – onto everyone not adhering to a narrow definition of atheism. This type of antagonistic othering has been described as an outcome of the affordances of Reddit in particular (Prakasam and Huxtable-Thomas 2021) and is one of the reasons why some argue that Reddit subverts any attempt to form a political identity or kick-start a political movement (Buyukozturk, Gaulden and Dowd-Arrow 2018).

This antagonistic othering was in both cases accompanied by articulations seeking to erase the projected other by emphasising the emptiness of atheism as a category and its naturalness as a state of mind. In this way, the atheist 'we' was established through negative projection of the irrational other as the only organising factor of what it means to be atheist. Communities forming through processes of antagonistic othering are fragile, as any nuanced articulation of the other threatens the coherence of the discursive formation. They can be understood as communities forged through hatred, and thus through a process whereby 'all that is undesirable [is projected] onto another, while concealing any traces of that projection, so that the other comes to appear as a being with a life of its own' (Ahmed 2014, 73). The central 'us' is thus established as the centre which implicitly needs to be protected from the threat of the other, through the hatred of the other: 'Those who hate excessively need their objects, because they become part of a community through this attachment. This hatred organizes bodies and spaces' (Chun 2016, 157). Agonism, by contrast, is the articulation of conflict as inhabiting a common symbolic space where interaction is based on mutual respect, and further seeks to harness pluralism for democratic purposes rather than attempting to erase it. Differences are not articulated as insurmountable or total, but as legitimate and necessary parts of a functioning social formation (Carpentier 2018; Mouffe 2013). As the above analysis shows, there are instances of agonistic discursive practices apparent in the comment section of Kasparian's video, as well as in the video itself. It should thus be emphasised that the particular discursive formation I have focused on is not necessarily characteristic of atheist discourse in general, and nor does it necessarily represent a majority of atheists on- or offline. However, it is a discursive formation that appears to have informed the negative stereotypes some atheists fight against.[6]

One aspect should be considered, however, before the types of practices discussed in this chapter are written off as simply communities of hatred. The first is how people relate to online content, especially /r/atheism, on which several users, responding to others calling the forum a circlejerk, declared that it was a place where atheists who are subjected to prejudices and discrimination in their everyday lives can vent frustration by laughing at caricatures of Christians. It is important to note that digital play was one of the marked characteristics of discourse on /r/atheism at the time, especially through the sharing of memes and short comments consisting of puns or pop culture references that are added to by others developing the joke. This type of collaborative digital play is a defining feature of interactions on various social networking sites (Lüder 2011), and present across a number of popular Reddit forums. On /r/atheism these instances of play functioned to foster a sense of belonging on Reddit in general, and on /r/atheism in particular, as they established a sense of interior and exterior. Thus, on /r/atheism, these antagonistic discourses were ways through which users expressed frustrations that were not necessarily meant for the eyes of the radically othered. By contrast, in the case of Kasparian this type of antagonistic atheist discourse was mobilised in an attempt to eradicate the position of the radically othered in a very explicit sense – an other that was in no way hostile to atheism. And indeed, there were examples of /r/atheism users being mobilised to harass specific people's social media profiles outside of Reddit after a story had been posted about them on /r/atheism.[7] This type of mobilisation links to larger discussions about the effect of violent online speech on democratic inclusivity (e.g. Jane 2014); even if online harassment is intended as a 'joke' by perpetrators, it may not appear as a joke to the victim, nor to people who want to participate in online spaces but feel unable to do so because of the proliferation of such practices. So while the intention may be to vent frustration, finding resonance in shared discontent may function to mobilise frustrations in a more directed way, for example through targeted online harassment.

Conclusion

The aim of this chapter was to explore the role of conflict in atheist community formation, looking at how anti-religious sentiments can be conceived vis-à-vis atheist community formation online in order to bring nuance to questions of if and how practices of engaging with atheist content online – or of 'reading with' – should be conceived of as participation in or formation of diffused communities. Using a discourse theory approach focusing on the framework of antagonism and agonism (Mouffe 2013), I have analysed the role of conflict in atheist discourse. The analysis showed what might be described as a type of antagonistic discursive formation, meaning a discursive formation that seeks to divide the discursive field into two binary poles via a process of radical othering (Mouffe 2013; Carpentier 2018). The atheist 'we' of this particular discursive formation was forged through the projection of the undesirable – in this case, irrationality – onto everyone not adhering to a narrow definition of atheism, and thus established through negative projection of the irrational other what it means to be atheist. The discursive formation was further characterised by a need to protect the implicit 'we' from the perceived threat of the other, mobilised via hatred and attempts to erase all difference, a hatred that can be seen as the primary organising principle of an antagonistic discursive formation. The characteristics of this discursive formation appear to be in line with what previous research has argued, namely that atheist identity is constructed in opposition to religious others (Guenther 2014; Guenther, Mulligan and Papp 2013; Smith 2011), and is deployed in order to signal a set of antagonistic presuppositions about religion which in turn works to empower atheists (Taira 2012; Lüchau 2010).

I would take this one step further and suggest that the 'we' of the particular antagonistic atheist discursive formation I have looked at radically others not just religion or religious people, but anyone who strays from the perceived objective, neutral definition of atheism. Thus, this discursive formation seems to correspond to the projected other of the 'progressive' atheist discursive formation that Laughlin (2016) identified as 'dictionary atheism', meaning an atheist discourse centred on atheism as nothing but the disavowal of a certain type of belief. What we see is thus something that appears paradoxical, namely a strong sense of coherence around the idea that atheism could not possibly be a community or a worldview. Recognising one's individual beliefs in the other is not necessarily about 'imagining community' but can be about reassuring oneself that although a great many people appear to be irrational, there are other rational people out there one can laugh along with. Distinguishing between communities proper – such as atheist organisations on- or offline – and this type of diffused engagement is, I think, crucial to understanding the difference between a wish to link up with like-minded people for various purposes and the impulse to use different online spaces as recursive echo chambers of atheist frustration and anger. While I show how the latter correspond to a particular discursive formation, it is less clear to me that this should be conceptualised as a community rather than simply a type of public discourse. While atheists on Reddit, for example, do appear to 'read with' and engage with like-minded strangers (Lundmark and LeDrew 2018), they do not seem to imagine themselves to be part of a community. Instead, they simply imagine themselves to be right, normal and rational. Looking at this as a form of publicness organised around the concept of atheism allows us to view it instead as a type of discursive tendency in a set of heterogeneous discourses centring on moral considerations or ideals, in this case identified as a complete rejection of belief in God (while maintaining that this complete rejection is in fact not complete) as the only normal way of being, thus rendering any opposing opinion not only wrong but completely absurd, much like believing that there are pumpkins at the centre of Mars.

Notes

1   A majority of YouTube and /r/atheism users were from the US (Erik [hueypriest] 2012a, 2012b; Google 2021). Furthermore, these particular social media technologies were created in and for the US market and are very reliant on US cultural norms and discourses (Lange 2007).
2   Quotations are always transcribed directly from the YouTube comment section or from reddit. com/r/atheism as they were written, including spelling errors. Usernames have been omitted.
3   The larger study looked at videos by 60 US women, gender-nonconforming vloggers and the accompanying comment sections. These videos were collected using the search terms 'My deconversion story', 'Why I'm an atheist', 'deconversion', 'deconverted', 'atheist' and 'atheism', and focused on the experiences of atheists and of non-religious people more broadly, though a majority of vloggers did identify as atheists in their videos (Lundmark 2019).
4   The video, which was five minutes long and titled 'Am I an atheist?', was published in January 2014 and had at the time of data collection (September 2016) received 21,1449 views, 4,887 upvotes, 513 downvotes and 5,148 comments.
5   It should be noted that 'gnosticism' in this chart appears to simply refer to 'knowledge' or 'absolute knowledge', that is, it is an antonym of agnosticism, rather than referring to Gnosticism as a religious or philosophical movement.
6   I have considered the positive content of atheist identity formation in a previous publication, which explores other forms of atheist discourse than the type discussed in this chapter (Lundmark 2019).
7   These practices were not encouraged by moderators and were one of the major reasons moderators would go in and delete content. Still, users would encourage each other to engage in these types of behaviour on several occasions.

References

Abbott, Dena M. and Debra Mollen. 2018. 'Atheism as a concealable stigmatized identity: Outness, anticipated stigma, and well-being.' *Counselling Psychologist* 46 (6): 685–707. https://doi.org/10.1177/0011000018792669.

Ahmed, Sara. 2014. *The Cultural Politics of Emotion.* Edinburgh: Edinburgh University Press.

Altemeyer, Bob. 2010. 'Atheism and secularity in North America', in *Atheism and Secularity. Volume 2: Global Expressions*, Phil Zuckerman, ed., 1–21. Santa Barbara, CA: Praeger.

Asad, Talal. 1993. *Genealogies of Religion: Discipline and reasons of power in Christianity and Islam.* Baltimore, MD: Johns Hopkins University Press.

Asad, Talal. 2003. *Formations of the Secular: Christianity, Islam, modernity.* Stanford, CA: Stanford University Press.

Brewster, Melanie Elyse, Brandon L. Velez, Elizabeth F. Geiger and Jacob S. Sawyer. 2020. 'It's like herding cats: Atheist minority stress, group involvement, and psychological outcomes.' *Journal of Counseling Psychology* 67 (1): 1–13. https://doi.org/10.1037/cou0000392.

Bullivant, Stephen. 2008. 'Research note: Sociology and the study of atheism.' *Journal of Contemporary Religion* 23 (3): 363–8. https://doi.org/10.1080/13537900802373114.

Buyukozturk, Bertan, Shawn Gaulden and Benjamin Dowd-Arrow. 2018. 'Contestation on Reddit, Gamergate, and movement barriers.' *Social Movement Studies* 17 (5): 592–609.

Carpentier, Nico. 2018. 'Diversifying the Other: Antagonism, agonism and the multiplicity of articulations of self and other', in *Current Perspectives on Communication and Media Research*, Laura Peja, Nico Carpentier, Fausto Colombo, Maria Francesca Murru, Simone Tosoni, Richard Kilborn, Leif Kramp, Risto Kunelius, Anthony McNicholas, Hannu Nieminen and Pille Pruulmann-Vengerfeldt, eds, 145–62. Bremen: Edition Lumière.

Chun, Wendy Hui Kong. 2016. *Updating to Remain the Same: Habitual new media.* Cambridge, MA: MIT Press.

Cimino, Richard and Christopher Smith. 2011. 'The new atheism and the formation of the imagined secularist community.' *Journal of Media and Religion* 10 (1): 24–38.

Cunningham, Stuart and David Craig. 2017. 'Being "really real" on YouTube: Authenticity, community and brand culture in social media entertainment.' *Media International Australia Incorporating Culture & Policy* 164 (1): 71–81. https://doi.org/10.1177/1329878X17709098.

Darwin, Helana. 2017. 'Doing gender beyond the binary: A virtual ethnography.' *Symbolic Interaction* 40 (3): 317–34. https://doi.org/10.1002/symb.316.

Edgell, Penny, Joseph Gerteis and Douglas Hartmann. 2006. 'Atheists as "other": Moral boundaries and cultural membership in American society.' *American Sociological Review* 71 (2): 211–34. https://doi.org/10.1177/000312240607100203.

Erik [hueypriest]. 2012a. '2 billion & beyond.' http://blog.reddit.com/2012/01/2-billion-beyond.html (accessed 15 April 2013).

Erik [hueypriest]. 2012b. 'Top posts of the year and best of 2012 awards.' http://blog.reddit.com/2012/12/top-posts-of-year-and-best-of-2012.html (accessed 15 April 2013).

Fader, Ayala. 2017. 'The counterpublic of the J(ewish) blogosphere: Gendered language and the mediation of religious doubt among ultra-Orthodox Jews in New York.' *Journal of the Royal Anthropological Institute* 23 (4): 727–47. https://doi.org/10.1111/1467-9655.12697.

Google. 2021. 'Press – YouTube.' https://www.youtube.com/intl/en-GB/about/press/ (accessed 30 March 2021).

Gorski, Philip S. 1990. 'Scientism, interpretation, and criticism.' *Zygon* 25 (3): 279–307. https://doi.org/10.1111/j.1467-9744.1990.tb00793.x.

Guenther, Katja M. 2014. 'Bounded by disbelief: How atheists in the United States differentiate themselves from religious believers.' *Journal of Contemporary Religion* 29 (1): 1–16. https://doi.org/10.1080/13537903.2014.864795.

Guenther, Katja M. and Kerry Mulligan with Cameron Papp. 2013. 'From the outside in: Crossing boundaries to build collective identity in the new atheist movement.' *Social Problems* 60 (4): 457–75. https://doi.org/10.1525/sp.2013.60.4.457.

Halpern, Daniel and Jennifer Gibbs. 2013. 'Social media as a catalyst for online deliberation? Exploring the affordances of Facebook and YouTube for political expression.' *Computers in Human Behavior* 29 (3): 1159–68. https://doi.org/10.1016/j.chb.2012.10.008.

Jane, Emma A. 2014. '"Your a ugly, whorish, slut": Understanding E-bile.' *Feminist Media Studies* 14 (4): 531–46. https://doi.org/10.1080/14680777.2012.741073.

Jürgens, Pascal and Birgit Stark. 2017. 'The power of default on Reddit: A general model to measure the influence of information intermediaries.' *Policy & Internet* 9 (4): 395–419. https://doi.org/10.1002/poi3.166.

Kaden, Tom and Thomas Schmidt-Lux. 2016. 'Scientism and atheism then and now: The role of science in the Monist and New Atheist writings.' *Culture and Religion* 17 (1): 73–91. https://doi.org/10.1080/14755610.2016.1160944.

Kidd, Ian James. 2017. 'Epistemic vices in public debate: The case of "New Atheism"', in *New Atheism: Critical Perspectives and Contemporary Debates*, Christopher R. Cotter, Philip Andrew Quadrio and Jonathan Tuckett, eds, 51–68. Cham: Springer.

Laclau, Ernesto and Chantal Mouffe. 1985. *Hegemony and Socialist Strategy: Towards a radical democratic politics*. London: Verso.

Lange, Patricia G. 2007. 'Publicly private and privately public: Social networking on YouTube.' *Journal of Computer-Mediated Communication* 13 (1): 361–80. https://doi.org/10.1111/j.1083-6101.2007.00400.x.

Laughlin, Jack. 2016. 'Varieties of an atheist public in a digital age: The politics of recognition and the recognition of politics.' *Journal of Religion, Media and Digital Culture* 5 (2): 315–38.

LeDrew, Stephen. 2016. *The Evolution of Atheism: The politics of a modern movement*. New York: Oxford University Press.

Lövheim, Mia and Evelina Lundmark. 2019. 'Gender, religion and authority in digital media.' *ESSACHESS: Journal for Communication Studies* 12 (2) (24): 23–38.

Lüchau, Peter. 2010. 'Atheist and secularity: The Scandinavian paradox', in *Atheism and Secularity. Volume 2: Global Perspectives*, Phil Zuckerman, ed., 177–96. Santa Barbara, CA: Praeger.

Lüder, Marika. 2011. 'Why and how online sociability became part and parcel of teenage life', in *The Handbook of Internet Studies*, Mia Consalvo and Charles Ess, eds, Chichester: Wiley-Blackwell, 452–69.

Lundmark, Evelina. 2019. '"This is the face of an atheist": Performing private truths in precarious publics.' PhD thesis, Uppsala University.

Lundmark, Evelina and Stephen LeDrew. 2018. 'Unorganized atheism and the secular movement: Reddit as a site for studying "lived atheism".' *Social Compass* 66 (1): 112–29. https://doi.org/10.1177/0037768618816096.

Manning, Christel. 2010. 'Atheism, secularity, the family and children', in *Atheism and Secularity. Volume 1: Issues, Concepts, and Definitions*, Phil Zuckerman, ed., 19–41. Santa Barbara, CA: Praeger.

Martin, David. 2014. *Religion and Power: No logos without mythos*. Burlington, VT: Ashgate.

Mouffe, Chantal. 2013. *Agonistics: Thinking the world politically*. New York: Verso.

Nash, Kate. 2014. 'Introduction', in *Transnationalizing the Public Sphere*, Kate Nash, ed., 1–7. Cambridge: Polity.

Olson, Richard G. 2008. *Science and Scientism in Nineteenth-Century Europe*. Urbana: University of Illinois Press.

Prakasam, Naveena and Louisa Huxtable-Thomas. 2021. 'Reddit: Affordances as an enabler for shifting loyalties.' *Information Systems Frontiers* 23: 723–51. https://doi.org/10.1007/s10796-020-10002-x.

Robards, Brady. 2018. '"Totally straight": Contested sexual identities on social media site reddit.' *Sexualities* 21 (1–2): 49–67. https://doi.org/10.1177/1363460716678563.

Scheer, Monique, Nadia Fadil and Birgitte Schepelern Johansen, eds, 2019. *Secular Bodies, Affects and Emotions: European configurations*. London: Bloomsbury Academic.

Smith, Christopher and Richard Cimino. 2012. 'Atheisms unbound: The role of the new media in the formation of a secularist identity.' *Secularism and Nonreligion* 1: 17–31.

Smith, Jesse M. 2011. 'Becoming an atheist in America: Constructing identity and meaning from the rejection of theism.' *Sociology of Religion* 72 (2): 215–37. https://doi.org/10.1093/socrel/srq082.

Starr, Chelsea, Kristin Waldo and Matthew Kauffman. 2019. 'Digital irreligion: Christian deconversion in an online community.' *Journal for the Scientific Study of Religion* 58 (2): 494–512. https://doi.org/10.1111/jssr.12599.

Stenmark, Mikael. 1997. 'What is scientism?' *Religious Studies* 33 (1): 15–32. https://doi.org/10.1017/S0034412596003666.

Taira, Teemu. 2012. 'More visible but limited in its popularity: Atheism (and atheists) in Finland.' *Approaching Religion* 2 (1): 21–35. https://doi.org/10.30664/ar.67489.

Taylor, Charles. 2007. *A Secular Age*. Cambridge, MA: Belknap Press of Harvard University Press.

Warner, Michael. 2005. *Publics and Counterpublics*. New York: Zone Books.

Wikipedia. 2021. 'List of most popular websites.' https://en.wikipedia.org/w/index.php?title=List_of_most_popular_websites&oldid=1023620874 (accessed 15 June 2021).

Zenk, Thomas. 2014. 'New Atheism', in *The Oxford Handbook of Atheism*, Stephen Bullivant and Michael Ruse, eds, 245–60. New York: Oxford University Press.

11
From 'talking *among*' to 'talking *back*'? Online voices of young Moroccan non-believers

Lena Richter

Introduction

I met Ikram, a student from Fès, by chance during a seminar. Only after we got to know each other better did she tell me, 'Hey, I actually fit into your research group about Moroccan non-believers,' and kindly offered to meet for an interview.[1] During our long conversation, the complexity, contextuality and fluidity of talking about non-belief became clear. For Ikram, her choice of words to talk about being non-religious depended on various factors, including her surroundings and the person she was talking to. She illustrated this with an example: 'I wouldn't go to the medina and cry out loud that I don't believe. I just seek dialogue with my closest friends and as far as possible with my family.'

In Morocco, in part because of the impact of social media and the February 20 Movement,[2] the number of non-believers has increased to 13 per cent of the population (Benchemsi 2015; Arab Barometer 2019, 13). Nevertheless, many are hesitant to publicly identify as non-religious, as the dominant public discourse is not in favour of people who leave or doubt Islam. Being outspoken about non-belief can lead to private, educational or professional obstacles. Legal aspects further restrict the possibility of being vocal, as everyone who promotes non-religious ideas risks being penalised for 'shaking the faith of a Muslim' (Penal code

§220). Consequently, non-believers are excluded from most formal talk shows and interreligious dialogues. Against this backdrop, social media remains one of the few places where non-believers can express themselves more freely (Mohammed 2019).

In the Moroccan diaspora in Western Europe, more members of the younger generation embrace a cultural interpretation of Islam. Yet the number of public non-believers remains very small (Saaf, Hida and Aghbal 2009). As Hussein, a young journalist and poet from Antwerp, told me: 'I'm only 26 years old and Muslims have been in Belgium for two, three generations, maybe even four. And it's a bit strange that in all this time I'm the first to make my non-belief public.' Shortly after he shared his story on Flemish television, the right-wing populist party *Vlaams Belang* tweeted: 'Congrats Hussein, for this brave decision to leave Islam.' That was the opposite of his intentions: 'I didn't want to make a statement against Islam – not at all, I just wanted to share my personal story to say "Hey, there are people like me, who grew up in a Muslim family but are not religious".'[3] Since only a few former Muslims speak out in public, those who do quickly find themselves in the spotlight, something which is accelerated by the fast and reactive nature of social media.

To further analyse the relationship between online spaces and non-religious expressions in Morocco and the Moroccan diaspora, I take inspiration from bell hooks's[4] book *Talking Back: Thinking feminist, thinking black.* Hooks (1989) defined talking back as an empowering act of speaking as an equal to those in power. For her, 'true speaking is not solely an expression of creative power; it is an act of resistance, a political gesture that challenges politics of domination that would render [the marginalised] nameless and voiceless' (hooks 1989, 8). While hooks's notion of talking back is based on the intersecting experiences of black women in the US, talking back has been proved to be a useful concept for other marginalised groups, such as Muslims in Western Europe (Van den Brandt 2019; Loukili 2021). In this chapter, I expand upon the idea of talking back to the experiences of Moroccan non-believers. Taking her theory as a starting point, I distinguish three different forms of talking: talking *among*, talking *back* and talking *with*. This approach begs the question 'Do online expressions of Moroccan non-believers remain a talking *among* like-minded people or do they constitute a talking *back* or even a talking *with* that seeks dialogue with fellow religious citizens?'

This question will be answered on the basis of my fieldwork about non-religious activism, which I conducted intermittently between 2016 and 2022 in Morocco and with the Moroccan diaspora in Western Europe. The hybrid ethnography also covered Facebook groups, such as *Atheists* in Morocco, *Marocains pour la Laïcité* (Moroccans for secularism) and *MALI*,[5] as well as *Atheist Antwerp* and *Ex-Muslims Belgium*.[6] My research group included young, educated non-believers[7] who mostly grew up in urban Muslim middle-class families in Morocco or within the Moroccan diaspora in Europe. While the majority of them do not see themselves as activists, their acts and words are often perceived as activism, as they challenge religious expectations. Therefore, my analysis applies an activist perspective, handling a broad understanding of activism that includes everyday acts of normalising non-religion. The insights in this chapter draw on the experiences of the research group as a whole while concentrating on the accounts of one female protagonist from Morocco, Ikram, and one male protagonist from Belgium, Hussein.

Thinking Arab, thinking Muslim?

The question of talking *back* is closely linked to power structures, as non-believers face multiple forms of interpellation. Althusser (1971) defines interpellation as the process of spreading systematic values and ideologies to the point that citizens consider them their own. In general, Moroccans are interpellated as being Muslims, regardless of their actual convictions (Quack and Schulz, in preparation). From an early age, they learn that Islam is not supposed to be questioned, neither publicly nor in private. While this interpellation is inevitable, one can decide whether to embrace, criticise or ignore this call to be Muslim (Bracke 2011).

Former Muslims, such as Ikram and Hussein, can rectify the assumption of *thinking Arab, thinking Muslim*, by showing that *thinking Arab* can also mean *thinking atheist* (P. Hecker, conversation, 2021). Their personal counter-narratives not only respond to clichés and stereotypes but also describe what it means to be non-religious. By doing so, they form a new counterpublic, as they not only oppose prevalent religious ideas but also embrace multiple alternative non-religious discourses (Smith 1993). As former Muslims are expected to remain silent about their deviant views, this mere act of speaking as a non-religious minority[8] to a religious majority can be seen as a challenging counter-conduct (Derrida 1982; Odysseos, Death and Malmvig 2016; Kaulingfreks 2015; Lorde 2018).[9] Those in power not only decide who is being addressed but also determine which statements are rewarded and which are met with disapproval (hooks 1989, 80). Despite being excluded from the public discourse, their voices often attract publicity (Fraser 1990; Fattal 2018), which shows that rather than being a passive and deprived site, the margin can be a space for resistance (Derrida 1982).

In Western Europe, the question of whether members of the Moroccan diaspora are religious or not is often not even posed. Instead, the question is to what extent their presumed Muslimness could become a threat to 'European' values, such as secular liberties (Benchemsi 2015). In this context, public former Muslims are often interpellated as secular subjects and receive unwanted praise as examples of successful integration. Against this backdrop, Hussein sees himself in limbo between the core (in terms of non-religious views) and the margin (in terms of being part of a diasporic minority). By not fitting into the simplified dichotomy of a population divided into 'secular Western Europeans' and 'bad Muslims', former Muslims continue to be othered on the basis of their alleged 'country of origin'.

Responses to these interpellations can take shape in myriad ways. Taboo topics, such as publicly leaving Islam, are often creatively communicated through art or music. For Hussein, poems offer him a creative way of expressing his views. Others communicate religious critique through humour, which is a central component of counterpublics (Warner 2002; Hecker, this volume; Gupta, this volume; Richter 2021). For a long time, stories of minorities have gone unwritten, miswritten or unread, but recently more marginalised groups have explored social media as an avenue of dissent to talk back to dominant power structures (Smith 1993; Mitra 2001; Peeren, Stuit and van Weyenberg 2016). These online expressions, which can range from one-liners to elaborated narratives, will be the focus of this chapter.

The impact of digitalisation on talking *back*

As counterpublics are text-based and evolve around a shared discourse, they emerge and change according to historically specific media practices (Hirschkind, de Abreu and Caduff 2017). In the past, a few thinkers, such as the poet Al-Ma'arri (973–1057), spread their critical thoughts on Islam. With the printing revolution, the possibility of reaching a wider audience increased, but the scope remained restricted to those privileged to read, write and print. Today, books are predominantly produced by a few well-known non-believers, many of whom publish under a pseudonym. For instance, the autobiography *Notes of a Moroccan Infidel* (2020) is written by Hicham Nostik, a pen name derived from 'agnostic'. In the diaspora, Dutch Moroccan Mano Bouzamour is part of a collective of writers, including Ayaan Hirsi Ali (2007) and Lale Gül (2021), who reflect on their Muslim upbringing.

In the digital age, some online platforms are used by only a few, vocal non-believers. YouTube channels such as *kafer maghribi* (Moroccan infidel) and podcasts like *Secular Jihadists* are mainly initiated and maintained by activist non-believers. Other platforms, such as private Facebook groups, offer a space for various non-believers to share their personal narratives online. In addition, Twitter hashtags such as #ExMuslimbecause have contributed to the new vocality of former Muslims.

Ikram experienced the impact of digitalisation at first hand: 'There were two different phases: before high school, I didn't even have internet. But after 2011, following the Arab uprisings, a lot of people, including non-believers, went on Facebook and Twitter. I was in different groups: *L'athée marocain*, the *AA* (*ArabAtheist*) and there was this online forum called *il7ad*, which means atheism in Arabic.' Such spaces were lacking for Hussein and other non-believers who grew up in the diaspora. Besides local groups, transnational Facebook groups exist that form a link between Morocco and the diaspora. This leads to a linguistic mix: sentences in Moroccan Arabic are intertwined with French terms, such as *laïcité*. In Darija (Moroccan Arabic), it is often more difficult to express non-religious views. One interviewee compared the lack of non-religious vocabulary to *1984*, the famous novel by Orwell: 'They developed a new dictionary, picking the new words so well, that it becomes impossible to formulate critique towards the party, so if you're disloyal you don't have the words to express that.' Moreover, non-believers often deliberately refrain from using certain keywords that might attract attention. For instance, they opt for blurred and symbolic expressions, such as *le7t lfota* (to throw in the towel) rather than *il7ad* (atheism). It is also common to share running gags and insider jokes, such as the ironic use of religious terms. This development of distinct phrases and sayings is a typical aspect of communication among counterpublics (Warner 2002).

As meeting in person can be difficult or even dangerous, many interviewees perceive it as less risky to express deviant opinions online, where they can choose whether, and with what level of anonymity, they wish to disclose their experiences (Fileborn 2014). Especially, closed Facebook groups allow a certain level of privacy. For this reason, the degree of publicity is complex. It is not always accurate to divide people into hidden (silent) and public (talking) non-believers. Even closeted non-believers might have some confidants to talk to, and more open non-believers may be hesitant about telling everyone their story. Many interviewees said that they opt for a stronger self-identification, such as atheist, online than they would do offline. This is also true of doubters from other religious backgrounds (Fader 2017).

The internet, and in particular platforms such as Facebook, have opened up new pathways for former Muslims to connect with one another anonymously. They can share personal and intimate thoughts about leaving Islam while keeping an anonymous distance (Chalfant, this volume). Consequently, the internet provides a space for strong counterpublics with the potential to stimulate a new image of non-believers (Fader 2017; Hirschkind 2006). According to Ikram, 'the internet changed a lot, but outside social media, you wouldn't find a lot of people who are courageous enough to say the same things, as they would probably face a lot of backlash.'

Speaking out online is not without its risks. While interpersonal communication is more ephemeral, what is said online lasts almost *ad infinitum*, eternally stored and findable. Other perils include online harassment, shaming, trolling and surveillance (Shayan 2016). Ikram reflected on this: 'I know that people trust Facebook, but you never know who reads it. Some people said bad things to me because of the things I posted about Islam and the Prophet.' In reaction, she blocked those who threatened her and sometimes restricted who had access to her posts: 'I used to write a lot about illogical *surahs* [verses]. I would just put it on my wall, but I don't let my family see what they don't need to see [*laughs*].' For a while, Ikram also preferred a pseudonym, which is, in combination with using a false picture, common among non-believers.

Why (not) talking?

The internet has created more space for marginalised groups to talk *back*, but what are the motivations to engage in talking? The reasons behind being vocal can be manifold and shift according to context, personal convictions and the intersectional position from which one speaks (Van den Brandt 2019). The main motive for sharing personal stories about how and why one left Islam is to talk *back* to misconceptions by providing a more nuanced, alternative and diverse understanding of non-believers. If many non-believers engage collectively in the act of talking *back*, they can create a counterpublic that resists dominant depictions of former Muslims (Dunajeva 2018). This unity of speaking is more viable in Morocco than in the diaspora, where internal differences can be pronounced. While some former Muslims incorporate anti-Islam rhetoric and become the spokespersons of right-wing groups, most former Muslims opt for disengagement or show solidarity with Muslims.

Disparaging statements which accuse non-believers of being immoral or lacking autonomous thinking are prevalent, especially about women. To counteract negative rhetoric, online storytellers seek more understanding and empathy from readers. By revealing their personal struggles they also raise awareness about the restrictive environment (Mulder 2018), which can motivate witnesses to become allies. Solidarity can thus be another aim of talking *back*. As hooks (1989) states, 'When we end our silence, when we speak in a liberated voice, our words connect us with anyone, anywhere who lives in silence.'

Not talking can also be mentally taxing. For Hussein, it was difficult to pretend to be religious: 'It is as if you're leading a double life and that means investing twice as much energy and thinking.' He adds: 'I had to lie, not because I wanted to lie, but because I thought it's for the best, for my parents and me; to have my freedom and to be able to do my thing without hurting anyone else.' Although he started questioning Islam at the age of 13, because he had never vocalised his doubts to others he sometimes had reservations about their validity. A few years later, speaking about his non-belief became a stepping stone for passing on his experience on to closeted non-believers. 'Every voice counts in making leaving Islam more negotiable and acceptable, so that parents like mine may become more tolerant towards their children.' Describing personal struggles in relation to structures of domination can also inspire and encourage others to do the same (Shayan 2016).

The choice to come out as a non-believer can initiate a shift from being invisible to being highly exposed, from carrying the burden of remaining silent to being compelled to talk. This means moving from non-interpellation, being made invisible, to negative interpellation, being hypervisible (Hage 2010; De Koning 2016). Constantly having to talk and explain oneself on and outside the internet can be burdensome. Hussein often gets asked why he is not fasting: 'It's sometimes tiring to explain it every time. I shouldn't have to justify why I drink water but somehow you have to do it because you can't walk around with a sign that says: "I'm not a Muslim".' The motivation to talk is also prone to change over the years. This was the case for Ikram:

> I had this phase where I was more active, I think everyone has that phase in the beginning [*laughs*] because you feel you're finally free to think whatever you want, so you want others, Muslim and non-Muslim friends, to know about it and understand your way of

thinking. But after 2012, I kind of stopped being active on Facebook. It became repetitive – you don't always want to talk about religion. I think I'm a bit over that phase of talking.

While there are many arguments for talking *back* some non-believers refrain from talking about their beliefs altogether, afraid of being misunderstood or disappointing others. The price for talking *back* can be high: from losing friends to being fired at work, or, in rare cases, getting arrested. This anxiety to talk is characteristic of the way those in a lower power position speak to those further up in the hierarchy (hooks 1989, 15). Being aware that it is risky to criticise Islam as part of the taboo troika: God, the nation and the king can lead to (self)censorship (Rahman 2012; Iddins 2020; Kettioui 2021). Silencing can happen in different situations, online and offline, and can come from different people, such as family, colleagues and strangers. Ikram stated that, although her private school was laid-back, she was often stopped when she posed critical questions.

Hooks (1989, 13) makes a key distinction: 'There is the silence of the oppressed who have never learned to speak and there is the voice of those who have been forcefully silenced because they have dared to speak and by doing so resist.' For hooks, remaining silent is more than a lack of speaking: it is a submissive act, which is viewed as the 'appropriate' role for the oppressed. For many, talking *back* remains a talking *among*. The anonymity of social media offers an outlet for people who do not want or cannot reveal their non-belief to those in their immediate social surroundings but wish to liberate themselves from keeping their identity completely hidden (Fader 2017). In non-religious Facebook groups, non-believers can share, empathise with and validate intimate opinions and thoughts.

Many non-believers also consciously and voluntarily decide not to talk *back*. They do not want to take part in this discourse, as they see atheism as a response to religion and argue that 'the whole concept of atheism is something religious people came up with'. By remaining silent, they ignore the expectation that they will engage in debate on the terms set by the dominant discourse, and focus their efforts elsewhere (Bracke 2011). Ikram, for example, considers dialogue important but thinks other approaches, such as education, are more effective means of achieving acceptance of non-religious viewpoints. The meaningful absence of talking is especially common in the diaspora, where former Muslims can potentially serve as 'living proof' for right-wing politicians that Islam is harmful. This appropriation of marginalised voices jeopardises the essence of counterpublics (hooks 1989, 14).

Who's talking?

As we have seen, in the digital era it has become possible for more non-believers to be heard. While not everyone has the opportunity or skills to write a book, it is relatively straightforward to post something on Facebook or Twitter. In spite of these developments, it is important to ask whether new digital forms of self-expression are truly inclusive. Who has the power to speak and to be heard? And who is not talking (hooks 1989, 129)? The barriers which hinder talking can be very tangible, such as not having internet access, or more indirect, such as not feeling safe enough to speak. Although online platforms offer a space for people of any conviction to express themselves, it continues to be chiefly activist non-believers who receive the most attention.

Often a combination of different intersecting factors is in play, affecting how people experience (dis)advantages when talking about non-religion (Yuval-Davis 2006; Crenshaw 2017; Salonen 2018). For instance, male non-believers seem to express themselves online more frequently. In general, talking *back* is perceived differently in relation to gender, as Ikram states:

> Women are supposed to be more obedient and honourable. So just the fact that you're thinking differently and dare to express that is not very accepted like it is for men. I was told that these are not my own ideas and that someone else is influencing me to think and talk like that. As a woman I get these reactions a lot: 'you were brainwashed' or 'someone is pushing you to do it'.

In Hussein's narrative, gender played a less focal role but was important in relations with women. He mentioned that his parents blamed his Flemish girlfriend for bringing him on the – supposedly false – non-religious path (see also Khazaal, this volume). A comparison of these two examples shows that women can be framed as both passive followers and active instigators (S. Loukili, conversation, 2021).

Former Muslims do not talk *back* in a single voice. Such heterogeneity in speech is distinctive among (minority) groups and even within individual narratives (Spivak 1988). A few collective narratives of non-believers use the we-form to stress common struggles. For instance, the

Moroccan MALI movement unitedly campaigns for the rights of non-believers, with slogans such as 'Stop Article 222', according to which public non-fasters can be arrested. Yet most narratives are written from an individual perspective. Especially in the diaspora, non-believers are less organised and opportunities to speak as a collective voice are harder to find. While most voices remain individual, they form a powerful and audible ensemble, contributing to the creation of a counterpublic.

What's the talking about?

The intersectional position of the narrator and the geopolitical context not only influence the choice of whether and where to speak but also the framing and emphases that are being made. The narrated experiences of a straight, upper-class, female non-believer might look different from the narrative of a queer, lower-class male. While Moroccan narratives might focus on the legal restrictions that are in place, those in the diaspora deal with the expectations of being a Muslim. As a more mixed group of non-believers are able to express themselves on online platforms, the topics of the narratives became more diverse.

The agenda of talking is still often set by those in power: topics are often a response to the interpellations of the majority. Thus, non-believers mainly respond to societal perceptions and interpellations of what being non-religious entails. The discussion is further guided by ad hoc reactions to major events, such as the arrest of non-believers, and rarely takes place on a more abstract meta-level. Yet the internet has also made room for more subtle, nuanced and alternative narratives, that describe doubts and the right to personal choice, as well as the postcolonial structures within which they were enculturated. The question remains as to whether these alternative voices are also heard (Van Zoonen, Vis and Mihelj 2010).

Expressions of anti-religious sentiment garner the most attention and are therefore perceived as the most dominant characteristic of people disavowing from Islam. Such sentiment resonates among others in the posts of some ex-Muslim organisations. Anti-religious discourse is often closely connected to ideas from the Enlightenment that oppose religion with science and rationality, criticising the supposedly illogical basis of the Qur'an. While this is assumed to be common ground among non-believers, many former Muslims dispute this generalisation, in which Islam is portrayed as misogynistic and backward.

However, many do criticise certain aspects of Islam and draw upon human rights issues when discussing their reasons for apostasy. Human rights are frequently referenced by online activists, especially when non-believers are arrested. Non-believers also vocalise their sense of discord between religious and legal texts and their ideas about gender and LGBTQ+ rights. In this case, talking *back* becomes talking *with*, as a means of showing solidarity with other minority groups which experience similar restrictions and call for more rights and reforms.

Much emphasis is also put on the struggles associated with being a non-believer in a Muslim-majority or -minority context. This notion resonates when talking *with* fellow Muslims as well as *among* non-believers. Problems can occur on personal, psychological, family and societal levels. Speaking out about the problems that come with identifying as non-religious can encourage others, regardless of their beliefs, to show empathy and back non-believers who face stigma.

Next to these more salient discourses, the internet offers a space for other more subtle ideas and views, where initial doubts can be voiced. As Ikram recalled, 'You cannot announce right away that you left Islam, you're more like, "Hey, I'm thinking about this particular Āyah [verse], what do you think of it?" People appreciate it when you start talking to them about Islam. They really want to explain it to you.' Those expressing doubts are often questioning everything, including their own non-religious stance, and do not want to convince others that they have found the truth. Instead, they stress commonalities with Muslims and challenge the dualistic categories and associations of being religious or not. This fluidity also permeates the narratives, which are not always clearly formulated or coherent but rather relational, syncretic and at times contradictory.

Another understated but pertinent discourse stems from the right of personal choice which stresses that being religious or not should be a free decision. Advocates of freedom of choice argue that parents and teachers should teach about different religions. This discourse was present in Ikram's account as well: 'Raising awareness is a good thing to do, we do need these kinds of conversations, but people are free to believe whatever they want. I don't want to be pushed in a certain way, so why would I try to do it to other people?' Those in favour of personal choice do not engage as much in public discussion because they deem it to be an individual decision, often favouring voluntary silence instead of talking.

Postcolonial discourse also plays its part within the narratives of non-believers and includes two core aspects: 1) deconstructing colonial thinking and structures and 2) finding local counter-narratives. Harnessing postcolonial thought can be seen as an act of talking *back* to claims that non-religion is something 'Western'. Many non-believers are critical of French secularism and cannot identify with the most vocal non-believers, who are overwhelmingly middle-aged Western men. They further criticise the colonial roots of several laws that restrict non-believers in Morocco, such as Article 222, which criminalises eating in public during Ramadan.

Dominant discourses portray non-religion as rooted in Enlightenment thinking and inflicted upon formerly colonised countries, such as Morocco. While critically acknowledging these aspects, non-believers also stress that non-religion can be something intrinsically Moroccan, referring to their Amazigh history or Arabic proverbs about freedom of (non-)religion (Ben-Layashi 2007). Additionally, they seek inspiration from non-religious YouTubers, activists and bloggers from the West Asia and North Africa (WANA) region. This was also visible in Ikram's narrative, in which she argued that Morocco should follow Tunisia in terms of secularism and further referred to the importance of the Moroccan February 20 Movement. For her, freedom of conscience is not a merely European concept: 'We have this saying in Arabic, and it's based on the Qur'an, that nobody can oblige you to do something that you do not want to do when it comes to religion.'

Looking at the diverse meaning-making processes of the less vocal majority shows that talking *back* is not simply about criticising Islam but also about talking *back* to more dominant and common conceptions about non-believers. Consequently, their purpose is to differentiate themselves from the religious majority as well as from the perceptions of more vocal non-believers.

Who is listening?

Looking at the diverse make-up of narrators and topics of talking *back*, we can come to the interim conclusion that the internet has set in place the basic conditions for a new counterpublic of non-believers. Against this backdrop, we can return to the question: do online narratives remain a case of talking *among*, or do they become a form of talking *back* to – or *with* – Muslim citizens? Exchange is a condition for change, something which hooks (1989, 16) explicitly calls for: 'We must be in dialogue. We must be speaking with and not just speaking to.'

Non-believers are compelled to deal with a multiplicity of audiences and their accompanying queries (Van den Brandt 2019). These target audiences, again, depend on the form of talking. Talking *among* happens inside the group of fellow non-believers. Talking *back* can address conceptions about former Muslims and Moroccan religious authorities or, in the diaspora, right-wing groups and Muslim citizens. Talking *with* can be multidirectional; it can be directed to other minorities, closeted non-believers and Muslim relatives or friends. Furthermore, the form of talking depends on the medium. More interactive media platforms, such as Twitter, allow more talking *with* than the one-directional communication of YouTube channels and podcasts.

Drawing on the case of Hussein, three main audiences can be distinguished. He aims to talk *back* to the Flemish audience and the Muslim minority yet envisions talking *with* other former Muslims. When he shared his story on television, these audiences reacted very differently. From non-religious Flemish viewers he received many supportive messages, which he considered, on the whole, well intentioned but unnecessary. Some responses were clearly against Islam, as the appropriation of his narrative by *Vlaams Belang* showed, which he paraphrased as follows: 'Look, here you have an ex-Muslim, do you see that Islam is bad and must leave Flanders?' Hussein considered it very opportunistic to appropriate his personal non-religious viewpoint as political propaganda. He immediately clarified his position, because, for him, 'if you see something, you cannot remain silent about it'. Ultimately, as the topic provoked too many unintended reactions and interpretations, he became less active about this topic on Twitter.

From the Flemish Muslim audience, Hussein mostly received a lack of understanding: 'The guy doesn't know what he's talking about! Why does he have to declare that on television? Couldn't he just do his thing and abandon Islam in silence?' He felt misunderstood: 'They see that as a kind of attack on their faith but miss the point of what I said. It is not because I want to attack Islam but because of the people who are at the turning point in their lives, to give them a little more clarity.' Hussein considers the latter group the most important audience: 'Everyone has their own story. And you can tell a story to someone who tries to understand it, or you can tell your story to someone who fully understands you and that gives much more fulfilment.' This is acknowledged in the many messages he received from young people who said, 'I recognise myself in your situation, I'm not a believer but my parents are believing Muslims and I don't know how to tell them.' As many former Muslims feel isolated, listening to the narratives of other non-believers can be an important source of comfort.

In Morocco, talking *with* each other mostly occurs at a family and friendship level. This kind of dialogue challenges mutual stereotypes and fosters understanding. Sometimes, interviewees brought religious friends with them to the interview or told me about crucial Muslim dialogue partners. Many interviewees first confided their doubts to people close to them who had extensive knowledge about Islam. For Ikram, who the interlocutor is matters in deciding how to talk: 'Sometimes you just say that you don't practise. You phrase it differently, you need to know how to react, to be aware of what to say to whom. Sometimes it's not very safe to say you're not religious, and sometimes it's fine. I wouldn't say it to someone I'd just met or who really practises religion and uses a lot of religious words. Also, abroad, people just assume that I'm Muslim and I just let them believe it.'

According to hooks (1989, 28), when a subaltern group speaks to those who dominate, the presence of the latter changes the direction and shape of their words. The public can thus influence and govern the language of talking. Depending on the audience, non-believers fluctuate between different identifications. In some conversations they prioritise their non-religious identity, while in others it is downplayed or denied. This manoeuvring of different narratives requires mental effort and is also visible in language (Cotter 2015). Hussein told me that in the presence of Muslims, he automatically says *Hamdulillah* ('Praise be to God'): 'It just happens without thinking.' This shows that non-believers do not live in a vacuum: growing up in a Muslim environment, their speaking is influenced by Muslim terms.

For hooks (1989), speaking does not suffice to overcome being silent; one must also be heard. Being heard does not require agreement but it does need an acknowledgement of one's position. Hussein described his trajectory as follows:

> For a long time, we never talked about it in a good conversation of 'sit down, what do you feel; what do you think?' My parents simply assumed that I'm a Muslim. There was no doubt about it. Of course I'm a Muslim, I was raised as a Muslim, why should I be anything else? Before telling them straight away, I first prepared them slowly. I went to live alone and then they realised that's not the usual course of things. I was almost 25 when I finally said to my mother, 'Look, there is something I have to say, something that comes from my heart – I'm not a believer.' That was a very difficult conversation, with a lot of frustration and incomprehension, but it was better because the hiding was just not healthy.

Hussein doubts that his mother really listened to him, as she often tells him, 'It is not too late, you can still take the right direction, become a good

Muslim, get married to a Muslim woman.' It is different for his older, non-religious sister, who is a close confidante: 'My sister is someone who understands me and that's very liberating. She really knows how and why, because we have taken the same "rebellious" path.' Some interviewees had the same experience with Muslim friends: 'And if we talk, it's not like we want to change each other's opinion. We're just talking, to understand each other, that's what talking is about.'

Talking on the internet has some peculiarities. Online narratives are often decontextualised and are heard by a wider public that goes beyond friends and family members. This makes it more difficult to anticipate the possible responses and attitudes of dialogue partners. The inexhaustible scale of social media can lead to a hazy overview of the audience. At the same time, this feeling of anonymity makes people feel more at ease when sharing their experiences. Sometimes it is easier to talk about this topic with a stranger than with a friend or family member.

The capacity to disseminate those stories in an already saturated online environment impacts the reach of stories. This explains why the narratives of ordinary non-believers often go unnoticed (Deseriis 2011). Online narratives that are more provocative, by being explicitly against Islam, have more outreach than more subtle narratives which focus on doubt or commonalities between Muslims and non-believers. This does not mean that the messages shouted the loudest actually reach the audience. Many interviewees pointed out that if you do not formulate your ideas thoughtfully, no one will listen to you. The struggle for attention between different narratives takes place not only among non-believers but also in relation to other groups. Non-believers are not the only ones who aim to talk *back* to the interpellations of religious authorities.

The internet is not always a suitable place to talk *with* others who have a different view. Because of algorithms and friendship networks, online echo chambers emerge. The degree of accessibility and intermingling between believers and non-believers also depends on the nature of the group. Some Facebook groups are not findable just by the group name and explicitly state that Muslims are not allowed to enter, to provide a safe space for Moroccan non-believers. Other groups do provide a meeting platform for Muslims and former Muslims. However, most of the talking *with* happens in face-to-face conversations.

Exchange in the form of talking *with* can also take place between different kinds of non-believers. In Facebook groups such as *Atheist Republic*, former Muslims interact with former Christians, Hindus and Buddhists. Often the administrators initiate dialogical questions, such as 'Did leaving religion impact your everyday life?' or 'Does being religious or not religious play a role in the choice of a potential partner?' These questions are widely discussed and gain considerable attention. In terms of their intersectional positions, non-believers can learn from each other when sharing personal narratives. While online groups are sometimes further divided into subgroups – for example of Amazigh or female non-believers – some assemble a mix of different people. Consequently, in talk *among* non-believers, sub-talking with different kinds of non-believers takes place.

Conclusions

Both in Morocco and in the Moroccan diaspora in Western Europe, former Muslims form a group that is often silenced, talked on behalf of or talked about, while rarely getting the chance to talk for itself. In this respect, they face a double interpellation. When they remain silent about their views, they are wrongly addressed as Muslim subjects. Once they identify openly as non-religious, they are confronted with new interpellations ranging from clichés about being non-religious in the Moroccan context to unwanted praise for being exemplary secular citizens in the diaspora.

Following the advent of social media, it has become easier for a larger and more diverse group of non-believers to talk *back* to these interpellations by sharing their personal narratives online. According to many interviewees, talking about non-religion might become even more acceptable because 'the future is in the hands of the next generation. The teenagers of today are edgier, they're going to decide the culture of talking.' Social media has already led to new publicity and a diversification of talking, as the internet has provided a platform for alternative stories. Dominant discourses and activists remain the most heard, such as those that focus on anti-religious claims, human rights and struggles. Yet, more subtle counter-narratives, which discuss doubt, personal choice and non-religion from a postcolonial perspective, have also found their space. Together they build an emerging counterpublic that consists of different sub-counterpublics.

The content, form and platform of online narratives depend on personal, situational and intersectional aspects, influencing whether people feel in a position to talk. As a result, remaining silent can be a voluntary or an involuntary decision. Being silenced happens as a reaction to the fear of being misunderstood, judged or instrumentalised. Remaining silent can also be a symbol of not taking sides or of expressing solidarity with Muslims by consciously not wanting to feed anti-Islam discourse prevalent in right-wing European movements.

Talking *among*, talking *back* and talking *with* address different audiences. Talking *among* takes place within the group of non-believers. In addition, sub-talking takes place between non-believers who have different intersectional positions. Talking *back* is mainly directed towards dominant discourses about non-believers and towards majority groups. In Morocco, this public consists of religious authorities and a substantial Muslim majority. In the diaspora, talking *back* addresses the expectations of religious members of the diaspora as well as society as a whole and political parties. At times, talking *back* can develop into talking *with* if all parties are willing. Talking *with* also takes place with other minority groups. In Morocco, these can include religious and sexual minorities, as well as non-believers from other religious backgrounds. In the diaspora, less allyship is visible between different minorities and talking *with* rather reaches out to closeted non-believers. The line between talking *among*, talking *back* and talking *with* is therefore fluid. Moreover, the same talking can simultaneously have multiple audiences and, hence, multifunctional forms of talking.

On a final note, while I have analysed exchanges in terms of talking *back* and listening, ideas move in a more circular way. It is not only about sending and receiving messages, but about multiple modes of talking and talking *back* (Warner 2002). There is no single voice or vocabulary with which non-believers can talk *back* to interpellations, and nor is there a single audience. While the voices of non-believers are diverse, they do form an emerging counterpublic which has barely been heard. This counterpublic is still in the making: the basis for it is formed in Facebook groups, where non-believers talk *among* themselves. Thus, this talking *among* does not need to be the final stage but can be a basis for future, more overt talking. Online platforms are spaces in a constant state of flux, whose dynamic changes influence how, where and with whom talking takes place. What started with just a few blogs has spread to social media and will continue to shift in tandem with the ever-evolving digital landscape.

Notes

1 Interview with Ikram, 6 April 2019, Brussels.
2 The February 20 Movement is seen as the Moroccan version of the Arab uprisings. Part of the movement asked for secular reforms.
3 Interview with Hussein, 28 March 2019, Antwerp.
4 The professor and social activist bell hooks purposely wrote her pen name in lower case to signify that the substance of her work is more important than the author herself.
5 *MALI* is the *Mouvement Alternatif pour les Libertés Individuelles* (Alternative movement for individual freedoms).
6 Names of people and hidden groups are pseudonymised.

7 Acknowledging the diverse identifications of this group, I use the broad terms 'non-believers' and 'non-religion', which also come closest to the Arabic term *lā dīnī*.

8 'Minority' does not refer to a numerically smaller group, but to the social construct of being a disadvantaged group.

9 Counter-conduct, a term coined by Foucault, is small-scale forms of resistance performed by citizens who refuse to be governed by the hegemonic principles that are set in place and find alternative ways of conduct.

Acknowledgements

I would like to thank my PhD supervisors Professor Dr Karin van Nieuwkerk and Dr Araceli González Vázquez, as well as the editors and reviewers for their fruitful comments. I am also thankful to my colleagues who shared their expertise on bell hooks with me, such as Dr Martijn de Koning, Dr Samira Azabar, Dr Margreet van Es, Dr Nella van den Brandt, Fouzia Outmany and Sakina Loukili. Moreover, I'm grateful to my interviewees for taking the time to share their thoughts on this topic.

References

Althusser, Louis. 1971. *Lenin and Philosophy and Other Essays* (trans. Ben Brewster). New York: Monthly Review Press.

Arab Barometer. 2019. 'Morocco country report'. https://www.arabbarometer.org/wp-content/uploads/ABV_Morocco_Report_Public-Opinion_Arab-Barometer_2019.pdf (accessed 24 June 2022).

Benchemsi, Ahmed. 2015. 'Invisible atheists: The spread of disbelief in the Arab world.' *New Republic*, 24 April. https://newrepublic.com/article/121559/rise-arab-atheists (accessed 24 June 2022).

Ben-Layashi, Samir. 2007. 'Secularism in the Moroccan Amazigh discourse.' *Journal of North African Studies* 12 (2): 153–71. https://doi.org/10.1080/13629380701201741.

Bracke, Sarah. 2011. 'Subjects of debate: Secular and sexual exceptionalism, and Muslim women in the Netherlands.' *Feminist Review* 98 (1): 28–46. https://doi.org/10.1057/fr.2011.5.

Cotter, Christopher R. 2015. 'Without God yet not without nuance: A qualitative study of atheism and non-religion among Scottish university students', in *Atheist Identities: Spaces and Social Contexts*, Lori G. Beaman and Steven Tomlins, eds, 171–93. Cham: Springer.

Crenshaw, Kimberlé. 2017. *On Intersectionality: Essential writings*. New York: New Press.

De Koning, Martijn. 2016. '"You need to present a counter-message": The racialisation of Dutch Muslims and anti-Islamophobia initiatives.' *Journal of Muslims in Europe* 5 (2): 170–89. https://doi.org/10.1163/22117954-12341325.

Derrida, Jacques. 1982. *Margins of Philosophy*. Chicago: University of Chicago Press.

Deseriis, Marco. 2011. 'Online activism as a participatory form of storytelling', in *Art and Activism in the Age of Globalization*, Ruben De Roo, Lieven De Cauter and Karel Vanhaesebrouck, eds, 250–63. Brussels: NAi Publishers.

Dunajeva, Jekatyerina. 2018. 'hooks, bell. (1989) *Talking Back: Thinking feminist, thinking black*.' (book review). *Critical Romani Studies* 1 (1): 128–31. https://doi.org/10.29098/crs.v1i1.18.

Fader, Ayala. 2017. 'The counterpublic of the J(ewish) Blogosphere: Gendered language and the mediation of religious doubt among ultra-Orthodox Jews in New York.' *Journal of the Royal Anthropological Institute* 23 (4): 727–47. https://doi.org/10.1111/1467-9655.12697.

Fattal, Alex. 2018. 'Counterpublic', in *The International Encyclopedia of Anthropology*, Hilary Callan, editor-in-chief. Hoboken, NJ: Wiley-Blackwell.

Fileborn, Bianca. 2014. 'Online activism and street harassment: Digital justice or shouting into the ether?' *Griffith Journal of Law and Human Dignity* 2 (1): 32–51.

Fraser, Nancy. 1990. 'Rethinking the public sphere: A contribution to the critique of actually existing democracy.' *Social Text* 25/26: 56–80. https://doi.org/10.2307/466240.

Gül, Lale. 2021. *Ik ga leven*. [I'm going to live]. Amsterdam: Prometheus.

Hage, Ghassan. 2010. 'The affective politics of racial mis-interpellation.' *Theory, Culture & Society* 27 (7–8): 112–29. https://doi.org/10.1177/0263276410383713.

Hirschkind, Charles. 2006. *The Ethical Soundscape: Cassette sermons and Islamic counterpublics*. New York: Columbia University Press.

Hirschkind, Charles, Maria José A. de Abreu and Carlo Caduff. 2017. 'New media, new publics? An introduction to Supplement 15.' *Current Anthropology* 58 (15): 3–12.

Hirsi Ali, Ayaan. 2007. *Infidel: My life*. New York: Free Press.

hooks, bell. 1989. *Talking Back: Thinking feminist, thinking black*. Boston, MA: South End Press.

Iddins, Annemarie. 2020. 'The digital carceral: Media infrastructure, digital cultures and state surveillance in post-Arab Spring Morocco.' *International Journal of Cultural Studies* 23 (2): 245–63. https://doi.org/10.1177/1367877919842575.

Kaulingfreks, Femke. 2016. *Uncivil Engagement and Unruly Politics: Disruptive interventions of urban youth*. Basingstoke: Palgrave Macmillan.

Kettioui, Abdelmjid. 2021. 'Sarcasm and taboo in the Moroccan mediascape after the February 20 movement.' *Journal of African Cultural Studies* 33 (4): 405–23. https://doi.org/10.1080/13696815.2019.1701426.

Lorde, Audre. 2018. *The Master's Tools Will Never Dismantle the Master's House*. London: Penguin Classics.

Loukili, Sakina. 2021. 'Making space, claiming place: Social media and the emergence of the'Muslim' political parties DENK and NIDA in the Netherlands.' *Journal for Religion, Film and Media* 7 (2): 107–31. https://doi.org/10.25364/05.7:2021.2.6 .

Mitra, Ananda. 2001. 'Marginal voices in cyberspace.' *New Media & Society* 3 (1): 29–48. https://doi.org/10.1177/1461444801003001003.

Mohammed, Wunpini Fatimata. 2019. 'Online activism: Centering marginalized voices in activist work.' *Ada: A Journal of Gender, New Media and Technology* 15: 1–11. https://doi.org/10.5399/UO/ADA.2019.15.2.

Mulder, Stephennie. 2018. 'Beeshu's laugh: The arts of satire in the Syrian uprising.' *Middle East Journal of Culture and Communication* 11 (2): 174–95. https://doi.org/10.1163/18739865-01102005

Nostik, Hicham. 2020. مذكرات كافر مغربي. [Notes of a Moroccan infidel]. Rabat: Dar Al Watan.

Odysseos, Louiza, Carl Death and Helle Malmvig. 2016. 'Interrogating Michel Foucault's counter-conduct: Theorising the subjects and practices of resistance in global politics.' *Global Society* 30 (2): 151–6.

Peeren, Esther, Hanneke Stuit and Astrid Van Weyenberg. 2016. *Peripheral Visions in the Globalizing Present: Space, mobility, aesthetics*. Leiden: Brill.

Quack, Johannes and Mascha Schulz. In preparation. 'Who counts as a "non(e)"? Non-believing, non-practicing, and non-identifying Hindus, Muslims, and atheists in contemporary South Asia.'

Rahman, Zahir. 2012. 'Online youth political activism in Morocco: Facebook and the birth of the February 20th movement.' *Journal of New Media Studies in MENA* 1: 1–13.

Richter, Lena. 2021. 'Laughing about religious authority – but not too loud.' *Religions* 12 (2), art. no. 73: 1–18. https://doi.org/10.3390/rel12020073.

Saaf, Abdallah, Bouchra Sidi Hida and Ahmed Aghbal. 2009. *Belgo-Marocains des deux rives: Une identité multiple en évolution*. Brussels: Fondation Roi Baudouin.

Salonen, Anna Sofia. 2018. 'Living and dealing with food in an affluent society: A case for the study of lived (non)religion.' *Religions* 9 (10), art. no. 306: 1–15. https://doi.org/10.3390/rel9100306.

Shayan, Zafar. 2016. 'Connectivity of online and offline activism.' *Journal of Turkish Weekly*, 5 September. https://www.kabulpress.org/article240000.html (accessed 24 June 2022).

Smith, Sidonie. 1993. 'Who's talking/who's talking back? The subject of personal narrative.' *Journal of Women in Culture and Society* 18 (2): 392–407.

Spivak, Gayatri Chakravorty. 1988. 'Can the subaltern speak?', in *Marxism and the Interpretation of Culture*, Cary Nelson and Lawrence Grossberg, eds, 271–313. Champaign: University of Illinois Press.

Van den Brandt, Nella. 2019. '"The Muslim question" and Muslim women talking back.' *Journal of Muslims in Europe* 8 (3): 286–312. https://doi.org/10.1163/22117954-12341404.

Van Zoonen, Liesbet, Farida Vis and Sabina Mihelj. 2010. 'Performing citizenship on YouTube: Activism, satire and online debate around the anti-Islam video *Fitna*.' *Critical Discourse Studies* 7 (4): 249–62. https://doi.org/10.1080/17405904.2010.511831.

Yuval-Davis, Nira. 2006. 'Intersectionality and feminist politics.' *European Journal of Women's Studies* 13 (3): 193–209. https://doi.org/10.1177/1350506806065752.

Warner, Michael. 2002. 'Publics and counterpublics.' *Public Culture* 14 (1): 49–90.

12
Ungodly visuals: confrontations, religion and affect in the everyday lives of atheists in India

Neelabh Gupta

In 2014, a Bollywood film titled *PK* made headlines for its engagement with 'non-religiosity'. The film tells the story of an alien and his (mis)adventures on earth in search of a medallion-like communicating device he needs in order to return home, a device that has found its way into the hands of a popular godman (spiritual guru). The film's major female protagonist, who belongs to a very religious family whose members are ardent disciples of the godman with the medallion, trusts the alien's story and becomes his quest companion. She begins to question the influence of godmen and religion in her personal life, including on her relationship with her estranged Muslim boyfriend from Pakistan, whom she met while living in Belgium. As the alien and the female protagonist race to locate the medallion, various social aspects of religion – communalism, blind faith, astrology and notions of God – are depicted critically. Throughout the film, the protagonist learns and unlearns various aspects of religion through encounters which generate humour and question contemporary practices within various religions. Clips of the film continue to circulate within the digital spaces I have been studying.

Though the atheists I discuss in the chapter are not aliens, their everyday experiences include many similar instances. This chapter is an attempt to understand the encounters atheists have with 'religious fields' in their everyday lives, in both online and offline contexts. It examines attempts made by atheists to publicise atheism, and their interactions with various aspects of religion, including an online religious public.

The religious field is shaped by socio-political contexts, both contemporary and historical, that mark out the space of atheistic expression. My notion of religious field is expansive, including direct and indirect ways in which religion becomes a relevant factor. Its meaning here is manifold. It is not simply a confrontation between religious belief and its denial, but an ongoing conversation that informs everyday lives. The intent is not to mark the boundaries of the 'religious field', because such strict boundaries will be hard to delineate. I will, instead, demonstrate various ways in which edges of the 'religious field' become visible by showcasing examples of visuals circulated in digital spaces such as closed Facebook groups and WhatsApp groups. When these different 'edges' are confronted, various affects come into place, informing the processes of becoming atheist and the expression of atheist views, including visual media in digital spaces. Affects here mean a complex of sensibilities and emotions that come into place, shaping navigation of the religious field on the part of atheists. Though particularities of religion and the religious field are important factors to consider when we try to understand how atheists experience religion after leaving it, my argument is focused more on atheist spaces of expression in everyday matters. I also examine confrontations that happen in varying forms governed by different sets of relations among groups such as family, religious publics, digital platform guidelines for religious content, and the state.

The focus of the chapter is on unorganised atheism in India, mediated through digital spaces, on atheists coming together in online spaces in different forms (groups, pages, channels, among other forms), and sharing and exchanging views, but living their individual lives in geographically dispersed socio-religious contexts that share similarities and differences. There is marked variation in how Indian atheists enact 'digital atheism' (Copeman and Schulz, this volume). It can be a simple extension of a social world online, a part of everyday life, where views are openly expressed. But I have found such expression to be quite rare for atheists in India. On the other hand, atheists may guard their digital activities carefully, and take measures to remain anonymous or hide their views and sharing of media from people they know personally. Ayala Fader's work among Hasidic Jews in New York who are critical of Judaic orthodoxy offers interesting insights into this kind of subject position. The heretics Fader studied enact almost parallel lives and online networks, remaining digitally anonymous or revealing their identities only after achieving mutual trust. They maintain digital anonymity because of the fear of being ostracised by their community (Fader 2020, 14–17). Similarly, many young atheists in India keep their online atheist lives separate from their physically known networks. But there are key differences as well. The atheists I have been working with do not hail from a single geographical location or community but from various parts of India and different religious communities. For example, in a WhatsApp group of around 20 atheists of which I am a member, members hail from different states of India, such as West Bengal, Uttar Pradesh, Assam, Odisha, Kerala, Delhi, Haryana and Punjab. They are also of different religious backgrounds: Hindu, Muslim, Jain and Sikh. Meanwhile, multiple other factors, such as state laws and online religious publics, contribute to regulating the digital expression of Indian atheists. Their digital activities range from a simple extension of their offline social life to the setting up of a parallel digital life in which they can freely discuss atheism and share ungodly visuals; this life is quite distinct from their offline one in which they maintain silence on these matters.

People use different terms for themselves in relation to their non-belief, such as rationalist, freethinker, non-believer, and also some regional words like *nastik* (Hindi for atheist),[1] *Vastvik* (loosely translated as materialist), *adharmi* (without religion) and *Mulhid* (Urdu for non-believer), with different connotations of non-belief. These identities are 'ambivalent', as they emphasise different aspects of non-belief and involve subtle political positioning as well (Lee 2015, 6–7). I am using the word 'atheist' in this chapter as an umbrella term for people on the spectrum of non-belief. Also, I am considering atheistic expression foregrounded in a relational approach towards non-religion (Quack 2014, 448–51), in which expression is regulated and influenced by the specific socio-political and geographic context of the religious beliefs atheists have grown up with and, to a large extent, still live in. Relationality of religion with non-religion can be understood in many ways, but I am describing it by using the word 'edge'. Edge here means a not so strict boundary, but at the same time it establishes a distinction between religion and non-religion.

I will describe the lives and experiences of young atheists who are mostly in their twenties. They are active participants in various digital media spaces for atheism in India. Making and sharing visual media, including but not limited to memes, informs the everydayness of these digital spaces. Usually such spaces are small, having only a few hundred active members. Many of my interlocutors are pursuing a degree, either living with or dependent on their parents and extended family. They usually do not have many atheists in their network of personal relations, which means that practising or expressing atheism is riddled with dilemmas. I do not put much emphasis here on the various ways through which non-religion is acknowledged or represented. Rather, I focus on everyday encounters with the religious field in which these atheists operate.

The sharing of visual media offers meaningful insights in locating encounters with the religious field and how it is navigated. I particularly focus on visuals, as they form a part of everyday media sharing, which gains importance in terms of atheistic expression in digital spaces (Richter 2021, 4–6). Visuals can be considered a part of conversations about atheism that are already happening in India, in which visuals are used to generate humour and other affects to signify shared experiences or commonalities. In any case, visuals shared in atheist spaces capture the complex entanglements of expressing non-belief within a society that is largely religious. Richter (this volume) notes a similar media-sharing practice among the young populace of Morocco, where memes about Islam are shared in closed private spaces. These visual media, which I call 'ungodly' visuals, may be blasphemous or simply provoke accusations of blasphemy, and they are often based on iconography of gods or refer to godly figures of various religions. Such visuals become a point of conflict between atheists and believers. These conflicts may remain confined to comment sections, but they harbour the potential to spark larger conflicts as well, including physical violence and legal action from the state. But, along with content, the process of regulating circulation in digital spaces is equally important for understanding atheistic expression, both online and offline.

Everyday encounters with religious 'edges'

In the late afternoon of a very cold Sunday in Delhi, I was anxiously waiting for an interlocutor's response to my messages about a scheduled interview call the same day. I had just begun my fieldwork and sent numerous messages to establish a network of online atheists to work with. While waiting for responses, I browsed through some notes from my previous conversations with some of these atheists. I had noticed reluctance on the part of some young atheists to come online and talk, particularly in a video-call format. The reluctance stemmed from concerns about privacy, which is understandable as many of them operate through anonymous (profiles with names such as 'Atheist' or 'Thinker') or pseudonymous accounts (profiles with fake names), with no trace of personal information. Conversing with an unknown person who claims to be a researcher could spell danger as they partake in sharing 'ungodly' visuals actively. But that was not the only concern. Many of my participants live with their families, who are blissfully unaware of their atheistic beliefs, let alone their activities in online spaces. Several times, concerns were expressed about attracting the unwanted attention of people at home, particularly parents, through being overheard in the house. They usually spoke to me very softly, censoring words every now and then or suppressing gleeful laughs, in order to avoid creating noise. I had been interviewing people during the pandemic, another potent reason for them to live in the confines of family homes. The kind of secrecy enabled by smartphone screens, then, becomes a blessing for atheists, who can thus express their views, rather vividly, on social media platforms. A similar thing happened in this interview, during which my interlocutor looked away from the screen every few minutes to listen for approaching footsteps.

I share with you a small excerpt from a chat with a person who manages a Facebook page named Atheists of South Asia. He agreed to talk to me, but only through text messages (figure 12.1). Since then, we have chatted many times about atheistic work online and, every now and then, about his personal life. He refused to meet me in person or even chat on a video call to avoid any confrontation with his family. He jokingly suggested that we can only meet once he is in his thirties, implying independence from parents. This palpable reluctance to talk in the presence of family points to various factors at play in the expression of non-belief outside digital media spaces. For online spaces, the choices of privacy settings offered by different platforms help in media-sharing practices, offering control over what becomes visible to family and other personal relations.

There have been some exemplary studies that have documented the everyday experiences of atheists in India. Stefan Binder, in his work with atheist activists in South India, employs the term 'ex-centricity' to refer to practices of making atheistic aspects of life visible in various ways, in public and in one's personal life (Binder 2020). He emphasises various ways of accomplishing this, such as making a wedding a subdued, secular affair, with no ritual element. My research with individual atheists connected via digital spaces shows that ex-centricity often becomes an aspiration, particularly in personal life. However, in online spaces, atheists find ways to express atheism, particularly through the ideological and atheistic media content shared. The personal accounts of atheists on different platforms usually have elements that outrightly convey atheism. This comes in the form of biographical description, profile pictures, pictures with logos of atheism, content shared through their profile and other forms of media sharing. But in offline lives, making atheism visible can be difficult.

12.1 Excerpt of chat with an interlocutor, translated from Hindi. Created using fakechatapp.com.

Along with making atheism visible, practising a rational, logical or reason-driven life may be complicated. Individually, atheists do try to make space for such practice, but within the domain of intimate familial relations there can be obstacles to overcome. Johannes Quack's work with organised 'rationalists' in the state of Maharashtra theorises 'modes of unbelief' in which atheist activists aspire to lead completely rational lives (Quack 2012a, 236–41). Arguments promoting rational ways of thinking are found in abundance in online spaces. It is worth noting that these two positions, ex-centricity and 'modes of unbelief', were defined in settings in which atheism is professed as social activism, with a strong support network present in the form of rationalist organisations. Further, it is often the case that males are in a position to be open about being atheists in a way that women cannot, since men are in general more able to assert authority and influence. Unorganised individual atheists, though sharing deep mediatised connections with other atheists, are often embedded in a religious field, where the scope for exhibiting and expressing atheism is limited. Here, ex-centricity and modes of unbelief turn into negotiation for atheistic expression within personal relations.

I have shared an old but popular meme (figure 12.2) which surfaces every now and then. In the meme, a woman has placed a hand on the mouth of her dog, in order to stop it from barking. The text adds meaning to the affect of forced silence, here in the context of atheism and religious conversations. For many of my atheist interlocutors, atheism is tied in with affective relations shared with family, a space where atheist beliefs are negotiated. Just a few months ago, as I was about to commence research on atheism, my mother asked me to pay for an online course on Hindu astrology. As an atheist, I did not want her to pursue it, but she argued that she accepts my non-belief and I should extend her the same courtesy. My case is not an isolated one, because many young atheists are embedded in this collective familial religiosity, within which the expression of atheism is actualised in the process of creating spaces of expression and marking boundaries, or trimming, even if only slightly, the edges of a religious field.

Collective religiosity is present in everyday lives as well as being reflected in events like life-cycle rituals relating to death. This has been noted, even among the established atheist activists, particularly with reference to death rituals. Opting not to have a funeral that accords with religious guidelines, either pre-planning for oneself or for some family member, meets with strong resistance from religious family and friends.[2] Negotiations take place to persuade people to donate the body to science instead of having a religious burial or conducting death rituals, which are

12.2   'Silenced dog' meme. Image taken from a closed Facebook group.

considered by atheist activists a Brahmanical form of monetary exploitation because of the price of conducting the rituals over several days and the social obligation to feed the Brahmins on the last day (Copeman and Quack 2015, 51). Other superstitions about the dead come into play: where the afterlives of the dead are assumed to be in jeopardy or worse, a form of haunting is expected if rituals are not completed (Copeman and Reddy 2012, 66). Such concerns about marriages, births, deaths and calendrical events such as festivals also constitute the religious field in everyday lives. One of my interlocutors, a queer ex-Muslim, vented about the pressure from his family to carry out religious ceremonies for his brother's wedding. Many fellow atheists came forward with sympathy and suggestions to help him navigate this familiar situation. His father did not dismiss his non-belief entirely but suggested that he perform the rituals anyway lest their omission raised questions from religious hard-liners within their community. Even though he did not want to perform those rituals, understanding the situation, he agreed.

It is not always a forceful assertion of religion or non-belief that creates confrontations in everyday life. Such confrontations are better understood as sensibilities of operating in a religious field, where space for expressing non-belief is negotiated within a balance of silence and argument. Also, the negotiations expand the space for atheistic expression as well as secure the space already present. Many atheists prefer to avoid conversations about religion and beliefs with their close family members and friends. Some even take part in rituals and festivities, in order to avoid hurting the feelings of family members or inviting unwanted arguments that slip into personal conflict. Another ex-Muslim, Tariq (pseudonym), in his late twenties, who works in a digital marketing firm, recounted many similar experiences. While coming to one of our physical meetings in Delhi, held during the brief spell of calm between coronavirus pandemic waves, he brought biryani cooked by his mother, at the request of a few members of the 'God Delusion'[3] WhatsApp group, a subset of twenty-odd people from a larger Facebook group. But his mother was not aware that he was going to meet atheists, nor that they were from an online group. Tariq chose to conceal this particular detail and simply referred to the group as friends, thus avoiding an argument that might have resulted in his missing the get-together. For another participant, a queer Dalit atheist, silencing came in the form of shushing or interrupting them while they were talking in order to prevent them from taking up some of the arguments in discussions with their neighbours. They were asked to avoid arguments about religion with neighbours as such disputes are not good for their image in the community. Such confrontations, resulting in forced silence for atheists, come from the religious field that becomes visible in everyday life in different forms. It is important to note that these young atheists, particularly those who do not express their atheist identity openly in front of their families, often feign interest in religious activities, in order to escape scrutiny. The closest that they can get to making their non-belief visible is in the form of religious indifference (Copeman and Quack 2019, 50), whereby they simply appear to be uninterested but non-critical about matters of religion.

I will illustrate the confrontations with the religious field through two examples. The first is the construction of the Ram Mandir (a Hindu temple) in Ayodhya, a coveted project of right-wing Hindu ('Hindutva') politics that commenced in August 2020, and the subsequent donation collection drive in January 2021, in various neighbourhoods of Delhi. The second is the everyday experience of non-straight/non-binary atheists.

On 5 August 2020, the prime minister of India, Narendra Modi, participated in a priest-led foundation ceremony (*Bhoomi pujan*) for the Ram Mandir in the city of Ayodhya, birthplace of the Hindu god Ram. In November 2019, the Supreme Court of India had legally paved the way for the construction of a Ram Mandir, in a major victory for Hindutva organisations across the country.[4] The building of Ram Mandir has been a fundamental ideological issue for many decades, provoking waves of communal violence in different parts of India. Since the Supreme Court judgement, it has been an active point of discussion in online spaces, making Ram Mandir almost indexical to the contemporary Hindu nationalist political regime. On the day of the foundation stone laying ceremony, various social media influencers who favour the ruling political party called for the lighting of five lamps in front of houses, as a mark of this 'holy' spectacle of the prime minister laying the foundation stone for a long-awaited religious, or rather political, achievement.[5] Many visuals and texts circulated on WhatsApp, reaching my participants, among others. In the evening, social media posts of lamps lit on the porches of houses or in windows and on balconies and terraces started circulating. Many atheists expressed a general disdain online by sharing screenshots of Instagram and WhatsApp stories or pictures of their neighbourhood, where lamps were in abundance. I was staying in South Delhi at that time, witnessing something similar there. Some atheists expressed concern about their own families participating in the ongoing celebration. Many expressed surprise, seeing the sheer number of people in their personal networks, whom they had never thought of as politically or religiously active, putting such stories[6] on social media platforms. Many atheists felt isolated and lonely, overwhelmed by the collective religiosity unfolding throughout their personal networks, both online and offline.

After that day, the phrase 'Jai Shree Ram' (Glory to Lord Ram) and references to Ram Mandir generally increased in atheistic digital spaces such as WhatsApp groups. A few months later, in January 2021, a drive to collect money for the construction of Ram Mandir was initiated by right-wing-affiliated Hindu organisations that supported the religious-political cause.[7] Soon, this collection drive reached many neighbourhoods of Delhi. People clad in saffron or bearing a symbolic saffron piece of clothing could be seen going around neighbourhoods, asking for small contributions (figure 12.3). These collectors soon reached the doorsteps of members of 'The God Delusion', the WhatsApp group, prompting the group to express derision at what was happening.

The discussion of the donation drive lasted for nearly three weeks on the WhatsApp group. Siddharth, one of the longest-standing members, shared his experience with the group. He resides in a gated community in Noida, an area south-east of Delhi, with his parents. They wanted to donate to the Ram Mandir construction, something quite typical of upper-caste families in India. He had persuaded his parents not to. His parents agreed, but were not entirely convinced. When he shared a snippet of his conversation with his father on the group platform, other members had similar stories to share from their own personal experiences. After a few days, Siddharth had another encounter. While going up in the apartment lift with his mother, he found himself trapped with two people who were collecting donations. They started talking to his mother, who was already interested in giving a donation for the temple. This time, he witnessed his mother eagerly agreeing to donate. She informed the donation collectors that she would prefer to donate online, which bought Siddharth time to persuade her otherwise. Apparently, she was inspired by the publicity of a famous Indian actor, Akshay Kumar,[8] who was rallying support for the same cause. Siddharth's partner, Aditi, also a group member, replied that she would talk to his mother. She did talk to her, suggesting she donate instead to a charity supporting education or feeding street dogs, but Siddharth's mother was not convinced. After a few days, Siddharth shared a post on a Facebook group expressing anguish at his own silence when all this happened. Some members of the Facebook group shared similar stories, about how they had not been able to stop their parents or friends from donating money. One of my interlocutors revealed that his family had donated 50,000 Indian rupees (around £500 or $650) for the temple because his grandfather was a former Member of the Legislative Assembly (MLA) for the Bharatiya Janata Party (BJP). He was repulsed by the fact, expressing absolute disgust towards his family members for doing it. He shared such sentiments on various occasions when the political and religious views expressed by his family made him feel alone, vulnerable and suffocated. He has been actively job hunting, which would enable him to move out of the family home and live an independent life. Those living by themselves or with friends were able to resist and did not donate, usually by ignoring the doorbell and shouts for them to come out. But those staying with their families faced multiple challenges, to varying degrees.

In between these conversations, running jokes about creating a fake donation drive were going on in our WhatsApp group. The plan was simple: a door-to-door collection in various neighbourhoods, wearing saffron clothes with devotional music in the background. The money gathered would be put to a productive use promoting science. The

12.3 Ram Mandir donation-drive bike rally, Delhi, January 2021.

thoughts about what to do with the money evolved over time, but the joke stayed for several weeks and neutralised tensions emerging from conflicting experiences in their personal lives. Here, the affect of silence was produced by the entanglement of atheists in the group in political religion, which was actively espoused by state and familial religiosity and decisions, where they had limited say. The silence was maintained in order to avoid confrontation, heated debates and possible violence, from family members and from the people collecting money for the temple. Silence becomes an important affect through which everyday religiosity is navigated by young atheists.

The Silenced Dog meme about family and religious conversations shows the nature of silence that atheists experience. The fact that it remains popular suggests an affective relation among atheists in online spaces, established through an understanding of the particularities of such silence. Silence becomes instrumental in the navigation of religious places, relations and the politico-religious activities of the state.

I will explore another meme (figure 12.4), which has been circulating in different digital spaces. In this meme, a disappointed and sad naked pubescent kid is sitting in bed with two naked women, a scene from *Rick and Morty*, a popular animated comedy show about the

12.4 Screenshot of meme shared in a secret Facebook group, with text caption.

adventures of a scientist and his grandchildren in a multidimensional intergalactic world.[9] The text in the meme uses the affective image to convey the dissatisfaction awaiting gay Muslims in *jannat* (heaven). The humour lies in the fact that a gay Muslim will not be happy with the afterlife reward of 72 female virgins or *hoors* in heaven, a reward suggested in Islamic texts.[10] As the text above the meme suggests, the visual questions the stance that many religions have taken on homosexuality. Some people commented on how difficult it was for them to come out, as since childhood they had been taught that homosexuality is a sin. A member cheekily commented that he would ignore the *hoors* and focus on *Farishtey* or angels, but a genuine discomfort with religion was visible in the ensuing discussions, with atheists criticising religious texts and moral stances that marginalise non-heteronormative choices. It brings out the complexities in dealing with familial relations in which being queer is already difficult and being an atheist adds a further strain.

Atheism and sexuality have a mutually complementing relationship for many of my non-binary, non-heterosexual interlocutors. Many have struggled with coming out both as an atheist and as a non-heterosexual/ non-binary person. In my research, I have come across many instances in which sexuality and the reasons for leaving a religion are affectively linked. For example, a queer atheist from Bengal told me a story that had formed part of his journey to atheism. As a child, around 10–11 years of age, they were experiencing conflicting feelings about their gender identity and sexuality, which led to a lot of frustration and unhappiness. They were unaware of how to make sense of these personal conflicts, and because of a staunch silence about gender and sexuality within their family and community, they had no one to talk to. Desperate for a solution, they prayed to God to eliminate all this turbulence, and just let them feel normal. When the feelings did not go away, they became angry with God and eventually started to question God's existence.

The affective relation between atheism and sexuality comes primarily from a sense of marginalisation and lack of visibility in public discourse (Brewster 2013). In atheist digital spaces, there are ample discussions about sexuality, gender identities and inherent patriarchy in religion, usually reflecting on difficulties faced by queer atheists living in a deeply religious society. This conflict of being a gay Muslim or Hindu or Sikh becomes a binary dilemma: either reconcile faith with your sexuality or deny the faith that does not accept your sexuality. Many queer atheists I was in contact with chose the latter. Through their experiences another edge of religious field becomes visible in everyday life, involving sexuality and prescriptive religious perspectives.

Some gay atheists shared their encounters on gay dating and meet-up apps in the group. While networking for intimate partners on digital apps one often comes across people who follow some religion. In addition to the usual forms of confrontation that being gay and being an atheist can invite, I became particularly fascinated by what happens in the intimate sphere of homosexuality when a gay atheist comes into contact with intimate partners who believe in God or follow some religion. One post in the same secret Facebook group mentioned that it was not easy to hook up with people around festivals such as *Navrati* or *Ramzan*, because some religious members of these dating apps chose to abstain from sex during these times, in order to preserve the religious sanctity of the festival. The creation of 'sacred' space and time, within a discreet queer marginalised network, regularly deemed sinful or immoral, shows another way in which the religious field operates. The 'edge' becomes visible in the choice between accommodating faith with sexuality and leaving faith because of sexuality. Another queer atheist activist, Prateek, shared a story with me of his encounter with a Muslim cleric in a town in Uttar Pradesh. When they asked the cleric why he engages in homosexual acts, when his religion clearly forbids it, the cleric replied that he has been possessed by *Jinnat* or an evil spirit and he cannot fight against it and has to submit to its demand. The cleric's reply left Prateek stupefied.

Here, the religious field operates through stigma around queer identities, which is shaped by strong moral undertones such as deeming gay sex sinful or unnatural. Similar notions were reinforced when the government of India opposed in the Supreme Court a legal plea to legitimise same-sex marriage.[11] The current Hindu right government, which takes into consideration the religious voter base, has described homosexuality as being against 'the Indian family unit concept', reiterating heteronormative notions about marriage and family, which come with a religious, moral undertone. This is not to suggest that homophobia does not exist among atheists, but to point out the everyday connections between religion and sexuality encountered by queer atheists.

The visuals that I have shown situate atheists in a religious field. But atheists use other visuals, such as Instagram reels or art, to critique religion, pushing against the religious field. More forms of religious edges become visible, which shape the everyday activism of atheists, particularly in digital spaces.

Pushing against the religious field

In this section I will focus on visuals that confront religion through critique, making visible the religious field through online religious publics, as well as the limits of atheistic expression in digital spaces. Visuals that mock religion, religious figures, norms, rituals, myths, gods and goddesses also inform the everyday digital feed of my atheist interlocutors. Most of the circulation happens either anonymously or in closed networks, but I will focus on the manner in which they circulate and what happens when 'ungodly' visuals get unwarranted public attention. Mocking religion is an important element of atheistic visual culture, so it is important to understand how these visuals are received and what their reception can tell us about the state of atheism in India.

Sushmita Sinha is a journalist in her mid-twenties residing in Delhi, and a vocal feminist activist. I came across her online profile on Instagram in late August 2020, when a video she shared as an Instagram reel, a short less than a minute long, went viral. In response, hashtags calling for her arrest trended on Indian Twitter. In atheist spaces online, various posts declared their support for her and called out people who were abusing her online for their bigotry and misogyny. The whole episode lasted for around two weeks, then people found new images to become outraged about (the next visual in this chapter).

Sushmita's reel focused on a book about the Hindu festival known as *Teej* or *Haritalika Teej*, a monsoon-related festivity in which women observe a fast for their husbands, celebrated in different forms across India. She had come across this book a year before she shot the video, when her family asked her to read it as part of the rituals the family had to perform. While reading this book, she could not stop laughing during the rituals as stories in the book were quite amusing to her feminist self. A year later, when the festival came round again, she decided to read segments of the stories from this book and put them on Instagram. In the film, she read a section and then made some humorous comments, and repeated this several times. For example, in one part of the video, she reads a story that suggests a woman would be reborn as some animal if she drank water and broke the fast during this time, and she comments on the absurd misogyny this fast symbolises. Curiously, the video has peppy background music, similar to music in pranks or viral funny videos on social media streams. In the end, she says 'I have wasted Rs.15 [Indian rupees] on this book; now I don't know what to do with this. I should use it as a tissue or toilet paper.' This served as the hook that made her video go viral for 'hurting Hindu sentiments', something akin to the outrage that Jaffrelot (2008, 2) suggests is a part of a 'discourse of victimization which is the very matrix of Hindu nationalism'. Later that day she uploaded a picture (figure 12.5) on her Instagram story, where the book is placed on what seems to be a toilet-roll stand.

12.5   Screenshot of viral Instagram story (Sushmita Sinha), with 'religious' book placed above a toilet roll.

Sushmita was not actively seeking to outrage people, she told me in our interview. She described the video as a humorous attempt to gain people's attention and highlight the misogyny in such practices as *Teej*. Her video went viral overnight and her account was flooded with notifications of all sorts. It was not a unique event, as many media objects go viral and gain attention. Facebook posts, stand-up comedy clips, images, texts and memes go viral, and create outrage of different sorts across South Asia, leading to unforeseen consequences. Such consequences were apparent in a case of student politics at a public university campus in Bangladesh, where a Facebook post had repercussions – fines and demotion – for a professor as things got heated (Schulz 2019, 10–12). Similarly, in India, political commentaries such as satire or stand-up comedy usually lead to controversies through social media's viral trajectory (Punathambekar 2015, 398), initiating legal cases or public outrage. This happened to Sushmita too; when her video went viral, there were calls for her arrest.

Two things are significant about the video that went viral. First, it was an edited clip of a video made by someone else, containing only the last bit, in which she equated the book with toilet paper. Second, screenshots of her Instagram story were circulated widely to portray her as 'anti-Hindu', indicting her for using a 'holy' Hindu book as toilet paper. Online trolls bombarded her with threats of sexual and physical violence. (Such abuse has become commonplace in political conversations on digital spaces, where *gaali* or abusive expletives form a repertoire of political expression and staunch beliefs (Udupa 2018b, 1515).) Outrage spilled over into the public domain over the next couple of days. She consulted some of her friends and made her account private on Instagram. But Sushmita struggled with switching to a private account as she did not believe there was anything wrong with the video. She switched her account back to being publicly visible. It is important to note this, because the sudden pressure from the online religious public left her scared. This kind of presence of an online religious public often comes from the organised online networks of the ruling party in India (Udupa 2018a, 465), among other, allied right-wing organisations such as Hindu IT Cell.[12] Legal cases were filed against her in Delhi, though they were eventually dropped as the judge in a local court did not find anything to substantiate the charges. But the fear of being persecuted and abused by the online religious public as well as the state machinery did stop her from sharing a few more, similar, videos that she had planned. Here, the edge of the religious field becomes visible in the form of a religious public online as well as in national laws about blasphemy and state persecution on religious matters.

The media Sushmita shared, particularly the Instagram story, were considered offensive by certain religious adherents. W. T. J. Mitchell argues that offending images have the ability to spark affective reactions through various elements. The media debacle took attention away from the critique of religion in the original video, shifting the focus towards 'anti-Hindu' rhetoric.[13] This particular screenshot of an Instagram story gained a meaning of its own, carrying an offence through disgust and contempt (Mitchell 2005, 125). Though not intended by Sushmita in this case, offence is an important affect, because it is through this 'offence' that atheistic visual cultures seek to break the silence around the critique of religion and religious institutions.

After a few days, Sushmita shared another video, urging her audience to watch the whole of the original video in order to understand the context of the viral short clip. A week later, she uploaded another video, this time of her wearing a T-shirt with Bhagat Singh's picture[14] and text reading 'why I am an atheist', urging people not to abuse her. Before she had uploaded the last video, calls for her arrest had been made, with members of ruling parties calling her Hindu-phobic on mainstream news channels. She had to flee from Delhi to her hometown in order to avoid the potential violence. After a couple of months, she stopped paying attention to whatever was happening and focused on her journalism covering elections in her home state Bihar.

The religious public, along with the organised online networks such as 'Hindu IT Cell' on Twitter or 'Internet Hindus' (Mohan 2015, 341), which are keen to make a spectacle of offence in order to create controversy, is another form in which the religious field becomes visible on the internet. It has been one of the primary reasons for many atheists refraining from sharing ungodly visuals publicly. The visuals that do appear are shared carefully, alterations in privacy settings offered by different platforms being used to limit their public reach. Many atheist spaces, to avoid such active conflicts, choose to remain private with some form of vetting, avoiding the religious public by sharing content that is a critique of religion using carefully worded posts. There are many like Sushmita who have much to say and share about religious beliefs in India. But the complexities of media sharing, in terms of controlling who can read the posts and avoiding giving offence, or curbing certain expressions, thus establish a limit on expression, in terms of both space and content. As controversy around Sushmita's particular video was reaching an end, another emerged, with a much greater impact on online atheists.

In the first week of September 2020 there was an explosion of tweets about atheism in India; #atheism trended in India, perhaps for the first and only time. Following the hashtag, I came across multiple tweets condemning an 'assault on Hindu beliefs'. The outrage had come after Armin Navabi, founder of Atheist Republic, tweeted about an artwork of Kali (figure 12.6),[15] a Hindu goddess. Atheist Republic is an atheist organisation with global networks on various digital platforms. The text

12.6   Screenshot of the 'Sexy Kali' image as tweeted by Armin Navabi, 3 September 2020.

of the tweet read 'Okay! I'm in love with Hinduism. I never knew you had sexy goddesses like these. Why would anyone pick any other religion? Source: bit.ly/2Z43qag.' Navabi's tweet shared the artwork from a digital comic art platform that is no longer available.

When I asked the CEO of Atheist Republic, Susanna Mcintyre, about this tweet, she laughed out loud and called it 'the sexy Kali episode'. Susanna is based in the United States, but she talked about the presence of Atheist Republic in India, which has a very active community, with private Facebook groups (whose content is visible only to the members) in multiple cities. As the organisation's digital media presence in India grew, its platforms, such as its Facebook page and YouTube channel, started to attract Hindu fundamentalists who enjoyed their memes/ visuals trolling Islam and Christianity. Before sharing this particular visual, Armin had posted a video in which he burnt the Qur'an, which was shared extensively in India. Susanna told me that they had not paid much attention to Hinduism before the response to the Kali post.

The decision to share the image of Kali was an attempt at 'shaking off the Hindu fundamentalist crowd that their media spaces had gathered'. The group had expected outrage and it was a calculated decision to go ahead with the tweet, but the scale of outrage was a surprise. The Sexy Kali image is not the first instance of religious authority being questioned through the sexualisation of images of gods or goddesses. As has been documented in relation to various artists in the preceding decades (Maheshwari 2018, 155–7), such as Maqbool Fida Husain for his nude representations of Bharat Mata (Jain 2010, 200–1; Juneja 2018, 166–9), there was an amplification of outrage caused by the intervention of right-wing Hindu organisations (Anderson 2015, 47). It was no different in this case. The Hindu IT Cell, founded by people associated with Hindu right-wing organisations, ran active campaigns on Twitter, tagging and inciting rage against Armin Navabi and Atheist Republic. The point of outrage was obvious: the goddess Kali and its pornographic representation. The mobs of digital religious people went on a rampage about Armin, morphing his mother's image with pornographic images. For a couple of months, the outrage continued in different forms.

This tweet sparked both scepticism and humour within the atheist spaces. Initially, people responded with 'haha' reactions and agreed that the artwork was indeed 'sexy'. But as the Twitter outrage escalated, the sense of threat grew. The fear was increasingly felt by covert atheist communities in India, particularly those constituted of young atheists. The debates, among other things, were about the timing of this tweet. Armin currently lives in Vancouver, and one user commented, '*Voh to*

Canada mein baitha hai, yeh humein jail bhijwayega' [He is sitting in Canada and we will end up in jail because of him]. Administrators of a particular group, associated with Atheist Republic though based in India, shared some guidelines (figure 12.7) with the members, three days after the tweet. They informed members about the existing blasphemy laws in India and the trouble that posting the image could invite, both for people based in India and for members of the group. Many people agreed with the guidelines and did not post the image publicly.

Interestingly, there have been nude representations of Kali in various art forms in the past and many users have shared similar memes (figure 12.8) to point out that outrage over nudity does not make sense. Armin shared this image knowing about this background. There were many opinions about the artwork, its timing and the growing outrage over atheism. But this image was shared mostly in closed spaces, not even

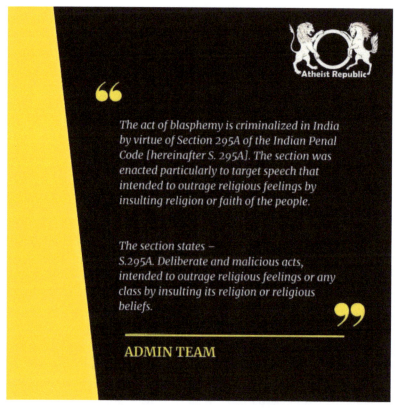

66

The act of blasphemy is criminalized in India by virtue of Section 295A of the Indian Penal Code [hereinafter S. 295A]. The section was enacted particularly to target speech that intended to outrage religious feelings by insulting religion or faith of the people.

The section states –
S.295A. Deliberate and malicious acts, intended to outrage religious feelings or any class by insulting its religion or religious beliefs.

99

ADMIN TEAM

12.7 A warning about blasphemy laws shared in a secret Facebook group affiliated to Atheist Republic.

appearing in the personal profiles of most of my interlocutors. This migration of a blasphemous artwork from Vancouver, Canada was an actively shared contention. A member of a closed Facebook group, a group with members across South Asia, when we met at a café in Gurgaon, Haryana later that month, shouted angrily: 'This man-child has no sensibilities of timing and difference in the context. He is sitting there safe with no blasphemy laws and here I am working in my office, with people

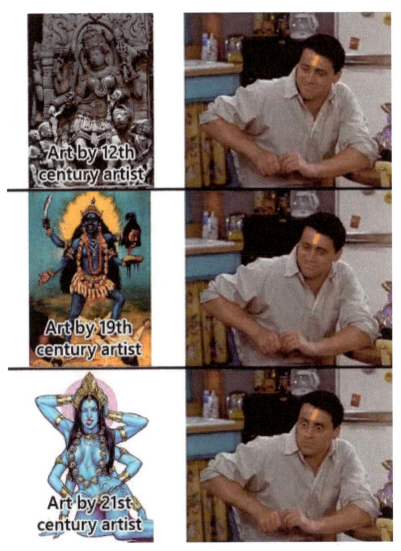

12.8   Meme shared in Indian atheist online spaces in support of Armin.

outraging over Sexy Kali!' She had to make an alternative profile to remain a member of other atheist groups, remove her profile pictures from public accounts and change privacy settings, just to hide her association in any form with Atheist Republic. Even Atheist Republic instructed its groups in India to change their privacy setting to 'hidden' on Facebook (where only members can look it up), and stopped taking new members.

Recent years have seen many such examples of 'outrage politics' throughout South Asia, in which religious publics interact with media critical of religion (Blom 2008; Frøystad 2019). Understanding the context of outrage enables us to see how blasphemous visuals work, but in the case of these atheist activists and their visuals a further meaning is present. When I talked to several content makers for atheist spaces, it became clear to me that they do not single out any particular community to target. Nor is the purpose to insult. Rather, through these visuals they are seeking to breach the silence about non-belief and are trying to normalise blasphemy. In the case of Atheist Republic, a digital art project has been developed, known as the blasphemous art project, in which artworks that combine gods and religious icons of various religions are mixed up and shown in a pornographic manner. Many of these themes can be deemed offensive, such as the one depicting a homosexually erotic act between Ram and Muhammad.[16]

After the outrage over the Kali meme died down, the government of India intervened and managed to get Armin's Twitter account suspended permanently, and a similar fate awaited the CEO of Atheist Republic. They both incurred permanent suspension for violating hate speech guidelines. The Facebook page of Atheist Republic is still banned in India, Pakistan being the only other country to ban it.[17] This particular incident was also cited in a public interest litigation case in the Supreme Court of India as a reason for regulating the content shared on online platforms, which has resulted in a new regulatory framework for social media platforms in India. In addition to following the existing guidelines, the platforms now need to comply with the regional laws about free speech and related matters.[18]

It is very common for atheists to come across warnings about community guidelines violations in relation to the content that they share on social media platforms. In one secret group on Facebook, there are guidelines about how to type certain words and phrases in order to avoid detection by Facebook or Instagram. The group has now disappeared because someone reported some content and Facebook deleted the entire group. Hence, atheists usually rely on multiple accounts and fake profiles, as they face censure whenever their content is reported and they are subject to account restrictions and, sometimes, deletion. In conversation, many interlocutors said that although these 'community guidelines' set out to protect individual religions, they prevented the critique of religion in general, which was just what they wanted to do. In fact, some atheists have argued that the guidelines constitute a limit on freedom of speech online. Also, the changes in political regime have made it more difficult for atheists to express views that are critical of religion, particularly Hinduism, in the past few years. The fear of state persecution has been documented in various South Asian and neighbouring countries, such as Indonesia (Duile 2020, 456) and Malaysia (Rashid and Mohamad 2019, 1–6).

In digital spaces, these images do not exist in isolation, but form a part of continuous stream of visuals and discussions about major religions and religious events, sharing affective relations. Here, the religious field comes in the form of community guidelines about 'hate speech and harmful content', limiting the circulation of 'offensive' atheistic visuals to closed or hidden digital spaces. While atheists see these images as part of a critique, digital platform guidelines consider them 'hate speech', which places limits on media-sharing practices in the context of India. In the case of the Sexy Kali image, these limitations spread as far as North America, when the image triggered the suspension of Armin's and Susanna's accounts, although many accounts based outside India which shared the same image are still present on Twitter.

The experience of everyday life and community or platform guidelines about sharing content pose a contentious challenge for atheists. When religious sentiments are so frequently expressed, and indeed predominate, on social media platforms, atheists understand that through the act of questioning they can hurt people. The religious sensibilities of online publics are borne in mind by many online atheists. There are multiple ways of dealing with this. The first is to frame arguments in an acceptable way, without abusive terms or generalised criticism of a community. This is particularly common in Hindi atheist groups, which put an emphasis on the art of effective argument. Many avoid sharing visuals in public, shield them from personal networks and share them anonymously. But fear of prosecution by the Indian state, unpredictable community guidelines and prevailing religious sensibilities about sharing 'offensive' images overlap and form another edge of the religious field, producing silence as affect through a policing of sorts.

Understanding silence

Writing of the Danish cartoon controversy that erupted in 2005 after a Danish newspaper published cartoons depicting the Prophet Muhammad, Saba Mahmood suggests that visualising the Prophet is not itself the cause of outrage; it is how this visualisation puts the individual Muslim's cherished relationship with the Prophet in jeopardy that creates a moral injury (Mahmood 2013, 62). Though the atheist visuals shared, particularly those of religious figures, can be considered an injury to religious sentiment, a question emerges, in my research, about the motivations of atheists in causing this offence. As I mentioned earlier, even though such visuals are common, their circulation remains limited for fear of a backlash. The Sexy Kali meme shared by Armin through a global media platform would be extremely hard for a person living in India to make and share for the reasons I listed above. For atheists, sharing blasphemous content is a way to break the silence and normalise criticism of religion. Moreover, for many, their critical views towards religion are shaped by bitter experiences with religion, in which they are deemed immoral for simply disagreeing with, or not conforming to, the norms of religiosity.

The pervasiveness of silence in different modes of atheistic expressions should be considered in a broader framework. It is not to suggest that silence gains more meaning or that silence itself is an act of resistance. Rather, I understand the prevailing silence as an affect which constitutes the process of becoming atheist, where transcending silence in everyday matters becomes important in the creation of space for atheistic expression. Veena Das writes of the importance of speech acts in everyday life that constitute the potential for violence: saying something can itself become an aggressive act (Das 2020, 70–6). In the case of atheists, silence has a similar function: the simmering silence in everyday life carries the potential for conflicts, arguments and even violence. The particularities of silence as affect are made visible through the visuals that I have talked about in this chapter. Silence is neither compelled nor a free choice, so how can we make sense of this silence that pervades everyday conversations, both online and offline? For example, carefully crafted and guarded digital spaces become cornerstones of 'free' expression, while the administrators of these spaces are vigilant to remove visibility from public sight. Silence here is a state of expression which bears affect that informs the sensibilities of being seen and heard as a non-believer. On a larger scale, this silence about atheism is visible in the fact that non-religious or atheist is not recognised as an official 'religious' affiliation in state documents such as the Census of India. A group of ex-Muslims are aspiring to file a Public Interest Litigation with the higher courts in India in an attempt to have 'atheist' recognised as an official category in state documents in which citizens have to fill in their personal details. The non-recognition of atheism is mirrored in the lack of public debate in popular media, and, as happened in the Sexy Kali episode, attention shifted from atheism as a non-belief position to the targeting of Hindu beliefs and to the obscenity of the visual. Though there are many organised rationalist organisations that have been working in India for many decades (Quack 2012b, 72–7), atheism is still not a mainstream position as it is in Western secular nations. When rationalists in India have gained voice and visibility in public, they have been subjected to a lethal form of silencing. Numerous rationalists have been assassinated in the last decade, and legal investigations are pending in almost all the cases.[19] These everyday acts of ungodly media sharing gain meaning in contemporary India to seek voice and resilience at the same time.

Conclusion

In this chapter, I have outlined various ways in which atheists operate and encounter the edges of the religious field. These edges operate through various means such as online religious publics, familial religiosity, and state laws about blasphemy or community guidelines for digital platforms. These edges overlap and pose multiple challenges for atheistic expression. Visuals that circulate within these atheist spaces are grounded in affective sensibilities connected with being an atheist in India. These digital formations of atheist spaces are situated within a broader religious field, where multiple checks and balances are used to control the circulation of atheist visuals. At the same time, these visuals are employed to challenge the hegemonic silence around atheistic expression through the sharing of blasphemous content. While seeking to secure space for sharing atheistic content, silence and humour as affects circulate widely, informing the everyday experiences of being an atheist in India, in both online and offline contexts.

Notes

1   For more on regional terms relating to atheism, and translation, see Quack and Binder (2018).
2   Also see Copeman and Hagström, this volume
3   The group is named after Richard Dawkins's book of the same name, very popular among atheists. The profile picture of this WhatsApp group was the cover of the same book.
4   For details of the judgement, see the BBC News report, 'Ayodhya verdict: Indian top court gives holy site to Hindus', 9 November 2019: https://www.bbc.co.uk/news/world-asia-india-50355775 (accessed 24 June 2022)

5   For details of the ground-breaking ceremony for Ram Mandir at Ayodhya, see Amrit Dhillon, 'Ayodhya: Modi hals "dawn of new era" as work on controversial temple begins', *The Guardian*, 5 August 2020: https://www.theguardian.com/world/2020/aug/05/ayodhya-narendra-modi-temple-foundation-stone-ceremony (accessed 24 June 2022).

6   'Stories' are visuals shared on various social media platforms that disappear after 24 hours. They have become a very common way to share everyday events as they offer much control over the audience, and allow overlapping of media (images, videos, effects, music, GIFs, stickers, etc.). Also, they are more interactive than public comments on normal posts and allow for private communication about a particular story.

7   There have been multiple donation drives in the past for the same cause. This was the latest donation drive, which collected money as the construction of Ram Mandir was about to commence. See Avaneesh Mishra, 'Nearly Rs 2,000 crore collected so far: Ram temple donation campaign concludes', *The Indian Express*, 28 February 2021: https://indianexpress.com/article/cities/lucknow/nearly-rs-2000-crore-collected-so-far-ram-temple-donation-campaign-concludes-7207863/ (accessed 24 June 2022).

8   Akshay Kumar has actively participated in many Hindutva campaigns, giving publicity to their cause and mobilising support. See 'The player', *The Caravan*, 1 February 2021: https://caravanmagazine.in/reportage/akshay-kumar-role-hindutva-poster-boy (accessed 24 June 2022).

9   See Bosman, this volume, for a detailed look at *Rick and Morty*, and atheism and nihilism as portrayed in the animated series.

10 When a man who has been an ardent and obedient follower of Islam dies and goes to Jannat, or heaven, his reward is 72 virgins. Many atheists quote references from religious texts to support the arguments they are making. For claims about 72 virgins, this link or its screenshot have been shared: https://sunnah.com/tirmidhi/38/40 (accessed 24 June 2022).

11 After the decriminalisation of homosexuality, when Section 377 of the Indian Penal Code was removed, activists are trying to gain civil rights for LGBTQ+ individuals, including the right to marry. See 'Same-sex marriage not comparable with Indian family unit concept: A timeline of Section 377', *The Indian Express*, 26 February 2021: https://indianexpress.com/article/india/timeline-of-section-377-7205718/ (accessed 24 June 2022).

12 Hindu IT Cell is an organised network of Twitter accounts, present also on other platforms, closely allied with the current regime. The purpose of this network is to find 'anti-Hindu' elements and hold them accountable over social media as well as legally. See more at Srishti Jaswal and Shreegireesh Jalihal, 'Inside the Hindu IT Cell: The men who went online to protect gods', *NewsLaundry*, 1 March 2021: https://www.newslaundry.com/2021/03/01/inside-the-hindu-it-cell-the-men-who-went-online-to-protect-gods (accessed 24 June 2022).

13 There were 'news' reports about her act, widely shared in online spaces to portray her as anti-Hindu. Many online news portals write reports to give more effect to the outrage. In the case of Sushmita, similar articles were shared online, for example *OpIndia*, 26 August, 'Journalist urges people to use Hindu religious book as toilet paper, netizens demand arrest over image of Teej Vrat book kept in toilet': https://www.opindia.com/2020/08/journalist-hindu-it-cell-complaint-social-media-hariyali-teej-book-toilet-paper-instagram/(accessed 24 June 2022).

14 Bhagat Singh is a celebrated atheist youth icon in India. His book *Main Nastik Kyun hun? (Why I am an Atheist)* is one of the most popular atheist texts in Hindi. For more, see Elam, this volume.

15 Many news portals carried the screenshot of Armin Navabi's tweet or shared the controversial image to report the incident. For example, OpIndia shared this news post in Hindi: https://hindi.opindia.com/social-media-trends/atheist-republic-founder-armin-navabi-insults-hindu-godess-kali/ (accessed 9 July 2022) and *India Times* reported it as well: Bobins Abraham, 'Atheist activist Armin Navabi who tore up Quran angers Hindus by calling goddess Kali sexy', 5 September 2020: https://www.indiatimes.com/news/india/atheist-activist-armin-navabi-who-tore-up-quran-angers-hindus-by-calling-goddess-kali-sexy-522084.html (accessed 9 July 2022).

16 See more at 'The blasphemous art project': https://www.blasphemousart.com/ (accessed 25 June 2022).

17 See a detailed report at Tushar Dhara, 'Facebook blocks Atheist Republic page on government directive, Twitter suspends founder', *The Caravan*, 8 February 2021: https://caravanmagazine.in/media/facebook-blocks-atheist-republic-page-twitter-suspends-founder-on-government-directive (accessed 25 June 2022).

18 Further discussion of this is beyond the scope of this chapter.

19 Read more in Ajay Sukumaran, 'Who killed Gauri, Kalburgi, Dabholkar, Pansare? The puzzle cracks, slowly', *Outlook*, 3 September 2018: https://www.outlookindia.com/magazine/story/who-killed-gauri-kalburgi-dabholkar-pansare-the-puzzle-cracks-slowly/300555 (accessed 25 June 2022).

References

Anderson, Edward. 2015. '"Neo-Hindutva": The Asia House M. F. Husain campaign and the mainstreaming of Hindu nationalist rhetoric in Britain.' *Contemporary South Asia* 23 (1): 45–66.

Binder, Stefan. 2020. *Total Atheism: Secular activism and the politics of difference in South India*. Oxford: Berghahn.

Blom, Amélie. 2008. 'The 2006 anti-"Danish cartoons" riot in Lahore: Outrage and the emotional landscape of Pakistani politics.' *South Asia Multidisciplinary Academic Journal* 2. https://doi.org/10.4000/samaj.1652.

Brewster, Melanie Elyse. 2013. 'Atheism, gender, and sexuality', in *The Oxford Handbook of Atheism*, Stephen Bullivant and Michael Ruse, eds, 511–24. Oxford: Oxford University Press.

Copeman, Jacob and Johannes Quack. 2015. 'Godless people and dead bodies: Materiality and the morality of atheist materialism.' *Social Analysis* 59 (2): 40–61. https://doi.org/10.3167/sa.2015.590203.

Copeman, Jacob and Johannes Quack. 2019. 'Contemporary religiosities', in *Critical Themes in Indian Sociology*, Sanjay Srivastava, Yasmeen Arif and Janaki Abraham, eds, 44–61. New Delhi: SAGE Publications.

Copeman, Jacob and Deepa S. Reddy. 2012. 'The didactic death: Publicity, instruction, and body donation.' *HAU: Journal of Ethnographic Theory* 2 (2): 59–83. https://doi.org/10.14318/hau2.2.005.

Das, Veena. 2020. *Textures of the Ordinary: Doing anthropology after Wittgenstein*. New York: Fordham University Press.

Duile, Timo. 2020. 'Being atheist in the religious harmony state of Indonesia.' *Asia Pacific Journal of Anthropology* 21 (5): 450–65. https://doi.org/10.1080/14442213.2020.1829022.

Fader, Ayala. 2020. *Hidden Heretics: Jewish doubt in the digital age*. Princeton, NJ: Princeton University Press.

Frøystad, Kathinka. 2019. 'Affective digital images: Shiva in the Kaaba and the smartphone revolution', in *Outrage: The rise of religious offence in contemporary South Asia*, Paul Rollier, Kathinka Frøystad and Arild Engelsen Ruud, eds, 123–48. London: UCL Press.

Jaffrelot, Christophe. 2008. 'Hindu nationalism and the (not so easy) art of being outraged: The Ram Setu controversy.' *South Asia Multidisciplinary Academic Journal* 2: 1–17. https://doi.org/10.4000/samaj.1372.

Jain, Kajri. 2010. 'Taking and making offence: Husain and the politics of desecration', in *Barefoot across the Nation: Maqbool Fida Husain and the idea of India*, Sumathi Ramaswamy, ed., 198–212. New Delhi: Routledge.

Juneja, Monica. 2018. 'From the "religious" to the "aesthetic" image, or the struggle over art that offends', in *Taking Offense: Religion, art, and visual culture in plural configurations*, Birgit Meyer, Christiane Kruse and Anne-Marie Korte, eds, 161–99. Paderborn: Wilhelm Fink.

Lee, Lois. 2015. 'Ambivalent atheist identities: Power and non-religious culture in contemporary Britain.' *Social Analysis* 59 (2): 20–39. https://doi.org/10.3167/sa.2015.590202.

Maheshwari, Malvika. 2018. *Art Attacks: Violence and offence-taking in India*. New Delhi: Oxford University Press.

Mahmood, Saba. 2013. 'Religious reason and secular affect: An incommensurable divide?', in *Is Critique Secular? Blasphemy, injury, and free speech*, by Talal Asad, Wendy Brown, Judith Butler and Saba Mahmood, 58–94. New York: Fordham University Press.

Mitchell, W. J. T. 2005. *What Do Pictures Want? The lives and loves of images*. Chicago and London: University of Chicago Press.

Mohan, Sriram. 2015. 'Locating the "Internet Hindu": Political speech and performance in Indian cyberspace.' *Television & New Media* 16 (4): 339–45. https://doi.org/10.1177/1527476415575491.

Punathambekar, Aswin. 2015. 'Satire, elections, and democratic politics in digital India.' *Television & New Media* 16 (4): 394–400. https://doi.org/10.1177/1527476415573953.

Quack, Johannes. 2012a. *Disenchanting India: Organized rationalism and criticism of religion in India*. New York: Oxford University Press.

Quack, Johannes. 2012b. 'Organised atheism in India: An overview.' *Journal of Contemporary Religion* 27 (1): 67–85. https://doi.org/10.1080/13537903.2012.642729.

Quack, Johannes. 2014. 'Outline of a relational approach to "nonreligion".' *Method & Theory in the Study of Religion* 26 (4–5): 439–69. https://doi.org/10.1163/15700682-12341327.

Quack, Johannes and Stefan Binder. 2018. 'Atheism and rationalism in Hinduism', in *Oxford Bibliographies in Hinduism*, Tracy Coleman, ed. New York: Oxford University Press.

Rashid, Radzuwan Ab and Azweed Mohamad. 2019. *New Media Narratives and Cultural Influence in Malaysia: The strategic construction of blog rhetoric by an apostate*. Singapore: Springer.

Richter, Lena. 2021. 'Laughing about religious authority – but not too loud.' *Religions* 12 (2), art. no. 73. https://doi.org/10.3390/rel12020073.

Schulz, Mascha. 2019. 'Performing the party: National holiday events and politics at a public university campus in Bangladesh.' *South Asia Multidisciplinary Academic Journal* 22: 1–22. https://doi.org/10.4000/samaj.6508.

Udupa, Sahana. 2018a. 'Enterprise Hindutva and social media in urban India.' *Contemporary South Asia* 26 (4): 453–67. https://doi.org/10.1080/09584935.2018.1545007.

Udupa, Sahana. 2018b. 'Gaali cultures: The politics of abusive exchange on social media.' *New Media & Society* 20 (4): 1506–22. https://doi.org/10.1177/1461444817698776.

Afterword: paradox laxity and unwordy indifference: non-religious figurations beyond emancipatory narratives and declamatory genres

Johannes Quack

The contributions in this rich volume are manifold. This afterword begins with an outline of how the volume both expands on and advances the study of non-religion. The volume does not only augment scholarly understanding of central questions within the interdisciplinary study of non-religion by illustrating and analysing the diversity of non-religion beyond the simple binary of the religious and the none. It also illuminates new avenues for exploring how sceptical publics are formed through the lenses of aesthetics and affects, emotions and embodiment, and materiality and media.

This afterword then takes up the volume's more implicit focus on silences and visibilities, normativities and normalisations and the implications that these subjects have for further research on sceptical publics. To that end it discusses the use of 'emancipatory' analytical vocabulary – awareness raising, silence breaking, coming out, reclaiming and self-empowerment – within the study of non-religion.

To conclude, and drawing on Joel Lee and Dorothea Weltecke's recent work, the afterword reflects on why and how we might seek to locate sceptical publics beyond organised atheism, secularist activism, other declamatory genres of self-representation and the respective public controversies or legal prosecutions. How do we approach non-religious figurations that are constituted by 'logophobic' and 'unwordy' ways of life? Which kinds of media and forms of publicity are at stake here?

Relations, objectives and contested values

This volume contributes to scholarly understanding of persistent questions within the study of non-religion by reconstructing different modes of non-religion in their societal contexts and underscoring the vast diversity of non-religious positionings and ways of being in the world. Non-religious 'figurations'[1] (Elias 1978) appear in this volume in a multitude of ways: as positions in and types of public discourse, as dispersed individuals who at times form affective or imagined communities, as organised groups, as instances of 'lived secularity' based on claims to and practices of being 'other-than-religious' (Binder[2]), and traditions perceived as 'distinct from, though sometimes in competition with, and at other times complementary to, the religious' (Bradbury and Schulz). Some chapters depict outward-oriented non-religious figurations, while others are described as inward-oriented (Hagström, Nash). Some talk *among* like-minded people or to a 'secularising public' (Hagström), while others talk *back to* as well as *with* fellow religious citizens (Richter). They have varying objectives: weakening the (religious) other; creating public controversies via humour and ridicule (Binder, Bosman) or transgression and insults (Gupta, Hecker); reaching out to new publics by proselytising; influencing the larger society through campaigning; inhibiting private quietism, fortifying existing communities or groups or consoling and comforting their constituency. They directly compete with, challenge and criticise religion (Copeman and Hagström), participate in processes of 'antagonistic othering' (Lundmark) and relate indirectly to religion, for example through certain styles and forms of artistic expression associated with secularism (Bradbury and Schulz, Hecker). Many strive not only for wider atheist or non-religious visibility vis-à-vis the religious mainstream but also for viability 'by giving [atheism] a coherent and defensible re-presentation' (Chalfant). In so doing, they negotiate and navigate different positionings and tactics, ranging from confrontation to assimilation and from compromise to dialogue and cooperation, often in very gendered ways (Khazaal).

As this volume exemplifies, understanding non-religion and scepticism requires both an investigation of the different relations and objectives of specific non-religious figurations and research on varying understandings of religion and secularism and contested values. The latter might include classical topoi like truth, enlightenment, rationality, scientific and critical thinking, and evidence-based lifestyles as well as questions of social justice, social equality, minority rights and individual liberty (for a systematisation of such relations, objectives and values, see Schuh, Quack and Kind 2019, 21–6).

Modes and medialities of non-religion

As this volume challenges us to think sceptical publics and non-religious figurations anew, its contributions place particular emphasis on the role of (new) media and materiality in the expression and production of non-religious affects, communities, imaginaries, practices, emotions and positionalities. The focus is not only on what the non-religious say and do but also on the media forms they employ and how such mediated representations change what as well as who they represent (see also Binder 2020). The discussions include themes like the evidence of the senses (Copeman and Hagström), how secular difference is made perceptible (Binder) and the importance of affects (Khazaal).

Such a focus on aesthetics and affects, emotions and embodiment, media and materiality might not be seen as something 'new'. After all, Talal Asad's influential work (which is not represented in this volume) focuses both on changing meanings of concepts and worldviews with respect to the secular and on the materialities and background conditions that preconfigure religious as well as secular publics. He asks how these are embodied and internalised and how they 'mediate people's identities, help shape their sensibilities, and guarantee their experiences' (Asad 2003, 14). But Asad – in contrast to many of this volume's contributors – gives insufficient attention to the diversity of religion's Others. That is to say, he does not ask whether and how 'heterogeneous and entangled secular and religious normative orders produce the diversity of both religious and non-religious concepts, institutions, and ways of being in the world' (Quack 2014, 442).

Although other volumes (e.g., Scheer, Fadil and Johansen 2019) have also set out to explore 'how certain groups of people use aesthetic or sensorially perceptible means to constitute themselves and their ways of living as different from, or not, religious' (Binder), the range of media investigated in this volume is unprecedented. It spans oral and rhetorical traditions, public lectures, superstition and miracle-exposure campaigns, conferences and training courses, pamphlets, newspapers, books, cartoons, comedy, theatre, music, dance, literature, painting, film, video, adult animated sitcoms and reality TV along with multiple and various online presences including blogs, Reddit, Facebook, Twitter, Instagram and YouTube. In selecting various sites of exploration, the contributors are able further to elucidate the diversity of non-religion, while, in their analyses, they convince.

How are these old and new media formats and technologies linked to changing secular styles, narratives, tactics and strategies? How are the respective modes and medialities of non-religion linked to the production and transformation of sceptical publics and publicities? To answer such questions, the individual chapters frequently draw on specific 'affordances' and implications of particular media or techniques, ranging from orality and rhetoric (Binder), to slow motion (Copeman and Hagström), the impact of moderation (Lundmark), ranking systems and algorithms (Chalfant, Richter), and the role of anonymity and pseudonymity (Chalfant, Copeman and Schulz, Gupta, Khazaal, Lundmark, Richter). Many chapters also point to the alleged downsides of new media, such as increased antagonistic othering (Lundmark), online harassment (Khazaal, Richter), shaming and trolling (Gupta, Richter), and the relationships between increased media visibility and unwanted publicity (Hecker) or other unintended side-effects, including increased violence (Copeman and Hagström).

Much ink has been spilt, or rather many keyboards have been pounded, to reflect on the impact of new media forms and formats in general. Taken together, the volume takes a balanced view of the widely discussed but intricate question of how the internet, and digitalisation more broadly, have impacted religious–non-religious entanglements. While some scholars (particularly Copeman and Schulz, Nash) question the emphasis of 'newness' in this matter, others point to important changes. As the contributions to this volume emphasise, the challenge is to acknowledge but not overstate various developments, particularly the striking differences between people who display their non-religiosity online but are silent offline (Gupta).

Another way to illustrate the importance and impact of the internet draws on the 'long-tail' metaphor, which has been used to explain why companies like Amazon make available for purchase books that are read by very few people, although they can barely be found on the offline market (e.g., Anderson 2006). Arguably this metaphor also helps to exemplify the significance of the internet for deviant religious as well as non-religious visibility. The internet's connectivity provided an opportunity for atheist and other non-religious individuals and groups to build upon their offline world by furthering the articulation, networking and perceptibility of less extroverted, more dispersed and unorganised non-religious positions. The polarisation of debates apparently also contributed to the visibility of deviant figurations (Stevens and O'Hara 2015). Richter contends that the 'internet has set in place the basic conditions for a new counterpublic of non-believers'. Possibilities of anonymity or pseudonymity are crucial here. As Chalfant notes (p. 246, this volume), these enable a

> way of cultivating a particular affect of stranger intimacy that serves not as a vehicle or platform for integration into the dominant public sphere, but as a counterpublic that provides an alternative space for the performance of (non-)religious identity as neither fully public nor fully private.

Although the internet did not create atheism, non-religion or other forms of sceptical publics, as these examples show, pseudonymity provided cover while possibilities for engagement expanded with increased visibility and new forms of perceptibility.

Silence, visibility and normalisation

These observations also point to a second, more implicit theme that threads this volume: a focus on visibility in connection to processes of normalisation that challenge enforced silences and problematise underlying normativities. This focus mainly draws on insights from the study of emancipatory social movements, such as activism around topics like racism, gender and feminism. To illustrate this point, I assemble a narrative of non-religious emancipation and problematisation. While such a narrative was not put forward by individual authors, it nonetheless emerges when several of the volume's chapters (particularly Chalfant, Gupta, Hagström, Khazaal, Lundmark and Richter) are read together.

These chapters describe and analyse how marginalised people, who have struggled with widespread silence, have formed non-religious figurations and sought public visibility. On the path from silence to visibility, they encounter the problem that people need to know that like-minded individuals exist. In many instances, such emancipatory processes start with attempts to raise awareness of each other – 'You are not alone, not anymore' (Chalfant, quoting O'Hair) – and initiate talking 'among themselves' (Richter). Like-minded individuals then begin to organise themselves by forming stronger communities and identities, thereby rendering 'atheism visible to a wider religious public' (Chalfant) or, more specifically, establishing 'an *apostate* politics of visibility' (Hagström), which makes it easier to further 'challenge the hegemonic silence around atheistic expression' (Gupta). To secure the space they have already carved out or to 'expand the space for atheistic expression' (Gupta), they not only need 'to overcome being silent', they also need to speak up so that they can be 'heard' (Richter, with reference to hooks (1989)). Representatives of these non-religious figurations not only want to become more vocal and visible but also to be acknowledged as valid actors with viable ways of thinking and acting (Chalfant).

Once the respective groups and communities reach a certain size and degree of coherence and self-confidence, they can further support their members. Such processes provide spaces for 'closeted non-believers' (Richter) to 'come out' and 'publicise the kinds of experiences, ambiguities and hardships that "closeted" atheists' (Hagström) experience. Indeed, Chalfant describes 'coming out' as one of the primary objectives of twentieth-century American atheist identity politics. Visibility enables individuals to 'reclaim' (Hagström) and 'reappropriate' (Binder) disrespectful labels and derogatory terms, which in turn further increases these marginalised groups' visibility and broadens awareness. Self-empowering steps towards reclamation contribute simultaneously to the 'normalisation' (Hagström, Gupta, Khazaal, Richter) of marginalised positionalities and ways of life. Accordingly, individuals are enabled to better navigate the 'balance' between 'silence and argument' (Gupta), to decide when, how and where they prefer to 'come out' or 'come in' to digital media spaces and to explore 'the relationships between visibility, identity and intimacy' (Chalfant), in whatever way they see fit.

All these mutually enforcing steps of community building, awareness raising, silence breaking, coming out, challenging, claiming, reclaiming and self-empowerment contribute to the subversion or problematisation of 'religio-normativity'[3] (Khazaal) and a 'normalisation' of non-religious deviance. Thus, the marginality and visibility of individual and collective non-religious figurations, as well as the normative orders within which these are situated, are at stake. Processes of problematisation can lead to a 'form of identity politics' that 'can be read as an attempt to expose the fiction that the public sphere is neutral towards public declarations of religious belief and disbelief' (Chalfant). Finally, such processes may eventually lead to the emergence of 'a religion-sceptical counterpublic' that challenges religious power (Hecker), a 'counterpublic which has barely been heard' (Richter).

These steps are not a linear process but are mutually reinforcing. They are also, to repeat the caveat I outlined above, my summation of the larger emancipatory narrative that emerged as I read the individual chapters and not necessarily shared by the authors I have cited in this section. For example, while Hagström writes of '"closeted" atheists', Richter does not use scare quotes when she speaks of 'closeted non-believers'; Chalfant explicitly states that he does not wish to argue that 'digital atheism is queer in any substantial sense'. This is also not my goal here. Instead, this section points to the apparently growing use of 'emancipatory' analytical vocabulary by non-religious figurations as well as within the study of these to stimulate a set of questions. Why are references to gender, sexuality and LGBTQ+ themes more prominent? Is this specific to certain movements, geographies or other factors of culture, class, age or religious environment? Is the focus on emancipation part of a larger narrative of 'ethical progress' (Keane 2016, 172–9) and 'enlightenment', of which many non-religious individuals and groups tend to see themselves as an important part? What are the reasons, advantages and disadvantages of doing so?

The increasing prevalence of emancipatory analytics can be traced to the ties that exist between non-religious and emancipatory movements (see also Blechschmidt 2018, 2019).[4] Indeed, such groups share similar, if not overlapping, structural positions. In some cases, both non-religious protagonists and the scholars who study them see such groups as emancipatory. In this volume, Gupta claims with reference to Brewster (2013) that the 'affective relation between atheism and sexuality comes primarily from a sense of marginalisation and lack of visibility in public discourse'. Richter describes how 'talking *back* becomes talking *with* [LGBTQ+ groups], as a means of showing solidarity with other minority groups which experience similar restrictions and call for more rights and reforms'. Other reasons for an increased conceptual borrowing from the study of emancipatory movements might be related to an increased public interest in 'identity politics', with such conceptual vocabulary particularly available in our current moment.

Three things must nonetheless be noted here. First, there are obviously analytical as well as political limits to such comparisons, to assumed commonalities and to the borrowing of analytical vocabulary. After all, there are not only important disparities in the way in which the differences are experienced, embodied and evaluated in everyday life but also disparities concerning the resulting forms of discrimination, exploitation (in connection with labour and capitalism), pathologisation and, indeed, dehumanisation. Second, it would be worthwhile to discuss whether we scholars build on unexamined premises if we tacitly adopt and reproduce narratives of emancipation and moral progress (and probably of enlightenment). Third, certainly not all non-religious figurations and transformations comprise stories of emancipation and empowerment.

Non-declamatory and paradox figurations

Joel Lee's book *Deceptive Majority: Hinduism, untouchability, and underground religion* (2021) reminds us that a lack of visibility should not always be equated with silence. Indeed, anthropological literature is littered with references to the tactics that vulnerable ('subaltern') groups use in the form of 'hidden transcripts' (Scott 1985) to deal with more powerful and dominant groups. Lee contributes to this literature by focusing on active and conscious 'ethics of [religious] self-disclosure sensitive to context and alert to the ways in which coercion structures social life' (2021, 271). Analogously to some of Bradbury and Schulz's observations in this volume, the tactics such groups employ range from the use of ambivalence, self-protective ambiguity and cultivated misrecognition to tactical retreat, which are at times coupled with active concealment and dissimulation (Lee 2021, 267–71).[5] More generally, Lee exhorts us to pay attention not only to 'declamatory' genres of speaking and self-representation but also to other semiotic traditions, including the use of non-verbal signs and other semiotic forms that are 'unwordy, unquotable, even logophobic' (2021, 264). It is for scholars of non-religion to think critically about where we might find non-religious figurations that do not struggle to make their existence visible through a 'declamatory publicity'.

In this volume, Nash laments that '[t]racing the very existence of what we would now call atheists, agnostics and freethinkers becomes more fraught with difficulty for historians the further back they go chronologically. Their visibility scarcely breaks the surface for a host of reasons'. This aptly describes a challenge masterfully tackled in Dorothea Weltecke's *'Der Narr spricht: Es ist kein Gott': Atheismus, Unglauben und Glaubenszweifel vom 12. Jahrhundert bis zur Neuzeit* ['The fool says in his heart: There is no God': atheism, unbelief and doubt from the twelfth century to the modern era] (2010). A landmark study of non-religious deviance in Europe between 1100 and 1500, it is not only rich in original historical sources and heuristic, conceptual and methodological clarifications but also provides much-needed, constructive historicisation of the academic discourse on atheism. In other words, it is a history of non-religion as well as a history of historical knowledge of atheism.

Before Weltecke's intervention, prominent and durable debates persisted about the existence of atheists in the Middle Ages. At their crux was the question of whether atheists remained underground (discrimination thesis) or whether it is anachronistic to speak of medieval atheism (anachronism thesis). Representatives of the anachronism thesis (most famously Lucien Febvre [1947] 1982) argued that the Middle Ages were a time of omnipresent and comprehensive faith, a period when the word 'atheism' was not commonly used and faith in God and corresponding religious ways of being in the world were – so the argument goes – exhaustive and inevitable.[6] Representatives of the opposing, discrimination thesis (e.g., Strauss 1952; Sommerville 1990) contend that while the Middle Ages were indeed notoriously religious, they were not exclusively so. They argue that the apparent lack of historical sources on medieval atheism is the product of persecution. Atheists thus faced such discrimination that they had to remain underground.

By contrast, Weltecke argues that discrimination does not explain the alleged absence of atheism in the Middle Ages. Despite the richness of judicial sources, there is no relevant historical evidence for a supposed underground non-religious subculture in legal history; thus, she declares the prosecution of atheism in the Middle Ages a 'modern myth' (Weltecke 2010, 55). At the same time, she cautions that this does not imply that there was an all-encompassing religiosity. To challenge the anachronism thesis, Weltecke discusses a whole range of alternative sources that show where and how people did not simply take the existence of God(s) and other such entities for granted, as well as moments when they doubted religious experts and rejected religious practices and ways of life.

My interpretation of Weltecke's findings can best be summarised in the distinction between doxa, paradox, heterodox and orthodox.[7] Many religious beliefs and practices attributed to the Middle Ages were indeed *doxa*, that is, generally taken for granted or regarded as common sense. They formed the basis for religious orthodoxies and religious heterodoxies' arguments. A widely shared view was that knowledge of God is natural. Or, in the words of a contemporary, the work of God is as palpable in the world as is the heat of fire (Weltecke 2010, 444). Paradox positions, which went past or beyond (*para*) such common sense (*doxa*), were nonetheless present. Accordingly, religiosity could not be comprehensive and inevitable. Such positions were not, however, prosecuted as heterodoxies, which explains the lack of mentions of atheism in legal sources. What, then, were these paradoxes?

Weltecke finds these paradoxical 'sceptical publics' not among the usual suspects but in other places and other terms. On the one hand, she identifies how critical reflections concerning, for example, the existence of God could be located at the heart of the orthodoxy (Weltecke 2010, 459), mostly in the form of abstract thought experiments that were, however, generally dismissed because of their 'obvious' stupidity and ignorance vis-à-vis what was considered common sense. On the other hand, and more importantly, Weltecke illustrates that it was not legal, scholastic or academic sources that discussed processes of alienation from religion and various kinds of religious doubt, but books used for spiritual edification and education which describe a vacuum of belief, spiritual despair or dismissive laziness concerning religious practice. As this does not reflect contemporary understandings of 'atheism' or 'unbelief', scholars must be open to other vocabulary and figurations such as a 'blasphemy of the heart' or the vice *acedia* (laxity). These confessional topoi were attributed to those who appeared ignorant of or indifferent to religious belief, behaviour and belonging, whose distance from faith and the church might eventually lead to contestations, conflicts and doubts (Weltecke 2010, 369–78). Pastoral care and spiritual guidance are needed to save the victims of such ignorance or indifference from the threat of *desperatio*. Because they did not propose an alternative worldview (an '-ism', such as scepticism or materialism), they were seen as neither philosophers nor scholars. They were also not treated as rebels or rivals (danger was ascribed to alternative religious convictions but not to a lack of belief), or criminals (as heretics were often considered to be), because they were seen as sinners and fools. Following the doxa of that time, their behaviour was commonly explained as the result of the devil whispering 'destabilizing thoughts' in people's ears (Weltecke 2013, 173).

In sum, such non-religious figurations were not seen as serious epistemological and political challenges, that is, not as heterodoxy.[8] Hence, the point was not to prove their arguments wrong or to lock them up for creating upheaval and turmoil but to offer them the pastoral care that would lead them back to the right path and save them from spiritual confusions that went past (*para*) common sense (*doxa*). As para- rather than heterodoxies, these examples were considered insignificant (Weltecke 2010, 463) at the time and thus remained below the radar of later historians.[9]

What both Lee's and Weltecke's work underscores is that a lack of visibility is not necessarily equivalent to silence. In consideration of the diversity and in/visibility of non-religion depicted in this volume, a next step would be to carefully consider where less vocal non-religious figurations might be found, to locate sceptical publics beyond organised atheists and secularist activism, beyond explicit political or philosophical confrontations, and beyond declamatory genres of self-representation and narratives of emancipation.

Conclusion

This afterword explores two key questions, one based on, and the other complementary to, this volume's fruitful discussion of pertinent themes in the study of non-religion, particularly concerning the importance of aesthetics, materialities and the use and impact of (new) media. The first question considers how the volume is shaped by themes of silence, visibility, problematisation and normalisation, by drawing on insights from the study of emancipatory movements, such as queer and feminist literature and studies of racism. Through this lens, the volume's contributions depict why and how non-religious groups try to raise awareness of their existence, and when and how non-religious groups align themselves with other, more or less marginalised, groups. How do they try to link isolated individuals across space and time to establish a sense of community and form (imagined) communities? How do they try to increase their visibility, circulate their ideas and make their position heard as well as recognised and viable? How do they try to cultivate shared sensibilities and establish a shared language and new forms of intimacy? How do they understand and display their difference from hegemonic positions? Do they try – and, if so, how – to form a counterpublic? While marginalised groups show similarities in their reactions to discrimination, this afterword also points to the analytical and political limits of such a comparison, given the important differences between forms of marginalisation, subordination and discrimination and the difficulties presented by unexamined commitments to a framework or narrative of declamatory forms of emancipation and their relationships to publicness.

Second, this afterword suggests that we may need to look for sceptical publics beyond organised atheists and freethinkers, secular movements and activism, or other forms of declamatory non-religion and respective public controversies or legal prosecutions. Lee's and Weltecke's work highlights that a lack of visibility, although it might be a concern for some actors, cannot be equated with silence. This invites scholars of non-religion to reflect further on why some non-religious figurations remain 'under the radar'. Lee discusses an ethics of self-disclosure that is sensitive to local contexts, asking us to look beyond declamatory genres of speaking and self-representation and to pay attention to non-verbal signs. Weltecke's work shows the importance of becoming sensitive to alternative non-religious figurations in other places. On the one hand, she displays how sceptical publics can also be found at the heart of orthodox positions. On the other, she argues – in my words – that we have to take paradox positions seriously.

My suggestion is not, however, simply to look for medieval-style paradoxa in the contemporary world, not least because the doxa constantly changes and is time- and place-specific. In many instances, non-religion is obviously seen not as paradox but as a means to participate in the public. The point is rather an invitation to listen to alternative voices and spaces that complement the focus on emancipatory (and enlightenment) narratives with unwordy and logophobic positions and genres, even if these do not seek visibility and therefore partake in publics in less obvious ways. Broadening our perspectives in such ways is also relevant to the apparently growing group of people largely indifferent to religion and religiosity (Quack and Schuh 2017), even if these do not feel marginalised or discriminated against, and even if their stance towards religious matters may be part of common sense (*doxa*). Indifference does not usually find its voice in declamatory genres but can be part of 'logophobic' semiotic forms. How do we approach non-religious figurations that are constituted primarily by shared secular habitus or that constitute 'unwordy' non-religious ways of life? Could sceptical publics also be based on shared indifference? What kinds of media and forms of publicity are at stake here?

Acknowledgements

My thanks go to Stefan Binder, Jacob Copeman and Mascha Schulz for helpful comments on drafts of this afterword and to Janine Murphy for correcting and improving my English. I also want to acknowledge the support of the European Research Council (ERC) under the European Union's Horizon 2020 research and innovation programme (grant agreement no. 817959).

Notes

1   The use of 'figuration' in this afterword is meant to signal a relational approach to non-religion. Relational thinking in the study of non-/religion can be operationalised differently; Bourdieu's field theory is but one of many possibilities (Quack 2014).

2   References without dates are to chapters in this volume.

3   The notion of 'religio-normativity' – inspired by the concept of heteronormativity – was developed to describe the 'means by which religion is experienced as carrying certain social orders' (Quack, Schuh and Kind 2019, 5), and was further elaborated by Schulz (2021).

4   But there are heteronormative and patriarchal tendencies also within many non-religious groups (Binder 2020). My research in India suggests a very strong generational gap in this

respect. Those non-religious groups dominated by people born after the 1990s tend to align with LGBTQ movements. Having said this, the large majority of organised non-religion across the world always was and remains a male-dominated sphere (Binder 2020, 196–227; Brewster 2013; Quack 2012, 290–3).

5 Lee thereby draws on the Shia concept of *taqiyya*, understood as an ethics that acknowledges that 'the stakes of self-disclosure can differ radically', depending on the social position of the people concerned, for example 'between landlord and labourer, colonizer and colonized, majority and minority' (2021, 272).

6 Atheism was supposedly, in Bernard Williams's words (Williams 1993, 60), a 'historical impossibility'.

7 My interpretation of Weltecke's book is inspired by Pierre Bourdieu's distinction between doxa, heterodoxy and orthodoxy and supplemented by my use of the notion paradox(a).

8 This afterword is not the place to operationalise how such paradoxes may eventually result in a heterodoxy. Standard accounts (often themselves part of an emancipatory narrative) suggest that from roughly the seventeenth century onwards one is able to speak of a (still) emerging non-religious heterodoxy in Europe, coupled with the gradually growing affinity between philosophy, science and atheism (Weltecke 2010, 44), the beginning of a more general and comparative 'history of religion' (Kippenberg 1997), and the establishment of an identity and community (partly based on the alleged discrimination during the Middle Ages) that was later coupled with themes like enlightenment, emancipation, progress, social reform, freedom and democracy (see Nash in this volume). Importantly, such shifts also led to changes in the *doxa* with respect to 'religion', for example with respect to the growing importance of belief rather than orthopraxy and loyalty, as well as with respect to the normativities associated with religion more generally.

9 Weltecke identifies clear exceptions. Another famous case (albeit after the time period Weltecke discusses) is Carlo Ginzburg's investigation of a Friulian miller in his book *The Cheese and the Worms: The cosmos of a sixteenth-century miller* (Ginzburg 2013). His views are – in my reading – not to be seen as 'the creation of a strange heterodox universe' (Nash) but as a paradox intervention.

References

Anderson, Chris. 2006. *The Long Tail: Why the future of business is selling less of more*. New York: Hyperion.

Asad, Talal. 2003. *Formations of the Secular: Christianity, Islam, modernity*. Stanford, CA: Stanford University Press.

Binder, Stefan. 2020. *Total Atheism: Secular activism and the politics of difference in South India*. New York: Berghahn.

Blechschmidt, Alexander. 2018. 'The secular movement in the Philippines: Atheism and activism in a Catholic country.' PhD thesis, University of Zurich.

Blechschmidt, Alexander. 2019. 'Collective nonreligiosities in the Philippines', in *The Diversity of Nonreligion: Normativities and contested relations*, Johannes Quack, Cora Schuh and Susanne Kind, eds, 77–104. New York: Routledge.

Brewster, Melanie Elyse. 2013. 'Atheism, gender, and sexuality', in *The Oxford Handbook of Atheism*, Stephen Bullivant and Michael Ruse, eds, 511–24. Oxford: Oxford University Press.

Elias, Norbert. 1978. *What Is Sociology?* (trans. Stephen Mennell and Grace Morrissey). New York: Columbia University Press.

Febvre, Lucien. 1947. *Le Problème de l'incroyance au XVIe siècle: la religion de Rabelais*. Paris: Albin Michel. Translated by Beatrice Gottlieb as *The Problem of Unbelief in the Sixteenth Century: The religion of Rabelais*, 1982. Cambridge, MA: Harvard University Press.

Ginzburg, Carlo. 2013. *The Cheese and the Worms: The cosmos of a sixteenth-century miller* (trans. John Tedeschi and Anne C. Tedeschi). Baltimore, MD: Johns Hopkins University Press.

hooks, bell. 1989. *Talking Back: Thinking feminist, thinking black*. Boston, MA: South End Press.

Keane, Webb. 2016. *Ethical Life: Its natural and social histories*. Princeton, NJ: Princeton University Press.

Kippenberg, Hans G. 1997. *Die Entdeckung der Religionsgeschichte. Religionswissenschaft und Moderne*. Munich: Beck.

Lee, Joel. 2021. *Deceptive majority: Dalits, Hinduism, and underground religion*. Cambridge: Cambridge University Press.

Quack, Johannes. 2012. *Disenchanting India: Organized rationalism and criticism of religion in India*. New York: Oxford University Press.

Quack, Johannes. 2014. 'Outline of a relational approach to "nonreligion".' *Method & Theory in the Study of Religion* 26 (4–5): 439–69. https://doi.org/10.1163/15700682-12341327.

Quack, Johannes and Cora Schuh, eds. 2017. *Religious Indifference: New perspectives from studies on secularization and nonreligion*. Cham: Springer.

Quack, Johannes, Cora Schuh and Susanne Kind. 2019. *The Diversity of Nonreligion: Normativities and contested relations*. New York: Routledge.

Scheer, Monique, Nadia Fadil and Birgitte Schepelern Johansen, eds. 2019. *Secular Bodies, Affects, and Emotions: European configurations*. London: Bloomsbury Academic.

Schuh, Cora, Johannes Quack and Susanne Kind. 2019. 'Concept: Non/religious constructions and contestations', in *The Diversity of Nonreligion: Normativities and contested relations*, Johannes Quack, Cora Schuh and Susanne Kind, eds, 7–34. New York: Routledge.

Schulz, Mascha. 2021. 'Convoluted convictions, partial positionings: Non-religion, secularism, and party politics in Sylhet, Bangladesh.' PhD thesis, University of Zurich.

Scott, James C. 1985. *Weapons of the Weak: Everyday forms of peasant resistance*. New Haven, CT: Yale University Press.

Sommerville, C. John. 1990. 'Religious faith, doubt and atheism.' *Past & Present* 128 (1): 152–5. https://doi.org/10.1093/past/128.1.152.

Stevens, David and Kieron O'Hara. 2015. *The Devil's Long Tail: Religious and other radicals in the internet marketplace*. New York: Oxford University Press.

Strauss, Leo. 1952. *Persecution and the Art of Writing*. Glencoe, IL: Free Press.

Weltecke, Dorothea. 2010. *'Der Narr spricht: Es ist kein Gott': Atheismus, Unglauben und Glaubenszweifel vom 12. Jahrhundert bis zur Neuzeit*. Frankfurt am Main: Campus Verlag.

Weltecke, Dorothea. 2013. 'The medieval period', in *The Oxford Handbook of Atheism*, Stephen Bullivant and Michael Ruse, eds, 164–78. Oxford: Oxford University Press.

Williams, Bernard. 1993. 'Moral incapacity.' *Proceedings of the Aristotelian Society* 93: 59–70.

Index

Muslims and Muslim faith 149, 294, 302–3; *see also* Islam

Namazie, Maryam 25
Narasimha Rao, P.V. 49
Nash, David xi, 12, 18–19, 195, 346
Nash, Kate 269
naturalness as a state of mind 281
Navabi, Armin 328–34
Nayak, Narendra 44
Nesin, Aziz 196–7
New Atheism 4, 15–16, 57, 147, 236
New Humanist (magazine) 227
newness 6, 15, 17, 29
Nietzsche, Friedrich (and Nietzschean standards) 97, 99, 114–18, 123
nihilism 98–9, 114, 122–3
Nişanyan, Sevan 200
'nones' xvii, 237–9, 339
normal way of being 284
normalisation 144, 189
normativity 341
nostalgia 123
nudity, women's 201, 204

occult practices 47
offensive behaviour 324, 333–4
O'Hair, Madalyn Murray 247–51, 254, 258
Omar Khayyam 198–9
online atheism *see* atheism: digital
online communication 294, 303–5
Open Society concept 228
oratory 136–8
Orsi, Robert 23
Orwell, George 291
othering 279–84
Oustinova–Stepanovic, Galina 149, 189
outreach 11, 24–5

Paine, Thomas 223–6
Pakistan 27, 177
Papineau, David 41
patriarchy 205–6, 210–11, 214
Penguen 202–3
periodicals 225
Philippines, the 147–8
philosophy 122
PK (film) 308
Plato 175
play 282
Pluto (planet) 104
Polat, Mehmet 201
polymedia 17
Popper, Karl 228
populism 214
Posen, Izzy 186
positivism 123, 178
'post-truth' 104
postcolonial discourse 299–300
posting 296; *see also* Facebook; meme; Reddit platform; social media
Prakasam, Naveena 271
Premanand, Basava 46–51, 56
present book, contents of 5, 8–9, 16, 20, 23
press coverage 177

privacy and privacy settings 6, 312–13, 326–9, 332
'progressive' discourse 270
Project Gutenberg 231
proselytising 340
proto-science 108–9
pseudonyms, use of 26, 145, 251–3, 264–5, 292, 311, 342
public opinion 196
public sphere 5–8, 12, 144, 164, 194, 237, 244, 249–50, 263, 344
generalised 5
publicity 4–6, 13–17, 26, 40–2, 146–51
and gender 150–1
publicness 269
publics 5–10, 14
characteristics of 8–9
plurality of 9
political nature of 10
and *the public* xvi, 245, 261–2
publishing 225–8
punishment for atheists 145
Pyrrho xvi

Quack, Johannes xii, 110, 134–5, 315
queer identity 256–7, 262–3, 322–3
the Qur'an 160, 165–6, 298, 329

racism 197
Rajagopal, Arvind 7
Rajamouli, S.S. 60–1
Ram Mandir temple 317–20
Rao, Naraasimha 49
rationalism and rationality 39–51, 55–64, 67, 278–84, 315, 335
Rationalist Press Association (RPA) 226–9
reading habits 227
reality tv 59
'realization humanists' 182, 189–90
Reddit platform 9–11, 15, 26–8, 42, 246–7, 252–5, 258, 261–4, 272–3, 282–5
religion
abandonment of 146
absence of xvii–xviii 3–6, 9–25, 28, 30, 39–41, 128, 131, 179, 336–44, 349–50
attacks on 99, 271
as a 'bad story' 121
as a coping mechanism 99, 108–9, 112
criticism of 197, 329–31, 33
definition of 23, 198
high-control form of 186
indifference to 347
interactions with atheism 310
and materiality 21
nature of 148
overt form of 99
reflections on 13, 147
Rick and Morty's view of 104, 109
and science 103, 105
and the state 130
study of 128–9
use of the term 149
waning of 237
religiosity 149, 239, 315, 320–1, 334, 347, 350
collective 318
popular or *lived* forms of 129

CPSIA information can be obtained
at www.ICGtesting.com
Printed in the USA
BVHW012105040523
663624BV00008B/32